Controlling Multinational Enterprises

Westview Special Studies in International Economics

Yoon S. Park, *Oil Money and the World Economy*
Karl P. Sauvant and Farid G. Lavipour (eds.),
Controlling Multinational Enterprises

Karl P. Sauvant studied at the Free University of Berlin and holds a Ph.D. from the University of Pennsylvania. He is at present an Associate Transnational Corporations Affairs Officer at the United Nations. Farid G. Lavipour holds a M.B.A. from The Wharton School of Finance and is now with the International Department of the Chase Manhattan Bank.

CONTROLLING MULTINATIONAL ENTERPRISES

ENTERPRISES

Problems, Strategies, Counterstrategies

edited by
Karl P. Sauvant and Farid G. Lavipour

Westview Press
Boulder, Colorado

to our parents

Copyright 1976 by Westview Press, Inc.

Published 1976 in the United States of America
by Westview Press, Inc.
    1898 Flatiron Court
    Boulder, Colorado 80301
    Frederick A. Praeger, Publisher & Editorial Director

Library of Congress Cataloging in Publication Data

Main entry under title:

Controlling multinational enterprises.

    Bibliography: p.
    Includes indexes.
    1. International business enterprises—Addresses, essays, lectures.
2. Industry and states—Addresses, essays, lectures. I. Sauvant, Karl P.
II. Lavipour, Farid G.
HD2755.5.C64   338.8'8   75-30824
ISBN 0-89158-020-4

Printed in the United States of America.

Contents

Part III
Counterstrategies

Preface

The present collection owes its genesis to an earlier effort in which the editors worked jointly with others to produce an annotated bibliography on multinational enterprises. The formulation of the general conception of this Collection and the selection of papers for it were a joint effort here as well. With respect to the preparation of introductions to the various parts, however, the editors would like to specify responsibility: Karl P. Sauvant is responsible for the general introduction and the introductions to Parts II and III and Farid G. Lavipour for the introduction to Part I.

We should particularly like to thank Andrew C. E. Hilton, Michael Morris, Franklin R. Root, and N. T. Wang, who prepared papers especially for publication in this volume. We wish to express our appreciation of the cooperation given us by authors and publishers of papers previously published elsewhere.

We also extend our thanks to Ursula Nunamaker for undertaking the arduous tasks of contacting publishers and authors for permission to reprint work which originally appeared elsewhere and patiently going through it in order to make it self-contained. Linda Young typed and proofread parts of the manuscript and helped in many other ways. Joel Millman standardized the format and checked the accuracy of the entries in the bibliography. Michael Moodie edited various drafts of the introductions. Ann Rogers offered valuable advice and criticism. And, finally, Vishwas Govitrikar assumed editorial responsibility for the introductions and, by pointing out a number of ambiguities, forced us to rethink and reformulate various passages. To all of them, and to the many others whom exigencies of space prevent us from mentioning individually, we should like to say: Thank you.

In addition, Karl P. Sauvant would like to thank the Multinational Enterprise Unit, the Wharton School, University of Pennsylvania, and especially its director, Howard V. Perlmutter, for generally facilitating work on the project. Farid G. Lavipour would like to thank the Foreign Policy Research Institute, and especially its director, Robert L. Pfaltzgraff, Jr., for providing time to work on this collection.

Needless to say, none of those mentioned above is in any way responsible for any errors on the part of the editors. The views expressed in this collection do not necessarily reflect those of the institutions—the United Nations in the case of Karl P. Sauvant and the Chase Manhattan Bank in the case of Farid G. Lavipour—with which the editors are currently affiliated.

New York, May 1975

Karl P. Sauvant
Farid G. Lavipour

Contributors

C. Fred Bergsten
The Brookings Institution
Washington, D. C.

Dale B. Furnish
College of Law
Arizona State University
Tempe, Ariz.

Andrew C. E. Hilton
World Bank
Washington, D. C.

Stephen D. Krasner
Department of Government
Harvard University
Cambridge, Mass.

Farid G. Lavipour
The Chase Manhattan Bank
New York, N. Y.

Michael Morris
Instituto Universitario de Pesquisas
Rio de Janeiro, Brazil

Franklin R. Root
Multinational Enterprise Unit
The Wharton School
University of Pennsylvania
Philadelphia, Pa.

Karl P. Sauvant
Centre on Transnational Corporations
United Nations
New York, N. Y.

N. T. Wang
Centre on Transnational Corporations
United Nations
New York, N. Y.

Thomas A. Wolf
Department of Economics
The Ohio State University
Columbus, Ohio

General Introduction

More than 10,000 enterprises control over 50,000 affiliates outside their home countries. These affiliates represent a book value of more than $165 billion. Approximately 80 percent of all multinational enterprises (MNEs), foreign affiliates, and their international direct investments originate in five countries: the United States, followed by the United Kingdom, France, the Federal Republic of Germany, and Switzerland. By including Japan and Canada, one can account for almost 90 percent of the international activities of MNEs.

A similar degree of concentration prevails among MNEs themselves. Not more than 150 enterprises, almost all of them headquartered in the seven countries just mentioned, control over half of all foreign affiliates and total international direct investment. Since assets and production of these enterprises are distributed over several countries, they are no longer dependent on any one country, including their home country. However, they are almost exclusively owned and managed by home-country nationals.

The internationalization of production has been accompanied by an internationalization of services. Not surprisingly, the structure of international banking, advertising, and business education is characterized by a similar or even higher degree of concentration.

This is the magnitude international business has achieved thus far. There is every indication of further growth. This collection, after briefly documenting the size and structural characteristics of international business, examines various attempts at controlling multinational enterprises, as well as the difficulties associated with these attempts.

Actually, MNEs are not a recent phenomenon. However, it is only since the 1950s, and increasingly during the past decade, that international production has become a major factor—or possibly *the* major factor—in international economics. For example, the book value of total U.S. foreign direct investment increased from $12 billion in 1950 to $33 billion in 1960 and exceeded $100 billion in 1974. Today, the volume of total international production surpasses in importance the volume of exports as a means of delivering goods to foreign markets.

Two factors, in particular, were responsible for this development. First, technological advances in communication and transportation facilitated the development of global business perspectives in an increasing number of enterprises and permitted the establishment of transnational unity in management policies and corporate organization. Second, the major market economies supported corporate internationalization by creating and maintaining an international environment favorable to the transnational flow of capital, entrepreneurship, and managerial and technical know-how. For their part, host countries initially perceived foreign direct investment as beneficial to their indigenous economic development. In the last few years, however, the unexpected growth, magnitude, and patterns of international direct investment have created the fear that the internationalization of production and attendant services may have undesirable economic, social, and political consequences for the host country—and sometimes even for the home country.

More specifically, these fears spring from the fact that MNEs are important—sometimes even crucial—allocators of values. This applies not only to human, financial, and physical resources, but also to attitudinal and behavioral patterns (including consumption patterns). In many instances, MNEs have the power to withhold, manipulate, or appropriate resources, and to decide the direction, type, and amount of those appropriations.

Concern over this power involves two aspects of the allocation process. First, many host countries find themselves in a weak position to bargain for foreign inputs which they think are necessary for their economic development, particularly when manufacturing facilities are involved. Large centralized MNEs, often generously supported by their home governments, are believed to be in a position to choose between competing host countries. Consequently, possibilities for host countries to influence the direction, content, type, and amount of any allocation are perceived to be limited. This is especially true in the case of developing countries, where other conditions usually tend to discourage the inflow of foreign capital. Naturally, governments have the sovereign power to prohibit the inflow of foreign direct investment.[1] But they do not have the power, beyond offering certain incentives, actually to bring foreign direct investment into the country. Even if the host government decides to renegotiate the operating terms of foreign firms already established, its options are limited, provided that its overall policy is to maintain a "favorable investment climate" in the interest of attracting further foreign inputs.[2]

To a lesser degree, the same observations apply to developed market economies as well as to centrally planned economies. Their relatively stronger bargaining position, however, is reflected in the increasing—although still rudimentary—trend toward monitoring inward investment in a way most beneficial to them.

The second aspect of the allocation process that is of major concern to host countries is the differences between the objectives and frames of reference of MNEs and those of governments. While MNEs aim to satisfy global corporate benefits and pursue this objective in a multinational framework, individual governments endeavor to satisfy (aggregate) national benefits and to pursue this objective in a national framework. Although the two objectives may often overlap, depending on the bargaining position of host countries and the degree of competition among MNEs, the nature, degree, and benefits of that overlap tend to be determined by MNEs. The point is not, however, that MNEs try maliciously to disadvantage any particular country; rather, any enterprise based on the principles of corporate efficiency and profitability and operating in a global environment characterized by an uneven distribution of the factors and conditions of production inevitably has to make selective allocative decisions. These decisions, again inevitably, will not be considered optimal by some countries—and certainly not by all. Therefore, under laissez-faire conditions in international direct investment, any major benefits that accrue to a country tend to be accidental. Only home countries, favored by the global distribution of factors and conditions of production, while capitalizing on the (still) prevailing practice of equating global corporate performance with that of the parent enterprise, can be reasonably sure of participating automatically and substantially in the benefits of international business.

Nevertheless, benefits do accrue to host countries. If this were not the case, MNEs would not be a problem: no enterprise would find it possible to expand beyond the borders of its home country. In fact, it is the basic contention of this collection that MNEs can indeed be useful agents of economic growth in host countries and will remain important as long as such growth is desired. However, not all growth is development. Frequently, deliberate and determined policy is required to improve the trade-off between costs and benefits in order to reduce, if not eliminate, undesirable effects.

The possible and actual differences in orientation between MNEs and states are the main cause of the increasing concerns of governments and of governments' efforts at controlling, or at least modifying, the activities of multinational enterprises.

It should be clear from the foregoing that MNEs are political actors in a very traditional sense: they help to determine, according to Lasswell's classical formulation, who gets what, when and how. By creating and controlling a formidable transnational network of interests, influences, and dependencies, and by allocating values through it, they have become powerful nongovernmental actors in international relations. But most of the research on MNEs to date has tended to ignore this fact. One of the reasons is that most research has been conducted by scholars in international business and economics. Their main interest has been directed toward the examination of the organizational, financial, and related behavior of these enterprises and the immediate economic costs and benefits. [3] Such an analysis, unfortunately, tends to obscure the profound sociopolitical and long-term economic implications of MNEs, which are perceived, in particular, by governments, labor unions, and the intelligensia of host countries. Political scientists, on the other hand, have not considered these implications either, although their neglect derives from different reasons. Traditionally, political scientists have directed most of their attention to public rather than private institutions as international transmitters of economic, social, and political influence.

However, this picture is changing. Increasingly, the activities of MNEs have become the subject of concern, discussion, and action in international organizations, governments, academia, labor unions, and the business community itself. This collection will focus on efforts at formulating and implementing counterstrategies toward MNEs, that is, policies designed to make MNEs accountable for their activities and to influence, if not direct, their behavior in the interest of the public (as opposed to corporate) good. The collection is organized in the following way:

Part I discusses the major international dimensions of MNEs and explores the extent to which MNEs contribute to the maintenance or the change of structures in the international economic system, most notably in relation to developing countries. Some correlates of MNE expansion, especially international banking and advertising and the diffusion of business cutlure, are introduced here. An attempt is also made to assess the expansion of MNEs into centrally planned economies.

Part II deals with some of the major factors constraining the formulation and implementation of counterstrategies toward MNEs, including, in particular, some of the tactics available to MNEs and some structural determinants, as well as the influence of public opinion regarding foreign direct investment.

Finally, Part III reviews various counterstrategies which have been initiated or are contemplated to counteract undesirable economic, social, and political consequences of MNEs. This section focuses primarily on the problems faced by governments at the national, regional, and international level as well as those encountered by producers' associations.

The function of the introductory essay in each part is to present the major issues under consideration and to integrate the individual selections into an overall framework. Readers who wish to pursue specific points further may refer to the bibliography at the end of the book. Additional references can be found in the individual contributions to this Collection; in a number of recently published bibliographies; and in the growing body of general literature on multinational enterprises. These works, as well as the complete references for the material referred to in the notes accompanying the introductions and the individual chapters can be found in the bibliography.

Finally, a word of caution. Extensive research on MNEs began, for the most part, only in the late 1960s. Many questions, notably those pertaining to sociopolitical aspects and the international system have barely been analyzed and systematically tested. Therefore, many of the observations made in this Collection are not final. They should be taken as such, questioned, and, if necessary, qualified and reformulated. Although research on MNEs is rapidly expanding and the literature is multiplying, much work, conceptual and empirical, has yet to be done before more than preliminary answers to these questions can be expected. If this volume stimulates such work, its purpose will have been fulfilled.

NOTES

[1]The issue is, of course, more complicated than that. If an open door policy is in the interest of the strongest power(s) in the international system, that (those) power(s) has (have) a number of ways in which to implement such a policy, at least to a limited extent. For instance, if a home country is reluctant to admit foreign direct investment, retaliatory measures may be threatened or actually taken against the country's MNEs. Plain political pressure can also be applied. In the recent "opening" of Japan, both approaches seem to have played an important role.

[2]An example of such a policy is the decision of the Chilean junta to return facilities and/or to compensate those foreign investors whose assets were alized by the Allende government.

[3]See, for instance, the survey undertaken by Lee Charles Nehrt, J. Frederick Truitt, and Richard Wright, *International Business Research: Past, Present and Future*, (1970), especially Chapters II and III.

PART I
Impact on the
International System

Introduction

It is difficult to quarrel with the assertion that the multinational enterprise (MNE) is today one of the important international vehicles for the transmittal of economic, political, and social inputs, and that in the process interpenetration between the states has been increased. It is equally difficult to quarrel with the assertion that little is known or that there is little consensus on whether this in fact is likely to increase or decrease world conflict, or whether it will help or retard the development aspirations of many of the developing states. The selections in Part I are aimed at acquainting the reader with some of the various dimensions of the MNE and how its activities are bringing about new forms of cross-national entities and interactions.

The controversy regarding the impact of the activities of the MNE has been, in part, colored by ideological perspectives. At one end of the spectrum, a school of thought concludes that the activities of the MNE will help bring about greater cross-national integration of economic structures worldwide, thereby leading to an interdependent world characterized by less extreme income inequalities. At the other end of the spectrum, a second school of thought thought concludes that, by gearing the economies of host countries—especially of the developing countries—to those of home countries, the activities of MNEs discourage the creation of widely based infrastructures that historically have been important for developmental takeoff. The result is likely to be the creation of a series of superordinate-subordinate relationships among states which aggravate existing inequalities, thereby increasing the likelihood of interstate conflict.

Chapter 1, in conjunction with the Appendix at the end of the book, presents basic data on the scope, geographic distribution, and ownership patterns of the MNE. It should be immediately clear that the nature of interdependence created by the MNE is likely to be different for developed, developing, and centrally planned economies. Among developed countries the main problems tend to be reflected in the fear host governments have of being unable to control foreign operations as related to general social-economic objectives. Among developing countries the fear tends to be associated with a sense of increasing dependence and of being locked as economic appendices to the developed economies—feelings which are buttressed by memories of colonial pasts. Among centrally planned economies the fears tend to stem from political and ideological distances and uncertainties represented by the multinational enterprise.

Chapter 2 summarizes recent findings on the research and development (R&D) activities of American MNEs. The R&D issue is a highly debated one because critics of the MNE have argued that there is little indication, if any, that one of the most flaunted benefits of the MNE—the transfer of technology—actually takes place. Chapter 2 concludes that most R&D is undertaken in the United States. This, coupled with the fact that most foreign operations are wholly owned, results in very little transfer of technology. The reader should ask himself whether for most countries the transfer of the most advanced technology referred to in Chapter 2 is at issue and whether the presence of the technologically advanced operations of MNEs will not in itself tend to raise the general technological level of these countries by requiring more sophisticated local products and services as inputs to run these foreign operations.

Chapter 3, by Karl P. Sauvant, examines the various ways in which the MNE contributes to the transfer of a home-country business culture to host countries. Sauvant provides some evidence that business culture does, indeed, get transferred and that the home-country business culture can serve as a competing, and at times dominating, agent of control and legitimization, at least for those individuals in host countries directly involved with it. One can ask, however, whether host-country business cultures tend to be passive recipients of foreign countries, able easily to be displaced. The reader should remind himself of the extent to which foreign business cultures have had to bend to local norms, as in the case of Japan, and ask whether certain aspects of the home-country business culture are in fact technology-specific rather than home-country-specific. To the extent that they are technology-specific, changes in host country business culture would change with technological development regardless of the presence or absence of foreign direct investment. Under this alternative formulation, MNE activities would simply hasten the process toward a cross-national technology-specific culture rather than generate it.

Chapter 4, by Thomas A. Wolf, summarizes the important structural linkages taking place between the centrally planned and market economies because of the particularly attractive attributes that MNEs present to the countries of Eastern Europe. One cannot but wonder whether East-West political relations have not at times lagged behind these new business developments between MNEs and the East European countries. And, if so, whether the increasing receptivity of East European countries to foreign operations will not create strong interests that may transcend and hasten to undermine ideological differences on both sides. The phenomenon of East-West interlinkages via the MNE also focuses on the issue of the equality of the ensuing partnership. Some critics have argued that it is harmful to the economies of the Eastern European countries, just as it is for developing countries in general, because it relegates them to the less technologically important tasks in the partnership.

Among the most important developments associated with the global expansion of the MNE has been the associated expansion of banking. Banks have followed their clients abroad in order to service the new global needs of these clients, needs which have included international monetary management techniques, advice on mergers and acquisitions in host countries, and general sociopolitical assessments of host countries' investment climates. By operating in numerous financial centers, banks have increased the integration of world money and capital markets as they have learned to manage their portfolios in ways that minimize the costs of their liabilities. The result has been a growing sensitivity of national financial markets to developments elsewhere. The reader is referred to the bibliography at the end of this volume for discussions on the recent developments in international banking.

Most states have assessed the impact of the MNE by taking a middle and eclectic course: they attempt to garner some of its perceived benefits and thwart some of its perceived costs. Toward this end most states have passed legislation relating to foreign operations in their economies appropriate to their particular circumstances; some have also joined in cross-national efforts aimed at controlling the impact of MNE activities on their economies. As will be noted in Parts II and III, while there are obstacles to constraining MNEs, each country's efforts are tailor-made, and no generalization can adequately summarize the variety of incentives and disincentives that exist.

Chapter
1
Dimensions of Multinational Corporations

United Nations Department of Economic and Social Affairs

Size and concentration

Although quantitative information on multinational corporations leaves much to be desired, and the wide disparities in methods of estimation among corporations, economic sectors, and countries introduce a considerable margin of error in the interpretation of all the essential economic magnitudes, a few general characteristics are discernible. A central characteristic of multinational corporations is the predominance of large-size firms. Typically, the amount of annual sales runs into hundreds of millions of dollars. Each of the four largest multinational corporations has a sales volume in excess of $10 billion, and more than 200 multinational corporations have surpassed the one billion level.

Indeed, for most practical purposes, those with less than $100 million in sales can safely be ignored.[1] The very size of these

Reprinted, with permission of the United Nations, from *Multinational Corporations in World Development* (New York, 1973), document no. ST/ECA/190 and Corr. 1, pp. 6-23.

See tables in Appendix for sources and explanation of quantitative information cited in this section. Sources for other quantitative information cited in the text and not contained in tables are indicated in separate notes following the text.

corporations as compared with other economic entities, including the economies of many nations, suggests an important source of power. Moreover, there are strong indications that the multinational corporations have grown dramatically, especially during the last decade. As a result, both their absolute and relative size has expanded.[2]

Closely related to their large size is the predominantly oligopolistic character of multinational corporations.[3] Typically, the markets in which they operate are dominated by a few sellers or buyers. Frequently they are also characterized by the importance of new technologies, or of special skills, or of product differentiation and heavy advertising, which sustains or reinforces their oligopolistic nature.

Another characteristic of the very large multinational corporations is their tendency to have a sizable cluster of foreign branches and affiliates. Although almost half of some 7,300 multinational corporations have affiliates in one country only, nearly 200 multinational corporations, among the largest in the world, have affiliates in twenty or more countries. The establishment of subsidiaries or the making of foreign investments, particularly in industries in which there is a high degree of industrial concentration, generally tends to be bunched in periods of relatively strong economic activity. These activities frequently reflect the need to react to or counter the activities of other multinational corporations.

A further central characteristic of multinational corporations is that they are in general the product of developed countries. Although the nonavailability of statistical information on multinational corporations in many developing countries obscures the overall picture, this fact in itself reflects the high degree of concentration of the location of parent companies in the developed countries. Eight of the ten largest multinational corporations are based in the United States. All in all, the United States alone accounts for about a third of the total number of foreign affiliates, and together with the United Kingdom, the Federal Republic of Germany, and France, it accounts for over three-quarters of the total.

The high degree of concentration of the origin of multinational corporations in the developed countries is even more clearly revealed by the distribution of the stock of foreign investment as measured by estimated book value. Of a total estimated stock of foreign investment of about $165 billion, most of which is owned by multinational corporations, the United States accounts for more than half, and over four-fifths of the total is owned by four countries, the United States, the United Kingdom, France, and the Federal Republic of Germany.

Moreover, foreign direct investment tends to be concentrated in a few firms within each home country. For the United States, about 250 to 300 firms account for over 70 percent. For the United Kingdom, over 80 percent of the total is controlled by 165 firms. For the Federal Republic of Germany, 82 firms control over 70 percent and the 9 largest foreign investors alone control 37 percent of the total. In the case of Japan, although there are some giant firms active abroad, many small firms appear to have participated in foreign investment activities.

The size of affiliates varies with the sector and area of operation. In the natural resources sector, for example, affiliates appear to be three to four times larger than in manufacturing. In the petroleum sector and in trade the average size of affiliates is somewhat larger in developing countries than in developed. In manufacturing, the size of affiliates in developing countries is only half that in developed, whereas in public utilities it is double.

Some changes in this pattern appear to have occurred over the last two decades. The size of U.S. affiliates in developed market economies doubled between 1950 and 1966. In the European Community the increase was almost threefold and in Japan more than fourfold. On the other hand, no change was recorded in the average size of U.S. affiliates in developing countries, except in Africa where the U.S. presence had previously been very limited. A similar trend suggests itself among United Kingdom affiliates, where an increase in average size in the developed market economies has not been matched by an increase in the size of affiliates in developing countries. The pattern reflects the fact that affiliates in developing countries often serve the local markets only, especially in the case of import-substituting manufactures, while the relatively larger affiliates in developed countries frequently serve bigger regional as well as national markets.

The dramatic growth of multinational corporations in the postwar period has been accompanied by unprecedented growth in the number of affiliates, the levels of capital flow, and the stock of investment. Between 1950 and 1966, the number of U.S. affiliates increased three times, from 7,000 to 23,000. The number of affiliates of the 187 main U.S. multinational manufacturing corporations

increased almost 3.5 times during the same period. The growth of
United Kingdom affiliates during this period was less dramatic, possi
bly a reflection, among other factors, of the sluggish growth of the
economy and the longer history in the United Kingdom of direct investment abroad. In the first twenty years after the Second World
War, the number of affiliates less than doubled. In contrast, the
more recent entry of Japan into the field has been marked by a
rapid rate of growth in the number of affiliates. Although no precise data exist, there are indications that the growth of French affiliates was somewhat higher than those of the United Kingdom,
while affiliates of the Federal Republic of Germany are growing
more rapidly than those of the United States.

The growth of foreign affiliates has been accompanied by an increase in direct investment and the accumulated stock of foreign
direct investment. During the last decade, the flow of direct investment from thirteen countries of the Organisation for Economic
Co-operation and Development rose from $2.9 billion to $7.9
billion a year. Among the countries with an above-average rate of
increase were Japan, the Federal Republic of Germany, Italy, the
Netherlands, and the Scandinavian countries.

The growth of investment flow has been reflected in the increase
in its cumulative stock. Between 1960 and 1971, the book value
of U.S. direct investment increased from $33 billion to $86 billion
and that of the United Kingdom from $12 to $24 billion. The
most dramatic increase, from less than $300 million to approxi-
mately $4.5 billion, was registered by Japan—a fifteenfold rise.
Recent indications show that this pace has continued if not accelerated. Almost equally impressive was the performance of the
Federal Republic of Germany, which exhibited an almost tenfold
increase of investment stock to $7.3 billion by 1971.

Geographical distribution

Although the network of multinational corporations is worldwide,
the bulk of their activities is located in the developed market economies.[4] Over two-thirds of the estimated book value of foreign
direct investment is located in this area where the advanced economic level and similarities in institutional and social structures have
facilitated the spread of the multinational corporate system.

Although the developing countries have received only about a third of the total estimated stock of foreign direct investment—that is, only half as much as the developed countries—the presence of foreign multinational corporations in the developing countries is generally of greater relative significance, since their economies account for much less than half of that of developed market economies.

Among the developing countries, the Western Hemisphere has attracted an estimated 18 percent of the total stock of foreign direct investment, Africa 6 percent, and Asia and the Middle East 5 and 3 percent, respectively. The distribution of affiliates (links) is roughly similar. Country variations reveal certain special relationships between the multinational corporations of some developed market economies and countries of investment.

The corporations of some of the smaller European countries with no colonial experience, such as Austria, Switzerland, and the Scandinavian countries, have a limited spread in the developing world. Faced apparently with a limited domestic market, and at times with trade barriers, corporations in these countries have invested in other developed countries with a view to enlarging the market for their products. On the other hand, the developing countries' share in the number of affiliates as well as the estimated stock of investment is relatively high for Portugal, France, the United Kingdom, Italy, Belgium, and the Netherlands. This pattern of distribution reflects the importance of former colonial ties. Thus, two-thirds of the French and Belgian affiliates in developing countries are in Africa, most of them in French-speaking countries. The more balanced distribution of the network of affiliates and stock of investment of the United Kingdom parallels to a large extent the geographical spread of the Commonwealth. One-third of United Kingdom affiliates, for instance, are in developing countries, 40 percent of them in Africa and 32 percent in Asia. Of the total stock of United Kingdom direct investment, 38 percent is in developing countries and is similarly geographically diversified. Sixty percent of it is equally distributed between Asia and Africa, 26 percent is in the Western Hemisphere and 13 percent— above the average of 9.5 for all Development Assistance Committee countries—is in the Middle East. The Japanese presence in the developing countries is also pronounced. Sixty percent of affiliates and investment stock is located in these countries, with a strong concentration in Central and South America and Asia. Central and South America is also the preferred region for affiliates as well as book value of investment in the case of the Federal

Republic of Germany. Canada, in particular, and Switzerland also, show a high concentration in the developing countries of the Western Hemisphere, while the Australian presence is felt almost exclusively in Asia.

A little more than one-quarter of U.S. affiliates and of the stock of direct investment is located in developing countries. Central and South America account for about 70 percent of the number of U.S. affiliates and of the book value of investment in developing countries, with the rest more or less equally distributed among Africa, Asia, and the Middle East.

Further light can be shed on this distribution of foreign direct investment among developing areas and the pattern of relationships between home and host countries by examining the distribution of investment by industrial sector.

Distribution by industry: natural resources and manufacturing

Historically, the activity of multinational corporations developed in the extractive and public utility areas before it became prominent in manufacturing. By the turn of the century, European and North American investors, attempting to secure their markets in petroleum, a field in which oligopolistic conditions were soon formed, had extended their vertical integration from the source of the supply to marketing. The entrenched United Kingdom and French positions in the Middle East were successfully challenged by U.S. corporations. Cartel arrangements concluded between multinational corporations before the Second World War were weakened in later years as the discovery of rich new fields in various parts of the world, in developing countries especially, encouraged the entry of new corporations into the field and brought about a large degree of market interpenetration among the largest multinational corporations in petroleum.[5] As the technology of production has become standardized and patents have expired, national corporations in developing countries, operating independently or in joint ventures with foreign multinational corporations, have been moving increasingly toward downstream vertical integration.

Market interpenetration and partnership have diluted the prewar international cartels in other extractive industries also, but the growth of multinational corporations experienced in the petroleum sector has not been matched by most metal industries. Where technology, economies of scale, and market control by the multinational corporations do not constitute formidable barriers, and the geographical distribution of the raw material source is limited, as in the case of copper, host countries have at times succeeded in increasing their participation or even wresting control from foreign multinational corporations. In other industries, such as aluminum, where not all these conditions are present, multinational corporations continue to play a primary role.

Manufacturing activities abroad, on the other hand, appeared later than operations in natural resources, either as the processing of raw materials or as the production of consumer goods. It appears that, initially, manufacturing operations increased faster in developed countries, later in developing countries, and in the last ten years their growth has again been more dynamic in developed countries, especially in Western Europe. Industrial sectors involving high technical skills have witnessed the fastest growth.

Manufacturing is at present the major activity of multinational corporations. It represents a little more than 40 percent of the total estimated stock of foreign direct investment of the main developed market economies. Petroleum accounts for 29 percent, mining and smelting for 7 percent, and other industries for 24 percent. A similar picture emerges from the distribution of U.S. affiliates among industrial sectors.

There is an asymmetry in the industrial distribution of multinational corporation activities in developed and developing countries. Whereas in developing countries half of the estimated stock of investment is in extractive industries and a little more than a quarter in manufacturing, in developed market economies half of it is in manufacturing, and about 30 percent is in extractive industries.[6]

Within a particular industrial sector, pronounced concentration in a few home countries is evident. Four-fifths of the estimated stock of investment in petroleum and in manufacturing originates in the United States and the United Kingdom.

Significant variations exist among major investing countries in the distribution of the stock of investment by sector. Although the largest investing countries, namely the United States and the United Kingdom, have a similar pattern in industrial distribution (one-third in extractive industries and 40 percent in manufacturing), both Japan and the Federal Republic of Germany show a different pattern of concentration; the former in trade and extractive industries, the latter in manufacturing. Japan's foreign direct investment appears to be aimed at securing raw material sources and export markets for the parent corporations. Even its investment in manufacturing (one-quarter of the total) is relatively heavily concentrated in lightly processed raw materials such as lumber and pulp and low-technology industries such as textiles and steel and nonferrous metals. In contrast to the Japanese structure, almost 80 percent of the foreign direct investment of the Federal Republic of Germany is in manufacturing and high-technology products such as chemicals, electrical products, and transport equipment. When compared with the dominant position of the United States and the United Kingdom in petroleum, the Federal Republic of Germany's investment in this area is almost negligible (3 percent in petroleum and 5 percent in mining).[7]

Concentration in high-technology industries is also a characteristic of U.S. investment and to a lesser extent that of the United Kingdom. Chemicals, machinery, electrical products, and transport equipment account for half of all the manufacturing investment of the United Kingdom and almost 60 percent of that of the United States. The technological strength of U.S. multinational corporations in the major chemical and automotive industries has given that country a dominant position in these fields. Much of the expansion of U.S. manufacturing affiliates abroad has been in the production of "skill-oriented" products, in which research and development is a relatively high percentage of sales and where an oligopolistic structure is prevalent.[8]

Multinational corporations have also been active recently in the service sector, especially in banking, tourism, and consulting. Banking in particular has grown spectacularly in recent years. Between 1965 and 1972, U.S. banks more than tripled their foreign locations from 303 to 1,009. In 1972 alone, U.S. banks opened 106 foreign locations (i.e., branches, representative offices and agencies, affiliates, and subsidiaries) while in the same year Japanese banks opened 25 new facilities, bringing the total to 145. The total number of foreign facilities of United Kingdom banks in 1972 amounted to 192, those of the Federal Republic of Germany to 103, and those of France to 91.[9] Foreign deposits represent an increasing share of total deposits of U.S. multinational banks. For example, for the larger New York-based banks foreign deposits increased from 8.5 percent of the domestic deposits in 1960 to 33.6 percent in 1968 to 65.5 percent in 1972.[10]

The expansion of the Eurocurrency market to $100 billion by the end of 1972, coupled with the phenomenal expansion of overseas branches, especially of U.S. banks, provides a readily available source of funds that can be shifted internationally, as well as the mechanism through which such shifts can be made. At the same time, they provide an important source of credit in several areas of the world, over and above what can be supplied by local banks.

Ownership patterns

By and large, multinational corporations exercise effective control over their foreign affiliates through complete or majority ownership, although at times such control can be exercised from a minority position. At least 80 percent of U.S. affiliates and 75 percent of United Kingdom affiliates are either wholly owned or majority-controlled. In terms of stock of investment, these two countries have placed about 90 percent in affiliates which are at least majority-owned. This desire for majority ownership and control appears to be a general characteristic of multinational corporations from other home countries, except in the case of Japanese multinational corporations, where a somewhat more sizable proportion of affiliates and stock of investment are minority-owned joint ventures. This difference in the ownership pattern is apparently influenced by differences in methods of control as well as in the industrial and geographical distribution of foreign activities. The predominance of trading activities and light industries in the case of Japanese multinational corporations suggests that relatively small affiliates may be adequate in many cases. Moreover, since a relatively high proportion of Japanese investment—made mostly in recent years— is located in developing countries, the ownership pattern may also have been influenced by a tendency of some Japanese multinational corporations to maintain a relatively low profile in some of those countries. This geographical influence on ownership patterns is also suggested by the somewhat lower share of wholly owned affiliates in the total number of U.S. corporations in developing countries as compared with that in developed countries. Over the last three decades, a slight increase in the proportion of minority ownership, particularly in developing countries, is suggested by U.S. data. There is also an indication that the longer the life of an affiliate, the more likely it is to be wholly owned. This tendency can, of course, be offset by pressures from host countries, as exemplified by recent trends towards increased local ownership in the OPEC and other countries.

Dimensions in the world spectrum

The enormous size and steadily growing importance of multinational corporations are clearly revealed when viewed in the context of world economic activities. Although the usual comparison of gross annual sales of multinational corporations with gross national product of countries exaggerates the relative importance of the activities of multinational corporations, the general conclusion that many multinational corporations are bigger than a large number of entire national economies remains valid. Thus, the value added by each of the top ten multinational corporations in 1971 was in excess of $3 billion—or greater than the gross national product of over 80 countries. The value added of all multinational corporations, estimated roughly at $500 billion in 1971, was about one-fifth of world gross national product, not including the centrally planned economies.

International production, defined as production subject to foreign control or decision and measured by the sales of foreign affiliates of multinational corporations, has surpassed trade as the main vehicle of international economic exchange. It is estimated that international production reached approximately $330 billion in 1971.[11] This was somewhat larger than total exports of all market economies ($310 billion).

Since the rate of growth of international production is estimated to have exceeded that of world gross domestic product or world exports, an increasing share of world output would be generated by the foreign production of multinational corporations if recent trends were to continue.[12] However, future developments will depend very much on the extent to which the problems raised by the operations of multinational corporations are dealt with by appropriate national and international measures which will permit continued growth in desired areas and directions, or by restrictive measures which will obstruct further growth. In addition, changing relationships between different groups of countries, for example increased cooperation and exchange between developed market economies and centrally planned economies, will influence the direction of multinational corporation activities.

Dimensions in developed market economies

If the worldwide integrative role of the multinational corporation is debatable, its importance to the interrelationship of the developed market economies is beyond doubt. Most of the developed market economies serve simultaneously as home and host countries. The United States, however, acts primarily as a home country, while certain others, such as Cyprus, Greece, Spain, Turkey, New Zealand, and South Africa, are almost exclusively hosts to foreign multinational corporations.

During the period of 1968-1970, inward direct investment flows were on the average only 20 percent of the outward flows for the United States, 30 percent for Japan, 63 percent for the United Kingdom and the Federal Republic of Germany, and 90 percent for the Netherlands. The reverse is the case with most of the other countries. In France inward direct investment flows were almost twice as high as the outward flows; in Italy and Canada a little more than twice; in New Zealand, three times higher; in Belgium, four times; and in Australia, Spain, Portugal, and South Africa, 7.5 to 12 times greater than outward flows.

As far as the United States is concerned, the preponderant position in the economy is occupied by domestic multinational corporations, rather than foreign multinational corporations whose presence is not as yet significant. More than one-third of the manufacturing output of the United States is represented by the top 187 U.S. multinational manufacturing corporations. In certain industrial sectors, such as automotive, pharmaceutical, and fabricated metal products, the consolidated sales of these corporations account for more than three-fourths of the sales of all U.S. firms, and in petroleum refining, chemicals, rubber, and electrical machinery, for more than one-half. A larger group of 264 multinational corporations is responsible for half of all U.S. exports of manufactures. In 1971, U.S. multinational corporations generated an outflow of capital of $4.8 billion for direct investment abroad and an inflow of approximately $9 billion in interest, dividends, royalties, and management fees. Furthermore, given the practice of extensive local borrowing, their control of overseas assets is substantially higher than the book value of long-term equity and debt held abroad.[13]

In contrast, the relative importance of foreign multinational corporations in the United States is limited. Foreign investment in the United States, while far from negligible, is mainly portfolio investment. The European investment in the United States, for instance, is about as high as the U.S. investment in Europe; but whereas 80 percent of the latter is in direct investment, 70 percent of the European investment in the United States is in portfolio form, almost equally divided between stocks and bonds. Thus, the book value of U.S. direct investment in other developed countries, with the exception of the Netherlands, is several times higher than the book value of direct investment of those countries in the United States.14 Multinational corporations from the United Kingdom, the Netherlands, and Switzerland are the leading investors in the United States, accounting for about 60 percent of total direct foreign investment. Although European and, more recently, Japanese corporations have penetrated the petroleum industry, manufacturing, and the service sector in the United States, there is no single industry in which they have assumed a preponderant role.

With the exception of Japan, the reverse is true in the case of the other developed economies, where foreign affiliates account for an important share of output, investment, employment, or exports.

In Japan, where regulatory policies have restrained foreign entry, firms with foreign capital participation represented in 1968 only 2.3 percent of total fixed assets and 1.65 percent of total sales in manufacturing. The share was much higher in the oil industry (60 percent) and in rubber (19 percent).15 Given the recent Japanese liberalization measures, the share of foreign affiliates (more than half of which are joint ventures) must certainly have increased.

In Canada, at the other end of the spectrum, the presence of foreign multinational corporations is pervasive, representing one-third of total business activity. Foreign affiliates account for 60 percent of manufacturing output and 65 percent of output in mining and smelting. The United States accounts for 80 percent of total direct foreign investment and the United Kingdom for most of the rest. In the United Kingdom, U.S. affiliates represent almost 70 percent of the total stock of foreign direct investment. They account for 13 percent of total manufacturing output, employ 9.2 percent of the labor force, and are responsible for one-fifth of all manufacturing exports.16 In Belgium, foreign affiliates are responsible for a quarter of the gross national product, one-third of total sales, 18 percent of employment, and 30 percent of exports. More than half of the total foreign direct investment is accounted for by U.S.-controlled affiliates.[17] In the Federal Republic of Germany, Italy, and France, foreign penetration is less pronounced, with the United States accounting for at least half of it, except in the case of France where its share is less than a third.[18]

The importance of multinational corporations in the developed market economies varies considerably by industrial sector. There is a high concentration in a fairly small number of industrial sectors characterized by fast growth, export-orientation, and high technology, sectors which are also regarded as key sectors by the host countries. It appears that in most of the developed market economies foreign-owned firms own very high (75 to 100 percent) or high (50 to 75 percent) sector shares in industries characterized by high technology. Thus, there is very high or high foreign presence in the oil refining industry in Canada, the Federal Republic of Germany, and Japan. Chemicals are under very high foreign ownership in Canada, high in Australia, and medium (25 to 50 to 50 percent) in the Federal Republic of Germany and Norway. The computer and electronics industries are under very high foreign ownership in the Federal Republic of Germany and the United Kingdom. Transport equipment is under very high foreign ownership in Canada and Australia, and medium in the United Kingdom. Electrical machinery is highly owned by foreign corporations in Austria, the Federal Republic of Germany, and Canada.

The presence of U.S. multinational corporations is also more pronounced in some sectors than in others. For instance, they control more than half of the petroleum industry in Belgium, approximately three-fifths of the food, tobacco, oil-refining, metal manufacturing, instrument engineering, computer, and technical manufacturing industries in the United Kingdom, and more than 15 percent of the production of semiconductors and 80 percent of computers and electronic data-processing equipment in the European Community. In the service sector, the U.S. presence is considerable in the hotel and recreation industries, consulting, public relations, and banking. It is estimated that in 1970 there were more than 30 U.S. banks operating in Europe, many of them having established affiliates jointly with European banks.

Another indication of the importance of U.S. affiliates in developed countries is their share in the gross fixed capital formation of these countries. In Canada in 1970 it amounted to one-third, in the United Kingdom to one-fifth, in Belgium, Luxembourg, and the Federal Republic of Germany to between 12 and 13 percent, and in France 6 percent. In certain industries, the share was much higher, e.g., in Canada it was more than 50 percent in chemicals, fabricated metals, machinery, and transportation equipment.

Dimensions in developing countries

In 1968 developing countries accounted for about one-third of the book value of foreign direct investment as opposed to only one-sixth of world gross domestic product and one-fifth of world exports, not including centrally planned economies. Half of foreign direct investment in developing countries was in the development of natural resources, a little less than one-third in manufacturing, and the rest in trade, public utilities, transport, banking, tourism, and other services.

Generally speaking, the relative importance of the multinational corporation in developing countries is rising in the manufacturing and services sectors and declining in the primary industries, in particular those connected with agriculture (plantations). On balance, the overall importance of the multinational corporation is growing. As a source of the net flow of resources to developing countries, private direct investment flows from such corporations represented about one-fifth of the total in the 1960s. During the same period, this flow increased at an average annual rate of nine percent. In six out of the twelve developing countries for which data were available, the stock of foreign direct investment increased faster than that of gross domestic product. In the second half of the 1960s, the slow growth of investment in some countries is attributable to the liquidation of foreign investment through nationalization.

The relative size of the accumulated stock varies by industrial sector and country, and the share of foreign affiliates' activity in output, employment, or exports varies accordingly. In some countries, the foreign content of the local economy is very high and at times concentrated in one sector, while in others it is less significant or more diversified.

In the Middle East, which accounts for 9.4 percent of the total foreign direct private investment in developing countries, petroleum accounts for approximately 90 percent of the total stock of foreign investment.[19]   In South America (36 percent of the total), on the other hand, 39 percent of foreign investment is in manufacturing, 28 percent in petroleum, and 10 percent in public utilities.   In Africa (20 percent of the total), 39 percent is in petroleum, 20 percent in mining and smelting, and 19 percent in manufacturing.   In Asia (15 percent), manufacturing has attracted 30 percent, petroleum 22 percent, and agriculture 18 percent of the total foreign investment stock.   In Central America (19 percent of the total), manufacturing has attracted 31 percent, petroleum 16, and trade 13 percent of the total.

This aggregate picture, however, does not reveal the fact that multinational corporations have tended to concentrate in a few developing countries.   Only a few developing countries have a stock of direct investment of more than $1 billion.   Thus, Argentina, Brazil, India, Mexico, Nigeria, Venezuela, and certain Caribbean islands[20] account for 43 percent of the total stock of investment in developing countries, which is roughly the same proportion as that of their combined gross domestic product to the estimated total for all developing countries.   According to OECD estimates for the end of 1967, in another 13 countries[21] in various developing regions the stock of investment was between $500 million and $1 billion, accounting for nearly another 30 percent of the total stock of investment in developing countries.   This concentration is related to the sector in which foreign investment is predominant.   In African countries and in Central and South American and Middle Eastern countries (Algeria, Libya, Nigeria, Zambia, Jamaica, the Netherlands Antilles, Trinidad and Tobago, Peru, Venezuela, Iran, Kuwait, and Saudi Arabia), it is the extractive industries which predominate.   In all these countries, the stock of investment in either petroleum or mining exceeds $200 million.   In several other countries, manufacturing is the predominant sector, more than $200 million being invested in manufacturing in Argentina, Brazil, India, Mexico, and the Philippines.   In India and Malaysia, investment in agriculture exceeds $200 million.

The activities of U.S. multinational corporations represent half of the total stock of foreign direct investment in developing countries.   In certain regions, however, such as Central and South America, the United States accounts for almost two-thirds of the total stock of foreign direct investment.   The rest of the stock is represented by the United Kingdom (9 percent), Canada (7 percent), the Netherlands (5 percent), and the Federal Republic of Germany (4 percent).   In Africa, on the other hand, the

United States accounts only for one-fifth of the total stock; the United Kingdom predominates with 30 percent, France following with 26 percent. Belgium, the Netherlands, and Italy account for 7, 5, and 4 percent, respectively, In the Middle East, the United States accounts for 57 percent, the United Kingdom for 27 percent, and the Netherlands and France for approximately 5.5 percent each. In Asia, the United Kingdom has the largest share (41 percent), the United States follows with 36 percent, France with 7 percent, and the Netherlands with 5 percent.

In some developing countries where the stock of investment exceeds $500 million, the foreign affiliates of a single developed market economy account for more than 80 percent of the stock of total investment.[22]

Data on the share of foreign multinational corporations in local production are limited. In Singapore, in 1966, affiliates from the main investing countries are estimated to have contributed one-third of the total value added in manufacturing.[23] It has been estimated that in the mid-1960s, sales of U.S. enterprises alone represented 17 percent of the gross value of industrial production of Mexico, 13 percent of that of the Philippines, and 11 percent of that of Argentina and Brazil.[24] In Central America, the output of foreign affiliates is estimated at 30 percent of the output of the manufacturing sector. Among the 500 largest manufacturing firms in Brazil, foreign affiliates controlled 37 percent of total assets.[25] In Mexico, among middle- and large-sized firms, weighted average foreign participation reached 45 percent in 1970. Foreign participation in the output of Mexican manufacturing industries, however, reached 100 percent in rubber products and transportation materials, and a weighted share of more than 75 percent in industrial chemicals and tobacco in 1970, while foreign participation in textile production was only 8 percent.[26]

Expenditures of multinational corporations on plant and equipment represent a varying share of the total gross fixed capital formation of developing countries. In 1970, the share of such expenditures by U.S. manufacturing affiliates was 9 percent in Mexico and 18 percent in Brazil. In some cases, such as electrical machinery in Brazil, the expenditure of U.S. affiliates on plant and equipment accounted for more than half of the total fixed capital formation in the industry.[27]

In addition to their dominant role in the export of products of the extractive industries, multinational corporations are in general playing an increasingly important part in the export of manufactures from developing countries.[28]   There is evidence of an overall increase in the exports of affiliates, both as a share of total sales and as a share of total exports by the host country.

Thus, exports of U.S. manufacturing affiliates in Central and South America accounted for 4 percent of their total sales in 1957, 7.5 percent in 1965, and 9.4 percent in 1968.[29]   Their share in the total exports of manufactures from these regions, which was 12 percent in 1957, reached 41 percent in 1966. This share varies by country; thus, in Argentina, between 1965 and 1968, exports of U.S. affiliates accounted for 14.5 percent of total exports. In Mexico, in 1966, U.S. manufacturing affiliates accounted for 87 percent of exports of manufactures, and in Brazil they represented 42 percent.

Sporadic data suggest that despite their visibility and presence in key sectors, the contribution of foreign affiliates to the total gross domestic product of developing countries remains relatively small in most host countries. This is because the bulk of the gross domestic product of most developing countries originates in agriculture and the service industries where, on the whole, the presence of the multinational corporation is relatively limited.

Dimensions in centrally planned economies

Although the centrally planned economies have attracted only a very small amount of direct investment and very few affiliates of multinational corporations, they are more involved in the activities of these corporations than a cursory examination of the standard data might indicate. The form in which the multinational corporations extend their operations in these economies differs from that taken in others. Equity participation in countries in which the private ownership of means of production is not congruent with the system is naturally uncommon. The major exceptions are a limited number of sales offices of multinational corporations and some minority participation, which is permitted by law in Romania and, on a very limited basis, in Hungary.[30]

Yet, apart from straightforward trade, the relationship between multinational corporations and the centrally planned economies has often involved cooperative arrangements in production, the development and transfer of technology, and marketing. Most of these arrangements are relatively recent in origin, reflecting the general trend in the centrally planned economies towards more outward-looking policies and a new emphasis on economic cooperation. Typically, a complex set of arrangements provides for technical help by the multinational corporation in plant construction (e.g., Occidental Petroleum and the proposed fertilizer complex in the USSR), exports and imports (e.g., the purchase by Occidental of the products of the plants, and sales to the USSR of Occidental products), and trade credit.

It has been estimated that there were about 600 industrial cooperation agreements with the developed market economies in force in Eastern European countries at the beginning of 1973. About one-third of these agreements have been concluded within the last two or three years, and continued fast growth is indicated. On the whole, these agreements account for a relatively small proportion of total trade with developed market economies. In some Eastern European countries, however, they already account for 10 to 15 percent of exports to the developed market economies in some branches of industry. In Hungary, for example, they are responsible for one-sixth of engineering exports to developed market economies.[31]

Similarly, while these agreements do not account for a significant share of the total output of Eastern European countries, they are important for certain branches. These are mostly industries requiring high technology or large investment. For example, over half of passenger automobile production in the USSR in 1975 is expected to come from Fiat, under one of the first industrial cooperation agreements negotiated with Italy. The current figure for Poland is two-fifths.

More recently, the role of multinational corporations in the exploitation of natural resources in the USSR has assumed particular importance. The copper project in Eastern Siberia being negotiated with multinational corporations would involve an investment of $1 to $2 billion, with an annual production of several hundred thousand tons. The natural gas project in Siberia, also involving the active participation of multinational corporations, would account for a major part of the entire natural gas production of the USSR by 1980. Moreover, as exports of these natural resources would continue to flow long after the foreign investments were paid off, import capacity would be correspondingly expanded. A further implication of these projects is that because of the vast outlay and the scope of activities involved, they will probably require the participation of very large multinational corporations or consortia of a number of them. Moreover, since many of these arrangements involve large deferred payments beyond the capacity of multinational corporations to finance, they will require financing from banks or export credit institutions.

Similar cooperative agreements have also been made between enterprises of the centrally planned economies and developing countries. Here, on the other hand, the centrally planned economies are usually the providers of technical aid, machinery and equipment, and credits, to be paid off with the products of the newly set-up plant.

In recent years, such cooperation has become a rapidly growing source of development assistance from socialist countries. Among the socialist countries' main partners are India and the countries of North Africa. Since 1971, there has been a tendency for a rapid spread to new partners in other regions and continents.[32]

NOTES

[1]Raymond Vernon, *Sovereignty at Bay: The Multinational Spread of United States Enterprises,* p. 4.

[2]See section on dimensions in the world spectrum, below.

[3]Frederick T. Knickerbocker, *Oligopolistic Reaction and Multinational Enterprise.*

[4]The discussion of the distribution of affiliates in this section refers to affiliate "links" as defined in the tables (see Appendix) except in the case of the United States.

[5]The nine largest U.S. multinational corporations in petroleum had crude oil operations in 1938 in 40 countries and in 1967 in 96 countries. Over the same period their subsidiaries in all types of operations related to petroleum increased from 351 to 1,442. Vernon, *Sovereignty at Bay,* p. 32.

[6]Investment in petroleum in developed market economies is mainly in refining and distribution.

[7]The radically different foreign direct investment structures of these countries reflect, to a certain extent, differences in endowments of factors and

natural resources, in industrial competitiveness, and in business traditions and orientation. In the case of Japan, the reemergence of large trading companies and the desire to secure raw materials have played a determining role; in the case of the Federal Republic of Germany, the major factors were the competitive strength of the IG-Farben successor corporations and apparent disinterest in building up a major domestically owned petroleum industry (approximately 90 percent of the petroleum industry of the Federal Republic of Germany is foreign owned).

[8]Vernon, *Sovereignty at Bay,* p. 63.

[9]Data supplied by the Chase Manhattan Bank.

[10]Frank Mastrapasqua, "U.S. Expansion via Foreign Branching: Monetary Policy Implications," pp. 23-25.

[11]Estimates of international production made in the literature vary according to the methodology used. J. Polk, on the basis of sales associated with direct investment and portfolio investment, estimates international production at $420 billion for 1968; see Judd Polk, "The Internationalization of Production." J. Behrman, on the basis of sales associated with direct and portfolio investment as well as licensed rights, estimates international production at $450 billion for 1971; see J. N. Behrman, "New Orientation in International Trade and Investment," in *Trade and Investment Policies for the Seventies: New Challenges for the Atlantic Area and Japan,* ed. Pierre Uri. Both authors, without adjusting for value added, evaluate the internationalized gross domestic product of market economies to be 23 percent for 1968 (Polk) and 22 percent for 1971 (Behrman). If the adjustment is made these shares would be considerably lower. S. Robock and K. Simmonds in calculating foreign production do not include portfolio investment or licensed rights; their figure for foreign production for 1970 is $230 billion, representing approximately 11 percent of market economies' gross domestic product. See S. H. Robock and K. Simmonds, *International Business and Multinational Enterprises.*

[12]Whereas between 1961 and 1971 gross domestic product of market economies at current prices rose at an annual average rate of 9 percent, international production, estimated on the basis of sales at current prices of U.S. foreign affiliates between 1962 and 1968, rose at an annual average rate of about 13 percent.

[13]U.S. net capital exports for direct investment abroad as a share of investment outlays of U.S. affiliates vary considerably by year, sector, and area of investment. In 1968, in Western Europe, the share was less than one-third; in a sample of 125 large multinational corporations (representing one-sixth of U.S. industry's ex-factory sales) only 6.7 percent of gross foreign investment was financed through a net capital outflow from U.S. parent companies, the principal source being foreign depreciation reserves, earnings, and borrowings. Business International, *The Effects of United States Corporate Foreign Investment, 1960-1970.*

[14]The U.S. stock of direct investment in the European Community is 3.5 times higher than the Community's investment in the United States; it is

7 times more in the case of Canada and almost 70 times more in the case of Latin America. Rainer Hellmann, *The Challenge to U.S. Dominance of the International Corporation.*

15Japanese Trade and Industry Ministry, *Special Report on Foreign Owned Firms in Japan.*

16John Dunning, *United States Industry in Britain.*

17D. van den Bulcke, *The Foreign Companies in Belgian Industry.*

18The foreign share in the total nominal capital of firms in the Federal Republic of Germany was 19 percent at the end of 1968, and in Italy in 1965, 15 percent. In France, out of a total of $707 million of direct foreign investment in 1967, the United States accounted for 30 percent, the European Community countries for 29 percent, and Switzerland for 22 percent. G. Bertin, "Foreign Investment in France," in *Foreign Investment: The Experience of Host Countries,* ed. I. Litvak and C. Maule.

19The discussion on the distribution of stock of foreign direct investment in developing countries is based on rough estimates made by the Organisation for Economic Co-operation and Development. See OECD, *Stock of Private Direct Investment by DAC Countries in Developing Countries, end 1967.*

20Leeward Islands, Windward Islands, Bahamas, Barbados, and Bermuda.

21Algeria, Libya, Jamaica, Panama, Trinidad and Tobago, Chile, Colombia, Peru, Iran, Kuwait, Saudi Arabia, Malaysia, and the Philippines.

22In 1968, in Chile, Colombia, Panama, Peru, the Philippines, and Saudi Arabia, more than 80 percent of the stock of foreign investment was owned by U.S. affiliates. In Zaire, 88 percent of total investment was made by Belgian affiliates.

23H. Hughes and Poh Seng You, eds., *Foreign Investment and Industrialisation in Singapore,* p. 192.

24Economic Commission for Latin America, *Economic Survey of Latin America,* p. 293.

25F. Fajnzylber, *Sistema industrial y exportacion de manufacturas: Análisis de la experiencia brasilera.*

26See C. Vaitsos, "Foreign investment policies and economic development in Latin America;" and Carlos Bazdresch Parada, "La politica actual hacia la inversión extranjera directa," p. 1012.

27United States Senate, Committee on Finance, *Implications of Multinational Firms for World Trade and Investment and for United States Trade and Labor.*

28The relative contribution of foreign affiliates may be affected by their orientation toward import substitution, which is enhanced by the restrictive tariff policies of host countries, and by the type of products manufactured in developing countries in connection with the global requirements of multinational corporations.

29U.S. Department of Commerce, *United States Business Investment in*

Foreign Countries, 1960 and *Survey of Current Business* Oct. 1970

[30]Yugoslavia is a special case. It was the first socialist country to permit minority participation by foreign enterprises. A constitutional amendment of 1971 goes so far as to offer a guarantee against subsequent expropriation and nationalization, once a joint venture contract has come into effect.

[31]United National Economic Commission for Europe, *Analytical Report on Industrial Co-operation among ECE Countries.*

[32]For further information, see "Centrally Planned Economies and the International Development Strategy," in United Nations, *Implementation of the International Development Strategy: Papers for the First Over-All Review and Appraisal of Progress during the Second United Nations Development Decade.*

Chapter

2

Research and Development in the Multinational Corporation

United States Senate Committee on Finance

This chapter discusses the allocation of research and development (R&D) functions and costs among the MNCs' worldwide operations. It seeks to answer the following questions. What are the MNCs' R&D policies? Can they be typified for the MNCs as a group? Do they provide results for the foreign affiliates at heavy cost to domestic R&D in the United States? Do they transfer U.S. technology to foreign hands?

The actual expenditures on R&D abroad by the MNCs are but a small fraction of the MNCs' R&D effort in the United States. Overall, in 1966 the MNCs in manufacturing spent about $7.6 billion on R&D in the United States and only $526 million abroad (or 6 percent of their total expenditures—see Table 1). The manufacturing total was about 90 percent of the R&D expenditures by MNCs in all industries. Most of the foreign R&D was conducted in three countries—Canada, the United Kingdom, and the Federal Republic of Germany—with the

Reprinted from U.S. Congress, Senate, Committee on Finance, *Implications of Multinational Firms for World Trade and Investment and for U.S. Trade and Labor,* Report to the Committee on Finance of the U.S. Senate and its Subcommittee on International Trade on Investigation no. 332-69, under Section 332 of the Tariff Act of 1930 (Washington, D.C., 1973), pp. 581-593.

Table 1
R&D spending by multinational firms in manufacturing
(in millions of dollars)

	1966 spending				
	In U.S.	Abroad	Total	Percent of total	
	Amount	Amount	Amount	In U.S. (percent)	Abroad (percent)
All manufacturing	7,598	526	8,124	94	6
Food products	136	18	154	88	12
Grain mill products	41	2	43	95	5
Other	95	16	111	86	14
Paper and allied products	64	3	67	96	4
Chemicals	1,258	74	1,332	94	6
Drugs	303	25	328	92	8
Soaps and cosmetics	66	13	79	84	16
Industrial chemicals	777	8	785	99	1
Plastics	31	12	43	72	28
Other	81	16	97	84	16
Rubber products	127	4	131	97	3
Primary and fabricated metals	312	10	322	97	3
Primary (excl. aluminum)	130	5	135	96	4
Fabricated (excl. aluminum, copper, and brass)	138	5	143	97	3
Primary and fabricated aluminum and other	44	0	44	100	0
Nonelectrical machinery	743	90	833	89	11
Farm machinery and equipment	119	13	132	90	10
Industrial machinery and equipment	184	44	228	81	19
Office machines	108	5	113	96	4
Electronic computing equipment and other	332	28	360	92	8
Electrical machinery	1,814	103	1,917	95	5
Electrical machinery and equipment[a]	1,100	13	1,113	99	1
Radio, TV, electronic components	685	28	713	96	4
Other	29	62	81	23	77
Transportation equipment	2,537	134	2,671	95	5
Textiles and apparel	29	0	29	100	0
Lumber, wood, and furniture	25	61	86	29	71
Printing and publishing	17	0	17	100	0
Stone, clay, and glass	103	4	107	96	4
Instruments	372	21	393	95	5
Other	61	4	65	94	6

[a]Includes household appliances.

[b]Estimates.

[c]Based on distribution of 1966 between domestic and foreign R & D in each industry.

[d]Based on (hypothetical) growth of 10 percent per year in R & D spending abroad.

Imputed 1970 spending						
In	Abroad	Abroad	Total	Total	Percent of total (B)	
U.S.[b]	(A)[c]	(B)[d]	(A)[c]	(B)[d]	In U.S.	Abroad
9,197	646	770	9,843	9,967	92	8
176	24	26	200	202	87	13
53	3	3	56	56	95	5
123	21	23	144	146	84	16
87	4	4	91	91	96	4
1,556	103	108	1,659	1,664	94	6
460	40	37	500	497	93	7
78	15	19	93	97	80	20
871	9	12	880	883	99	1
54	21	17	75	71	76	24
93	18	23	111	116	80	20
169	5	6	174	175	97	3
363	11	15	374	378	96	4
152	6	7	158	159	96	4
160	5	8	165	168	95	5
51	0	0	51	51	100	0
984	120	132	1,104	1,116	88	12
157	17	19	174	176	89	11
246	58	64	304	310	79	21
138	6	7	144	145	95	5
443	39	42	482	485	91	9
2,172	111	151	2,283	2,323	93	7
1,325	13	19	1,338	1,344	99	1
826	34	41	860	867	95	5
21	70	91	91	112	19	81
2,790	147	196	2,937	2,986	93	7
36	0	0	36	36	100	0
30	73	89	103	119	25	75
21	0	0	21	21	100	0
150	6	6	156	156	96	4
590	31	31	621	621	95	5
73	5	6	78	79	92	8

Source: All-firm data from National Science Foundation, *Research and Development in Industry, 1969*, NSF 71-18, and Highlights, NSF 71-39; MNC data are from U.S. Department of Commerce, Bureau of Economic Analysis, International Investment Division.

remainder spread rather thinly around the rest of the world. The following tabulation illustrates, showing the percentages of R&D conducted outside the United States in various countries by manufacturing MNCs in 1966:

Canada..27
United Kingdom...25
Federal Republic of Germany...............................20
France..8
Other, including Australia, Belgium, Italy, and
the Netherlands in particular.............................20

Table 1 (pages 30-31) contains two alternative estimates of the MNCs' R&D expenditures in 1970. These are not intended to be definitive, but rather to show simply that, even under fairly generous assumptions about how fast the MNCs' foreign R&D spending may have grown after 1966, it probably still remained quite small compared to R&D outlays by the MNCs in the United States and worldwide. Estimate A, which is based on the notion that the foreign portion of the MNCs' R&D outlays merely kept up with the growth of spending by the MNCs in the United States, shows the foreign total for manufacturing MNCs at $646 million, 6 percent of the estimated worldwide total, as in 1966. Estimate B posits that the foreign portion expanded at a steady 10 percent per year between 1966 and 1970; on this assumption, the foreign share of the worldwide total rises to a still-small 8 percent, or $770 million.

Table 1 outlines the distribution of domestic and foreign R&D expenditures by the MNCs among industries. In most industries the foreign share of worldwide outlays is low, but in a few it rises rather high. To facilitate discussion of R&D spending in these industries, the following tabulation lists those in which the foreign share is 10 percent or greater, with the recorded share noted:

"Other" electrical machinery.........................77
Lumber, wood, and furniture.......................71
Plastics...28
Industrial machinery and equipment......................19
"Other" chemicals.......................................16
Soaps and cosmetics......................................16
Food products (excl. grain mill products).............14
Farm machinery and equipment.........................10

Some of the relationships revealed by these figures are spurious, and they can be ignored with a fair degree of confidence that they result from misspecifications of where the R&D funds were spent, especially on the U.S. side. This applies to the two catchall "other" categories; lumber, wood, and furniture; and plastics. In each case, domestic R&D expenditures properly allocable to these industries were listed under other industries, so that the proportions of world-wide expenditures "accounted for" by foreign R&D spending were inflated. In all these cases, the misspecifications are not large enough to alter materially the relationships shown in Table 1.

The foregoing eliminations leave for serious discussion the industrial and farm machinery industries, soaps and cosmetics in the chemicals group, and the food products industry. All have one essential characteristic which "explains" relatively higher levels of foreign R&D spending than in the rest of manufacturing: the existence of a high level of product differentiation based on special factors that differ rather widely among countries. For soaps, toiletries, and food products this characteristic is especially important. Here, "tastes"— meaning cultural factors that determine demand patterns—play a key role and require heavy expenditures on tailoring products to meet local consumers' requirements (real or imagined) in the host countries. In the two machinery industries listed, a similar kind of phenomenon prevails but it is more fundamental than merely differences in "tastes." Industrial machinery designs often need to be fitted to the systems and production conditions prevailing in local plants, and these can differ from those found in the United States. Similarly, foreign modes of agricultural production different from those found in the United States require altered—and sometimes entirely different—farm machinery designs. In all of these cases, the problems of product differentiation are sufficiently large—and sufficiently exclusive to the host-country environment—that it is economic to perform the necessary R&D, product testing, and market testing on the spot, under local conditions and probably with knowledgeable local staff. Often, the "R&D" involves little more than the alteration of a basic U.S. product—modifying the design of a machine or tractor, for example, or altering slightly the formula for a laundry soap or shampoo—but in other cases it can take more fundamental forms.

Surveys of multinational companies show that practically all of the basic research of U.S. industry is done in the central research headquarters in the United States. The few companies which have established overseas laboratories do more development work there than research. A few, notably IBM, farm selected research projects out to the foreign affiliate. Duplication of efforts by the parent and the foreign affiliates is shunned because of the high cost of research.

Most of the development tends to be in the United States also, because the U.S. market is large and provides perhaps the best testing ground for new products (excepting products like food and cosmetics where national tastes and cultures are very different). European companies with affiliates overseas have an even tighter centralization of R&D efforts than American MNCs—with Royal Dutch Shell providing a notable exception.

Centralization of research also is governed by the prevailing view that R&D professionals work better when there is an aura of success within the group. This feeling of success is more readily gained within a large organization working on many projects, at least some of which are successful. If one of the research divisions is in another country and fails to produce, not only does the company fail to attract good men there, but also the estimation by the parent of the desirability of continuing the work or maintaining the research affiliate might be more negative than if it were located in the central organization. At one time, research directors as a group felt that the optimum number of professionals in an R&D unit was between 1,000 and 5,000. More recent surveys have turned up several companies which now feel that groups of as many as 6,000 are economic and efficient.

There are other problems with having separated research units. If a foreign research facility does produce some striking and useful results, the problem arises of where they should be "innovated." Should they be production tested first in the United States or abroad? Where should they be market tested? To keep an élan in the foreign country where the research was successful, some managers have felt it almost necessary to permit initial production and marketing there. But that market might not be the best for testing in either the short or long term. Such problems are avoided by proceeding with the development in the parent's facilities and then deciding where the best foreign location should be for later innovation or production.

Considerations such as the foregoing ones on the part of the MNCs have led to a pattern whereby new products are normally introduced first in the market of the parent, and only later, usually after an interval of several years, are they passed on to the foreign affiliates. Often, however, pressure by a host government or minority partner of an affiliate may cause the transfer abroad of some part of the innovative process.

The few companies which do maintain fairly sizable foreign research facilities can cite several reasons for doing so. Pressures and encouragements by host governments often are a deciding factor. Many governments judge that creative, company-sponsored research in their economies will accelerate efforts in other areas of scientific activity and innovation. Indeed, the presumed possibility of the injection of new technology into the local environment, with its stimulative effects on the rest of the economy, often is viewed as a reason for encouraging MNC activity despite disadvantages which host governments see in such activity on other grounds. Many governments even go so far as to offer subsidies to companies establishing research facilities within their borders; Canada is a good example. Nevertheless, the view that MNC R&D activity is a positive contribution to the host country is not unanimous. Some countries (notably France) have argued that MNC-sponsored research can stifle the creation of a domestically owned research base.

Conducting research abroad often costs less. Professionals and technicians may work for lower pay, and subsidies—where they exist—clearly have a bearing here too. However, lower direct costs can be and often are offset by difficulties of communication and coordination of research.

A final justification for doing R&D abroad lies in the simple observation that the host country may actually have a more advanced technology in particular industrial fields than that to which the MNC has access domestically. The MNC has a better chance of obtaining some of that technology if it has an R&D operation on the spot. More broadly, a worldwide R&D network can widen the firm's scope and increase the probabilities that innovations will be found. Good ideas for new products or processes are scarce. Well-dispersed research operations not only will contribute to their creation, but also can perform intelligence functions by being alert to new ideas generated in local universities, among customers on the local scene, and even among competitors.

The costing of R&D within the corporation comes within the province of internal accounting. Because neither law nor the stockholders or other influential groups require detailed revelation of the R&D phase of a company's business, companies generally publish—

or otherwise reveal--descriptions of only a tiny fraction of what goes on. Company attitudes in this respect are similar to corporate secrecy on other "internal" administrative matters such as salary administration for supervisory and management personnel, or transfer-price policies for products made in one division or affiliate and "sold" or transferred to another part of the business.

As discussed earlier in this chapter, centralized R&D facilities are the rule rather than the exception in large MNCs. This centralization tends to govern R&D costing policies. Inasmuch as the companies themselves have difficulty in precisely matching the expenses of R&D against the actual results and locations in which its fruits are realized, there is a strong tendency to cover the costs of research simply by fixed assessments—often based on sales volumes—against all operating affiliates, domestic and foreign. In those cases where previously developed technology that can also be well defined—such as a product design or a process--is assigned to a specific operating affiliate for production, the "overhead" fee for supporting the budget of the central R&D organization may be supplemented by a fixed royalty payment. In companies which disperse their R&D activities, the operating affiliates usually share the total costs on the same sort of basis as in the case of centralized research. It is possible, however, that a firm which places strong organizational stress on geographical differentiation, with "national" companies forming the core of its organization, may give a measure of proprietary control over R&D to its separate national or regional affiliates. Thus, the "French company" within the MNC's universe may set up and run a research facility on its own, charging fees and royalties to other affiliates or the parent only when usable technology is developed and transferred.

As a general rule, management attention is not focused primarily on R&D costing policies. Pro forma sharing of total R&D costs of the worldwide firm continues to be a largely mechanical, nonpolicy matter--until some "special situation" arises to demand management attention. These "special situations" often have little to do with technology; more often, management finds in royalty and fee arrangements a convenient way to extract profits from a subsidiary when other avenues are closed. For example, if an affiliate is located in a high-tax country or one that limits profit repatriations, inflated fees and royalties (including "management" fees) furnish a simple way of getting the profits home without calling them such. Another example: an MNC whose affiliate is partly owned by foreign citizens or governments could rig the profit split in its own favor by overcharging the affiliate for technology or management services. Royalties and fees remitted abroad come off the top of the income statement as costs, thus reducing the eventual declared profit on which taxes must be paid and out of which foreign shareholders must be recompensed with dividends.

In the current state of knowledge about how R&D is conducted, it is not possible to evaluate with even a semblance of definitiveness the extent to which the R&D costing policies of the MNCs may or may not have the effect of "giving away" U.S. technology. The best that can be done is to suggest some sensible approaches to looking at the problem.

Perhaps the most important point is that in the MNC context, as opposed to technology transfers under licensing and similar agreements with unrelated foreigners, neither ownership nor proprietary control of technology pass from American hands. To the extent, therefore, that affiliates receive and pay for U.S.-developed technology, that technology remains a possession of U.S. citizens. Thus, a clear distinction must be made between the ownership of technology and the locus at which it is employed in production. Clearly, there are greater direct economic benefits to the United States in cases where ownership and production location are both domestic. But *if* technology moves abroad, the loss probably is less if it flows to an affiliate than if it is sold or rented to a foreigner. The affiliate may pay no more than the foreigner would in royalties, but (a) returns in the form of profits from production using the technology accrue to U.S. citizens; and (b) diffusion of the technology to the proprietary ownership of foreigners is longer delayed than in the case of a direct transfer to an unrelated firm. Thus, the U.S. firm, if it is an MNC, tends to capture more of the fruits of technological advance than does the non-MNC, while it can rapidly achieve a greater presence in the foreign market without rapidly turning over its technology to foreigners for exploitation.

Because most of the MNCs, especially those in high-technology industries, conduct centralized research for their worldwide operations in the United States, and because they usually finance R&D costs by assessments against all affiliates, it is possible for foreign affiliates to pay for R&D in the United States from which they receive no benefit or only delayed benefit. Much R&D leads to dead ends; that is why it is carried as an overhead cost. Current R&D spending may produce results only in the distant future, yet operating affiliates pay for it on a current basis. As a general rule, therefore, the larger proportion of a MNC's sales that is realized outside the United States, the higher the share of foreign affiliates in U.S.-based R&D costs. A plausible but hypothetical example of how R&D costs are shared in a particular firm might be the following. Suppose that a given firm has a $100 million R&D budget of which 25 percent is financed by federal government funds, the rest with company funds. Suppose, in addition, that half its sales are generated abroad by foreign affiliates. The cost of the R&D operation may therefore be shared in the proportions of 25 percent by the federal government, 37.5 percent by domestic operating subsidiaries, and 37.5 percent by foreign operating affiliates. Thus, the lower the share of the U.S. government and the higher the proportions of sales generated abroad, the greater will be the share of domestic R&D in the United States borne by the foreign part of the business. This, clearly, is an input to U.S. technological muscle, not an extraction from it.

The extraction comes, however, in the form of U.S.-developed technology that is made available to foreign affiliates for production abroad. Theoretically, all the technology available to the parent MNC is available to its affiliates. In practice, this is rarely the case. The foreign affiliates may have less immediate access to U.S.-developed technology than do domestic operating affiliates in the United States, so that, if they share R&D costs equally with the domestic subsidiaries, they may pay for more than they get. This can occur for several reasons. As a matter of strategy, large firms with semimonopolistic market positions (which are characteristic of the important MNCs) will introduce new products to their markets only when older products cease to generate acceptable returns. If a firm is technologically superior to its foreign competition, it may hold back on transferring its first-line technology even to its own affiliates until either (a) a slightly older technology ceases to provide sales growth at a satisfactory rate; or (b) competition by foreign firms forces the introduction of the new technology as a means of protecting a market share.

To sum up, in the interaction of the MNC's affiliates' bearing of R&D costs and the benefits that accrue to them in the form of new products and processes, there is a possibility that the affiliates (at least in some industries) may contribute more to R&D in the United States than they take from it—and a virtual certainty that their net withdrawal of technology from the United States (if it exists) is not as large as the gross amount which is transferred.

Chapter

3

The Potential of Multinational Enterprises as Vehicles for the Transmission of Business Culture

Karl P. Sauvant

In a study on the export of sociocultural patterns to the Federal Republic of Germany by affiliates of U.S. parent enterprises, Heinz Hartmann observed that, "except for the special case of military occupation, there is probably no linkage through which the features of one society can be transferred as rapidly and effectively to certain sectors of another society"[1] as the linkage provided by foreign affiliates. Surprisingly, however, little or no attention has thus far been paid to the role of multinational enterprises (MNEs)[2] in transmitting home-country culture, and especially headquarters business culture, to host societies. This is true not only of the general literature on MNEs, but also of the literature on imperialism.[3] This neglect is astonishing since foreign direct investment consists not only of capital investment but is usually accompanied by sociocultural investments.[4]

This paper attempts to investigate the potential of MNEs for transmitting sociocultural patterns. Three crucial aspects of this potential will be investigated: (1) the magnitude and distribution of international business; (2) the nature of the linkages between

The author gratefully acknowledges the support of the Multinational Enterprise Unit, Howard V. Perlmutter, Director, for the preparation of this paper. The views expressed here do not necessarily reflect those of the United Nations Secretariat, with which the author is currently associated. Parts of this paper have been previously published in the *Journal of Peace Research* 13, no. 1 (1976).

headquarters of MNEs, their foreign affiliates, and their host countries, and (3) the extent to which MNEs instigate the creation of a
foreign-determined business infrastructure, especially regarding
business education and advertising services.

Conceptual framework

"Culture" is defined here as a society's body of historically
learned, shared, and transmitted values and patterns of behavior.
Thus, such concepts as "business culture" and "political culture"
refer to the respective subbodies of learned, shared, and transmitted values and behavioral patterns associated primarily with the
economy and the polity. Culture develops through recurrent social relationships which form patterns that are eventually inter-
nalized by a number of individuals. Since most social relationships
are determined by economic conditions, these conditions strongly
influence not only other subcultures but culture as a whole, thereby contributing substantially to the shaping and reproducing of
social order, i.e., of the specific relational system of interaction
among individuals and collectivities.[5] The overall impact of economic conditions is intensified by the fact that nearly every individual is continuously involved in the production process, while
acting at the same time as a member of other subcultures and
occupying roles in various institutions of the social order. Thus,
although it may be useful for analytical reasons to distinguish between different subcultures, it has to be borne in mind that economic conditions (particularly as expressed in the modern corporation) have a predominant influence not only on other subcultures, but on culture and the social order as a whole.[6]

Given that the economic subculture plays this crucial role, the
successful introduction into it of novel business values and behavioral patterns can be expected to have a profound impact both
on culture as a whole and on the social order.[7] Probably the most
important vehicles for such an introduction are MNE affiliates. In
the first place, they directly and immediately influence the actual
economic conditions of the host country by adding to and shaping
its production apparatus and by introducing, demonstrating, promoting, and disseminating new modes of operation and behavior.
Second, they usually instigate the creation of a business infrastructure geared to their needs, but also available for indigenous
use, notably in regard to the demand for and supply of specific
managerial talents and the establishment and use of advertising
services.[8]

The critical element in this respect is that foreign direct investment does not consist only of capital investment but is usually
accompanied by sociocultural investments. A recent study by the
government of Canada identified some of the precepts and values
which are often associated with long-term capital inflows from
the United States, but which are probably also typical of most
other headquarters countries:

> individual responsibility; equalization of opportunity; social and
> geographic mobility; [free enterprise system, i.e.,] ideological op-
> position to state intervention (except for protection from "unfair"
> competition); use of the employer-employee relationship (e.g., col-
> lective bargaining) rather than general legislation to achieve certain
> social goals; skill training; growth and expansion of output; ex-
> ploitation of resources as soon as discovered; technological advance;
> planned obsolescence; product innovation and differentiation; in-
> creased consumption through mass marketing techniques, including
> want creation and "hard-sell" advertising if necessary; emphasis on
> packaging and branding.[9]

As the study notes, the issue is not—although it might very well
be—whether these, or most of these, precepts and values would
not have developed in the absence of foreign affiliates. In fact, a
number of them, at least in their general tendency, are probably
unavoidable concomitants of Western-style industrialization. The
issue is whether or not foreign affiliates can be expected to adapt
them in such a way as to meet specific local demands, whether
for cultural identity or for the appropriate use of scarce economic resources. The transmission and subsequent assimilation of
home-country values and behavioral patterns might well be a
crucial factor for the modernization of host countries, particularly that of developing countries;[10] but, at the same time, it
might mean imposing undesirable and inappropriate sociocultural models on these societies. Furthermore, two fundamental questions need to be asked: How symmetrical is the diffusion of culture—i.e., do all the countries involved have an equal
opportunity (to use one of the precepts above) to determine its
content? And what are the likely consequences of a small number of countries being the only suppliers of values and behavioral
patterns to most other countries?

An investigation of the role of multinational enterprises in diffus-
ing culture, and particularly business culture, must be concerned
with three major factors: (1) the magnitude and distribution of
international business; (2) the nature of the linkages between the
headquarters of MNEs and their foreign affiliates ("intercountry

linkages") and between the foreign affiliates and their host countries ("intracountry linkages"); and (3) the extent to which MNEs
instigate the creation of a foreign-determined business infrastructure. The first two factors refer to the direct role of MNEs in
transferring business culture; the third one concerns their indirect
role. A comprehensive study would also have to determine the degree to which diffusion of culture actually takes place and has an
impact on a host country's business culture and its cultural and social system in general. This aspect is not pursued in this chapter
although, toward its end, some pertinent empirical findings (from
the very scarce literature on this subject) will be introduced to indicate that the various linkages are, in fact, not dormant but appear to have a powerful effect on host-country business culture.
Instead, the chapter will concentrate on the three major factors
identified at the beginning of this paragraph. Properly speaking,
therefore, I will be dealing primarily with the *potential* of MNEs
and their attendant institutions to serve as a vehicle for the transmission of business values and behavioral patterns to host societies; it is obvious, however, that this potential constitutes the basis
for any actual diffusion and impact.[11]

I shall begin by outlining the size and distribution of multinational
business, with respect both to parent enterprises and foreign affiliates. This factor is important because it determines the magnitude,
and thereby the relevance, of the intercountry linkages. To limit
the discussion, no attention will be paid here to the *relative* importance of multinational enterprise activities in individual host
countries. Numerous country-case studies have been written on
this topic; suffice it to say that, as a rule, MNEs control a substantial and sometimes dominating share of key industries in host
countries.[12]

Next I shall deal with the nature of the linkages between headquarters of MNEs, their foreign affiliates, and their host countries.
Three variables appear to be crucial: control of foreign affiliates;
control of parent enterprises; and integration of foreign affiliates
into host countries. In the case of the first variable, ownership
patterns, organizational structures, and the presence of expatriate
executive staff in key positions of the foreign affiliate are crucial
elements since they determine the tightness of the intercountry
linkages, and, consequently, their potential effectiveness for the
transmission of business values (e.g., business philosophy) and behavioral patterns (e.g., organization, standard operating procedures). In the case of the second variable, I shall be concerned

with the extent to which the ownership and management of the parent enterprises reflect the international involvement of the enterprise as a whole and, in particular, the extent to which foreign affiliates are involved in key corporate decision-making, including the determination of the content of the values and behavioral patterns transferred. Finally, I shall make some brief observations regarding the integration of foreign affiliates into the host country.

Since it is not intended in this chapter to pursue the last point much further, some methodological comments are in order, because this is the crucial linkage for the actual dissemination of imported sociocultural investments. Foreign affiliates are linked with the host country by a variety of mechanisms, notably "status-sets" and "organization-sets".[13] In the first case, the linkage is effected by the employees of the foreign affiliate who are simultaneously members of other subcultures and occupy roles in a number of the host country's societal institutions; they are potential agents for the transmission, in a multiplying fashion, of the values and patterns of behavior embedded in the foreign affiliate. In the second case, the linking mechanism consists primarily of the complement of local organizations with which the foreign affiliate has recurrent interactions. Particularly relevant here are forward and backward linkages with the local economy and the extent to which the foreign affiliate structures these interactions, for example, by encouraging certain supply and demand patterns or by insisting on the introduction, by its local suppliers, of new standards, different production methods, etc. Both types of linkage can be expected to vary among industries, being least important in the case of "enclave" operations.[14]

Last, the issue of a foreign-determined business infrastructure and its content will be discussed in terms of the supply of business education and advertising services. Business education derives its importance from the fact that the establishment of affiliate schools abroad (or the foreign imitation of major home-country schools) often involves the acceptance of the content of this education as far as (business) values and behavioral patterns are concerned. Furthermore, business education is intimately linked to the extent to which English has become the *lingua franca* of international business. The importance of advertising lies in its direct appeals to a society's value orientations, especially as they concern consumer values.[15] The major characteristics of the advertising industry in its international context will be outlined, and the importance of the industry will be assessed, with respect to both its absolute size and to its relative importance in a number of host societies.

The conceptual framework outlined in the previous pages is schematically summarized in Figure 1 (pages 46-47). We will now turn to the discussion of the three major factors which, it was suggested, determine the potential of multinational enterprises to transmit business culture.

Magnitude and distribution of international business

At the beginning of the 1970s, more than 7,000 enterprises in the United States and Western Europe, and about 3,000 in Japan, Canada, and Australia, controlled assets outside their home country,[16] the book value of which amounted to about $165 billion. More than two-thirds of these enterprises have their headquarters in the United States (which accounts by itself for one-third in the North Atlantic area and over 50 percent of international direct investment), the United Kingdom (about 20 percent of the headquarters and 15 percent of international direct investment), the Federal Republic of Germany, France, and Switzerland.[17]

This high concentration is accompanied by a similarly substantial concentration in the number of multinational enterprises actually responsible for most foreign direct investment.[18] As Table 1 shows, about 150 enterprises in all account for approximately three-fifths of some of the major countries' foreign direct investment. Overall, these 150 enterprises appear to be responsible for one-half of international direct investment.[19] In the context of this paper, this finding is important since it further limits, and at the same time concentrates, the range of influences potentially transferred to host countries.

Elsewhere[20], it has been estimated that the total number of foreign affiliates linked to parent enterprises is about 55,000. The distribution of these affiliates in terms of countries of origin is again characterized by a high degree of concentration: parent enterprises of the five major headquarters countries mentioned above control more than 80 percent of them.[21] In addition, these affiliates are not evenly distributed among host countries. About two-thirds are located in developed market economies while the remainder are distributed across developing countries in a pattern which largely reflects the historical interests and preoccupations of particular home

Table 1
Parent enterprise concentration of foreign direct investment

	Concentration				
Home country[a]	Stock of foreign direct investment, 1971 (in millions of dollars)	Number of multinational enterprises	Year	Percentage of foreign direct investment accounted for	Amount of 1971 stock of foreign investment accounted for by specified number of enterprises (in millions of dollars)
United States	86,000	50	1966	55	47,300
United Kingdom	24,000	52	1962[b]	71	17,100
Federal Republic of Germany	7,300	24	1964	52	3,900
Switzerland	6,800	7	1965	65	4,400
Canada	5,900	13	1963	70	4,200
Japan	4,500	20	1972[b, c]	28	1,300
Sweden	3,500	5	1965[d]	50	1,700
TOTAL	138,000	171		58	79,900
World	165,000	over 10,000	1969-1970	100	165,000

Source: United Nations, *Multinational Corporations in World Development;*
W.B. Reddaway, *Effects of U.K. Direct Investment Overseas,* Interim Report;
Monthly Report of the Deutsche Bundesbank, December 1965; Svenska Handelsbanken, *Economic Review,* 1969; Max Iklé, *Die Schweiz als internationaler Bank-und Finanzplatz;* Toyo Keizai, *Statistics Monthly,* August 8, 1973; Government of Canada, *Foreign Ownership and the Structure of Canadian Industry;* and material made available by the U.S. Department of Commerce, Bureau of Economic Analysis.

Note: The figures for the number of enterprises and the percentage of foreign direct investment for which they account are for the years in column 3. In applying the respective percentage ratios to 1971 foreign direct investment book values, it has been assumed that the degree of national concentration in foreign direct investment has not changed significantly in recent years. This assumption appears to be supported by data for the United States: in 1966, 50 enterprises accounted for 55 percent of that country's foreign direct investment; in 1957, 45 enterprises accounted for 58 percent. See Department of Commerce, *U.S. Business Investments in Foreign Countries.*

[a]Arranged in descending order of stock of foreign direct investment.
[b]Mining and manufacturing.
[c]In the case of Japan, another observation has to be made: many of the foreign direct investment projects are joint undertakings of several Japanese firms. Frequently, one of the partners is one of the ten largest trading companies. If these joint undertakings, or a number of them, were allocated to the trading companies, the concentration ratio of Japanese foreign direct investment would be considerably higher.
[d]Percentage of foreign direct investment accounted for refers to sales of foreign affiliates.

46

Figure 1. Schematic summary of conceptual framework

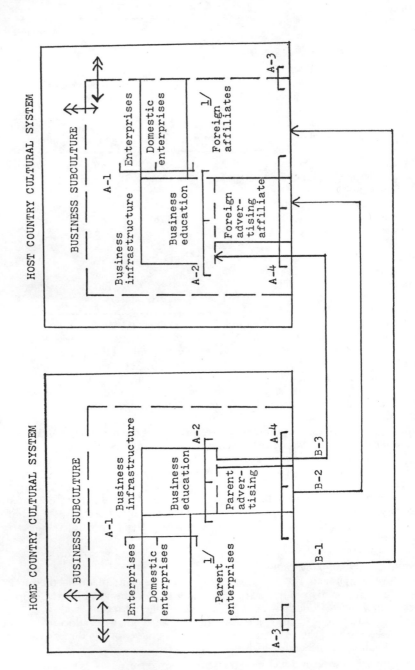

1/ Magnitude, importance, distribution.

(Figure 1 continued)

Explanation of linkages:

A. Intra-country linkages

A-1 Forward and backward linkages with the economy ("organization sets"); content: standards of performance, demand and supply patterns.

A-2 Demand for and supply of talent; content: values (e.g. business philosophy) and behavioral patterns (e.g. managerial skills).

A-3 Employee linkage with other subcultures and position in the social system ("status-sets"); content: enterprise experience.

A-4 Marketing and consumer linkage; content: consumption patterns.

B. Inter-country linkages

B-1 Ownership and management control of parent enterprises and foreign affiliates; content: supply of values (e.g. business philosophy) and behavioral patterns (e.g. organization, standard operating procedures).

B-2 Ownership and management control; content: supply of values (in particular consumer values) and behavioral patterns (e.g. organization; standard operating procedures).

B-3 Organizational dependency or imitation; content: supply of values (e.g. business philosophy), behavioral patterns (e.g. managerial skills) and language.

countries. Approximately 70 percent of France's developing-country affiliates are in Africa, and 90 percent of these in former French colonies. The United Kingdom's affiliate network in developing countries is almost evenly distributed over Africa (40 percent), Asia (32 percent), and Latin America (28 percent); again, in each area, a concentration can be observed in former colonies: 89 percent of the United Kingdom's affiliates in Africa, 73 percent of those in Asia, and 47 percent of those in Latin America are in former colonies. Latin America, finally, is the preferred area for enterprises of the United States and the Federal Republic of Germany, accounting for 75 percent and 50 percent, respectively, of their affiliates in developing countries. The United States alone accounts for over half of all foreign affiliates in Latin America.

In summary, the activities of MNEs and their foreign affiliates constitute an important element in international economic relations; international production has already surpassed the exports of the market economies as the most important vehicle for the delivery of goods to foreign markets. Moreover, these activities are highly concentrated, as far as the number of home countries, the number of parent enterprises, and the distribution of foreign affiliates are concerned. In addition, most of the major home countries share essentially the same culture. It can be expected, therefore, that under conditions of close headquarters control over foreign affiliates, the predominance of home-country nationals at headquarters, and integration of foreign affiliates into the host country, the MNE network should represent a powerful potential for profoundly influencing the cultural and social fabric of the societies in which it is entrenched.

The nature of the linkages between headquarters of MNEs, foreign affiliates, and host countries

Ownership and control of foreign affiliates

Most affiliates—on the average, about 80 percent—are majority-owned by their respective parent enterprises. For instance, 91 percent of U.S. affiliates and 72 percent of Japanese affiliates abroad are majority-owned in terms of numbers; for the United Kingdom, the figures are 76 percent in terms of numbers and 91 percent in terms of value.[22] This pattern seems to apply to home countries generally, and, if recent U.S. figures are indicative, it is not likely to change.[23]

Parent-enterprise ownership is usually accompanied by integrated management, hierarchically structured and presided over by the top executives of the headquarters. There seems to be an initial period, usually immediately after entry into the foreign market, during which foreign affiliates enjoy a certain degree of overall autonomy.[24] However, this phase appears to be followed very shortly by a period of consolidation, usually accompanied by the establishment of an international division at the headquarters of the parent enterprise. Finally, enterprises move typically into a third phase after top executives have perceived that gains are to be realized from the coordination of corporate activities on a worldwide scale. This results in structural changes which can be classified in three major types: (1) global production divisions, in which worldwide responsibilities are assigned to the previous domestic product divisions; (2) area divisions, in which each division is responsible for all affiliates in one particular geographical region of the world market; and (3) a combination of the product and area approaches, in which some product lines are managed on a worldwide basis and others by area divisions.[25] A fourth phase may already be discernible in which worldwide product and area divisions share responsibility over foreign affiliates, thereby creating a "grid" of multiple reporting relationships which, through their own combination, further increase the integration of all affiliates into a global network.[26]

Naturally, the degree of centralization varies, depending on the specific corporate functions involved. It is usually strongest in the central areas of finance; budget preparation (particularly the planning of investment expenditures); product planning, design, and development; sourcing, purchasing, and rationalization; and pricing.[27] Affiliate autonomy is usually highest in the area of salaries and personnel policy at the lower levels. This pattern is attested to by a number of empirical studies. A survey of foreign enterprises in Belgium[28] determined, for instance, that over four-fifths of the U.S. affiliates and three-quarters of the European Community affiliates included in the sample needed authorization from headquarters for decisions regarding investment expenditures;[29] in an additional 12 percent and 11 percent, respectively, headquarters influence was reported to be moderate. High or medium influence was usually found in not less than 50 percent of all U.S. and European Community affiliates in the areas of budget decisions, planning and organization of production, and pricing. On the other hand, only 1 percent of the U.S. and 20 percent of the European Community affiliates were subject to strong headquarters control in the area of salaries and personnel policy, with an additional

30 percent and 26 percent indicating moderate control.[30] Interestingly enough, even in cases of minority participation in Belgian enterprises, decisions regarding investment expenditures were strongly influenced by headquarters.[31]

Parent-enterprise control is, as a rule, reinforced by the presence of expatriate staff in key positions in affiliate firms. In Canada, for instance, in 1962, only 44 percent of the directors of a sample of large majority-owned foreign affiliates and 45 percent of the presidents were Canadian citizens.[32] Similarly, in the Federal Republic of Germany in 1966, only 44 percent of the executive management *(Geschäftsführung)* of a sample of U.S. affiliates had a purely West German executive management.[33] Finally, in Belgium, only 28 percent of the members of the boards of directors *(conseils d'administration)* of foreign affiliates were Belgian,[34] there being no difference in this regard between U.S. and European Community affiliates. This percentage increased with decreasing foreign ownership, but even where the parent enterprise held only a minority interest, hardly more than half of the board members were Belgian.

Ownership and control of parent enterprises

Both factors, majority ownership and managerial control by the parent enterprise—either directly by headquarters, or by headquarters personnel in top posts in foreign affiliates, or by both—in combination with the structural integration of the affiliates into the global enterprise network, increase the effectiveness of the linkage between parent enterprises and their foreign affiliates as far as the transmission of home-country sociocultural pattern is concerned. This degree of control is further increased by the fact that parent enterprises are, as a rule, almost exclusively owned and managed by citizens of the home country.

There are, of course, several exceptions to this rule. With respect to ownership, the most important (perverse) exception has already been alluded to: a number of parent enterprises are in fact themselves foreign affiliates of third-country enterprises, in particular those of the United States (see note 17). Another (real) exception is the transnational ownership of a few enterprises, notably Unilever, Shell, Dunlop-Pirelli, Hoesch-Hoogovens, VFW-Fokker, Polygram-Gruppe, Porsche, and Agfa-Gevaert. In spite of these exceptions, however, no appreciable general movement toward multinationalization of ownership is discernible. Home-country resistance is frequently the major reason. In the case of Nestlé, for instance, a multinational enterprise with 90 percent of its assets outside Switzerland, only Swiss nationals are allowed to buy voting shares. In any case, it should be kept in mind that even if the multinationalization of ownership should increase, such a development would probably only involve nationals from a very limited number of developed countries.

With respect to senior management, the lack of foreign (including host-country) participation in parent enterprises is similarly pronounced. One of the major reasons for this situation may have been epitomized by the following comment of a former chairman of a United Kingdom multinational enterprise: "We have to be able to speak freely together, and trust each other implicitly . . . [and] if we had a foreigner here [on the board in London], his loyalties would be divided. He might sometimes be tempted to give undue weight to the interests of his own national subsidiary, or to tell his home government of our deliberations."[35] Whatever the reasons, the actual number of foreigners in top managerial positions is minimal. The following figures briefly document the situation.

In a study of 2,859 managers in 38 of the largest 500 corporations in the Federal Republic of Germany, it was found that only 1 percent (33 managers) were non-German, and that among these almost one-third were Austrian.[36] At the same time, these companies did, on the average, about 30 percent of their business abroad. Similar findings emerged for U.S. corporations in a 1966 study of the national origins of the top management of the 150 largest industrial corporations of that country. Although about one-fifth of the total employment of those firms was abroad, only 1.6 percent (59 persons) of the 3,733 top corporate officers and directors on whom data could be obtained were nonnationals, that is, had entered the United States as foreigners at age 26 or over (34 of them) or had served in top managerial positions outside the United States (25 of them); this proportion was found to be independent of the degree of the company's foreign involvement.[37]

A 1972 survey by the Conference Board of corporate directorship practices of 855 of the largest U.S. manufacturing and nonmanufacturing companies further substantiated the findings for the United States.[38] Of the 5,962 directors of 514 manufacturing companies, only 117—or 2 percent—were non-United States citizens;[39] the corresponding figure for 4,798 directors of 341 nonmanufacturing companies was 29—or 0.6 percent. In other words, of the 10,760

directors of 855 large U.S. companies, only 146—or 1.4 percent—
were not citizens of the United States. In addition, the study pointed out that noncitizen directors more often came from outside the
company than from within the employee ranks—in about a 2 to 1
ratio—a further indication that it is somewhat difficult for foreigners to advance to top decision-making positions *within* their multinational enterprises.[40]

In short, the internationalization of business operations has not
been accompanied by an internationalization of parent-enterprise
ownership or top management. Rather, ownership and top management positions are almost exclusively in the hands of nationals of
the home country, and no trend can be identified which would indicate any basic change in this situation. It is, therefore, unlikely
that foreign affiliate managers or, for that matter, non-home-
country nationals in general, will, within the next decade or so, be
able to introduce their concerns and attitudes to any appreciable
extent into headquarters decision-making on the major issues confronting the enterprise system and its affiliates. On the other hand,
headquarters are tightly in control of their foreign affiliates.

Integration of foreign affiliates into host countries

It was mentioned earlier that foreign affiliates are linked to the host
country by a variety of mechanisms, notably status sets and organization sets. It is not the aim of this paper to pursue this linkage
much beyond its conceptualization in the introduction. With respect to the organization set linkage, i.e., forward and backward
linkage, in particular, the reader is referred to various country-case
studies (see note 12). This aspect is by no means unimportant:
for instance, roughly 90 percent of the sales of U.S. manufacturing
affiliates abroad are made locally.[41]

To appreciate the importance of the status set linkage, one only has
to consider the number of persons employed in foreign affiliates.
U.S. foreign affiliates engaged in extraction and manufacturing employed (in 1966) about 49,000 Americans and about 5.5 million
local workers[42] and U.S. foreign direct investment has increased
since 1966 by about 60 percent. In the case of the Federal Republic
of Germany, 24 of the major foreign investors in the chemical, electrical, automotive, and machinery industries employed about
336,000 workers abroad in 1971.[43] Swedish manufacturing affiliates abroad employed 180,000 workers in 1970.[44] When the direct

employment of foreign affiliates of other countries is added, the resulting number of directly employed workers abroad is probably about 13 to 14 million.[45] If persons indirectly linked to foreign affiliates, especially through forward and backward linkages, are included, the total number of employees directly or indirectly connected with foreign affiliates, and therefore potential multipliers of exogenous values and patterns of behavior, is probably considerably higher.

In summary, foreign affiliates are, as a rule, highly integrated into the parent system. They are subject to close headquarters control through a variety of mechanisms, notably majority equity ownership, managerial control in key decision areas, and the presence of expatriate personnel among the senior staff of the affiliate. Consequently, the transmission of business culture will encounter hardly any resistance from the affiliate. Given the ownership and control situation of parent enterprises, the content of the business culture transmitted is almost exclusively determined by home-country nationals. Finally, the strong intercountry linkages are complemented by various intra-host-country linkages, thereby completing a chain of mechanisms which in its totality and magnitude constitutes a formidable potential for the diffusion of cultural influences.

The establishment of a foreign-determined business infrastructure

The supply of business education and language

The potential sociocultural impact of international business is not limited, however, to the direct linkage, "headquarters-foreign affiliate-host society." One of the effects accompanying the internationalization of business has been the internationalization of (home-country) business education.

Local employees of MNE affiliates are brought into contact with imported values through their experience within these affiliates. They can be expected to imitate, learn, or internalize values and patterns of behavior embedded in these affiliates, and they can be expected subsequently to disseminate them into the host societies.

With respect to managers, an additional factor has to be taken into account, both for those working for foreign affiliates and those employed by indigenous firms. Home-country business schools, especially those in the United States, led by the Harvard

Business School and the Wharton School, have played a crucial
role in educating managerial personnel from and for a great number of foreign enterprises, thereby infusing home-country business
values and behavioral patterns into management practices in other
countries. But the teaching influence of these schools, which are
almost exclusively located in the major home countries and sometimes financially supported by MNEs of the home countries, is not
restricted to the education of students in the home country alone.
The Harvard Business School, for instance, has recently set up an
affiliate management school in Lausanne.[46] Lausanne is already
the home of IMEDE, a management school that is financially independent of the Harvard Business School (it is heavily supported by
Nestlé), but its intellectual offshoot. Other major European management schools include INSEAD at Fontainbleau (with its new
satellite, CEDEP, created on the initiative of the French companies L'Oréal and BSN); CEI at Geneva (heavily supported by the
Canadian multinational enterprise ALCAN); NEMI near Oslo; the
Management Centre Europe at Brussels (an offspring of the American Management Association); and the Foundation for Business Administration at Rotterdam (established by Unilever, Akzo,
Royal/Shell, the Amro Bank and others). In all these schools,
staff and alumni from Harvard and Wharton are an influential if
not dominant group within the faculty, and, in most cases, teaching and reading reflect a decidedly American business ethos. The
coming generation of top managers in Europe, all more or less similarly trained to put the commercial interests of their enterprises
above other considerations, are increasingly divorced from their
particular national framework and reflect, if anything, the business philosophy of the ruling U.S. schools.[47]

The spread of business schools and business literature has further
enhanced the ascendancy of English as the *lingua franca* of international business. Table 2 lists countries in which in 1968/1969
foreign languages were used, either exclusively or partly, for instruction in local management-training programs. Clearly, English
emerges as the dominant language. In some countries, business
training is only available in English: Cyprus, Ethiopia, Ghana,
India, Jamaica, Kenya, Lebanon, Malaysia, Nigeria, the Philippines, Tanzania, Thailand, Trinidad, and Uganda. French, on the
other hand, is used exclusively only in Tunisia. It should be noted
that even in Bulgaria, Romania, and Yugoslavia, English and
French are used coequally with the indigenous languages. Finally,
Japan merits some comment. Two institutions offer courses in
English only. One of them, the Asian Productivity Organization,

Table 2.
Language(s) of instruction of management-training programs,
by country, 1968-69
(Number)

Country	Total number of institutions[a]	Number of institutions using foreign language(s)	Language(s) of instruction[b]
Belgium	9	4	2 Du, E, F
			1 Du, F
			1 E, F, G, I
Bulgaria	1	1	(1 E, F)
Cyprus	1	1	1 E
Ethiopia	1	1	1 E
Finland	3	1	(1 Sw)
France	13	3	2 E, (1 E)
Ghana	1	1	1 E
India	12	12	12 E
Iraq	1	1	(1 E)
Italy	9	1	1 E, F, Sp
Jamaica	2	2	2 E
Japan	10	4	2E, (2 E)
Kenya	3	3	3 E
Lebanon	1	1	1 E
Malaysia	2	2	2 E
Netherlands	8	2	2 E
Nicaragua	2	1	(1 E)
Nigeria	1	1	1 E
Norway	7	1	(1 Da, Sw)
Pakistan	4	4	3 E, (1 E)
Peru	4	2	(2 E)
Philippines	8	7[c]	7 E[c]
Romania	1	1	(1 F)
Senegal	1	1	1 E, F
South Africa	5	5	4 E, 1 E, Af.
Spain	7	1	(1 E, F)
Switzerland	4	4	3 E, 1 G
Taiwan	1	1	(1 E)
Tanzania	2	2	2 E
Thailand	2	2	2 E
Trinidad	1	1	1 E
Tunisia	1	1	1 F
Uganda	2	2	2 E
United Arab Republic	3	3	(2 E), (1 E, F)
Yugoslavia	2	1	(1 E)

Source: Compiled from Nancy G. McNulty, *Training Managers: The International Guide* (New York, 1969).

a The criteria for including management-training institutions were as follows: (1) courses in management for midcareer executives in the subject areas of general management, functional management, and personal skills; (2) regularly scheduled programs; and (3) programs structured around a syllabus (see

serves a regional dissemination function: its objective is "to increase professional skills and change attitudes and behavior," and
its participants, who are recruited from 13 Asian countries, are expected to serve as trainees and consultants for small business, to
"produce a 'multiplier' effect."[48] Another case is the Keio University Business School, Tokyo. This university has several different programs, one of which—the "Keio-Harvard Advanced Management Program"—is offered in English and Japanese. However, it is
taught exclusively by faculty trained at the Harvard Graduate
School of Business.[49] Another program of the Keio University is
taught in Japanese but completely patterned on Harvard's M.B.A.
program, all the faculty members being Harvard-educated. The
basic orientation of this education is summed up in the following
quotation from Keio's course guide: "The theory of management
taught is premised on the continued development of free enterprise."[50]

It is not surprising then, that more and more enterprises should
have made adjustments in regard to the language question. Managers of U.S. and British affiliates abroad—which account for about
two-thirds of all foreign affiliates—have always had to report to
their headquarters in English. It seems, however, that non-Anglo-
American enterprises cannot escape the trend; several Swedish
multinationals, among them SKF, have adopted English as the official company language for all international publications, charts,
manuals, head office announcements, and all correspondence involving more than one affiliate; Nestlé uses French and English
as the enterprise's two languages.[51] Finally, Philips has gone so far
as to adopt English as the language for all internal correspondence.

Business education directly instills managers with home-country
values and behavioral patterns independent of experience with or
exposure to the demonstration effect of foreign affiliates. At the
present time, business education can to all intents and purposes be

---

McNulty, *op. cit.*, p. 4).

b Language abbreviations: Af = Afrikaans; Da = Danish; Du = Dutch; E =
English; F = French; G = German; I = Italian; Sp = Spanish; Sw = Swedish.
Teaching is either entirely or partly in the language(s) specified. If part of
the teaching is also done in the indigenous language, the number of institutions to which this applies and the respective foreign language(s) have been
put in parentheses. Where the entire teaching of a given institution is carried
out in the foreign language(s) only, no parentheses have been used.

c The language of instruction of the eighth institution could not be
ascertained.

equated with American business education, and it is frequently a-
vailable only in English. In general, English has become the *lingua
franca* of international business and its ascendancy may also facilitate, or even spur, the acceptance of nonbusiness aspects of the culture which it expresses. It may be expected that foreign managers,
after being trained in home-country business schools and adopting
the home-country language, would perform crucial model functions with important multiplying effects when they are sent to
foreign affiliates or return to their independent firms.

The international advertising industry

The other major dimension of a business infrastructure created in
many host countries by the international expansion of multinational enterprises is the establishment of advertising services. The
internationalization of production has been accompanied, quite or-
ganically, by an internationalization of advertising and public relations, both on the part of multinational enterprises themselves
and on the part of the advertising industry.[52] Frequently, agencies operating abroad start out with a few major clients already
served by the parent agency at home. In fact, as a study on the
Canadian advertising industry found, "the backbone of foreign
controlled agencies is still the *common account,* i.e., the head
office of the advertiser is served by the head office of the same agency."[53] The study continued: "of the top 70 advertisers in Canada, 78 percent of the advertising placed through foreign-controlled agencies were either accounts common to the parent agency
or placed directly by a United States based agency."[54] In other
words, a foreign-controlled shop is often awarded accounts merely
because its parent handles the account of the foreign-controlled
parent of the advertiser. Such practices are entirely sound from a
business point of view, but they put local agencies at a competitive disadvantage—particularly since foreign clients or their parent
companies as a rule budget comparatively large accounts. Given
the strong position of U.S.-based multinational enterprises in international direct investment, and the superior knowhow of U.S. advertising agencies, it can be expected that American shops have a
prominent position in international advertising. In fact, as the following data will demonstrate, U.S. agencies dominate the industry
almost completely.

The extent to which international advertising agencies have penetrated the mechanisms of national marketing has led, in many

countries, to fundamental changes in the "cultural ecology," in
that "a changed communications structure increasingly transmits
and reinforces attitudes that fit nicely with the requirements of
the multinational goods producers that are financing the new system."[55] Change in the communications structure can best be observed in the commercialization of television; in recent years, following the American example, most European countries have permitted commercials on their broadcasting networks. France did so
in 1968, and in 1973 the United Kingdom granted time for commercial radio. At the present time, the only Western European
countries without commercial television and radio are Belgium,
Sweden, Norway, and Denmark. Otherwise, however, "the number of homes capable of receiving commercial tv has nearly
reached saturation in all countries except France, Italy, Spain,
and Switzerland."[56]

It should be noted that advertising does more than merely sell
products and form consumption patterns: it informs, educates,
changes attitudes, and builds images. For purposes of illustration,
we may quote the statement of a marketing manager who answered the basic marketing question, "What do we sell?" in the
following way: "Never a product, always an idea."[57] In other
words, the function of advertising agencies is to seek "to influence
human behavior in ways favorable to the interests of their clients,"
to "indoctrinate" them.[58]

Advertising is an important and rapidly growing industry. World
advertising volume was estimated at $33.1 billion in 1970.[59]
The United States accounted for $19.6 billion (59 percent), Ca-
nada for $1 billion (3 percent), Western Europe for $8 billion
(24 percent), Asia for $2.4 billion (7 percent—$2.1 billion in Japan alone), Latin America for $1.1 billion (4 percent), Australia
and New Zealand for $0.5 billion (2 percent), and the Middle East
and Africa for $0.3 billion (1 percent). In terms of per capita ex-
penditures, this volume represents $91.3 for the United States/Ca-
nada, $23.9 for Western Europe, $2.3 for Asia, $4.5 for Latin Am-
erica, $34.9 for Australia and New Zealand, and $1.3 for the Middle East—a tremendous amount of funds, even in areas not exactly characterized by an abundance of resources. In addition to
the United States, the Federal Republic of Germany, Japan, the
United Kingdom, Canada, and France spent (in 1970) $1 billion
or more for media advertising. These six countries alone account
for over four-fifths of worldwide expenditures. Twenty years ago,
the United States still held a share of about three-fourths of the

world total; but from 1961 to 1970, spending outside North America almost doubled, from $6.8 billion to $12.5 billion.[60] *Advertising Age* observed that "American companies, both advertisers and advertising agencies, have provided the fuel for some of this explosive growth in international advertising."[61]

The growing commercialization of the cultural ecology of an increasing number of countries is, in the context of this chapter, of particular importance, since, even more so than in the case of international business in general, advertising agencies of the United States dominate the highly concentrated industry.

As Table 3 (pages 60-61), shows, in 1973 seven of the world's top ten independent agencies were entirely American; two agencies, International Needham Univas and SSC and B, Inc., had strong U.S. participation; and one was Japanese. The biggest advertising agency in the world is the Interpublic Group of Companies, to which McCann-Erickson alone contributes 70 percent of the billings. Of the world's 25 biggest agencies, 21 belong in the United States (19 of purely U.S. nationality and 2 with strong U.S. participation), 2 are Japanese, and 1 is French. Finally, of the 50 largest agencies, 34 have their headquarters in the United States, 8 in Japan, 2 each in Canada, the Federal Republic of Germany, and France, 1 in the United Kingdom, and 1 in Switzerland. The largest agency entirely based in Europe, Publicis Conseil (French), is only one-fourth the size of the largest U.S. agency.

Although Japanese agencies perform rather well among the top 50, their business is almost entirely domestic and consequently they are not, so far, a factor in international advertising. This reflects rather accurately the fact that until very recently, Japanese enterprises had not made a substantial amount of direct investment abroad. Since this situation is changing rapidly, it can be expected that Japanese agencies will soon capture a greater share of international billings. The European agencies, on the other hand, have a considerable foreign content, but, comparatively speaking, they are much too small to have more than regional importance. The large U.S. agencies, finally, generate a considerable share of their business abroad. For the ten largest, foreign billings average almost half of their total billings; and for the ten next biggest, the foreign content amounts to an average of 40 percent. The remaining smaller U.S. agencies, as a rule, do hardly any business abroad.

Table 3.
The world's 50 biggest independent advertising agencies,
by country, size, and foreign content, 1973

Rank	Agency	Nationality[a]	Total billings (millions of $)	Billings abroad (percentage)
1	Interpublic Group of Cos.[b]	US	966	57
2	Dentsu Advertising	J	923	3
3	J. Walter Thompson	US	845	54
4	Young & Rubicam	US	650	40
5	International Needham Univas[c]	F/UK/US	552	37
6	Leo Burnett	US	512	35
7	Ted Bates	US	496	51
8	SSC & B[d]	UK/US	483	72
9	Batten, Barton, Durstine & Osborn	US	458	26
10	Ogilvy & Mather International	US	458	55
11	Grey Advertising	US	414	33
12	D'Arcy-McManus & Masius	US	396	51
13	Dancer-Fitzgerald-Sample	US	345	54
14	Doyle Dane Bernbach	US	334	26
15	Foote, Cone & Belding Communications	US	326	28
16	Benton & Bowles	US	293	42
17	Hakuhodo	J	246	about 1
18	I.M.A.A.[e]	US	229	90
19	Publicis Conseil	F	226	about 60
20	Compton Advertising	US	200	48
21	Norman, Craig & Kummel	US	193	64
22	Wells, Rich, Greene	US	190	4
23	Daiko Advertising	J	179	—
24	N.W. Ayer & Son	US	175	—
25	William Esty	US	167	—
26	Kenyon & Eckhardt Advertising	US	164	35
27	Ketchum, McLeod & Grove	US	131	17
28	Marsteller	US	119	21
29	Cunningham & Walsh	US	106	—
30	Euro-Advertising International	F	100	69
31	Campbell-Mithun	US	78	—
32	Clinton E. Frank	US	77	—
33	WPT Group[f]	— —	77	...
34	Ross Roy	US	76	—
35	Troost Werbeagentur	FRG	75	40
36	Yomiko Advertising	J	75	—
37	Tokyo Advertising	J	74	—
38	Dai-Ichi Kikaku	J	72	—
39	Bozell & Jacobs	US	69	—
40	Tatham-Laird & Kudner	US	65	2
41	Dai-Ichi Advertising	J	63	—
42	Post-Keyes-Gardner	US	63	—
43	McCaffrey & McCall	US	61	—
44	Grant Advertising[g]	Can	60	85
45	Warwick, Welsh & Miller	US	60	7
46	Dr. Hagemann	FRG	58	...

47	Chuo Senko Advertising	J	57	–
48	Collett, Dickerson, Pearce	UK	55	...
49	McLaren Advertising	Can	55	16
50	Griswold-Eshleman	US	52	4

Source: Compiled from *Advertising Age,* in particular February 26, 1973; March 26, 1973; February 25, 1974; and March 25, 1974; *Anny,* January 25, 1974; *Werben und Verkaufen Poster,* 1973; various newspaper and magazine reports and direct inquiries.

[a]Nationality abbreviations: Can = Canada; F = France; FRG = Federal Republic of Germany; J = Japan; UK = United Kingdom; US = United States.

[b]The most important member of this group is McCann-Erickson with, in 1973, $681 million billings, of which 70 percent were abroad.

[c]International Needham Univas consists of three partners:

	Nationality	Billings (millions of $)	%age foreign	%age Share in INU
Havas Conseil Group	F	245	52	37.5
Needham, Harper and Steers	US	213	22	37.5
KMPH/Pemberton	UK	94	31	25.0

The basis of International Needham Univas is an international cooperation agreement, with Needham responsible for the Western Hemisphere; Havas for the Continent of Europe, the Middle East, and parts of Africa; and Pemberton for the United Kingdom, parts of Africa, and Asia. The percentage of billings abroad refers to billings outside the three home countries.

[d]SSC & B Inc., New York, owns 49 percent of SSC & B-Lintas International. Since SSC & B Inc., New York, effectively participates in the management of SSC & B-Lintas International, the billings of the two agencies have been combined.

[e]International Markets Advertising Agencies (I.M.A.A.) is a holding company jointly owned by agencies in 15 countries. The largest among them are I.M.A.A./Man-Non-Sha (Japanese; billings 1973: $83 million) and I.M.A.A./Van Brunt (U.S.; billings 1973: $23 million). The U.S. agency owns about 50 percent in the holding company; I.M.A.A. is incorporated in New York.

[f]WPT is a Zürich-based holding company jointly owned by several agencies, the most important of which are Wilkens/WPT (FRG) and Publinter-WPT (Italy).

[g]Grant Advertising was originally based in Chicago. It was purchased in March 1972 by Comcore Communications Ltd., a Toronto-based holding company. Grant is therefore regarded as a Canadian agency.

Despite the presence of a number of non-U.S. advertising agencies among the world's 50 biggest, international and national advertising in general, with the exception of such countries as Yugoslavia, Japan, Greece, and Ireland, is completely dominated by U.S. agencies. Table 4 (pages 64-65) documents the presence of foreign affiliates among the five largest shops of 73 countries in 1973. In the following countries, all three of the largest advertising agencies are foreign majority-owned: Australia, Dominican Republic, Federal Republic of Germany, Indonesia, Italy, Malaysia, Nigeria, Peru, Portugal, Singapore, and the United Kingdom. More generally speaking, in 44 of 73 countries, the largest advertising agency is foreign majority-owned—in 39 of these by parent agencies which are either entirely American or have strong U.S. participation (Table 5, page 66). In an additional 6 countries, foreigners, in this case U.S. agencies, have acquired an often substantial minority interest in the largest agency. In all, in only 23 (or 32 percent) of the 73 countries is the biggest agency entirely owned by nationals.

If one examines the five largest agencies in the countries on which data were available, a distinct pattern emerges: except for the fifth-largest shop, the high the ranking, the more likely it is that the agency is foreign and that means, with only sixteen exceptions, U.S.-owned, through either minority or, in most cases, majority participation. The percentages (those for foreign *majority*-controlled agencies in parentheses) are: largest agencies, 68 percent foreign participation (60 percent foreign majority-controlled); second-largest agencies, 66 percent foreign (56 percent foreign majority-controlled); third-largest agencies, 58 percent foreign (54 percent foreign majority-controlled); fourth-largest agencies, 56 percent foreign (51 percent foreign majority-controlled); and fifth-largest agencies, 75 percent foreign (68 percent foreign majority-controlled). Conversely, across the same rankings, 32 percent, 34 percent, 42 percent, 44 percent, and 25 percent of the agencies were *entirely* domestically owned.

Upon closer inspection, it further emerges that only a very limited number of agencies account for most foreign shops: five agencies are the parents of over half of all foreign majority-controlled shops, and ten agencies are responsible for over four-fifths (Table 6, page 67). Among the ten parent agencies found most often, seven are entirely U.S.-owned, two have very strong American partners, and one, Grant Advertising, was transferred from American to Canadian ownership in 1972. Of the 151 majority-owned foreign agencies—which represent, as it will be recalled, close to 60 percent of the aggregated top five agencies in 73 countries—84 (or 56 percent) are controlled by five agencies: the Interpublic Group of Cos. (27), SSC & B Inc. (20), J. Walter Thompson Co. (18), I.M.A.A. (10), and Grant Advertising (9). If another five agencies are added, the number increases to 125, or 83 percent. This percentage, however, is not constant across foreign-owned agencies as they appear in their host-country ranking. Rather, the higher the host-country placements, the more likely it is that they are occupied by affiliates of the ten most found parent agencies: they account for 91 percent of the foreign shops in the first, 85 percent in the second, 81 percent in the third, 76 percent in the fourth, and 74 percent in the fifth placements.[62] In short, the international advertising industry, even more than international direct investment, is highly concentrated, with only ten parent agencies accounting for over four-fifths of all foreign majority-controlled shops.

Given the size and tremendous concentration of the international advertising industry and its domination by U.S. agencies, the pattern-setting potential of foreign affiliates in their various linkages with the host country receives powerful additional support from advertising in a converging encroachment on national culture and its remodeling according to the values of headquarters countries.[63]

Some empirical findings

It appears inevitable that in a culture-diffusion process, the U.S. variety of business culture should be the most influential one. Empirical research in this area is scarce, although some evidence exists to support this expectation. For instance, Hartmann's study, which is particularly interesting since it does not focus on the relationship between a developed and a developing country (where one would expect strong elements of asymmetry), sought to discover whether U.S. capital investments in the Federal Republic of Germany were accompanied by such sociocultural investments as techniques of organization, ideologies and philosophies, and such concrete manifestations as (business) language, professional literature, clothing, and mannerisms.[64]

As a general observation, Hartmann's research showed that, even if the parent enterprise tried to avoid any export save that of capital, a certain amount of U.S. business culture, or some part of it, was

Table 4
The five largest advertising agencies in 73 countries, by country of origin, 1973

Country	Placement of agency[a]				
	Largest	Second	Third	Fourth	Fifth
Argentina	US (3)	US (1)	D(xUS11)	D	D(xUS 10)
Australia	US (7)	US (1)	US (3)	F/UK/US (5)	US (6)
Austria	D	UK/US (8)	US (3)	US (1)	D
Barbados	D (xUS 20)	D	...	...	...
Belgium	US (1)	D(xxUS 16)	UK/US (8)	US (3)	FRG (35)
Bermuda	D (xxUS 20)	...	...	...	...
Bolivia	US (26)	...	...	...	...
Brazil	US (1)	US (3)	D	D	F/UK/US (5)
Burma	D	...	...	...	...
Canada	D (44)	D (49)	D	US (13)	US (3)
Chile	D	US (26)	...	...	...
Colombia	US (6)	D	D	D	US (1)
Costa Rica	D	US (1)	...	...	...
Denmark	US (7)	D	UK/US (8)	D	US (10)
Dominican Republic	US (4)	US (26)	US (1)	...	...
Ecuador	US (1)	US (18)	...	...	...
Egypt	US (18)	...	...	...	...
El Salvador	US (1)	...	...	...	...
Finland	US (1)	D	D	Bel.	D
France	D (19)	F/UK/US(5)	D	US (7)	D
Federal Republic of Germany	UK/US (8)	US (1)	US (3)	D (35)	US (9)
Ghana	UK/US (8)	...	...	...	...
Greece	D	D	D	D	UK/US (8)
Guatemala	D	US (1)	D	...	...
Honduras	US (1)	D	...	...	...
Hong Kong	US (7)	D	US (1)	D	US (13)
India	D (xxUS 3)	D (xxUS 1)	US (10)	D	UK/US (8)
Indonesia	UK/US (8)	US (7)	US (13)	...	...
Iran	US (18)	D	...	...	...
Ireland	D	D	D	F/UK/US (5)	D
Israel	D	D	US (18)	D	D
Italy	US (1)	F/UK/US (5)	US (4)	UK/US (8)	US (26)
Jamaica	US (1)	US (21)	D(xUS 20)	D	US (26)
Japan	D (2)	D (17)	D (23)	US (18)	D (37)
Kenya	US (10)	Ca (44)[b]	D	...	...
Kuwait	D	...	...	...	...
Lebanon	F/UK/US(5)	US (4)	D	Ku	D
Malaysia	US (6)	US (10)	US (1)	UK/US (8)	Ca (44)[b]
Mexico	D	US (1)	US (3)	D(xxUS20)	US (4)
Morocco	F/UK/US(5)	...	...	...	...
Netherlands	F (19)	US (9)	D	UK/US (8)	US (3)
Netherlands Antilles	D	US (26)	...	...	...
New Zealand	D(xxUS 1)	D(xxF/UK/US5)	US (10)	D	UK/US (8)
Nicaragua	D	US (1)	...	...	...
Nigeria	UK/US (8)	US (10)	Ca (44)[b]	D	D
Norway	US (7)	D	D	D (xxUS 4)	UK/US (8)

Placement of agency[a]

Country	Largest	Second	Third	Fourth	Fifth
Pakistan	UK/US (8)	US (18)	D	...	...
Panama	D	US (1)	Ca (44)[b]	...	...
Paraguay	D	...	...	...	...
Peru	US (1)	US (3)	US (26)	US (18)	...
Philippines	US (3)	D(xxUS20)	D	US (1)	US (18)
Portugal	UK/US (8)	US (21)	US (6)	US (18)	F (19)
Puerto Rico	US (4)	D(xxUS20)	D	US (3)	US (15)
Rhodesia	US (6)	US (3)	...	...	...
Sierra Leone	UK/US (8)	...	...	...	...
Singapore	Ca (44)[b]	US (6)	US (10)	US (13)	D(xxUS20)
South Africa	F/UK/US(5)	US (3)	D	D	UK/US (8)
South Korea	D	D	...	...	...
Spain	D(xxUS16)	D	US (3)	US (26)	UK/US (8)
Sri Lanka	Ca (44)[b]	...	...	...	...
Sweden	US (10)	D	D	D	D(xxUS20)
Switzerland	F (19)	D	US (13)	D	D
Syria	D	...	...	...	...
Taiwan	D	D	US (18)	D	Ca (44)[b]
Thailand	UK/US (8)	D	US (1)	Ca (44)[b]	US (6)
Trinidad	US (1)	D(xxUS20)	US (21)	US (26)	US (16)
Turkey	D	FRG (35)	D	...	...
United Kingdom	US (3)	US (1)	US (10)	US (12)	US (6)
United States	D (1)	D (3)	D (4)	D (5)	D (6)
Uruguay	US (3)	US (1)	...	...	...
Venezuela	D(xxUS10)	US (3)	US (4)	D	US (6)
Yugoslavia	D	...	...	...	...
Zambia	Ca (44)[b]	...	...	...	...

Source: See Table 3.

[a]In terms of 1973 billings. For each rank placement, the following information is provided: (a) if the agency is 50 percent or more owned by an agency outside the respective country, the country of origin is indicated; if the agency is a domestic one, the entry is "D"; (b) the rank of the parent agency among the world's 50 biggest advertising agencies follows, in parentheses, the country-of-origin entry; this rank corresponds with the ranking in Table 3; (c) if a foreign agency holds a nonmajority interest in a national agency, this is indicated in parentheses, by an "x" (minority interest) or an "xx" (substantial minority interest) after the "D" entry and before the country-of-origin entry plus the world's rank of the parent corporation. For instance, the entry "D(xUS11)" reads: "The agency in this particular placement is a nationally-owned one, but the U.S. agency Grey Advertising (11) has a minority interest in it."

The country-of-origin abbreviations used are Bel = Belgium; Ca = Canada; F = France; FRG = Federal Republic of Germany; Ku = Kuwait; Sw = Sweden; UK = United Kingdom; US = United States.

[b]The information available regarding the foreign affiliates of Grant Advertising indicates merely "partly owned"; it is assumed that this indicates majority ownership. See also footnote g in Table 3.

Table 5
Foreign and domestic ownership of national advertising agencies, by placement, 1973

	Placement of agency					Total First to Fifth
	Largest	Second	Third	Fourth	Fifth	
Total number of entries for each placement[a]	73	59	48	41	40	261
National ownership						
Total	29	26	22	20	13	110
Entirely national	23	20	20	18	10	91
Majority national	6	6	2	2	3	19
Foreign ownership						
Total foreign participation	50	39	28	23	30	170
Majority ownership	44	33	26	21	27	151
US only	39	31	24	18	23	135
Minority ownership	6	6	2	2	3	19
US only	6	6	2	2	3	19
Total foreign participation as percentage of total entry	68	66	58	56	75	65
US only	62	63	54	49	65	59
Total foreign *majority* ownership as percentage of total entry	60	56	54	51	68	58
US only	53	53	50	44	58	52

Source: Based on Table 4.

Note: SSC & B Inc. ("UK/US") and International Needham Univas ("F/UK/US") are considered as U.S. agencies.

[a] The number of countries for which Table 4 provides information on each particular placement.

inevitably transmitted to its German affiliates; in other words, some ideas and practices will always be adopted by the affiliate. In fact, all the U.S. affiliates in the Federal Republic investigated by Hartmann exhibited, in one way or another, American characteristics in response to extensive headquarters contact. This applies especially to their organizational structure, which usually differed from that of local companies and almost always copied, often in detail, that of the parent enterprise. The particular organizational structure, in turn, "reflects typical American values," for instance, the official emphasis on informal relationships within the framework of a strict hierarchy, and the emphasis on marketing. Similarly, U.S. techniques in various areas of management—e.g., production, accounting and finance, executive leadership, advertising, and public relations—were introduced by affiliates. Finally,

Table 6

Concentration in foreign majority-owned advertising agencies: the ten parent agencies encountered most frequently, 1973

Rank	Agency	Placement of agency					Total First to Fifth
		Largest	Second	Third	Fourth	Fifth	
1	Interpublic Group of Cos.	10	10	4	2	1	27
8	SSC & B	8	1	2	3	6	20
3	J. Walter Thompson	4	5	5	2	2	18
18	I.M.A.A.	2	2	2	3	1	10
44	Grant Advertising	3	1	2	1	2	9
	Subtotal: above 5	27	19	15	11	12	84
6	Leo Burnett	3	1	1	–	4	9
10	Ogilvy and Mather International	2	2	4	–	1	9
26	Kenyon and Eckhardt Advertising	1	3	1	2	2	9
5	International Needham Univas	3	2	–	2	1	8
7	Ted Bates	4	1	–	1	–	6
	Subtotal: above 10	40	28	21	16	20	125
	Other American	2	4	5	3	5	19
	Others	2	1	–	2	2	7
	Total	44	33	26	21	27	151
	Top 5 as %age of total	61	58	58	52	44	56
	Top 10 as %age of total	91	85	81	76	74	83

Source: Based on Table 4.

Hartmann particularly noted the growing use of Americanisms in the business language and a general increase in the use of English, knowledge of which was often a prerequisite for advancing to certain positions in the management hierarchy.

Taken together, Hartmann observed, these components reflected a "business philosophy" or "management philosophy" (both concepts have no precise conceptual equivalents in German) which are distinctly American, and which imply a set of attitudinal patterns that determine the behavior of company managers with respect to their corporation, colleagues, and employees, as well as the place of business in society. Hartmann also noted that this business philosophy was not confined to the top management, but was disseminated, in different degrees and through various mechanisms, both inside and outside the affiliate. Consequently, the author concluded that "it seems that the significance of the socio-cultural export process derives, to a considerable degree, from the fact that foreign affiliates constitute the German bridgehead of a transatlantic connection from which American achievements are further disseminated. . . . According to the testimony of our respondents, our own observations, and the data of other countries, it is more than probable that the demonstration of American management style in United States foreign affiliates substantially affects the attitudes and behavior of extra-corporate observers."[65]

One can place these findings in a larger perspective. In theory, non-home countries, and especially developing countries, are faced with a sociocultural impact of American, European, and Japanese origin. However, assuming the validity of Hartmann's findings, one would have to conclude that the business culture exported by enterprises of the Federal Republic of Germany—and probably by other European enterprises as well—is increasingly Americanized. European enterprises, then, would play a supportive intermediary role in the global diffusion of U.S. business culture.

Some other empirical findings are relevant in this context and of importance for the topic of the chapter in general. It has been found that, if data from multinational enterprises based in the Federal Republic of Germany can be generalized, a substantial percentage of parent-enterprise managers actually recommend the imposition of headquarters business practices on their foreign affiliates. Almost two-thirds in a sample of 2,701 managers employed in enterprises of the Federal Republic of Germany answered the question whether German business customs should serve as guidelines in German subsidiaries abroad in the affirmative.[66] These managers, in other words, are not particularly interested in developing and applying system-wide standards abstracted from the (different) experience of the individual parts of the enterprise system, but, instead, exhibit a clear bias towards customs of headquarters, i.e., home countries, and recommend their application abroad. Given the structure of the multinational enterprise system, these intentions can easily be carried out. And assuming the validity of Hartmann's findings, the content of these customs is increasingly Americanized.

Summary and conclusions

Let us briefly review the material presented on the potential of multinational enterprises to serve as vehicles for and disseminators of home-country business culture. We found that the ability of foreign affiliates to influence and shape a host country's business culture—and through it the entire cultural and social system—is based on two factors: first, on their direct capacity to add to and shape the production apparatus of the host country and to introduce, promote, and disseminate new modes of operation and behavior; and, second, on the impetus they give to the creation of a supporting (foreign-controlled) business service structure geared to meet the needs of foreign affiliates. The crucial common element in these factors is that the capital investments underlying international business are accompanied by sociocultural investments, that is, values and behavioral patterns associated with the parent enterprise (or agency) and its home country. More concretely, it was suggested that the degree of foreign-affiliate impact depended on three factors, the discussion of which constituted the body of the chapter: the magnitude and distribution of international business; the nature of the linkage between multinational enterprise headquarters, their foreign affiliates, and the host country in which they are operating; and the extent to which MNEs instigate the creation of a foreign-determined business infrastructure. Overall, we found that the configuration of all three factors is such that foreign affiliates possess a powerful potential for exerting a considerable impact on a host-country's business culture.

We observed first of all that more than 10,000 multinational enterprises own a minimum of 50,000 foreign affiliates. About two-thirds of these affiliates are located in developed market economies. The distribution of the one-third of affiliates located in developing countries closely reflects the historical interests and preoccupations of their major home countries, with the result that a considerable share of these affiliates is concentrated in former colonies or other spheres of influence, thereby increasing the probability of a similar type of impact. The importance of MNEs is compounded by the fact that they are highly concentrated in terms of number of home countries, number of parent enterprises, and number of foreign affiliates. The United States, followed by the United Kingdom, the Federal Republic of Germany, France, and Switzerland, are the home countries of most of the approximately 150 MNEs that control about one-half of the approximately $165 billion of international investment. In addition, all but one of the major headquarter countries share basically the same culture, in particular business culture, although it must be concluded that the U.S. variation of this culture, based on its overall share in international business and supported by its predominant position in international advertising and the supply of business education, is more than *primus inter pares.*

With respect to the linkage between headquarters, foreign affiliate and host country, we found that the overwhelming majority of foreign affiliates are highly responsive to headquarters policies owing to a variety of formal and informal control mechanisms. Most significant among these are majority ownership of foreign affiliates by the parent enterprise, prerogatives of headquarters in key decision-making areas of their affiliates, and the presence of expatriate personnel in top managerial positions of the affiliate, who not only exercise a valuable control function but also fulfill an important social model function vis-à-vis members of the indigenous society. The unidirectionality and asymmetry of this relationship, already inherent in a hierarchical business organization, is further accentuated by the absence of any representation of the interests of the foreign affiliates (or host countries) in the parent enterprise: parent enterprises are almost exclusively owned and managed by home-country nationals, and in no way reflect the international involvement of the enterprise system as a whole. On the other hand, foreign affiliates are directly linked to the host society by a variety of mechanisms, notably forward and backward economic linkages and the employment of indigenous labor. The relevance of the second linkage has been illustrated by the estimate that foreign affiliates directly employ approximately 13 to 14 million indigenous workers.

The spread of foreign affiliates has created a demand for local infrastructure, particularly with respect to the supply of trained personnel and advertising services. The special importance attributed to these factors by U.S. enterprises, in combination with their financial strength, probably accounts for their international predominance in these fields; and their success probably explains the increasing tendency in other countries to replicate and imitate them. As regards the supply of business education, almost all major business schools are either established, staffed, or inspired by the major American schools. The content of their teaching, as far as values and behavioral patterns are concerned, reflects a decidedly Western, or, more precisely, U.S. approach. This situation also affects independent indigenous firms, because a rising number of their managers are trained in these institutions; they are, therefore, directly inculcated with home-country values and behavioral patterns, independent of exposure to the demonstration effect of foreign affiliates.

The close ties between foreign affiliates and their headquarters are also mirrored in the use of the parent-enterprise language in intra-firm communications. A number of examples, moreover, seem to suggest that intra- and interenterprise communications, even of non-Anglo-American enterprises, tend increasingly to be carried out in English. The emergence of English as the *lingua franca* of international business accurately reflects the Anglo-American preponderance in international business together with the American dominance of its infrastructure.

The expansion of foreign affiliates has also been complemented in recent years by an internationalization of advertising, a concept which is, in itself, basically American. International advertising is almost entirely an American industry: 21 of the largest 25 agencies in the world are U.S. agencies or strongly linked with them and most of them generate about half of their billings abroad. In other words, the larger the advertising agency, the more likely it is to be a U.S. agency or to have a strong U.S. partner. Foreign majority-owned shops are the largest in 44 out of 73 countries; 39 of them are affiliates of American or American-related parents. And in an additional six countries, U.S. parents have acquired an often substantial minority interest in the largest agency. More generally speaking, the bigger an agency within a country, the more likely it is to be under (usually majority) foreign (and, as a rule, American) control, with this likelihood not falling below 70 percent for the first placement. Moreover, while U.S. agencies are omnipresent, non-U.S. shops are either entirely domestic (Japan) or of only regional significance (Western Europe). Finally, among foreign majority-owned agencies, the higher the ranking in the host country, the more likely it is that they are affiliates of only ten parent agencies, with this probability exceeding 90 percent for the foreign-held first placements in host countries. Nine of these ten parents are U.S. agencies or have strong U.S. partners, and one was only recently transferred from U.S. to Canadian ownership.

One can expect the international advertising strategies of foreign-owned agencies to be largely influenced by home country values. The consumer values and consumption patterns they propagate, and the images and aspirations they build in the service of their primarily multinational clients, are usually not of local provenance. Rather they reflect the achievements of the parent enterprise which, in turn, are based on R & D almost entirely conducted in (and frequently also for) home-country markets. In view of this function, advertising agencies are more than a mere service structure for foreign affiliates; they are independent agents with great potential for influencing and shaping host-country values and behavioral patterns.

Special attention must be drawn to the directionality of the various linkages discussed above. Central to the nature of the relationship between headquarters, foreign affiliates (or agencies), and societies is the fact that the linkage between them is not only strong but clearly unidirectional, flowing from the home country to the host country. Some of these linkages, moreover, contain elements of coercion: the strictly hierarchical structure of business organizations, and the use of a variety of formal and informal control mechanisms, place headquarters in the position of being able (within the boundaries of self-defined global economic rationality) to impose their values and behavioral patterns on their affiliates, and this without necessarily having to take into account any specific local needs such as cultural identity or appropriate (national) usage of scarce economic resources. And, as empirical evidence indicates, home-country managers consciously advocate the usage of headquarters business practices in their foreign affiliates. Thus, influences flowing from a host-country's business subculture to other components of its cultural and social structure can be expected to be highly foreign-determined. Since this pattern, because of the unidirectionality of the linkages involved, is not replicated in the home country, the relationship between host countries and home countries in the transfer of business culture is asymmetrical, i.e., it is not a relationship between equals.

Taken together, the magnitude of international business and the nature, directionality, and content of the linkage mechanisms involved suggest that the foreign-affiliate network of MNEs, further supported by the associated structures of business education and advertising, constitute a substantial potential for the transmission and dissemination of home-country culture, and specifically for Western business culture, American-style. Evidence presented with respect to the impact of U.S. affiliates on the business culture of the Federal Republic of Germany seems to indicate that this potential is, in fact, powerful, and inevitably affects, in and by itself and even without any conscious attempt on the part of the parent enterprise, those coming in contact with it.

If this is the case with respect to Western Europe, one can only speculate about the degree to which the pattern-setting potential of these factors and mechanisms, in their convergent encroachment on national culture followed by its subsequent remodeling according to the values and behavioral patterns of headquarters countries, is further magnified in developing countries, where the difference between indigenous (business) culture and the culture of foreign affiliates is even more marked. It seems, in fact, that the values and behavioral patterns in question have been accepted and are being imitated almost on a world-wide basis.[67]

The success of a few home countries in supplying the content of an emerging world culture is such that even societies whose overall economic conditions are completely different from those of the countries whose economic development is reflected in its content attempt to sustain and share this culture.[68] This acceptance also includes the adoption and internalization of the goals embodied in this culture, notably those involving the type, direction, and speed of material progress. Since a number of these goals, particularly in the case of developing countries, cannot be attained autonomously in the time span desired, or require continued inputs from abroad, dependency on countries and their institutions that can help to fulfill these aspirations becomes almost unavoidable. In this sense, the acceptance of the values of a few home countries may lead to "self-colonialization" and may become an important correlate of the "nonviolent" perpetuation of structures of intersocietal dependency.

NOTES

[1]Heinz Hartmann, *Amerikanische Firmen in Deutschland*, p. 11.

[2]The term "multinational enterprise" is used here merely as a label referring to enterprises centrally controlling assets in two or more countries; it is not implied that these enterprises are, for instance, multinationally owned or managed.

[3]See, for instance, a recently compiled bibliography on imperialism literature in Dieter Senghaas, ed., *Imperialismus und strukturelle Gewalt. Analysen über abhängige Reproduktion*, pp. 379 ff.

[4]MNEs are, of course, not the only agents of cultural diffusion; exchange programs, travel, general education, the media, and other taste-forming industries are also relevant. Nonetheless, MNE operations, given their magnitude and their direct, multifaceted, and continuing linkages with host societies, are of special importance in promoting the homogenization of world culture.

[5]For a brief review of the distinction between "social" and "cultural" phenomena, see A. L. Kroeber and Talcott Parsons, "The Concepts of Culture and of Social Systems," *American Sociological Review*, pp. 582-583.

[6]This is not to deny the possibility of effects in the other direction, but the contention is that these are less important.

[7]This is particularly true of developing countries, where traditional values and patterns of behavior are challenged in the process of industrialization. This increases their receptivity to new influences, e.g., to those introduced by MNEs.

[8]The establishment of a foreign-controlled financial infrastructure (e.g., banks) will not be considered here.

[9]Government of Canada, *Foreign Direct Investment in Canada,* p. 294.

[10]In the context of developing countries, the values and behavioral patterns introduced might also be understood in terms of Parsons' pattern variables, in addition to those mentioned in the study by the government of Canada cited above. Osterberg and Ajami argue along these lines. See David Osterberg and Fouad Ajami, "The Multinational Corporation: Expanding the Frontiers of World Politics," *Journal of Conflict Resolution,* pp. 457-470.

[11]Another paper investigates the extent to which home-country managers in fact consciously recommend the utilization of this potential. See Karl P. Sauvant and Bernard Mennis, "Zum Managerbewusstsein in multinationalen Unternehmen vor dem Hintergrund europäischer Integration," in *Zur Multinationalisierung des Kapitals,* ed. Klaus Jürgen Gantzel.

[12]Most of these studies are listed and annotated in David Burtis, Farid G. Lavipour, Steven Ricciardi, and Karl P. Sauvant, eds., *Multinational Corporation—Nation-State Interaction: An Annotated Bibliography;* OECD, *Foreign Investment and Its Impact in Developing Countries;* and OECD, *Private Foreign Investments and Their Impact in Developing Countries.*

[13]R.K. Merton, *Social Theory and Social Structure;* William M. Evan, "The Organization-Set: Toward a Theory of Interorganizational Relations," in *Approaches to Organizational Design,* ed. James D. Thompson, pp. 175-191; and Evan, "An Organization-Set Model of Interorganizational Relations," in *Interorganizational Decision Making,* ed. M.F. Tuite, Roger Chisholm, and Michael Radnor, pp. 181-200. Further developments of these mechanisms are treated in William M. Evan, *Organization Theory: Systems, structures, and Environments.*

[14]A more comprehensive framework for an empirical analysis of the linkages between foreign affiliates and developing host societies has been elaborated in a research proposal by William M. Evan, Andrew C. Hilton, Patrick H. Irwin, Taghi Saghafi-nejad, and Karl P. Sauvant, "The Effects of Multinational Enterprises on the Modernization Process of Developing Countries: A Comparative Study."

[15]As a result, host countries, in particular developing countries, often reproduce the consumption patterns of the developed home countries, which correspond, of course, to far higher per capita incomes and therefore tend to distort national economic development. See, for instance, Economic Commission for Latin America, *Economic Survey of Latin America.*

[16]The figure for the United States and Western Europe is from the *Yearbook of International Organizations,* 13th ed., 1970-1971. The *Yearbook* compilation does not provide data for Australia, Canada, and Japan. In 1972, 510 Australian enterprises had 973 affiliates abroad (data obtained from the Australian Commonwealth Bureau of Census and Statistics). In the case of Canada, 713 enterprises are reported to have had foreign affiliates in 1968; see Canadian Department of Industry, Trade and Commerce, "Canada's International Investment Position, 1926 to 1967." For Japan, the *Quarterly Survey of Japanese Finance and Industry* (vol. 23, Oct.-Dec. 1971, published by the Industrial Bank of Japan) reports, for 1968, 1,608 enterprises which had acquired securities abroad; 366 cases in which claimable assets had been acquired; and 33 cases of acquisition of real estate. The number of Japanese affiliates abroad is reported to be 3,935 for 1970 (Toyo Keizai, *Statistics Monthly,* vol. 32, June 1972). The figures, particularly those for Japan, are not strictly comparable to the *Yearbook* figures.

[17]The share of the major foreign direct investment countries, notably that of the United

States, is actually higher than indicated in most figures, owing to indirect foreign direct investment. For instance, in 1964, 43 percent of the total book value of Canadian foreign direct investment was accounted for by foreign affiliates in Canada; U.S. corporations alone controlled 38.9 percent of the total (Canadian Department of Industry, Trade and Commerce, "Direct Investment Abroad by Canada, 1964-1967." A similar situation probably exists in Switzerland; U.S. direct investment in Switzerland in 1971 totalled $1,884 million; 77.4 percent of this amount was in "other industries," a category which accounts for only 22.7 percent of *all* U.S. foreign direct investment (*Survey of Current Business,* Nov. 1972). It can be assumed that a substantial share of this investment is in holding companies which in turn control foreign affiliates officially regarded as Swiss.

[18] Foreign direct investment figures are used as an approximate measure of multinational enterprise assets, although the identity is not complete: in the case of the United States, for example, multinational enterprises account for over 80 percent of the value of total U.S. foreign direct investment (U.S. Department of Commerce, *The Multinational Corporation, Studies on U.S. Foreign Investments,* vol. 1.)

[19] In the light of the preceding discussion, Dunning's estimate that the 50 largest world multinational enterprises probably account for one-half of the total international investment and the next 50 largest for an additional 25 percent, appears to be too high. See John H. Dunning, "The Determinants of International Production," *Oxford Economic Papers,* pp. 289-336. It is, however, entirely possible that the concentration ratio in international direct investment is higher than estimated here. For instance, the increments added by any Canadian enterprises over the largest 10 Canadian foreign investors are very likely to be (much) smaller than those added by a number of U.S. enterprises not included in the first 45 of Table 1. In other words, the foreign direct investment of the 45th largest U.S. foreign investor is probably higher than the combined foreign direct investment of the 10th to 13th Canadian foreign investors. In spite of possibilities for these adjustments and the additional consideration of indirect foreign direct investment (note 17), it is unlikely that fewer than 150 enterprises account for much more than one-half of international direct investment.

[20] Karl P. Sauvant and Bernard Mennis, "Corporate Internationalization and German Enterprises: A Social Profile of German Managers and their Attitudes Regarding the European Community and Future Company Strategies."

[21] In the discussion of the distribution of affiliates, percentages refer to host-country links and not to the actual number of affiliates. Source: *Yearbook of International Organizations,* 13th ed., 1970-1971. Australia, Canada, and Japan are excluded because the available data are not comparable.

[22] United Nations, *Multinational Corporations in World Development,* pp. 152-155.

[23] See John B. Rhodes, "Upturn in Foreign Activity by U.S. Business," *Columbia Journal of World Business,* p. 23.

[24] See John M. Stopford and Louis T. Wells, Jr., *Managing the Multinational Enterprise.*

[25] Stopford and Wells, *Managing the Multinational Enterprise,* pp. 26-27.

[26] For a highly instructive account of the evolution of business organizations to their present structure, see Alfred D. Chandler, *Strategy and Structure.*

[27] See Business International, *Organizing the Worldwide Corporation,* p. 80. Research and development is carried out almost entirely in the home country.

[28] D. van den Bulcke, *Les entreprises étrangères dans l'industrie Belge.* The following figures are drawn from this study.

[29]In a number of affiliates, the limit below which autonomous decisions could be made was between $5,000 and $10,000.

[30]Van den Bulcke found, however, that a number of U.S. affiliates needed headquarters authorization for hiring and for increasing the salaries of middle and upper managers. An incident in which the personnel director of a U.S. affiliate, upon intervention from headquarters, had to reduce an increase in salary for a secretary from $150 to $70 was found to be exceptional.

[31]In 60 percent of the U.S. and 33 percent of the European Community cases. In other decision areas, headquarter influence was, however, considerably lower.

[32]Government of Canada, *Foreign Direct Investment*, p. 143.

[33]DIVO Institut für Wirtschaftsforschung, Sozialforschung und angewandte Mathematik GmbH, *Amerikanische Tochtergesellschaften in der Bundesrepublik*. Twenty-five percent had a purely American executive management, and the rest was mixed.

[34]Van den Bulcke, *Les entreprises étrangères*.

[35]Quoted in Christopher Tugendhat, *The Multinationals*, p. 195. It would be interesting to know if the former chairman would agree with the corresponding interpretation that he has a bias in favor of his (the home-) country's operations and his government. Nestlé's policy, on the other hand, is different, at least to a certain degree: non-Swiss have an equal opportunity to be promoted to top management—except for the chairmanship.

[36]Sauvant and Mennis, "Corporate Internationalization and German Enterprises." "Managers" include the lowest level management; one of the companies did not belong to the 500 largest corporations. Similar figures are reported for the 25 largest European corporations. See Lawrence G. Franko, "Who Manages Multinational Enterprises?" *Columbia Journal of World Business*, p. 39.

[37]Kenneth Simmonds, "Multinational? Well, Not Quite," *Columbia Journal of World Business*, pp. 115-122. Simmonds found that of the 34 who transferred to the United States, only 13 were previously employed in a foreign subsidiary of the parent corporation, and 22 of them (two-thirds) were British or Canadian; only 1 top manager came from a developing country—Mexico—and he had a degree from the Massachusetts Institute of Technology. Among the 25 members of top management who had not transferred to the United States, 19 were Canadian and 3 British.

[38]Jeremy Bacon, *Corporate Directorship Practices: Membership and Committees of the Board*.

[39]Since Simmonds' study, as discussed in the previous paragraph, did not include non-manufacturing corporations, only this figure can be compared with his findings. Furthermore, it should be kept in mind that Simmonds also included nondirector top-managers.

[40]As far as future developments are concerned, the study points out that more than nine out of ten companies which do not yet have foreigners on their boards of directors have not considered electing such individuals. It is asserted, however, that "the absence of a non-U.S. citizen director rarely reflects a company policy" (p. 6). One might quote Simmonds in this context, who found that a group of executives interviewed in the course of his study emphasized on the one hand that "the firm should always look for the 'best' man regardless of nationality," but, on the other, were quite contented if this usually meant an American (Simmonds, *"Multinational?"* p. 120).

[41]Local integration of mining affiliates is substantially lower, hardly amounting to 20 percent of affiliate sales.

[42]Raymond Vernon, *Sovereignty at Bay*, p. 156.

[43]R. Jungnickel, G. Koopmann, K. Matthies and R. Sutter, *Der Internationalisierungs-*

prozess der deutschen Industrie.

44Data obtained from the Swedish Ministry of Industry.

45United Nations, *Multinational Corporations in World Development,* p. 52.

46The Wharton School is setting up a branch in France.

47The influence of U.S. business philosophy is, of course, not restricted to Europe. The American University of Beirut, for example, has a department of business administration which, according to the *Financial Times* (October 3, 1973), "As the Middle East's 'Harvard' . . . provides the local intellectual cream for the area." Courses are styled on American business school methods, although certain adaptations are made.

48Nancy G. McNulty, *Training Managers: The International Guide,* p. 401.

49*Ibid.,* p. 48. Each year, two members of the Keio faculty are sent to Harvard for training.

50Ibid., p. 468.

51Business International, *Organizing the Worldwide Corporation,* p. 70.

52In fact, the concepts of "advertising" and "public relations," in their present form, originated in the United States; and the style, concepts, techniques, and often also the technology, of advertising have, over several decades, been an American export.

53Kates, Peat, Marwick and Co., "Foreign Ownership and the Advertising Industry," p. 111.

54*Ibid.* On the other hand, 79 percent of the advertising by Canadian-controlled enterprises is placed by Canadian-controlled agencies.

55Herbert J. Schiller, "Madison Avenue Imperialism," *Trans-Action,* p. 53.

56*Advertising Age,* Oct. 29, 1973, p. 56.

57Quoted in Hartmann, *Amerikanische Firmen in Deutschland,* p. 180.

58Quoted from Paul C. Harper, Jr. (Needham, Harper and Steers), "The Agency Business in 1980," *Advertising Age,* Nov. 19, 1973, p. 35. Tom Dillon, the President of Batten, Barton, Durstine and Osborn, the world's ninth largest advertising agency, understands the function of advertising in a broader political framework (it is not suggested, however, that his views are representative). In an article on "Freedom must advertise, or it surely will lose itself" (*Advertising Age,* Nov. 21, 1973) he declares that, "without the financial support of advertising, not only would there be no practical freedom of economic choice, but there is also a very serious question whether there would be any practical freedom in politics and religion" (p. 210). This is so because advertising guarantees the independence of the media, in particular that of the press; after all, in the July 6, 1776, issue of the *Pennsylvania Evening Post,* the Declaration of Independence was followed by ten ads. Advertising, therefore, is "as vital to the preservation of freedom in my country as the free exercise of publishing a newspaper or the free exercise of building a church or the free exercise of the right of trial by jury" (p. 210).

59International Research Associates and International Advertising Association, *1970 World Advertising Expenditures.* The following figures in the text are from this source.

60*Advertising Age,* Nov. 21, 1973.

61*Advertising Age,* Nov. 21, 1973, p. 192.

62It is not surprising, then, that governments in a number of countries should be trying to reduce the number of foreign-produced commercials. But the results are questionable, although predictable. For instance, Procter and Gamble Co. of Canada, which imported a number of its commercials from the United States, in reaction to Ottawa's pressure on foreign affiliates in Canada to produce broadcasts and print advertising locally, replaced two of its U.S. commercial suppliers—with three Toronto shops owned by U.S. agencies (*Advertising Age*, Nov. 12, 1973).

63Most MNEs also engage in public relations, the function of which, even more so than that of advertising, is to create favorable attitudes towards their products and services and the corporations themselves. The objective is to promote the image of the company and the values it stands for, in order to gain its acceptance by the respective host societies. The most effective way of this is by stressing—or creating—communities of interest, values and aspirations.

64Hartmann, *Amerikanische Firmen in Deutschland.*

65*Ibid.*, pp. 184-185.

66See Sauvant and Mennis, "Managerbewusstsein." To give the exact distribution of the answers: 4 percent said "certainly yes"; 60 percent "probably yes"; 23 percent "probably no"; and 13 percent "certainly no."

67See Talcott Parsons, "Order and Community in the International Social System," in *International Politics and Foreign Politics*, ed. James N. Rosenau, pp. 120-129.

68The result is, of course, polarization in host countries, in particular in developing countries. The modern sectors, which absorb almost all foreign direct investment, are oriented to or integrated into the world economy and reflect its advanced standards, while the traditional sectors, especially the rural sector, remain engaged in underdeveloped subsistence activity. This aspect of the consequences of multinational enterprise activities is receiving increasing attention. See, for instance, Osvaldo Sunkel's classic article, "Intégration capitaliste transnationale et désintégration nationale en Amérique Latine," *Politique Etrangère*, pp. 641-700.

Chapter

4

East-West Economic Relations and the Multinational Corporation

Thomas A. Wolf

Multinational banks and financial consortia are finding new opportunities in East-West trade. The growing import requirements of the socialist countries, together with the deferred-payment feature of many plant, equipment, and technology sales, has created an increasing need for Western credits. Such banks as Chase Manhattan have recently opened special units in Western Europe to handle East-West business, and Chase, France's Credit Lyonnais, and the Deutsche Bank and Dresdner Bank of West Germany are setting up representative offices in Moscow.

Among Western companies currently or potentially involved in East-West commerce, the multinational corporation has particular advantages in doing business with the socialist countries of Eastern Europe (SCEE). One reason, mentioned by both Eastern and Western observers, is that MNCs may be contemplated with less suspicion in the SCEE because of the relative independence from parent-country political influence that they allegedly enjoy.

Reprinted with permission of the Center for Multinational Studies, from *East-West Economic Relations and the Multinational Corporation*, Occasional Paper no. 5 (Washington, D.C., 1973), pp. 56-62 and 65-73. The author wishes to acknowledge financial support from the New York University Project on Multinational Enterprises and the U.S. and World Economies.

Perhaps more important is the relatively large size of many of the MNCs. This has several implications for dealing with the socialist countries. First, their size puts them in a somewhat better bargaining position when negotiating with Eastern foreign trade monopolies or large industrial combines. Second, in general the larger and more "multinational" a company, the greater its financial resources and access to varied sources of capital for its operations. Given the deferred-payment feature of many East-West transactions together with the increasing frequency of massive projects (particularly in the USSR) requiring enormous amounts of credit, this size advantage can be very important.

Third, the MNCs are seen by many Eastern ministry and enterprise officials as more suitable partners in the event of sudden production bottlenecks or threatened shortfalls in meeting annual investment or consumption plans. It is typically easier to contract for large deliveries with big, flexible MNCs, rather than having to spread the order over a number of smaller Western firms, any one of which is unable to meet the entire request out of current production.

A further possible advantage of the multinational firms, and this may hold particularly for American corporations with major operations in Western Europe, would appear to rest in these firms' concentration in manufacturing, particularly the production of machinery and transport equipment. Indeed, as we have seen, SCEE demand for Western manufactured products, particularly machinery and equipment, has been especially strong in recent years, and their new five-year plans indicate an accelerated emphasis on international specialization and the import of plant, equipment, and technology. The favorable position of U.S.-based MNCs in this respect may be inferred from the heavy concentration of their West European subsidiaries in machinery and transport equipment relative to their West European competitors (53 percent of total manufacturing sales by U.S.-controlled companies versus 40 percent for total West European manufacturing exports and 32 percent for total West European production).[1] This conclusion is only tentative, however, as there are other factors suggesting a relative disadvantage for U.S.-controlled firms doing business with the East. For example, most American MNCs do not have the long experience and continuity of relationships with Eastern partners which many of their European competitors possess, and this is a factor found to be particularly important in a recent ECE study of this subject.[2]

Other advantages of the multinational corporations in East-West commerce arise from the persistence of various structural problems in this trade, particularly the bilateralism constraint and the asymmetrical commodity structure of East-West trade. It is of course true that the need for each of the SCEE to bilaterally balance their trade with individual Western countries has diminished over the postwar period. This is in part because of the movement away from inconvertibility of the West European currencies in the late 1940s and 1950s, but also because of the expansion of strong Eastern trade contacts to a wider range of Western countries, and the increased possibilities for financing Eastern trade deficits for longer than one year. As a result, the number of governmental bilateral clearing agreements (under which deficits had to be offset within very short periods through an expansion of exports or reduction in imports) between East and West have declined to a very low level.[3] Most East-West trade relations are now carried out on a basis of multilateral settlements; that is, simply in terms of one or more of a number of convertible Western currencies.[4]

Hard currency earnings from Western tourists are also playing an ever more significant role in many East European countries' balance of payments. It has been estimated, for instance, that Hungary's 1972 earnings from over 1 million Western tourists, $60 million, more than covered its interest expense on borrowings from the West.[5] While there has been a growing availability of government and government-guaranteed or uninsured private Western credit for exports to the SCEE in recent years, the debt burden for many of these countries is considerable and rising. This is demonstrated in Table 1, which gives 1970 estimates for this debt, as well as total SCEE exports to the West and recent trade balances. A more recent Eastern estimate of combined SCEE indebtedness to Western sources (presumably including the IBEC loans) is $5-5.5 billion, which shows the acceleration of the growth in this debt burden over time.[6]

The low proportion of relatively income-elastic manufactured exports in the SCEE trade structure, together with less than optimistic Eastern prospects for near-term rapid expansion of these exports, will make it difficult for these countries to earn the desired amounts of foreign exchange in the near future. Tourist receipts, while growing, are still relatively small in most SCEE. Furthermore, there is inevitably an upper limit on the amount of new credit which will be forthcoming from the West. The bilateralism constraint therefore continues in East-West trade, but in a

Table 1
Eastern European Debt Burdens
(in millions U.S.$)

	Debt to Western sources Dec. 1970	1971 Exports to industrialized West	Trade balance with West	
			1970	1971
Bulgaria	250	341	(51)	(46)
Czechoslovakia	400	1,019	(90)	(77)
Hungary	350	691	(72)	(225)
Poland	600	1,198	69	8
Romania	700	776	(167)	(102)
Subtotal	$2,300			
USSR	...	3,127	(327)	(82)

Source: Robert S. Kretschmar, Jr., and Robin Foor, *The Potential for Joint Ventures in Eastern Europe*, p. 38; and Economic Commission for Europe (ECE), *Economic Bulletin for Europe*, vol. 24, no. 1, pp. 24-28.

somewhat changed form. The principal need now is for each socialist country to strive for a balancing of its Western import needs with its *total* earnings of Western currencies, regardless of the export source (regional bilateralism). The attempt to bilaterally balance (or at least to not run a bilateral deficit) with each Western country will probably still be strong, however, so as to not incur a permanent and growing deficit with individual nations, which might represent an unwelcome sign of dependence for many Eastern countries.

In this continuing "structural" dilemma in East-West trade would appear to lie further competitive advantages which the MNCs may have in their dealings with the East, above and beyond the characteristics of size and alleged independence discussed earlier.

First, the multinational firm generally has the advantage of multinational sourcing. When selling to an Eastern country, an MNC may often be able to comply with an Eastern request to supply products from a particular Western country with which the Eastern partner may happen to be running a relatively small bilateral deficit or even a bilateral surplus. This is of obvious benefit to MNCs operating with subsidiaries or affiliates in two or more West European countries. Little attention has been placed in the literature so far, however, on the potentialities of multinational sourcing for the American-based MNC confronted with the bilateralism constraint as it appears in U.S. trade with individual Eastern countries.[7]

It is generally believed that a large portion of many American MNCs sales to the SCEEA have traditionally been carried out by their West European affiliates. This trade existed in spite of the fact that the comprehensive U.S. export control system also in theory included foreign affiliates. With the apparent dramatic relaxation in these controls over the past four years, there has been a general expectation of significant increases in U.S. exports to SCEE.[8] Yet, with the possible exception of future Soviet fuel and raw materials sales to the United States, it is likely that other Eastern countries' export growth to the United States will fall behind their growth in demand for dollars to pay for American products, even after taking into full account the positive effects of MFN (should it be extended to the remaining SCEE), and Eximbank credit support. Consequently, one might expect a portion of the expected U.S. export surge to be realized in practice by West European affiliates of U.S. companies. This result is suggested by the relatively more favorable Eastern balance of trade with some West European countries (for example, Soviet trade with Sweden and the United Kingdom), and lower transport costs for many potential exports from Western to Eastern Europe.

A further advantage possessed by the MNC is a worldwide distribution network. This is potentially of great importance in light of the problems many of the SCEE seem to be having in selling their products successfully in Western markets. While poor product quality and inadequate market research may be important, many of their problems appear to arise on the distribution side as well. One Polish economist, for example, has suggested that a major obstacle faced by that country is simply a shortage of trained and knowledgeable people to market Polish products in the West.

While the establishment in the West of joint marketing ventures with Western companies is one way to expand the effective distribution network for Eastern products, another possibility is the use of existing marketing systems of MNCs. Multinational corporations with diversified product lines would seem to be in a particularly advantageous position to meet the need to accept from Eastern partners certain products in exchange for export sales to the Eastern market. The smaller firm, with a more limited distribution network, may be forced to dispose of these goods by bearing the costs of using the switch traders and other middlemen who have a peculiarly prominent role in East-West trade.

Still another advantage of the MNC in East-West trade arises from its experience in making foreign investments, and particularly, in undertaking joint ventures. This is an advantage because of the growing trend of so-called industrial cooperation agreements in East-West commerce, including some signs of a movement towards joint ventures in several SCEE on a limited basis. The Eastern countries are increasingly recognizing long-term arrangements for coproduction, product specialization, and joint research and development as a means to acquire Western machinery and technology without having to increase their indebtedness to the West. At the same time this expands their potential for changing the structure of their exports in the direction of a higher proportion of those finished manufactures characterized by relatively high-income elasticity of demand in the industrialized West. The phenomenon of industrial cooperation, including joint ventures, is explored in more detail below.

There are a multitude of types of so-called "industrial cooperation,"[9] and while any attempt to classify them is bound to be arbitrary, it may be convenient to deal with the following broad categories: subcontracting, sale of licenses (both of these are usually considered "lower" forms of cooperation), coproduction, product specialization, joint marketing, project cooperation, joint tendering, and research and development.[10]

A *subcontracting* arrangement in East-West trade is similar to many such agreements in the West. That is, a Western firm, perhaps confronted with a short- or medium-term shortage in production, may subcontract out production runs to Eastern enterprises with excess capacity. Subcontracting, particularly in cutting and finishing garments for Western markets, is an important device for earning foreign exchange in Hungary. Total Hungarian revenue from East-West subcontracting was $100 million in 1972 and is expected to reach $140 million in 1973.[11] Yugoslavia also has found subcontracting to be a profitable means for utilizing surplus capacity, notably in the rubber, iron and steel, footwear, and furniture industries. Some 180 Western companies signed such agreements with Yugoslav enterprises in the first half of 1972. Poland is another important subcontractor for the West. Most subcontracting agreements run for only relatively short periods, and typically the transfer of technology is negligible. While subcontracting can be mutually profitable in the short run, it is not seen as a particularly useful form of industrial cooperation for the longer term by most socialist countries.

The sale of Western product or process *licenses* to the SCEE often involves a greater degree of ongoing cooperation among the partners than results from similar sales in the West. This results from the shortage of hard currencies in the East which may preclude payment of royalties in cash. One solution to this problem is for the Western company to take up part of the product licensed. For example, the agreement by which Sweden's Ericsson AB has licensed the production of relay devices for railway signal boxes requires the Polish partner to pay one-half of the license fees in the form of deliveries of these devices to the Swedish company. In another agreement, under which a Polish agricultural machinery plant is to produce heavy tractors under an International Harvester license, part of the product will be marketed in third countries on a joint basis.

So-called *coproduction* agreements involve dividing the production of a particular product, with the Western firm typically supplying some production technology to the Eastern partner while it continues to manufacture the more technologically sophisticated components. A by now classic case of coproduction is the agreement between Austria's Steyr-Daimler-Puch and Ikarus of Hungary for the production of buses under the "Steyr-Ikarus" trade name. The Austrian company produces the bus motors and frames, and the buses are assembled in Hungary. Similar, but not identical buses are then marketed both within the SCEE and in some Western countries.

East-West *specialization* agreements can develop under several circumstances. Under one type of arrangement the Western partner retains production of one part of a product line and the Eastern enterprise specializes in the other. Often each partner will offer the full product line in its own (or own regional) market. A West German manufacturer of diesel engines, for instance, concentrates on the production of its larger series of diesel engines, as well as on the manufacture of cylinders and valves common to both series. Its Yugoslav partner specializes in certain labor-intensive components of the smaller series, which make up between 60 and 65 percent of the value of this series. Another example is the agreement between Olympia-Werke of West Germany and Unis of Yugoslavia. On the basis of a long-term license and know-how contract, the Yugoslav partner will produce 250,000 typewriters a year, of which 200,000 will be delivered to Olympia. Unis is to be in charge of marketing all Olympia products in Eastern Europe.

In other cases, East-West specialization is not based upon the transfer of technology per se, but instead arises from the need of producers in small markets to realize economies of scale in production. This type of arrangement appears to be particularly important for firms in small countries which are geographically close. Austrian and Hungarian chemical companies, for example, have found it mutually beneficial to exchange surpluses of important intermediate products.

Joint marketing arrangements often evolve from the sales of Western licenses to the East. Because of inadequate socialist marketing skills and contacts in the West, the two partners may establish a joint venture (in the West) to sell the Eastern firm's output of the licensed product on Western markets. These agreements may also be a vehicle for Western sales based upon technology developed in the socialist countries. An example is the recent 50-50 joint venture set up by Hungary's Intercooperation Ltd. (formed by a group of Hungarian banks and enterprises with the objective of coordinating and stimulating cooperation agreements) and two U.S. firms, MGA Technology Inc. and Intercontinental Resources. With offices in Amsterdam and Curacao, the new company will attempt to market a new Hungarian fabric, as well as licenses for its production, in the West. Another example is the Hungarian textile foreign trade enterprise (FTE) Hungarotex, which has established joint ventures with companies in Spain, the United Kingdom, and West Germany for the purpose of marketing Hungarian textiles and ready-made clothing in Western countries.

The most spectacular examples of East-West industrial cooperation have of course been the *project* agreements by which a Western firm, or group of companies, is responsible for the development of new industrial facilities in Eastern countries. Fiat's construction of the $800 million Togliatti automobile factory in the Soviet Union is the classic case, as well as the emerging Kama truck complex. Numerous smaller-scale projects, ranging from chemical plants to nuclear reactors, have been undertaken in the USSR and other SCEE.

In these projects, Western firms typically provide the plant designs and technology, and supply most of the more sophisticated equipment. The Eastern partners take much (or all) of the responsibility for construction and often supply the simpler equipment. Such industrial projects usually require credit financing, with ultimate payment made in cash in the form of service fees or royalties. Other large ventures may involve payment in kind. For example, the Mannesmann sales of wide-diameter pipes to the Soviet Union for natural gas pipeline construction will be paid for by natural gas deliveries to Ruhrgas AG.

Because of the enormous size and long time horizon involved in such projects, the problems and financial risks may be greater than for other types of cooperation agreements. The Togliatti project, for example, has been controversial. This is due not only to the political undertones surrounding the project, but also because of its questionable profitability to Fiat, as well as to the logistical difficulties in dealing with the Soviets. In another instance, Italian engineers from the Pirelli Tire Co. were reportedly prohibited from even visiting the $50 million plant the Soviets were constructing under license.

Still another form of East-West cooperation involves the *joint tendering* for the construction of complete plants or processing lines or the undertaking of large civil engineering projects. A variety of arrangements between the partners are possible. For example, the Western firm or consortium may subcontract to the Eastern partner, as is the case with the Uhde-Siemens syndicate's agreement with Poland's Polimex to supply a chemical plant in Morocco. The Polish partner will deliver a sulphuric acid still and the Uhde-Siemens group will supply a reduction facility for the plant, which will produce phosphoric acid. On the other hand, the socialist partner may be the main contractor. This is the case, for instance, in the joint delivery of a polyacryl-nitril fibers plant by the Romanian FTE Petrom and West Germany's Büttner-Schilde-Haas (a member of the Babcock Group) to North Korea.

A further form of cooperation involves cooperative *research* and *development* of products or processes. While joint R&D is a feature of a growing number of coproduction and specialization arrangements, there have also been numerous recent agreements signed between large Western companies and Soviet authorities exclusively dealing with the exchange of scientific documentation and technical experts. Examples are General Electric's agreement concerning joint R&D on electric power-generating equipment and long-term USSR agreements with West German companies such as AEG-Telefunken, BASF, Siemens, Hoechst, Henkel, and Friedrich Krupp.

Patterns and growth of industrial cooperation

The Economic Commission of Europe has compiled considerable data on the pattern of East-West industrial cooperation, both by industrial branch and by category, based on a sample of 202 cases involving the SCEE countries (i.e., excluding Yugoslavia).[12] The distribution of reported industrial cooperation (IC) agreements by industrial sector in five SCEE is shown in Table 2. The preponderant share of IC arrangements are accounted for in most countries

Table 2

Percentage distribution of East-West industrial cooperation agreements
by industrial branches
(percentages)

	Total	Czecho-slovakia	Hungary	Poland	Romania	USSR
Chemicals	19.3	20.0	14.0	24.5	14.3	31.8
Transport equipment	17.3	26.7	20.9	11.3	28.6	13.6
Machine-tools	8.4	13.3	3.5	11.3	10.0	9.1
Mechanical engineering (excluding machine-tools)	22.3	20.0	29.1	22.6	4.8	4.6
Electrical engineering and electronics	16.3	13.3	18.6	13.3	14.3	18.2
Other	16.4	6.7	13.9	17.0	28.0	22.7
	100	100	100	100	100	100

Source: ECE, "Analytical Report on Industrial Co-operation Among ECE Countries," p. 7. Based on a sample of 202 agreements.

by the mechanical engineering, transport equipment, and chemical industries, with the electrical engineering, electronics, and machine tool branches also accounting for a high number of agreements.

The distribution of industrial cooperation within selected manufacturing sectors by type of cooperation is also noteworthy. As Table 3 shows, specialization-coproduction and licensing (with full or partial payment in licensed products) arrangements are particularly popular within manufacturing generally, and also within the transport equipment and mechanical engineering branches. In the chemicals sector, plant delivery ("project") agreements are also important.

Table 3

Percentage distribution of East-West industrial cooperation within selected
industrial branches by type of agreement
(percentages)

	Licensing	Plant delivery	Coproduction-specialization	Subcontracting	Joint venture projects	Total
Total manufacturing	28.2	11.9	37.1	7.9	14.9	100
Chemicals	20.5	23.1	33.3	2.6	20.5	100
Transport equipment	29.0	5.3	50.0	15.8	–	100
Mechanical engineering (excluding machine tools)	28.9	4.4	48.8	8.9	8.9	100

Source: ECE, "Analytical Report on Industrial Co-operation Among ECE
Countries," p. 8. Based on a sample of 202 agreements.

The ECE study also suggests some industry characteristics which
may be particularly conducive to industrial cooperation. One such
feature is the degree of "segmentability" of technology in an industry. This would explain the high proportion of agreements in the
engineering branches and the importance of specialization-coproduction arrangements within these activities. In the chemicals
branch, on the other hand, plant deliveries and joint projects (including marketing and joint tendering) are of relatively greater
significance. Other important characteristics are the degree to
which production is serial rather than custom-made, and whether
the segmentable production processes are subject to increasing returns to scale. Both features would tend to encourage East-West
coproduction and specialization. Furthermore, the extent of
price competition in Western markets faced by potential Western
partners is undoubtedly important, as significant cost reductions
may be made possible by setting up production within the SCEE.[13]

Industrial cooperation is a relatively new feature in East-West commerce, with most of the growth in the number of these agreements taking place in the past five to ten years. A 1969 study by
the United Nations Conference on Trade and Development included information on 135 IC arrangements (excluding Yugoslavia)
and in April 1971 the *Financial Times* estimated the existence of

some 200 agreements.[14] They appear to have proliferated at an accelerating pace in the past couple of years, as Hungary alone has been reported as having 164 IC agreements by mid-1972. The ECE secretariat has recently estimated that some 600 industrial cooperation agreements are now in force in the SCEE, of which perhaps 200 have been concluded since 1970. In some manufacturing activities such as engineering, industrial cooperation is estimated to already account for some 10 to 15 percent of several SCEE countries' exports to the West.[15] Hungary and Poland seem to have been particularly active in concluding IC arrangements, with the most frequent Western partners being firms located in West Germany, France, the United Kingdom, Austria, and Sweden.

While hundreds of IC arrangements have been concluded in recent years, many of the agreements signed in the past are undoubtedly now without life. In some cases the partners are simply not able to successfully implement their initial plans for a mutually beneficial continuing relationship. Nevertheless, there are numerous cases in which an IC agreement has led to an ever deepening relationship between partners (e.g., joint R&D), as well as having established a basis for expanded conventional trade. Consequently, industrial cooperation must be seen in another dimension as well, as a catalytic force for expanded East-West economic relations.

NOTES

[1]ECE, "Analytical Report on Industrial Co-operation among ECE Countries," Annex 1, May 4, 1973, p. 17.

[2]*Ibid.,* Annex 2, April 9, 1973, p. 4.

[3]*Eastern Europe Report,* vol. 1, no. 5, Geneva, Business International, Sept. 8, 1972.

[4]The author is indebted to Heinrich Machowski for comments concerning this issue.

[5]*Eastern Europe Report,* vol. 2, no. 10, May 18, 1973.

[6]*Eastern Europe Report,* vol. 1, no. 12, December 15, 1972.

[7]See, however, Thomas A. Wolf, "A New Era in East-West Business," *European Business,* 1973.

[8]See Thomas A. Wolf, *U.S. East-West Trade Policy: Economic Warfare Versus Economic Welfare,* chapter 8.

[9]Much of the discussion in this subsection draws directly from Wolf, "A New Era in East-West Business."

10For a slightly different form of classification and a much more extensive discussion, see ECE, "Analytical Report on Industrial Co-operation among ECE Countries,"including Annex 1.

11*Eastern Europe Report,* vol. 2, no. 9, May 4, 1973.

12ECE, "Analytical Report on Industrial Co-operation among ECE Countries."

13*Ibid.,* Annex 2, pp. 1-8.

14Eva Sarosi, "Zur industriellen Kooperation zwischen Österreich und Ungarn," *Forschungsberichte* no. 2.

15ECE, "Analytical Report on Industrial Co-operation among ECE Countries."

PART II
Constraints on
Counterstrategies

Introduction

So far, this collection has examined the dimensions of MNEs and their impact on the international system. Since this impact, significant as it often is, is frequently perceived to be uncontrollable, unfavorable, or undesirable, governments are increasingly beginning to formulate and implement counterstrategies, defined earlier as policies designed to make MNEs accountable for their activities and to influence, if not direct, their behavior in the interest of the public (as opposed to corporate) good. In Part III some of these counterstrategies will be discussed and evaluated.

Before turning to them, however, it is necessary to consider some of the broad parameters constraining counterstrategies so as to understand the general difficulties involved in their formulation and implementation. Therefore, this part of the collection will look at some of the alternative strategies open to MNEs to protect their interests; it will review some of the structural determinants that were investigated in the previous part, and, finally, it will consider briefly some limitations resulting from mass attitudes towards foreign direct investment.

Many of the alternative strategies open to MNEs to protect their interests are a result of the flexibility associated with their global structures and the option space these provide them in a decentralized world of often competing national jurisdictions. This flexibility has frequently been recognized and discussed with respect to host countries and, in fact, has been one of the main concerns of these countries. At the same time, the (usually implicit) assumption is often made that MNEs are fully responsive to the policies of home countries. This is, however, an assumption that is far from obvious. In principle one would expect that the more multinational an enterprise becomes in terms of the distribution of its production facilities, the greater becomes its ability to also ignore the policies of its home country. If this were indeed the case, it would constitute an important development: on the one hand, it would further increase the importance of MNEs as independent international actors, while on the other hand it would create certain communalities of interests between host and home countries with a view of controlling the activities of these entities. Franklin R. Root deals with this problem in Chapter 5. Specifically, he investigates to what extent rising corporate internationalization is associated with perceptions, on the part of top executives, of increased autonomy for decision-making relative to the objectives of home-country public policy. Root examines this question with regard to various key corporate decision-making areas in relation to alternative public policy worlds.

In cases where MNEs cannot ignore the policy of their home countries, they may be prepared to take an even more drastic step and move their headquarters abroad. Such a move is all the more tempting if it has financial (notably tax) benefits associated with it. For instance, *Business International* reported that, "when threatened by [an unfavorable] tax reform . . . close to a dozen Canadian-based international firms have transferred their domiciles to other countries."[1]

Beyond these more reactive alternatives, MNEs have also developed sophisticated strategies to protect their assets abroad and to decrease their vulnerability. In this attempt, manufacturing MNEs (under conditions of virtually unlimited alternatives for manufacturing sites) enjoy the crucial advantage of commanding access to important markets—a most decisive barrier, for competitors, to enter into production. The tremendous difficulties involved in establishing a recognized brand name and a large distributing and servicing network constitute a formidable constraint on host countries, particularly on developing ones, in dealing with MNEs. The situation is hardly improved if foreign affiliates produce primarily for the host-country market but remain sensitive to technological progress in their manufacturing processes: since virtually all research and development is carried out in home countries, MNEs maintain a high degree of indispensability. Finally, even the potential vulnerability of enterprises engaged in international specialization at the component level is offset by the cautious establishment of alternative sources of supply for the same product, be it at home or in third countries.[2] In none of these situations would a takeover of such affiliates serve much purpose since they would not be viable production units on their own.

Enterprises operating in raw materials, on the other hand, are, by their very nature, more vulnerable to host-country pressures, in spite of the latter's high dependency on MNEs for capital, technology, processing facilities, and marketing outlets. Theodore H. Moran's analysis of Kennecott's reaction to demands for Chileanization in 1964 showed, however, how a company can successfully protect itself by creating a set of transnational stakes in its continued well-being. Kennecott insured its assets under a U.S. AID program (later OPIC) and then raised further expansion capital "by writing long-term contracts for the new output with European and Asian customers and then selling collection rights on these contracts to a consortium of European banks . . . and to a consortium of Japanese institutions." In the words of a company executive, the aim of this strategy was "to insure that nobody expropriates Kennecott without upsetting relations to customers, creditors, and governments on three continents."[3] When President Allende later nationalized Kennecott's facilities, international pressures were, indeed, forthcoming. As a result, the Chilean government assumed most of the international obligations of the affiliates and, furthermore, agreed to a settlement in excess of the net worth of the 1964 operation. Anaconda, on the other hand, had not taken any of these precautions and was nationalized without compensation payments.[4]

Other strategies commonly pursued by raw-material MNEs to decrease their vulnerability involve the location of more advanced processing facilities outside countries considered to be poor investment risks while, at the same time, geographically diversifying sources of supply of lower-stage products. If advanced processing facilities constitute the major barrier to entry of production and if alternative supplies are plentiful, vulnerability to nationalization or expropriation is reduced considerably.

These strategies are illustrated by Michael Morris, Farid G. Lavi-pour, and Karl P. Sauvant in Chapter 6. This essay examines the evolution of Guyana's attempt to reformulate its relationships with Alcan, one of the major multinational aluminum corporations that was operating on Guyana's territory. The chapter discusses this conflict in the larger framework of the international aluminum industry which is, in its structure, in many ways typical for raw-material industries in general. It discusses how the structure of this industry makes, on the one hand, a re-formulation of relationships highly desirable for the host country, while constituting, on the other hand, one of the most important parameters for such a reformulation attempt. This chapter also analyzes some of the means at the disposal of a MNE in the event that a conflict with a host country should erupt, and points out the restraints imposed on a host country which is dependent on in-ternational marketing and financing institutions for the operation and expansion of its mining facilities and which is dependent on official development assistance flows for its modernization programs.

The structural patterns in the international aluminum industry, of course, only reflect the structure of the international economic system in general. As discussed in Part I, a highly limited number of enterprises, headquartered in a few countries, dominate its ma-jor dimensions, the most important of which are production, tech-nology, finance, advertising, and business culture. Since these di-mensions of the international economic system are interrelated to form one dominance structure, it is very difficult for peripheral countries to emancipate themselves and move from dependence to interdependence. The recent emergence of a few additional major headquarters countries does not fundamentally change the situa-tion of most countries; at most, it offers them the option of di-versifying their dependence. The very structure of the internation-al economic system, therefore, is one of the most important para-meters for the successful implementation of any counterstrategy.

Finally, host countries' internationalization of home-country val-ues and aspirations further imposes constraints on the formulation and implementation of counterstrategies. As has already been pointed out in Chapter 3, by accepting desiderata which cannot be fulfilled autonomously, most host countries bring themselves into (or keep themselves in) a position dependent on those who can fulfill or help to fulfill these values and aspirations. This is particu-larly true in the case of former colonies as Andrew C. E. Hilton shows in Chapter 7. In his study of Nigeria, Hilton finds a high awareness of the presence of foreign direct investment in the national economy and a decidedly favorable attitude towards it, at least so far as the investment originates in the principal metropolitan countries. Such attitudes may restrain the government from taking decisive actions against MNEs, a conclusion which is supported by findings reported for Canada: although an increasing percentage of Canadians feel that (U.S.) foreign direct investment is a "bad thing"—notably because of loss of indigenous control required to make decisions strictly in the interest and benefit of Canadians—this attitude varies widely enough "so that a policy which would appeal to all sectors would be almost impossible to formulate."5

In summary, many counterstrategies face various constraints. This is not to say that such constraints cannot be overcome, at least in the long run. In fact, one of the functions of a well-designed counterstrategy is precisely to do this. Nevertheless, these constraints must be kept in mind when looking at ongoing efforts aimed at counteracting some of the negative implications of MNEs.

NOTES

1*Business International* (May 11, 1973), p. 145. The reform stipulated, *inter alia,* that the earnings of Canadian-owned holding companies located in low-tax countries would be taxable regardless of whether the funds were repatriated or not. This stipulation drew so much criticism that the implementation of the bill was postponed. Massey-Fergusson, the fourth largest Canadian-owned company, threatened to consider alternative domiciles if the bill should actually be enacted (*ibid.,* p. 152).

2For the U.S. semiconductor industry, an industry with substantial assembly operations abroad, a survey by Y.S. Chang found that enterprises are "extremely anxious" to reduce the likelihood of any disruption abroad. Chang observed: "One of the methods most often used is to maintain sufficient backup assembly operation of the U.S. plants to take care of the emergency needs. . . . The other often used method is to geographically diversify a number of assembly plants at offshore locations. . . .Many firms flatly refuse to locate a second plant in the same country. In other words, the economy of single site offshore operation is being sacrificed to reduce the risks of disruption" (see Y.S. Chang, *The Transfer of Technology: Economies of Offshore Assembly. The Case of Semiconductor Industry,* pp. 38, 36).

3Both quotes in Theodore Moran, "Transnational Strategies of Protection and Defense by Multinational Corporations: Spreading the Risk and Raising the Cost for Nationalization in National Resources," *International Organization,* pp. 279-280.

[4]*Ibid.* Moran concluded (p. 283), "The only reasonable course for Anaconda's board of directors—which it took—was to fire the entire top management...."

[5]J. Alex Murray and Mary C. Gerace, "Canadian Attitudes Toward the U.S. Presence," *Public Opinion Quarterly*, p. 396.

Chapter
5

Independence and Adaptation:
Response Strategies of U.S.-
Based Multinational
Corporations to a Restrictive
Public Policy World

Franklin R. Root

The literature on the political role of multinational corporations
points to an inherent conflict between corporate and national interests. It is asserted that MNCs act to achieve corporate goals in
a global arena, while governments act to achieve national goals in
a national arena. Hence, the resulting clash of interests generates
tensions and conflicts that cannot be resolved in any ultimate
sense.

This perspective, with its implication that MNCs operate outside
the constraints imposed by national policies, is not shared by multinational managers. From their perspective, MNCs must necessarily adapt to the world as they find it by pursuing appropriate strategies in response to market opportunities, costs, competition, and
government policies. Multinational managers, therefore, perceive
as significant only those actions of national governments that
create actual or potential opportunities and constraints for their
operations. In such situations they must decide how to respond in
a way that would sustain or strengthen the viability of their company, both immediately and in the future. For the corporate de-
cision-maker, then, the central question is not whether he should
respond or adapt to government actions, but whether he has real
choice in his response strategy. If he has a choice of two or more
viable response options, then it follows he is in some degree

"independent" of government actions. That is to say, his "response option space" is large enough to enable him to choose a course of action that sustains his corporate interests regardless of the policies of a particular government.

The MEPP study

How independent of public policies are MNCs? Which factors influence their response strategies to shifts in public policies? To answer these and other related questions, the Multinational Enterprise Unit of the Wharton School has undertaken a study analyzing how U.S.-based multinational corporations would respond to alternative public-policy futures as depicted in four scenarios.[1]

The fundamental purpose of MEPP is to provide government policymakers, in this case the United States, with information on the probable response strategies of MNCs to alternative public policies and the implications of these strategies for the United States and the world economy. Such information constitutes a systemic "advanced feedback" on the probable consequences of a given public-policy environment that may be contemplated by policymakers but has not yet come into existence. MEPP is a continuing research effort.

Each of the four scenarios describes a different potential behavior of the United States, the European Economic Community (EEC), and Japan in international trade and investment. The policies of these three political entities are assumed to collectively determine the critical public policy environments for manufacturing MNCs in the 1970s. Scenario I—"Global Restrictive"—depicts a world environment in which the United States imposes tariffs, quotas, and investment controls, and in turn faces a similar retaliation from Japan and the EEC. Scenario II—"Global Supportive"—depicts a situation which is the converse of "Global Restrictive." Scenarios III and IV are mixes of Scenarios I and II, namely, "U.S. Restrictive-EEC/Japan Supportive" (Scenario III) and "U.S. Supportive-EEC/Japan Restrictive" (Scenario IV). This chapter deals mainly with corporate response to the Global Restrictive World which is shown as Exhibit 1.

All four scenarios were presented to 174 top executives in 42 U.S.-based manufacturing companies which have foreign operations. These companies belong to fourteen industry groups (two-digit

Exhibit 1
Global Restrictive World
(Scenario I)

We ask you to imagine a world (emerging in the 1970s) in which the policies of the United States, the EEC, and Japan become progressively more restrictive with respect to the behavior of multinational enterprises. Public policies in this world may be generally characterized as *divisive, distrustful, retaliatory,* and *ethnocentric.* In this restrictive world, we would expect some (if not all) of the following policy initiatives and responses by the United States, the EEC, and Japan:

The United States
—imposes protectionist tariffs and quotas on most manufactured products (including reentry of U.S. made components)
—intensifies investment controls, particularly with respect to the EEC and Japan
—abolishes foreign tax credits and requires payment of U.S. taxes on foreign income when earned
—imposes high withholding rate on dividends repatriated outside the U.S.
—taxes and (at times) restricts technology transfer from the U.S.
—starts "antitrust drive" on MNCs
—supports attacks by labor and other groups on U.S. MNCs
—accuses the EEC and Japan of "unfair treatment" of U.S. exports

The European Economic Community
—retaliates with extensive import restrictions on U.S. goods
—sets out to "curb the American business presence in Europe "
—pressures U.S. MNCs to "disinvest" out of European subsidiaries either entirely or by becoming minority partners in joint ventures
—prohibits all acquisitions of European companies by U.S. MNCs
—places limitations on repatriation of earnings to U.S. parents and use of local capital sources by their European subsidiaries
—limits employment of American technicians and managers in Europe

Japan
—retaliates against U.S. policies in much the same way as the EEC
—instructs all U.S. MNCs to reduce any ownership interests in Japanese affiliates to 25 percent
—prohibits all new investment by U.S. companies
—imposes exchange controls on dollar transactions

In brief, in the 1970s the non-Communist world economy is beginning to break up into three blocs: A U.S. bloc, an EEC bloc, and a Japanese bloc.

SIC numbers) with corporate sales ranging from $150 million to well over $10 billion and with percentages of after-tax corporate income derived from foreign operations ranging from less than 10 percent to over 40 percent. Forty of the sample companies are listed in the *Fortune* directory of the 500 largest U.S. industrial corporations. In personal interviews, each scenario was discussed with an executive until he indicated his comprehension of the kind of world it portrays and was able to "internalize" it. He was then asked a series of questions concerning how his company would most probably respond to this world in the decision areas of corporate strategy and development, production, personnel, finance, research and development, and marketing.

It is not possible in this chapter to examine corporate responses in all the decision areas taken up during the interviews. Instead, selected corporate responses to a Global Restrictive World will be used to show that, given the "option space" available to MNCs, certain national policies can be rendered "countereffective" in terms of government objectives. Moreover, the countereffective consequences of such national policies are associated positively with the degree of multinationality of the firm as measured by its anticipated involvement in foreign operations.

MNC response strategies in production and R&D

The response strategies of the sample corporations to a Global Restrictive World for production and research and development are presented and discussed in 3 x 3 matrices below. Each cell of the matrices is identified as "effective," "noneffective," or "countereffective" from the perspective of U.S. policymakers. The response presence of corporations in countereffective cells is used to demonstrate the difficulty the U.S. government would have in its attempts to control the operations of U.S.-based MNCs; the converse holds for responses in effective cells. On the other hand, responses in noneffective cells demonstrate the insensitivity of some U.S.-based MNCs to U.S. government policies aimed at influencing their behavior.

In a Global Restrictive environment, U.S.-based MNCs are faced with a government policy aimed at containing all their operations within the United States and forcing them to service their foreign markets through their domestic operations. With respect to production, U.S. policymakers would want U.S.-based MNCs to increase their U.S. production while, at the same time, decreasing (or at least not increasing) their production abroad. The result would be an absolute or relative shift in their production to the United States.

Table 1 indicates corporate production strategies in response to a Global Restrictive World. A majority of the responses would be countereffective for U.S. policy. Only six companies would increase their U.S. production while decreasing their EEC/Japan production and only two companies would increase their U.S. production while not changing their EEC/Japan production. In contrast, eighteen companies would anticipate a decrease in U.S. production. If the U.S. policy objective were simply to increase U.S. production, then only ten companies would make effective responses. If, as we assume here, the U.S. policy objective were to make U.S.-based MNCs shift out of EEC/Japan production in favor of U.S production, then the responses of only six companies would be clearly effective and the responses of two companies would be marginally effective (increase in the United States, no effect in EEC/Japan). For several companies the relationship between their U.S. production and their EEC/Japan production is complementary rather than substitutive because they support their sales in EEC/Japan with U.S. production via exports. This relationship (together with anticipated lower sales) explains the high number of decrease/decrease entries in Table 1.

Table 1
Global Restrictive World: Production response strategies
(Number of companies)

U.S. \ EEC/Japan	Decrease (D)	Increase (I)	No effect (NE)	
Decrease (D)	15 (Countereffective)	3 (Countereffective)	0 (Counter effective)	18
Increase (I)	6 (Effective)	2 (Countereffective)	2 (Effective)	10
No effect (NE)	4 (Noneffective)	0 (Countereffective)	2 (Noneffective)	6
	25	5	4	34

Corporate response strategies in research and development expenditures are depicted in Table 2. If the objective of U.S. policy were to strengthen U.S. R&D capabilities vis-à-vis EEC/Japan by restricting the outflow of technology, then the response strategies of only two companies would clearly serve that objective by simultaneously increasing their R&D in the United States while decreasing it abroad. Another six companies would serve that objective only in a relative sense by decreasing their R&D in EEC/Japan but not changing their R&D in the United States. In contrast, many corporate response strategies would serve to strengthen the R&D capabilities of EEC/Japan vis-à-vis the United States. In particular, six companies would increase R&D abroad while decreasing R&D in the United States. Three response patterns (D-I, I-I, NE-I) involving twelve companies represent a strategy to sustain EEC/Japan production by providing more local R&D in the face of restrictions on U.S. technology outflows. Almost certainly, U.S. policymakers would perceive these countereffective responses of the majority of companies (20 companies out of 35) as indicators of MNC "independence" that opposed U.S. national interests.

Table 2
Global Restrictive World:R&D expenditure response
strategies
(Number of companies)

U.S. \\ EEC/Japan	Decrease (D)	Increase (I)	No effect (NE)	
Decrease (D)	7 (Countereffective)	6 (Countereffective)	1 (Counter effective)	14
Increase (I)	2 (Effective)	1 (Countereffective)	1 (Effective)	4
No effect (NE)	6 (Effective)	5 (Countereffective)	6 (Noneffective)	17
	15	12	8	35

Multinational involvement and independence

The option space of a *national* company in responding to shifts in its public policy environment is confined to the home country. In contrast, the option space of MNCs contains not only response options in the home country but in host countries as well. Does this option space become larger for MNCs in step with the growth of their foreign involvement? There can be no simple answer to this question; the decision-making autonomy of a MNC is the result of many factors. Moreover, the response option space of MNCs will vary by decision variable.[2] Nonetheless, the general answer, supported by the data collected in the MEPP study, would appear to be in the affirmative. The greater the multinational involvement of a corporation, the greater the number of real options it has with respect to decisions on market entry, location of production, and research and development; the movement of products, managers, technology, and funds; and (potentially) the location of corporate headquarters. From the perspective of government policymakers, higher multinational involvement (and correspondingly larger corporate response option spaces) is perceived as an expansion in the autonomy of corporate decision-making relative to public policies.

Indeed, the higher the multinational involvement of a company, the greater the likelihood it would adopt a countereffective strategy in response to restrictive policies that sought to constrain its operations. Table 3 offers evidence in support of this proposition.

Table 3
Global Restrictive World: corporate response strategies
in production and R&D expenditures by foreign-source income
groups
(Number of companies)

Response strategy	Low	Middle	High
Production in U.S.:			
Increase	4	2	2
Decrease	3	7	7
No Effect	3	3	4
Total	10	12	13
R&D in U.S.:			
Increase	1	1	2
Decrease	2	4	6
No Effect	7	7	5
Total	10	12	13

The sample MNCs are classified into three groups in accordance with the percentage of foreign-source income expected in 1980: a "low" group (less than 26 percent of income from foreign sources), a "middle" group (26 to 40 percent of income from foreign sources), and a "high" group (more than 40 percent of income from foreign sources). It is evident that a significantly higher proportion of the response strategies of the middle and high groups as compared to the low group would have countereffective results for U.S. restrictive policy.

Data gathered in the MEPP study also reveal a drive towards higher levels of multinational involvement by the majority of sample companies. The tenacity of this drive is most evident in responses to the Global Restrictive World. In responding to a world breaking up into protectionist blocs, MNCs have two broad options: (1) withdrawal to the home country or (2) adaptation to a fragmented world. MEPP data indicate that most U.S.-based MNCs would choose the second option: they perceive the cost of pulling out of foreign operations to be very high ("catastrophic" or "permanent damage" for 25 of 41 companies; "major adjustment" for 13 companies) and they perceive, at the same time, substantial benefits from greater multinational involvement. Thus the majority of MNCs anticipate a higher share of foreign-source income in 1980 than in 1972, and many would plan, for example, to bring more foreign nationals into corporate headquarters regardless of a Global Restrictive World. In effect, this adaptive response sustains the strategy option space of MNCs by rejecting a withdrawal to a uninational posture.

In general, the drive toward higher levels of multinationality results in greater independence with respect to the home government.[3] Contemporary MNCs are still, however, more oriented towards home countries than host countries since corporate headquarters are located in the former, and almost all of top corporate managers are likely to be home-country nationals, as are the majority of stockholders. Moreover, except for MNCs headquartered in small countries, such as Switzerland and Sweden, the largest single national share of MNC assets, sales, and employees is still located in the home country. Hence MNCs remain "hostages" to the home country to a higher degree than the host countries, notwithstanding the recent experience of the international petroleum companies.

The MEPP interviews show that the most drastic response to home government policies contemplated by MNC executives would be to change the national identity of the MNC and shift corporate headquarters to another country. Only two companies in the sample indicated they would consider moving corporate headquarters outside the United States in response to the Global Restrictive World where the policy environment is hostile to MNCs in both the United States and EEC/Japan. But in another scenario, where U.S. policy is restrictive but EEC/Japan policies are supportive of MNCs, five out of sixteen companies stated they would consider this dramatic response. This latter finding illustrates that the independence of MNCs with respect to a particular government's policies is partly dependent on the degree to which those policies diverge from the policies of other governments.

Present and anticipated multinational involvement is positively associated with a strategy of adaptation. U.S. corporations with larger multinational involvement would be more likely to respond to a Global Restrictive World by (1) increasing the number of foreign stockholders in the parent corporation; (2) increasing the percentage of foreign nationals at worldwide headquarters, regional headquarters, and in foreign affiliates; (3) increasing the duplication of production activities in different countries; (4) using more local funds to finance new long-term investments abroad; (5) letting each foreign affiliate handle its own cash management; (6) decentralizing decisions in marketing; and (7) increasing research and development expenditures in EEC/Japan.

For the most part, then, the adaptation strategy to a Global Restrictive World involves a decentralization of decision-making to regional or country levels in order to make regional and affiliate operations more self-sufficient. In effect, MNCs would match a fragmentation of the world environment with a fragmentation in their operations while, at the same time, retaining system-wide planning and control at the parent headquarters. In the Global Restrictive World, the drive toward higher levels of multinationality would be slowed down but it would not be reversed for the majority of MNCs. They would continue to sustain their global strategies and operations (with necessary adaptations) even in the face of hostile public policies.

NOTES

[1]Other articles relating to MEPP have appeared in the *Columbia Journal of*

World Business (Fall 1973), *MSU-Business Topics* (Autumn 1973), and *Business Horizons* (Apr. 1974). Cooperative research efforts using the methodology of MEPP have been initiated by Lars Otterbeck and Gunnar Hudlund in Sweden (Stockholm School of Economics) and by Peter Banting in Canada (McMaster University). Associate Directors of MEPP are Howard V. Perlmutter and Franklin R. Root.

[2]MEPP data reveal that corporate sensitivity to a restrictive environment is highest in decision areas relating to current operations (earnings, sales, production, and employment) and lowest in ownership and the nationality mix of personnel at corporate levels. See Franklin R. Root, "Public Policy and the Multinational Corporation," *Business Horizons*, Table 3, p. 72.

[3]*Ibid.*

Chapter 6

The Politics of Nationalization: Guyana vs. Alcan

Michael Morris, Farid G. Lavipour, and Karl P. Sauvant

In their efforts to implement counterstrategies to reshape their relationships with multinational enterprises in extractive industries, host-country governments are confronted with a number of difficulties. These difficulties stem, in part, from the general global structure of extractive industries and relate specifically to the industries' degree and nature of concentration and the locational patterns of various stages of their operations. To a large extent, these factors define the constraints within which any counterstrategy by host countries vis-à-vis enterprises in extractive industries unfolds; they also define the pressure that both parties can mobilize in pursuit of their interests. In addition, each side can attempt to improve its bargaining strength by mustering allies in support of its position, thereby expanding the conflict beyond its immediate host government/multinational enterprise headquarters context.

The conflict between Alcan (one of the world's largest aluminum companies, headquartered in Canada) and Guyana—a conflict that

Research for this article was assisted substantially by interviews of one of the authors with Canadian and Guyanese officials and members of the private sector. These interviews were usually not for attribution and therefore are not cited directly. The views expressed in this paper do not necessarily reflect those of the institutions with which the authors are currently affiliated.

eventually led to the nationalization of Alcan's assets in Guyana—highlights the difficulties facing a raw-material-producing country in its efforts to redefine its relationship with a multinational enterprise. This paper intends to examine various aspects of these difficulties against the backdrop of the characteristics and confinements of the international aluminum industry. Specifically, it will briefly outline (a) some characteristics of the international aluminum industry; (b) the position of Guyana and Alcan in this structure; and (c) the manner in which these positions defined the benefits accruing to both parties, shaped the dynamics of the conflict between the two, and contributed to the nature of the final outcome of the conflict. Over the years before the actual outbreak of the final conflict, and even more so during the conflict itself, the interaction between the host-country government and the multinational enterprise developed its own momentum and finally led to a crystallization of the interests of both parties into positions which proved to be irreconcilable, resulting in an impasse which was eventually ended by the sovereign act of nationalization. In the analysis of the crisis itself—beginning in November 1970 and ending with nationalization in July 1971—special attention will be paid to the bargaining strategy of each party and, in particular, to their attempts to mobilize outside pressure in support of their respective positions.

The structure of the international aluminum industry

Table 1 (pages 114-119) summarizes the main characteristics of the international aluminum industry. The aluminum industry is highly concentrated, with six major enterprises controlling roughly two-thirds of the bauxite, alumina, and aluminum capacity in the market economies. Second, concentration is similarly high among the bauxite-producing countries. Jamaica, Surinam, and Guyana alone produce about 40 percent of the bauxite of market economies, and Australia (also a member of the International Bauxite Association) another 22 percent. Table 1 furthermore shows the interdependence between bauxite-producing countries and aluminum enterprises: while almost all of the major aluminum enterprises depend on only a few countries for the bulk of their bauxite supplies, the same countries are also largely dependent on the same enterprises as the major (if not only) recipients of these supplies.[1] Third, the industry evinces tight vertical integration: only a small percentage of the total value of all transactions for any of the six major companies takes place outside the corporate networks.[2]

Fourth, the cost of entry into the industry is extremely high, due to heavy capital investments required (over two-thirds of them for smelting)[3] and the need to enter all stages of operations (bauxite, alumina, aluminum, and fabrication) simultaneously. The overall result of these factors is to make entry into the international aluminum industry very difficult.

Furthermore, the international aluminum industry exhibits distinct locational preferences for various stages of the production process. While overall nearly two-thirds of the mining operations are located in developing countries, this share decreases rapidly with higher stages of production: overall, 23 percent of the alumina capacity is located in developing countries, 7 percent of   the primary aluminum capacity, and 2 percent of the fabrication capacity. For several of the six majors, this distribution is even more pronounced (see Table 1).

The above facts are important because they lay down the parameters of the industry and host-country relationships. But not all of these parameters are inviolable. In particular, the geographic location of the stages of production noted above is not inherent to the industry for either technological or economic reasons.[4] Host countries, in fact, have argued that a number of economic considerations favor the location of advanced processing facilities near the site of mining; for instance, transportation costs savings could be realized since the average tonnage ratio between the various stages of production decreases progressively (approximately 4.5 short tons of bauxite are required to produce 2 short tons of alumina and 1 short ton of aluminum). Certain home-country government measures, on the other hand, appear to have played an important role in determining the location of different stages of operations of the industry. Subsidies for electric power, tax concessions for regional development, and tariffs, to name just a few, create incentives for aluminum enterprises to locate their advanced processing operations within developed countries. The structure of tariffs (see Table 1) is particularly illuminating: while all the major developed countries do not level import tariffs on the raw material, bauxite, and while only the European Community has tariffs on alumina imports, all major industrial countries tax the import of aluminum and even more so the import of fabricated products.[5] Under these circumstances it is difficult for an aluminum enterprise to locate advanced processing facilities outside a major market if any of its competitors is located inside.

Table 1: The structure of the world aluminum industry: patterns of location and distribution of benefits, 1971

Table 1A

Level of production	Value added (ratio)	Year/country	Import Tariffs Percentages in terms of value	Tonnage ratio	Market economies production a/ (tons and percent)
Bauxite	1	1961: Canada EC e/ Japan U.S.A. 1973: Canada EC e/ Japan U.S.A.	- 0 - 0 - 0 - 0 - 0 - 0 - 0 - 0	4.5	Total: 55.7 mil.t. = 100% DMEs - 38 France - 6 Greece - 6 U.S.A. - 4 Australia - 22 DCs - 62 Jamaica - 23 Surinam - 11 Guyana - 7 Guinea - 5 India - 3
Alumina	2.5	1961: Canada EC e/ Japan U.S.A. 1973: Canada EC e/ Japan U.S.A.	- 0 - 11.1 - 0 - 0 - 0 - 5.6 - 0 - 0	2	Total: 19.3 mil.t. = 100% DMEs - 77 U.S.A. - 38 Japan - 8 France - 6 Canada - 6 Australia - 14 DCs - 23 Jamaica - 9 Surinam - 5 Guinea - 3 India - 2 Guyana - 2

Primary aluminum	8	1961:
		EC e/ – 9
		Japan – 15
		U.S.A. – 5.3
		
		1973:
		Canada f/ – 4 approx.
		EC e/ – 7
		Japan – 10.4
		U.S.A. f/ – 4 approx.
			1	Total: 8.6 mil.t. = 100%
				DMEs – 93
				  U.S.A. – 42
				  Canada – 12
				  Japan – 11
				  Norway – 6
				  F.R.G. – 5
				DCs – 7
				  India – 2
				  Ghana – 1
				  Brazil – 1
				  Surinam – 1
				  Cameroon – 1

Fabricated aluminum products g/	17	1961:
		Canada – 15-20
		EC e/ – 15-20
		Japan – 20
		U.S.A. – 15-20
		
		1973:
		Canada e/ – 10 approx.
		EC e/ – 10 approx.
		U.S.A. e/ – 10 approx.
			1	Total: 7.2 mil.t. = 100%
				DMEs – 98
				  U.S.A. – 55
				  Japan – 12
				  F.R.G. – 9
				  France – 5
				  U.K. – 5
				DCs – 2

(Table 1 continued)

(Table 1 continued)

Table 1B

The six major aluminum companies: distribution of company-owned capacities b/

Level of production	Alcan	Alcoa	Alusuisse	Kaiser	Pechiney Ugine Kuhlmann	Reynolds

Bauxite	Total:5.6 m.t.=100%
	IMFs - 9
	  France - 9
	
	DCs - 91
	  Jamaica(25) - 55
	  Guinea - 15
	  Malaysia - 10
	  India - 7
	  Brazil - 4
		Total:12.3 m.t.=100%
		DMEs - 31
		  U.S.A. - 8
		  Australia(30)- 23
		DCs - 69
		  Surinam(90) - 37
		  Dominican Rep.- 12
		  Jamaica - 11
		  Guinea - 7
		  Brazil - 2
			Total:3.4 m.t.=100%
			DMEs - 73
			  France - 9
			  Australia - 64
			DCs - 37
			  Sierra Leone(95) - 24
			  Guinea - 3
				Total:11.9 m.t.=100%
				DMEs - 40
				  Australia(30)c/- 40
				
				DCs - 60
				  Jamaica (25) - 58
				  India - 2
					Total:4.5 m.t.=100%
					DMEs - 84
					  France(95) - 61
					  Greece - 23
					DCs - 16
					  Guinea - 16
						Total: 7.8 m.t.=100%
						DMEs - 16
						  U.S.A. - 16
						
						DCs - 84
						  Jamaica(25) - 57
						  Guyana - 17
						  Haiti - 9
						  Ghana - 1

Alumina	Total:3.2 m.t.=100%
	DMEs - 55
	  Canada - 38
	  Japan - 8
	  Australia - 9
	DCs - 45
	  Jamaica - 35
	  Guyana - 5
	  India - 3
	  Brazil - 2
		Total:4.4 m.t.=100%
		DMEs - 72
		  U.S.A. - 57
		  Australia - 15
		DCs - 28
		  Surinam - 27
		  Brazil - 1
			Total:0.5 m.t.=100%
			DMEs - 85
			  F.R.G. - 85
			DCs - 15
			  Guinea - 15
				Total:2.4 m.t.=100%
				DMEs - 89
				  U.S.A. - 68
				  Australia - 21
				DCs - 11
				  Jamaica - 9
				  India - 2
					Total:2.1 m.t.=100%
					DMEs - 91
					  France - 58
					  Greece - 21
					  Australia - 12
					DCs - 9
					  Guinea - 9
						Total:2.4 m.t.=100%
						DMEs - 86
						  U.S.A. - 83
						  U.K. - 3
						DCs - 14
						  Jamaica - 14

	Total:1.4 m.t.=100%	Total:1.6 m.t.=100%	Total:0.5 m.t.=100%	Total:1.0 m.t.=100%	Total:0.7 m.t.=100%	Total:1.1 m.t.=100%
Primary aluminum	DMEs - 93 Canada - 65 Norway - 13 Japan - 10 Spain - 2 Australia - 2 DCs - 7 India - 4 Brazil - 3	DMEs - 94 U.S.A. - 86 Norway - 5 Australia - 3 DCs - 6 Surinam - 4 Mexico - 1 Brazil - 1	DMEs - 100 F.R.G. - 26 U.S.A. - 18 Switzerland - 14 Norway - 13 Italy - 12 DCs - 0	DMEs - 83 U.S.A. - 66 New Zealand - 4 F.R.G. - 3 U.K. - 3 Australia - 5 DCs - 17 Ghana - 13 Bahrain - 2 India - 2	DMEs - 95 France - 59 Greece - 19 Netherlands - 13 Spain - 4 DCs - 5 Cameroon - 5	DMEs - 97 U.S.A. - 77 Canada - 13 U.K. - 6 Norway - 1 DCs - 2 Ghana - 1 Venezuela - 1
Fabricated aluminum products/	Total number of facilities: At least 59 in 29 countries DMEs At least 41 in 18 countries DCs 18 in 11 countries	Total number of facilities: At least 38 in 9 countries DMEs At least 35 in 6 countries DCs 3 in 3 countries	Total number of facilities: At least 26 in 8 countries DMEs At least 24 in 7 countries DCs 2 in 1 country	Total number of facilities: At least 45 in 13 countries DMEs At least 38 in 11 countries DCs 7 in 7 countries	Total number of facilities: At least 35 in 17 countries DMEs At least 24 in 8 countries DCs 11 in 9 countries	Total number of facilities: At least 48 in 15 countries DMEs At least 40 in 10 countries DCs 8 in 5 countries

Sources: (1) Value added, tonnage ratio, tariffs: Norman Girvan, in *The Caribbean Bauxite Industry;* John W. Stamper, "Aluminum," *Mineral Facts and Problems, 1970;* Francis K. Topping, *Comparative Tariffs and Trade: The United States and the European Common Market; Tariff Schedules of the U.S.; Official Journal of the European Communities; Canadian Customs Tariffs;* OECD, *Problems and Prospects of the Primary Aluminum Industry;* Japan Tariff Association, *The Customs Tariff of Japan, 1962;* UNCTAD, *The Kennedy Round Estimated Effects on Tariff Barriers.* (2) World and company figures: U.S. Department of the Interior, Bureau of Mines, *Minerals Yearbook, 1971;* Bundesanstalt für Bodenforschung and Deutsches Institut für Wirtschaftsforschung, *Untersuchungen über Angebot und Nachfrage mineralischer Rohstoffe. Aluminium;* World Bureau of Metal Statistics, "World Metal Statistics," Feb. 1974; *Metal Statistics 1961-1971* (Frankfurt: Metallgesellschaft Ag., 1972); OECD, *Problems and Prospects of the Primary Aluminium Industry;* company reports and inquiries.

[a]The totals are broken down into developed market economies (DMEs) and developing countries (DCs). Tons are metric tons.

According to the tonnage ratio column, 4.5 tons of bauxite are required to produce 2 tons of alumina. As can be seen from the volume column, the figures do not seem to support this ratio. The reason is that in any particular year some bauxite might be stockpiled, sales might be deferred, etc.

[b]All figures refer to company-owned capacity; purchases from third parties, in other words, are not included. The bauxite estimates are for 1973; the other figures for 1971. Bauxite mines usually work at approximately 80 percent of their capacity.

The six major aluminum companies account for approximately 60 percent of all bauxite mining capacity of market economies, 70 percent of all alumina, and 60 percent of all aluminum capacity.

[c]Reynolds also has small mines in Guinea and France.

[d]In the case of the bauxite mining countries, an attempt has been made to provide a second percentage figure, written in parentheses. This figure refers to the proportion of a country's bauxite exports which is accounted for by a specific company. For instance, in the bauxite/Kaiser cell, the expression "Australia (30) 50" reads: "30 percent of Australia's bauxite exports is accounted for by Kaiser; and the same amount constitutes 50 percent of Kaiser's world wide bauxite capacity."

Overall, the direction of the bauxite and alumina exports of the major producing countries is as follows:

	Bauxite	Alumina
Jamaica	100% to U.S.	89% to U.S., Canada, Norway, U.K., Sweden
Surinam	96% to U.S., Canada	88% to U.S., Netherlands, Norway, F.R.G.
Guyana	95% to Canada, U.S.	70% to Norway, Canada, U.S.
Australia	89% to Japan, F.R.G.	100% to U.S., Japan, Canada

Perhaps the most important considerations for locating the higher stages of production outside the (developing) bauxite-mining countries, however, are political. The aluminum companies have been reticent to establish benefication and especially costly smelting operations in countries possibly inclined towards nationalization. In fact, by locating advanced processing facilities outside the reach of such governments, each aluminum company decreases the temptations to nationalize mining assets while, at the same time, increasing leverage over the bauxite-mining countries, in particular under conditions of diversified supply.[6]

The importance of this geographic distribution of production facilities is that the benefits associated with production increase with each higher step of processing. For instance, the amount of value added at each stage of production increases at a ratio of approximately $1:2.5:8:17$—that is, one ton of semifabricated aluminum yields a gross income which is seventeen times higher than that created by mining.[7] As a result, only about 4 percent of the total value added of the industry as a whole is created at the mining level, i.e., in developing countries.[8]

A related factor severely limiting the contribution of the aluminum industry to host economies is that mining operations, as a rule, are not integrated into the national economy and instead exhibit the typical characteristics of an enclave. Hardly any forward or backward linkages to the rest of the economy exist because, on the one hand, production is, as a rule, exported, while, on the other hand, the equipment required for mining is technologically too sophisticated to be manufactured locally. Moreover, investment in infrastructure usually is limited and specific to the needs of the mining operations; and upgrading of skills remains company-specific and tends not to be disseminated throughout the economy.[9] Thus, despite some positive inputs into the host economy as a whole in the form of employment, government revenue,

---

[e]Excluding the U.K., Ireland, and Denmark.

[f]The Canadian and U.S. tariffs are given as 1¢/lb. The ratio of 4 percent approximately is based on the 1973 price of primary aluminum of 25-30¢/lb.

[g]With respect to the six aluminum companies, the number and distribution of company production facilities (including those in which these companies have major participations) have been provided. Facilities in developing countries generally are relatively small, as indicated by the share of these countries in the world consumption of fabricated aluminum.

and foreign exchange, mining operations are more integrated into the worldwide operations of the parent company than into the economic system of the host country. The implications of such a situation are that the enclave country not only foregoes substantial income but also the beneficial spin-off effects associated with advanced production.[10]

Guyana vs. Alcan

Demba, Alcan's subsidiary in Guyana, had many of the characteristics of an enclave. Mackenzie, the community where Demba is located, was isolated from the rest of Guyana to such an extent that it was not even accessible by road until December 1968.[11] Nevertheless, Demba, which was managed until the 1960s almost entirely by expatriates, represented the largest business operation in Guyana's economy. In 1968, for instance, Demba accounted for approximately 14 percent of Guyana's GDP, 10 percent of total government revenues, 9 percent of annual fixed investment, and averaged between 40 and 50 percent of Guyana's exports.[12]

Faced with a situation in which most of the benefits of the country's natural resources materialized outside the country, it is understandable that Guyana initiated efforts to gain greater control over Demba and attempted, among other things, to convince Alcan to locate advanced processing facilities in the country. Until 1966, such attempts, however, were severely limited by the country's status as a British colony. Cheddi Jagan, the leader of the (leftist) People's Progressive Party (PPP) and the head of several governments before independence, had favored nationalization of all foreign assets as part of the process of political and economic emancipation. But his policies were frustrated by several interventions on the part of Britain, fully supported by the United States. In 1964, Jagan was deposed and Forbes Burnham, the leader of the People's National Congress (PNC), became the head of government and later the country's first Prime Minister after independence (1966).

Although Burnham had indicated some desire to assert greater control over Demba, his relatively weak political position and his dependence on a coalition partner, the procapital United Force, did not allow a vigorous policy. Nevertheless, when the Demba issue became highly politicized in the final months before independence, the future Prime Minister reportedly indicated that unless

Demba would locate a smelter in Guyana, bauxite exports to Canada would be discontinued. Disturbed by this report[13], Alcan requested Burnham to come to Canada to clarify the matter. The result was an agreement (July 1966) which stipulated that the United Nations should carry out a study on the economic feasibility of certain hydroelectrical power sites in Guyana; if judged economically feasible, Alcan agreed to use a significant portion of the power capacity Guyana would build to smelt aluminum for export.[14]

In August 1968, the United Nations study was released, concluding that "it is technically and economically feasible to construct a hydroelectric power development."[15] Alcan, however, claimed that it had never been shown that aluminum could be produced economically at competitive world prices. Guyanese officials, on the other hand, wondered if Alcan had not decided in principle against building a local smelter and was merely trying to gain time in order to diversify its bauxite sources and decrease its dependence on Guyana.[16] The conviction grew that greater control over Demba was necessary if advanced production facilities were ever to be built. The issue, therefore, increasingly became one of participation in Demba.

By 1969, the stage was set for a renewal of confrontations. But by that time the bargaining situation of both parties had changed considerably. In Guyana, the elections of December 1968 provided Burnham with a stronger power base and a government no longer dependent on a coalition partner. However, the elections also left the country badly divided between various ethnic and political groupings. The only question on which all major groups agreed was that greater national control over Demba was necessary—an issue particularly promoted by a militant black group and the PPP.[17] Aided by Alcan's apparent bad faith concerning the recent smelter agreement, popular feelings against Demba rapidly built up. As a result of his own stronger position, pressures from other political groupings, and a certain need to embrace an issue of broad popular concern, Burnham now adopted a more assertive stance vis-à-vis Alcan. The primary government objective, however, was still limited to increasing processing in Guyana and to allowing Guyanese participation in Demba. In spring 1970, the pressure was stepped up when Burnham officially adopted a policy of seeking "meaningful participation" in the bauxite industry. At the same time, the specter of nationalization, always promoted by the rival PPP, was first raised officially when a committee of a summit conference of the heads of the Caribbean Commonwealth governments recommended nationalization of the bauxite and other key industries in the area.[18]

Events moved rapidly toward formal negotiations when, on November 16, 1970, Alcan accepted a Guyanese invitation to hold talks about participation, commencing December 7, 1970. Then, on November 28, 1970, Prime Minister Burnham delivered a nationwide address, in which he presented the government's "main proposals" for participation in Demba. They included the following: (1) the government's participation shall be a majority one and shall confer on the government the control which inheres in such majority holding; such participation shall be by means of the purchase of a share in Demba's assets; (2) evaluation of assets will be no greater than book value; (3) payment will be made out of future after-tax profits of the joint undertaking; and (4) the agreement finally arrived at between Demba and the government shall be deemed to take effect on January 1, 1971. In a confidential letter of the same date from the Office of the Prime Minister to the President of Demba, the same proposals for participation were declared to be "not negotiable."

Alcan responded in a press release on November 30, 1970, referring, however, to the Prime Minister's confidential letter rather than to his public and less categorical speech. By disclosing that the "proposals" had been termed "not negotiable" in the letter, the Burnham government was now committed in public to a tough stand. Any major concessions would thus appear to be a capitulation on the part of the Guyanese government and would thereby demonstrate to other bauxite-producing countries the powerfulness of the major aluminum companies.

Formal negotiations between Guyana and Alcan began on December 7, 1970, and continued through February 22, 1971. Guyana's nonnegotiable conditions governed her responses to Alcan's proposals throughout the negotiating period. During the negotiating period, Alcan made several proposals for expansion of the calcined bauxite sector; all of them called for the Guyanese government to raise the necessary funds. All of Alcan's proposals also provided for the replacement of Demba by a new bauxite enterprise in whose management Guyana would share. Differences in the proposals largely centered around variations in the formula for organizing and controlling the new expanded bauxite entity. Alcan's last proposal of February 22, 1971, for example, agreed to 51 percent Guyanese participation in the new enterprise, while previous proposals were on the basis of 49 percent Guyanese government participation. However, the Guyanese government still felt that the February 22 Alcan proposal did not meet its demands, and on February 23 Prime Minister Burnham terminated negotiations and declared the Government's decision to nationalize Demba.

In March 1971, the "Bauxite Nationalization Bill, 1971" was approved by parliament. The enabling legislation mentioned an unspecified "Vesting Day" when the nationalization of Demba would become effective; in April, this day was set for July 15, 1971. After protracted discussions, a compensation agreement was reached on July 14, 1971. Before moving into an analysis of the negotiations, however, a brief review of Alcan's position and interests is in order.

Given Alcan's worldwide integrated operations, Guyana's demands for increased participation in all stages of aluminum processing created a number of concerns. Alcan had developed an operational structure which capitalized on its own financial and technological strength, Canada's and Norway's sources of cheap hydroelectric power, and large resources of Caribbean bauxite. Alcan contended that it was this division of operations based on the advantages of each party that made Caribbean bauxite of real marketable value. In this scheme, Jamaica and Guyana provided bauxite (and alumina) to Canada and Norway, Trinidad provided transshipment and storage facilities, and the (Alcan-owned) Saguenay Shipping Company and Sprostons Ltd. provided shipping and related services.

This division of operations and the nature of the world aluminum market vested an important strength in Alcan: control over its far-flung operations. Its heavily capital-intensive smelting operations were out of the jurisdictional reach of Guyana, while, at the same time, the small world market for unprocessed bauxite made Guyana dependent on Alcan for the marketing of its bauxite output. By minimizing the proportion of value added to the total operation that could be made hostage to Guyana, Alcan, in effect, reduced the bargaining strength of any Guyanese government bent on nationalization. As Alcan's position in Guyana became increasingly politicized shortly before and after the country gained independence, Alcan attempted to reduce the exposure of its assets committed to Guyana, both by refusing to commit any new resources for higher levels of processing and by a determined policy of diversifying its bauxite sources, first away from Guyana, and later away from the Caribbean in general.

Alcan's diversification policy began in the late 1950s. Up to the mid-1950s, Alcan was 100 percent dependent on Guyana for its bauxite supplied via intracompany transactions. This heavy dependency alone made it prudent for Alcan to diversify its bauxite sources. Strong arguments for diversification also included the anticipated growth of world demand for aluminum and the fact that Guyanese bauxite, compared to bauxite from other sources, was relatively expensive due to its heavy overburden resulting from the extra transportation cost associated with the relatively inaccessible inland terrain where it is mined. Initially, Alcan's diversification strategy concentrated mainly on the Caribbean, namely Jamaica. By 1960, Jamaica provided more than 30 percent of Alcan's bauxite exported to other affiliates—a percentage about equal to that of Guyana's in the same year (see Table 2).

Beginning in the 1960s, Alcan modified its diversification strategy because of its increasing concern over the political risk its assets were exposed to in the Caribbean. The company was particularly concerned about the "demonstration effect" that would be created in Jamaica if Alcan's assets in Guyana were either nationalized or Alcan's equity control substantially diluted.[19]   Table 2 shows Alcan's gradual diversification out of the Caribbean, and particularly out of Guyana, into Australia, Guinea, and Brazil.

While Alcan was taking steps throughout the late 1950s and 1960s to reduce its dependency on Guyanese metal-grade bauxite, there was little it could do about its dependency on the increasingly profitable calcined bauxite operations also carried out by its Demba subsidiary. By 1970, calcined bauxite yielded slightly more than 40 percent of Demba's total output. Calcined bauxite is produced by heating (calcining) selected grades of Guyana's low-iron-content bauxite. Besides having a higher market value than metal-grade bauxite, calcined bauxite has a ready use in the continuously expanding abrasive and refractory industries of the world. Not only is the technology required to produce calcined bauxite relatively unsophisticated, but all of Alcan's calcined bauxite operations were located in Guyana. Moreover, the unique characteristics of Guyana's bauxite made the duplication of the calcining process developed by Alcan extremely difficult and left Demba with a near world monopoly in the product. Thus, by nationalizing

Table 2

Alcan's diversification of bauxite sources
(percentages)

Source	Early 1950s	1955	1960	1965	1970	1971	1973	Late 1970s (projected)a
Guyana	Up to 100	Up to 80	Over 30	Under 30	Under 30	20b	About 10b	—
Jamaica	Minimal	Over 10	Over 30	Over 30	Over 30	Over 30	Over 40	35
Australiac			Planning began early 1960s		5	Over 5	15	At least 15
Brazild	Minimal	Minimal	Minimal	Planning for export began mid-1960s	Minimal	Minimal	3	At least 20
Guinea				Planning began mid-1960se			10	At least 20
Other sourcesf	Minimal	Minimal	About 30	About 40	About 35	About 40	About 20	About 10

Source: Alcan Corporation, various issues of annual reports, and other Alcan documents.

aProjections by the authors on the basis of 1973 data.

bAfter Demba's nationalization in July 1971, Alcan agreed to purchase more than 50 percent of the full capacity of metal-grade bauxite from Guybau (formerly Demba) for 1971. Alcan also agreed to buy limited quantities in 1972 and 1973.

cAlcan does not own bauxite mines in Australia, but it has a 22 percent share in Queensland Aluminium, Ltd.

dAlcan had long owned a small bauxite-aluminum operation in Brazil, supplying the domestic market. Only in the mid-1960s were efforts made to explore for additional bauxite reserves for export purposes.

eAlcan had owned a small bauxite operation in Guinea which had been nationalized in 1961.

fIncludes bauxite not exported and bauxite bought from noncompany sources. Alcan controls mines in India (since before the Second World War; production is refined and smelted locally); Malaysia (since 1956; output is exported to refining facilities in Japan, jointly owned by Alcan and Nippon Light Metal Co.); and France (output is sold in Europe).

Demba, Guyana would not have to anticipate any major difficulties for at least 40 percent of its bauxite production. On the other hand, Alcan was anxious to maintain the valuable market it had cornered for calcined bauxite.[20]

Analysis of the negotiations

In the following analysis of the negotiations between Alcan and Guyana, the importance of the different perspectives and interests guiding the behavior of each party will be noted. In addition, the differing abilities of each to mobilize pressure to its side will be investigated. As pointed out in the previous pages, each party had its own overriding interests which it brought into the bargaining situation and which it promoted within the context given by the international structure of the aluminum industry and the dynamics of internal Guyanese politics.

Alcan's primary interest was to maintain the integrity of its international network which required control over each of its elements. Consequently, Guyana's quest for greater participation in all phases of the aluminum process, in particular its insistence on participation in Demba, constituted an imminent and important threat. Alcan furthermore feared that concessions to Guyana might create a demonstration effect for other countries, specifically those in the Caribbean. Such a demonstration effect, with a possible resulting "domino effect," therefore, had to be avoided. Finally, Alcan had, of course, no interest to commit any further resources to what had become a poor investment-risk country.

Guyana's main interest, on the other hand, was to increase the benefits it could gain from its natural resources and to integrate their utilization into the economic structure and development of the country in general. Participation in the management of Demba, therefore, became of paramount importance.

Although the basic interests of the two parties were incompatible, a number of areas of common interest existed. Both wanted to maintain an ongoing relationship; in fact, even during the negotiations, Demba's operations were not discontinued at any point in time. Guyana needed the income generated by Demba, and felt that it would continue to need Alcan's technology and markets, at least in the short run. In addition, Guyana was concerned over the potentially adverse effects on the inflow of foreign capital to support its development plans should it nationalize Demba. Alcan, on the other hand, still received a considerable share of its metal-grade bauxite from Guyana and therefore wanted to avoid the dislocations associated with a complete rupture. Moreover, it was especially interested in preserving its calcined bauxite operation.

During the negotiations, however, and as discussed in the following section, both parties tried to mobilize as much pressure as possible in the pursuit of their interests. But both parties remained aware of the larger context within which their conflict was being enacted, and both pitched their strategies, at least in part, to that larger context.

Prenegotiations

Alcan felt that the "not negotiable" terms set out in the November 28, 1970, confidential Guyanese letter ran counter to vital corporate interests, and indeed left no important issues for negotiation. The company also regarded the letter as a unilateral, irresponsible act. On November 16, Alcan had already accepted a Guyanese invitation (of November 9) to hold talks about participation, which presumably provided for the conventional give-and-take of negotiations. Accordingly, in the press release of November 30, 1970, Alcan stated that it had been presented nonnegotiable conditions, which constituted an effort to dictate rather than negotiate a solution to outstanding differences. By referring to the "not negotiable" demands of the Guyanese letter rather than to Burnham's less categorical speech, Alcan forced the issue, while, simultaneously, portraying itself as a reasonable party wronged at the hands of a radical nationalist government. Alcan thus tried to capitalize on an important vulnerability of the Burnham government—Guyana's reputation as a radical state, acquired during Jagan's rule. Burnham himself was aware of Guyana's dependency on international financing and marketing institutions should a break with Alcan occur. The November 30 press release also attempted to step up pressure against Guyana by stressing Alcan's decreasing dependence on Guyanese bauxite: "If the supplies of alumina and metal grade bauxite from Guyana are affected, Alcan believes alternative sources of supply can be arranged."[21]

In turn, Guyana regarded Alcan's public reference to the "not negotiable" conditions in the confidential letter rather than to the "Government's main proposals" in the speech as an act of bad faith.[22] Alcan's public reference to the nonnegotiable part of the letter made Guyana's position seem more extreme than it desired, and was clearly designed to compel Guyana to reassess the course of its action. Guyanese officials have subsequently described their own reference in the letter to nonnegotiable conditions as a bargaining chip—used in the confidence of negotiations—to place Guyana in a favorable initial position.

Both sides failed to achieve the objectives they had apparently set out to accomplish during prenegotiations. Alcan did have some success in portraying the Guyanese presentation of nonnegotiable demands as a unilateral, irresponsible act, but certainly did not achieve its much more important objective of compelling Guyana to reassess the course of its action. Guyana, for its part, elicited a tough response from Alcan rather than compliance with its nonnegotiable demands. Both parties also failed to assess correctly the impact of Guyanese public opinion on the negotiations. Alcan appears to have been much more aware of, and interested in, the potential which publication of the letter presented for mobilizing world opinion against the Guyanese government than of the provocative effect a tough corporate position would have on Guyanese public opinion. To be sure, Burnham's speech was designed to mobilize public support for the negotiations. But once the content of the confidential letter was publicized it became extremely difficult for Guyana to back down from, or even to compromise about, the so-called "not negotiable" demands. Instead of leading public opinion, the Burnham government often found itself responding to pressures for harsher measures against Alcan.[23]

Negotiations about participation

While the attempt to foist "not negotiable" conditions on Alcan in large part backfired, Guyana's public statement of the basic bargaining terms in the November 28 speech nevertheless worked in its favor. The Guyanese demand for majority participation through the purchase of a share in Demba's assets was generally accepted as a legitimate national aspiration for control. Alcan itself acknowledged Guyana's sovereign right to control its own natural resources, and was therefore placed on the defensive throughout this negotiating phase.[24] Since Guyana stated its avowedly legitimate demand for participation at an early date, Alcan bore the onus of developing some kind of plan which would meet Guyanese approval. A constant source of pressure on Alcan was then that unless it approximated Guyana's basic negotiating demands sufficiently, it would most probably be nationalized. The state of Guyanese public opinion added credibility to this implicit threat.

Alcan was still able to further its objectives by claiming that Guyana was merely playing politics because majority local participation and a Guyanese aluminum smelter had great national political appeal but little economic justification.[25] Alcan, in contrast, claimed its objective was to run a profitable operation according to good economic sense, and on this ground it opposed local participation (meaning ultimate operating control) and a Guyanese smelter.[26]

Important political considerations underlay Alcan's position, in spite of its ostensible economic rationale. Implicit in the Alcan proposals was a desire to increase gains at minimum risk. Details concerning the organization of the new bauxite enterprise were modified in subsequent proposals, but in all of them Alcan would not invest new risk capital. The Guyanese government would have to raise 50 million Guyana dollars from the World Bank or elsewhere for the expansion of calcined bauxite production.[27] Alcan's contribution to the new company would be in the form of Demba's assets as a loan.[28] In essence, Alcan's plan would allow it to determine the course of expansion of the enterprise into calcined bauxite rather than aluminum and to benefit from a more profitable enlarged calcined bauxite operation without new investment.[29]

Changes in form rather than substance characterized Alcan's willingness to compromise about participation formulas. Only on February 22 did Alcan agree to 51 percent instead of 49 percent Guyanese participation. Even after this concession was made, hedges were provided to prevent full Guyanese operating control. A chief executive officer was to be nominated by Alcan and appointed by the board of directors. Guyana would enjoy majority participation on the board of directors, but the Alcan-nominated chief executive officer would have extensive management responsibility.[30] And, of course, the new company would only control the static bauxite/alumina operation without any power over decisions affecting aluminum production, while the expanded calcined bauxite sector would operate separately from Alcan's worldwide integrated aluminum network.

Negotiations about compensation

Some details of Alcan's final February 22, 1971, proposal were shaped more to Guyana's liking, although Guyana's basic demands still were not met. Consequently, on the very next day, the Guyanese government announced that it intended to nationalize Demba. February 23 was also a political occasion—the anniversary of Republic Day—chosen, apparently, in response to internal pressures for more forceful action. Even at this point, however, not all possibilities were foreclosed. After passing the enabling legislation for nationalization within ten days—obviously to step up pressure on Alcan—the government took more than one month to name the "Vesting Day." Similarly, Alcan's president, during a shareholder meeting on April 1, only spoke of "prospects" of having Demba nationalized.[31]

With the decision to nationalize Demba, the advantage during subsequent formal and informal discussions about compensation passed to Alcan. Since Guyana was anxious to have international circles well disposed to its independent bauxite operation, it now bore the onus of developing a compensation formula which would meet Alcan's approval. Alcan held that the compensation formula included in Guyana's nonnegotiable demands—evaluation of Demba's assets at book value with payment made out of future after-tax profits—violated the principle of prompt, adequate, and effective compensation for nationalized property and was subject to many contingencies. Alcan had accepted these methods of reimbursement in the context of joint participation in an expanded calcined bauxite operation, but not as compensation for nationalization. Throughout the negotiations about participation, Alcan had made it clear that nationalization would entail harsher compensation terms and denial of its cooperation in operating Demba's successor. Alcan was more concerned about the demonstration effect of the nationalization and compensation arrangements than the size of immediate financial rewards. A rigorous schedule of compensation payments and denial of Alcan cooperation was expected to generate serious Guyanese difficulties in running the new bauxite company, and thereby deter political leaders in other countries flirting with nationalization measures.

In spite of this hard line, Alcan could still convincingly portray its own actions as moderate and those of Guyana as immoderate. The Guyanese Constitution[32]—which had provided for "adequate and prompt" compensation in cases of nationalization—was amended after the decision to nationalize and the relevant provision was changed to "reasonable compensation." In contrast, Alcan's reply to Burnham's announcement of the decision to nationalize stressed its own moderation: "Alcan will make every effort to ensure that such transition [to an independent bauxite operation] will be effected in an orderly way."[33] The theme of Guyanese immoderation and Alcan's moderation exerted a strong influence in pushing Guyana away from its "book value/future after-tax profits" compensation formula toward more generous conditions of repayment.

Alcan first proposed that Demba's assets be valued by a mutually acceptable independent appraiser, with payments to be made in equal annual installments with interest. Alcan recognized that its compensation formula (stressing prompt, adequate, and effective compensation) was generally accepted in international business circles and would probably be endorsed in large part by a third-party appraiser. Involvement of a third party in the dispute would also complement Alcan's effort to call as much international attention to the compensation negotiations as possible in order to pressure Guyana to accept conventional formulas for compensation. In this manner, Alcan would have been able to sever all ties with Guyana while still retaining considerable assurance of generous compensation terms. Guyana, therefore, rejected this proposal on the ground that it would unnecessarily inject a third party into the negotiation.

Alcan's attempt to portray Guyana's behavior as radical and even illegal did gain considerable international sympathy. For instance, when nationalization was announced, the sympathy of the international press—generally supportive of Guyana in the past—shifted to Alcan.[34] Ironically, however, the U.S. rather than the Canadian government exerted pressure on Guyana to accept the principle of prompt, adequate, and effective compensation.[35] The U.S. government did not become alarmed about Guyana's behavior until the February 23, 1971, enabling legislation was passed. The nationalization bill contained provisions which the United States felt would be tantamount to expropriation without compensation, a view which coincided with Alcan's. The strong convergence of interests between the U.S. government and Alcan substantially enhanced Alcan's bargaining position during the compensation stage of negotiations. The U.S. government expressed its disapproval of the Guyanese compensation formula by abstaining in a vote on a $5.4 million World Bank loan for Guyana. Since the Guyanese legislation was not seen to assure prompt, adequate, and effective compensation, the United States argued that the loan must be withheld.[36] U.S. concern was not merely to protect the interests of Reynolds, the (small) U.S. aluminum operation in Guyana,[37] United States shareholders in Alcan, or even the interests of all U.S. aluminum companies in the Caribbean, but more broadly to uphold the principle of adequate, prompt, and effective compensation at a time when the principle was being challenged elsewhere in Latin America. Although approval of the loan was given in June before the final Demba compensation agreement was arranged, Guyana was shaken by U.S. opposition to its compensation formula.

On a number of occasions, Alcan made representations to the Canadian government to play a more active role in the conflict. The Canadian government, however, only sent two letters to Prime Minister Burnham requesting fair, nondiscriminatory treatment for Alcan. The Canadian government's concern with the size and influence of U.S. investment in Canada has led it to favor a hands-off attitude on the part of all governments towards their private overseas investors.[38] Consequently, the sizable Canadian bilateral aid program to Guyana continued throughout the crisis, and Canada voted for the World Bank loan to Guyana. Nevertheless, if Demba would have been expropriated, Canadian officials did suggest (in interviews) that the Canadian aid program to Guyana would have been affected adversely—a possibility certainly not absent from Guyanese concerns.

Alcan also benefited from a strike of Demba workers in late April 1971 against the Guyanese government. Demba workers had traditionally received relatively high salaries and pensions. It had become uncertain, however, to what extent Alcan's Retirement Income and Life Assurance (RILA) fund—the contributions to which had been invested in Canada—would continue to benefit Guyanese employees after nationalization. The protest of Demba's workers to the Guyanese government about possible adverse effects of nationalization on their welfare benefits worked to Alcan's advantage. The Guyanese government wanted both employer and employee RILA contributions repatriated to a new trust fund in Guyana. Alcan attempted to maintain a position of "benevolent neutrality" in this matter by claiming that power to transfer the funds to Guyana resided with its consulting actuaries in Canada. About $4.5 million of pension funds held by Alcan in trust for Demba employees were eventually repatriated to Guyana, but only after some of the risks of nationalization and limitations of the Guyanese government had been made painfully evident.[39]

While Guyana's ability to pressure Alcan was weaker during the compensation stage of negotiations than during the participation stage, Guyana still had some bargaining power.[40] After it had become apparent that Guyana was bent on nationalization, Alcan was interested in eliciting compromises from Guyana about compensation in order to minimize unavoidable losses. For example, in response to Guyanese demands, Alcan kept Demba functioning at a normal production level throughout the crisis. For its part, Guyana managed to blunt Alcan pressure somewhat by alternating ambiguity with forcefulness. Ambiguities in Guyana's enabling legislation left Alcan unsure of Guyana's intentions as late as April 1, when Alcan's president, Nathanael Davis, addressed the company's annual meeting. Davis noted that since the enabling legislation for nationalization had not yet been implemented, a participation agreement still might be possible, or, failing such an agreement, the possibility of an agreed settlement on compensation also remained.[41] On April 4, however, the Guyanese minister of mines and forests clarified the government's view that Alcan's earlier refusal to accept the basic terms of participation had definitively terminated negotiations in February and that no further negotiation for participation was contemplated.[42] Guyana subsequently named the "Vesting Day"—the day when the nationalization of Demba would be effective—as July 15, 1971. Naming of the Vesting Day before a settlement on compensation had been arranged set a deadline, in effect, for compensation negotiations and helped Guyana regain some of the bargaining initiative.[43]

The compensation settlement of July 14, 1971, tended to favor Alcan, although it did not receive as generous terms as it had desired. Demba's gross value (undepreciated) was about U.S.$114 million, which was considered by Alcan as the fairest basis for compensation. Demba's book value, for Guyanese tax purposes, was U.S.$46 million, which Guyana had proposed as the proper amount of compensation. Total compensation provided by the final agreement was about U.S. $80 million ($53.5 million basic compensation and about $26.5 million from interest payments minus withholding tax.) While this amount was below Alcan's expectations, the company felt that the principle of prompt, adequate, and effective compensation had been defended since both of Guyana's relevant "not negotiable" conditions had been significantly modified. The figure set was considerably higher than book value written down for tax purposes; and payment was to be a charge on government revenue, rather than to be made out of future profits.

The aftermath

Both Alcan and Guyana experienced costs and benefits from the crisis. Alcan lost the profitable calcined bauxite operation and a valuable source of bauxite and alumina, but was nevertheless able to adjust to Demba's nationalization. Its previous preparations to diversify bauxite sources facilitated the transition to a new supply network. The company may even be able to utilize elsewhere the calcined bauxite technology it developed in Guyana. In May 1973, Alcan and Billiton International Metals of the Netherlands announced that they would undertake a feasibility study for a joint project to produce refractory-grade calcined bauxite in Surinam.[44] Guyana has faced a number of difficult problems in running an independent bauxite/alumina operation; but no problem has proved insurmountable. In the immediate aftermath of the nationalization, Alcan denied Guybau, the new name of the nationalized bauxite enterprise, the use of its transshipment facilities located in Trinidad (which Demba had previously used). Trinidad, however, overruled Alcan's decision.[45] With respect to the managing of Guybau, P. A. Thompson, chairman of the enterprise, listed eight major problem areas faced by the enterprise in shifting to an independent bauxite/alumina operation: staffing and organization, production, maintenance of equipment, maintaining stock levels, finance, personnel administration and industrial relations, marketing, and shipping.

A temporary closure of Guybau's alumina plant for six weeks in the summer of 1972—due to oversupply of aluminum in the world market—added to problems in most of these areas; but solutions are being worked out. For example, Philipp Brothers of New York City and Switzerland have been contracted as a marketing agent; and Samincorp of New York has been employed as a purchasing agent. The agreement with both agencies provides for training of personnel in the marketing and purchasing areas.[46] Plans are also being made for the expansion of calcined bauxite production; and trading relations with centrally planned economies in bauxite products have expanded. Finally, the recent decision of Trinidad and Tobago, Jamaica, and Guyana to build a Caribbean smelter may be a positive development if it proves to be within the means of the Caribbean governments.[47] Overall, there is a general sense of relief that the immediate economic costs of nationalization were not greater and a conviction that national control of the bauxite industry will ultimately benefit Guyana more than foreign control.

Since Guybau has not suffered unbearable difficulties and, in fact, has performed quite well, the demonstration effect of the nationalization on other states has been detrimental to Alcan. Alcan expected the economic costs of nationalization to be so great that other countries would be deterred from taking similar measures. But Guybau's viability since July 1971 may justify the nationalization to many in Guyana and elsewhere. Alcan's inflexible bargaining strategy may then have led to several Pyrrhic victories. Alcan never yielded from the principle that greater participation and processing would only occur on its own terms, although this insistence led to nationalization. Alcan insisted as well that the principle of prompt, adequate, and effective compensation be respected, and here Guyana was forced to make significant compromises. But the cost that had to be paid by Guyana may not be the most lasting effect of the crisis. Instead, other developing countries often seem to have been most impressed with Guyana's determination to obtain greater control of national resources in spite of numerous vulnerabilities. Jamaica, in particular, appeared to have been quite impressed by Guyana's success. After a change in government in 1972, the country took a considerably more active stance vis-à-vis the foreign bauxite companies.[48] In recent years, in fact, increased efforts of host countries have concentrated on changing the locational patterns of the operations of the aluminum industry and on sharing more of the equity of local operations. Host country insistence on greater participation in all stages of the aluminum industry has been aimed at obtaining more of the profits of the total operations and at integrating aluminum operations more closely into the rest of their economies, thereby erasing the detriments of stringent enclave-type mining operations. The aluminum enterprises, in turn, are resisting these locational demands. Not only are they afraid of exposing large assets to potential nationalization, but they also fear that different locational patterns of operations would increase the general leverage that host countries have on total operations and policies and thus make global coordination difficult. At the same time, the aluminum enterprises had to be somewhat conciliatory because of their dependence on host countries as the primary source of bauxite ore.

In pursuing their strategies, there is a temptation for both the host country and the multinational enterprise to expand the immediate conflict by mustering allies to their side. In the case of the host country this usually means the mobilization of domestic opinion and of like-minded governments faced with, or likely to face, similar conflicts. In the Alcan/Guyana conflict, Guyana was only able to capitalize on a reservoir of antiforeign sentiment that was associated with the movement toward independence. At the same time that it utilized that reservoir, however, it also became its prisoner, at least to a certain extent. Similarly, Alcan's preoccupation with the possible demonstration effect of the Guyana solution reduced its room for maneuver.

Eventually both parties got caught up in the momentum of the crisis and arrived at an outcome which both of them originally had neither anticipated nor desired. Both sides had preferred to continue cooperation if certain basic issues could be settled. But unresolved questions about participation and processing tended to become aggravated, and reconciliation of interests became increasingly difficult at successive stages of the crisis. Both parties, however, had fairly explicit negotiating strategies and both appear to have been fully aware of their divergent and common interests. Proposals and counterproposals were carefully structured to protect corporate or national interests while holding out the promise of mutual benefits.

The Alcan/Guyana conflict also highlights the very real outside pressures that a multinational enterprise can muster against a host country, particularly when operating in the highly oligopolistic and vertically integrated framework of a raw material industry. Picturing a host country as "radical" can be effective in temporarily halting the inflow of new investment and technology into that country. Also, the more or less convergence of interest between a multinational enterprise and its home country—and to a lesser extent that of all headquarter countries—is clear. No home government can afford to portray for too long an image of indifference to the interests of its business abroad. The unwillingness of the Canadian government to support Alcan was due more to the contingencies of an overriding policy interest in the Caribbean than to a lack of concern over Alcan's interest and, perhaps even more importantly, to its own position as an important host country.

NOTES

[1] In recent years, however, enterprises have adopted diversification strategies that decrease their dependence on individual (traditional) supplier countries. For one, most enterprises have actively explored and developed bauxite

reserves in alternative countries (notably Australia), and second, many of these new ventures have been brought on stream as consortia projects, thereby spreading risk and increasing (via home countries) insurance.

[2]A "list of some 'arm's-length' metal grade bauxite purchases of which we have knowledge," an appendix to a confidential Alcan memorandum entitled "General Comment on the 'Caribbean Bauxite Industry' by Norman Girvan," contains only seven items. The amount involved probably does not surpass 20 percent of world production. The rest, in other words, are non-arm's-length deals, i.e., intracompany transactions.

Alusuisse noted, in its 1971 Annual Report, p. 6: "The degree of integration of the Group increased from 59% in 1970 to 73% in 1971. Approximately three quarters of the Group's output of primary aluminum is therefore processed in our own plants."

[3]Norman Girvan, *The Caribbean Bauxite Industry,* p. 2, estimates that a bauxite mining capacity of 1 million tons costs about U.S. $20 million, the complementary alumina processing capabilities require an investment of about U.S. $125 million, and the smelting capacity about U.S. $250 million; power to supply such a system would cost about U.S. $120 million. This gives a grand total of approximately U.S. $515 million. Alcan company files confirm this estimate. See also Martin S. Brown and John Butler, *The Production, Marketing, and Consumption of Copper and Aluminum,* pp. 5, 72-73.

The bauxite/alumina production of Demba, Alcan's subsidiary in Guyana, was of about the size used in this example; the estimates, therefore, provide a rough idea of how high capital expenditures would have been to produce aluminum in Guyana.

[4]Locational determinants are discussed, for instance, in H. D. Huggins, *Aluminium in Changing Communities;* and Sterling Brubaker, *Trends in the World Aluminum Industry.* Girvan, *The Caribbean Bauxite Industry,* also contains a brief but interesting discussion of this question.

[5]Brubaker, *Trends in the World Aluminum Industry,* p. 235, estimates that tariffs maintained at rates of 5-9 percent in major industrial countries is the equivalent of 2-3 mills in power cost, "by itself sufficient to compensate for most or all of the power cost advantage which might be anticipated in less-developed states."

[6]Different barriers to entry in a number of other mineral-extraction industries have tended to place much greater bargaining power in the hands of natural-resources-producing states. In the copper and oil industries, Theodore Moran has reasoned that developing countries control the crucial mineral-extraction stage of production that establishes the oligopoly power of the industry and therefore negotiate from strength with multinational enterprises. In the case of industries such as aluminum, he adds, the point of oligopoly control—that is, control of the stage where the greatest barriers to entry are located—lies at the smelting stage, so that the bargaining position of ore producers is relatively weak. See Theodore H. Moran, "New Deal or Raw Deal in Raw Materials," *Foreign Policy,* pp. 124-129.

[7]See Girvan, *The Caribbean Bauxite Industry,* p. 3. Girvan's calculations are corroborated by data from Alcan's files. Applied to output in 1964, Girvan (*ibid.,* p. 10) calculated the following distribution of GDP created by processing of Caribbean metal-grade bauxite (millions of U.S. dollars).

| | GDP created by | | | | | |
in	Mining	Benefication	Smelting	Semifabrication	Total U.S.$	%age
Caribbean	89	33	—	—	122	6
North America and						
rest of world	—	119	568	1,117	1,804	94
Total	89	153	568	1,117	1,924	100

Of the 6 percent income created in the Caribbean, one has to subtract the net profits, dividends, and interest repatriated by the aluminum companies "so that the real Caribbean share is more likely to be in the region of 4 percent." (*ibid.,* p. 11).

[8]See note 7.

[9]For a charting of industries potentially based on and linked with bauxite see Norman Girvan, *Foreign Capital and Economic Underdevelopment in Jamaica,* p. 77. Some quantitative material on linkages is contained in Girvan, *The Caribbean Bauxite Industry.*

[10]For a discussion of such spin-off effects see Johan Galtung, "A Structural Theory of Imperialism," *Journal of Peace Research,* pp. 81-118. The three major U.S. aluminum companies, for instance, have all their R&D operations located in the parent country. See, in this context, also the literature on the international division of labor cited in the bibliography of this Collection.

[11]Demba was incorporated in Guyana in 1916 and started exporting in 1919. A former Demba assistant manager, R. E. Rosane, characterized the accessibility of Mackenzie as follows: "Earlier transportation was by air which was expensive or by river which was slow and arduous." This same official described the foreign enclave nature of Mackenzie: "Finally, an important perspective is to study Demba in Guyana as an *international* enclave. The scope of Company operations and the variations in income flow which it generates, and most particularly the phasing of its programs of investments for growth, are determined primarily by its international economic circumstances. The need to fit these variables into the less flexible national development program . . . underlies the national concern with the relative lack of national control over an important part of the economy. The influence of international political groupings also has a significant bearing on the company-government relationship, particularly where the firm has a strong link with one or more foreign governments that are also major aid donors." R. E. Rosane, "Bauxite in Guyana: The Role of Demerara Bauxite Company, Limited in Guyana Over Fifty-Three Years," pp. 6, 8-9.

For a more comprehensive account of Demba's relations with the community of Mackenzie, see Cedric Grant, *Company Towns in the Caribbean: A Preliminary Analysis of Christianburg-Wismar-Mackenzie.*

12Rosane, "Bauxite in Guyana," passim.

13At that time, Alcan was still heavily dependent on Guyanese bauxite.

14See the "Joint Statement by Guyana Prime Minister and Alcan on Aluminium Smelting in Guyana," Alcan press release, Jul. 19, 1966: "Mr. Davis ' [president of Alcan] recalled that in July 1965 an Alcan statement affirmed the company's serious interest in the use of power for aluminium smelting in Guyana. As a result of today's meeting, Mr. Davis confirmed that the Company believes that aluminium smelting for export would be in the economic interest of both Guyana and Alcan, and assuming current power studies give assurance of economic power costs, Alcan wished to negotiate with the Guyana government for the purchase of power for smelting when such was available."

15Shawinigan Engineering Company Ltd. "Power Development Survey in Guyana for United Nations, Tiboku Hydro-electric Development Feasibility Study." Shawinigan, a Canadian company, carried out the study for the United Nations. In Alcan's interpretation of the July 19, 1966, press release (see previous note), however, it was the responsibility of Guyana to develop the necessary power facilities and to approach Alcan, in due course, with an offer of power supply at a proposed price.

16Alcan's production of metal-grade bauxite in Guyana was hardly expanded between 1956 and 1968.

17For a careful account of the internal conflicts in Guyanese politics and their relationship to foreign influences in Guyana, see Colin Henfrey, "Foreign Influences in Guyana: The Struggle for Independence," in *Patterns of Foreign Influence in the Caribbean,* ed. Emanuel de Kadt, especially pp. 77-80.

18From April 1970 through fall 1970, the government demonstrated its seriousness to Alcan by making extended, careful preparations for the impending negotiations. Norman Girvan, one of the two West Indian academicians who were involved in an advisory capacity in the events leading up to nationalization, described these preparations in his "Bauxite: The Need to Nationalize, Part II," *Review of Black Political Economy,* pp. 81-101.

Alcan officials privately dismissed "the nationalization talk as a roundabout approach to induce Alcan to operate an aluminium smelter in Guyana." (*Financial Post,* July 25, 1970). But the mounting resentment toward Demba finally compelled Alcan to publicly justify its policies. J. G. Campbell, president of Demba, tried to set forth the record of the company's contribution to Guyana in a speech over Georgetown radio stations in August 1970. Portions of Campbell's address, as well as supporting documents, were subsequently compiled in pamphlet form for distribution in Guyana and elsewhere ("Where did the money go? The Demba record in Guyana 1919-1969," Demerara Bauxite Company, Ltd., Republic of Guyana, September 1970).

19A sympathetic account of Alcan's concern about the demonstration effect of the crisis is presented in "Who is the Winner in Guyana?" *Executive,* June 1971, pp. 34-37.

[20]The calcined bauxite market was of particular interest for Alcan at the beginning of the 1970s since the world market for aluminum slid into a depression at that time. Beginning in mid-1960, production capacity of aluminum began to outpace demand; and that imbalance was expected to continue at least into the mid-1970s. The major aluminum companies attempted to bring supply and demand back into equilibrium by operating their home-country smelters below full capacity and deferring additional projects. Alcan was especially hard-hit by the problems of overproduction due to its heavy reliance on exports. In this situation, a Guyanese smelter would have led directly to additional cut-backs in Canadian aluminum production and thus would have further compounded Alcan's problems.

[21]Alcan press release, Nov. 30, 1970.

[22]This became very apparent in several interviews with Guyanese officials.

[23]Girvan quoted Burnham as saying: "I prefer to take on Alcan rather than the people of Guyana." (Girvan, "Bauxite: The Need to Nationalize," p. 70.)

[24]During prenegotiations and subsequent negotiations about compensation, however, Alcan did muster considerable support by claiming Guyana was taking a radical position.

[25]While the negotiations focused on the participation issue, the question of processing, in particular the construction of an aluminum smelter in Guyana, was implicit in the debates. Majority control of Demba would permit the government to decide for itself about a smelter, since it felt that Alcan would not otherwise undertake such a development. With the exception of calcined bauxite, Alcan opposed an expansion of processing in the country.

[26]To prove its point, Alcan buttressed its proposals with extensive economic data and reasoning and essentially argued that what was good for the economic health of its international network was also good for Guyana.

[27]As interviews indicated, Guyana felt that Alcan had long been skimming off huge profits by taking out natural resources in an unprocessed state, and now not only refused to consider further processing of bauxite into aluminum but also wanted Guyana to worry about financing expansion of only one sector of the industry.

[28]Alcan's proposal closely resembles Kennecott's expansion plan in Chile, which Theodore Moran describes as part of a company strategy aimed at spreading the risk and raising the cost of nationalization in natural resources. See Theodore H. Moran, "Transnational Strategies of Protection and Defense by Multinational Corporations: Spreading the Risk and Raising the Cost for Nationalization in Natural Resources," pp. 273-287. It is noteworthy that each company—Alcan and Kennecott—offering an expansion plan on this basis had previously resisted any major changes in operating procedures. While such an expansion plan was ostensibly in the host countries' interest it actually was self-serving on the companies' part. In each case, the enterprise would take no new financial risk, but would end up with 49 percent holdings in a much more profitable enterprise. Nevertheless, Kennecott's program did provide for a broad-based expansion of the national copper industry even if Chile had to worry about financing it. Alcan's plan of only expanding

calcined bauxite operations, however, deemphasized Guyana's bauxite/alumina operation and indefinitely shelved the idea of a Guyanese aluminum smelter.

Girvan indicates that the Guyanese officials were aware of the self-serving nature of the participation agreements negotiated in Chile (and Zambia). By drafting the nonnegotiable conditions, they were determined to avoid repeating the same kind of host-country errors. See Girvan, "Bauxite: The Need to Nationalize," pp. 89-90, 92.

29Within the general guidelines of this plan, Alcan was willing to make some compromises. For instance, according to an early proposal, the debt the new company would owe Alcan for Demba's assets would need to be repaid by annual installments at a commercial rate of interest. Later Alcan was willing to contribute Demba's assets at their written book value and agreed that repayment of these assets would be made out of the future cash flow of the new company. But Alcan was only willing to thereby lock itself into the future operation of the new company as long as it did not have to contribute new capital and Guyana would finance expansion of the calcined bauxite sector.

30This condition—to maintain ultimate control—was crucial to Alcan and, at the same time, unacceptable to Guyana.

31Nathanael V. Davis, "Alcan's Present Situation in Guyana: Remarks Concerning Guyana by Nathanael V. Davis, President of Alcan Aluminium Limited, at the Annual Meeting of the Company's Shareholders," Montreal, April 1, 1971, mimeographed.

32Alcan's president, Davis, in his remarks to shareholders (see note 31) emphasized that the enabling legislation "abrogates, for the bauxite industry alone, the provisions of the Guyana Constitution guaranteeing adequate and prompt compensation in the event of nationalization . . . ." He did not mention, however, that the constitution had been drafted in England before independence.

Guyana argued that prompt compensation would be onerous for a small state. Repayment would not be onerous to Guyana if it were commensurate with the volume of future profits. This would also make Alcan dependent on the future welfare of the new bauxite company so that continuing cooperation would be likely. Regardless of the possible political merits of the Guyanese compensation formula, prompt, adequate, and effective compensation for nationalized properties was a generally recognized principle in international financial and marketing circles. Since the success of Guyana's independent bauxite/alumina operation depended on the goodwill of these circles, Guyana was vulnerable to Alcan's pressure to adhere to the standard compensation formula of promptness, adequacy and effectiveness.

33Alcan press release, Mar. 3, 1974.

34Cedric H. Grant—besides Girvan the only other academic advisor to the Guyanese negotiating team—has examined international pressures on Guyana which Alcan was able to exert or encourage. See his "Political Sequel to Alcan Nationalisation in Guyana—The International Aspects," *Social and Economic Studies*, pp. 249-271. Some of the following discussion is based on this source. Grant does not, however, discuss Guyana's strategies or the internal pressures of the Guyanese society.

35Maybe not all that ironical: in 1970, U.S. residents held 47.8 percent of Alcan's common shares (1971: 39.4 percent) and Canadian residents 40.6 percent (1971: 48.8 percent).

36See Charls Walker, "Expropriation of Foreign Private Investments."

In interviews, Guyanese officials maintained that Alcan and Alcoa (the largest U.S.-based aluminum company and formerly Alcan's parent) colluded in trying to convince the U.S. government to block the World Bank loan. It was also maintained that Alcoa attempted to have Guyana's U.S. sugar quota cut.

37Guyanese officials explained (in interviews) their delay in negotiating about participation with Reynolds by the unexpected consequences of the Demba nationalization: since in its aftermath all local personnel trained for the bauxite industry were occupied by the new national enterprise, and all available funds were needed for payment of compensation, the redefinition of Reynolds' role had to be deferred. On January 1, 1974, however, Prime Minister Burnham announced that the government had begun negotiations for ownership and control of the bauxite mines and plants owned by Reynolds Mines Guyana, Ltd. *(New York Times,* Jan. 2, 1974).

38At the same time, Canada was reshaping its general policy toward the Caribbean, attempting to acquire a more progressive image. Interference in Guyana would have seriously damaged such a policy.

39Grant, "Political Sequel to Alcan Nationalisation," maintains that Alcan's strategy was to yield on the RILA issue only as a condition for a satisfactory settlement of the compensation question.

40Norman Girvan's article, "Why We Need to Nationalize Bauxite and How," in *Readings in Political Economy of the Caribbean,* ed. Norman Girvan and Owen Jefferson, pp. 232-233, mentioned as part of a nationalization strategy for bauxite the formation of an organization of bauxite-exporting countries "to collectively exercise a reasonable amount of bargaining power in relation to the major using countries. The basic aim of such an organisation would be to facilitate a takeover by the participating countries of the production and marketing of their bauxite, processing it locally into alumina and aluminium as far as possible." It is unclear to what extent Guyana actually explored this possibility in any active manner. Jamaica's reaction certainly was not very encouraging: in the midst of the negotiations between Alcan and Guyana, Prime Minister Shearer of Jamaica went so far as to disassociate himself from Guyana's policy and to reaffirm his policy of encouraging foreign investors.

41See Davis' remarks, "Alcan's Present Situation in Guyana."

42Guyanese government press release, Apr. 4, 1971.

43Alcan also felt constrained in exerting any severe pressure on Guyana due to the possibility of placing the lives of Alcan's expatriate employees in danger. This danger increased as the crisis escalated. Anti-Demba (and even anti-Canadian) feelings were running so high during the spring of 1971 that one violent incident did occur. Demonstrators in Guyana stoned the Canadian

High Commissioner's home in Georgetown on April 30, 1971, to protest the conviction by a Montreal court of several West Indian students who had participated in the student occupation of Sir George Williams University in 1969.

[44]Alcan, *Annual Report,* 1973.

[45]In interviews, Guyanese officials did express the belief that Alcan probably would have been most satisfied if Demba would have collapsed after nationalization—as an example for all leaders bent on nationalization. Some of Alcan's actions do suggest that this may have been an objective.

[46]Guybau, *Annual Report,* 1972.

[47]*New York Times,* June 11, 1974.

[48]In fact, the bauxite-producing countries—led by Jamaica—have commenced, in early 1974, to actively reshape their relations with the major aluminum companies. The questions of participation and control played a major role in ongoing negotiations.

Chapter
7
Perceptions of Foreign
Investment in Nigeria
Andrew C. E. Hilton

Notwithstanding significant exceptions, it is generally true that, in relatively developed countries, societal cleavages tend to cut across, rather than to reinforce, one another. It is also true that in these more or less homogeneous societies the entry of the MNE does not usually represent a radically new social, political, or economic input. In relatively less-developed countries, on the other hand, ethnic, linguistic, religious, urban-rural, and economic cleavages tend to be mutually reinforcing—with the concomitant result that the political structure is fragile and that the circulation of elites is rapid and often violent.[1]

Within these societies—of which Nigeria, with its ethnic fractionalization and history of political instability, is a paradigm case—the MNE, by virtue both of its size and the value-clusters with which it is associated, is bound to have a more profound impact than in societies accustomed to large-scale industry and ostensibly committed to Weberian norms of rationality and bureaucracy.

This study, data collection for which was made possible by the Danforth Foundation and by a grant from the University of Pennsylvania, should in no way be taken to represent official policy of the International Bank for Reconstruction and Development, with which the author is currently associated.

This chapter, therefore, deals with the position of direct foreign investment in a country deeply divided by ethnic, linguistic, and religious cleavages and which epitomizes the most extreme problems of development. It presents some conclusions, generated by data collected in 1972, and addresses itself to three major points: (1) the levels of awareness of foreign investors shown by respondents, (2) the degree of favorableness shown toward investment by different national groups, and (3) the possibility that hostility toward certain foreign groups might serve a positive function both as a means of securing in-group cohesiveness and as a way of diverting hostility from other potentially more vulnerable expatriate communities.[2]

The question of foreign investment is not of merely academic interest in Nigeria. While the situation of 1949—where indigenous traders controlled only 5 percent of imports and the three largest expatriate companies accounted for 49 percent of all traded items[3]—no longer exists, the 1968 Industrial Survey of 625 manufacturing establishments estimated that, out of a total paid-up capital of $179.8 million, private non-Nigerian sources accounted for almost $126 million—or 70 percent.[4] Of this figure, approximately 51 percent was British, 20 percent was American, and 22 percent was Western European. The remainder—only 7 percent of the total—was divided between such groups as the Lebanese and Indians.[5]

The economic and psychological impact of such a large foreign presence is compounded by the privileged position of expatriates within—or rather parallel to—Nigerian society. In the first place, most Western European and American expatriates are geographically contained within what are essentially white ghettos. Few Nigerians in Lagos can afford the annual house rent of up to $8,400 in Ikoyi, Apapa, or on Victoria Island. Second, the distribution of wealth in Nigeria is highly skewed: of 87,714 employees interviewed in the 1968 Industrial Survey only 2,040 (2.3 percent) were non-Nigerians, yet this expatriate group accounted for 25.1 percent of all wages and salaries, and received 63.4 percent of all "nonmonetary" rewards. Finally, given that at least 56 percent of the indigenous labor force is engaged in small scale agriculture, and that estimates of urban unemployment run as high as 20 to 25 percent, the economic position of the expatriates as a highly privileged and virtually inaccessible elite is further enhanced. After all, the average foreigner earns eight times as much as the most privileged Nigerian—those with jobs.[6]

Awareness of foreign investment

Notwithstanding these glaring social and economic inequalities, the tendency for foreigners both to live and work in relatively narrowly defined enclaves, and to interact with the indigenous population only minimally and almost exclusively on a master-servant basis, would seem to make widespread awareness of the extent of foreign investment *a priori* unlikely. To test this hypothesis, respondents were asked two sets of questions: (1) to ascertain whether certain specific firms were felt to be domestic or foreign, and (2) to assess their ability to link particular companies with their individual national origins.

In the first case respondents were asked whether they thought five well-known, larger firms were "at least 51 percent owned by foreigners." Of those chosen, three were in fact expatriate and two were owned and controlled by Nigerians, but as is illustrated in Table 1, four out of the five were assigned correctly by a majority. The sole exception can perhaps best be attributed to the extremely sophisticated market strategy employed by West African Breweries to compete against long-established and very popular foreign-owned beers, such as "Star" "Heineken," and "Guinness"—all of which are bottled by the foreign-owned Nigerian Breweries.

Table 1
Awareness of domestic or foreign status of specific companies

Company	Actual status	%age of those choosing each category	
		Foreign	Domestic
Nigerian Breweries	Foreign	55.1	44.9
Henry Stephens and Sons	Domestic	34.1	65.9
West African Breweries	Domestic	72.4	27.6
Kingsway Stores	Foreign	82.6	17.4
Nigerian Tobacco Co.	Foreign	51.0	49.0

While only 16.6 percent of respondents identified every company correctly, almost 75 percent were able to identify three or more accurately and, even among manual workers and the unemployed, over half made less than two errors. Moreover, there was a clear association between socioeconomic status and level of awareness— for example, 63 percent of respondents earning over $1,960 per annum, and only 44.3 percent of those earning less, identified four or five correctly,[7] but such a correlation is less important than the overall inference of a population highly aware of the presence of foreign investors.

On the second question, when respondents were asked to give the nationality of companies identified to be foreign, in only one case was the modal response not the correct one—a situation shown in Table 2. Furthermore, in the case of U.T.C., its Swiss origins might not be apparent even to sophisticated observers.

Table 2
Awareness of foreign companies by specific national origin

| Company | Correct origin | Countries listed (%age of those responding) | | | | |
		U.K.	U.S.	France	Switzerland	Nigeria
U.T.C.	Switzerland	67.2	1.4	4.3	15.8	1.5
Lever Brothers	U.K.	85.7	3.1	2.8	0.2	2.9
Total Oil	France	26.7	29.6	31.4	—	1.4
Mobil Oil	U.S.	31.7	56.9	3.4	—	1.1

What is perhaps equally interesting is the perceived dominance of British business and the extent to which the United States has come to be associated with the petroleum sector. Thus, U.T.C.—a Swiss company in the traditionally British trading sector—was thought by over two-thirds to be British, and Total Oil was thought by almost 30 percent to be American.

Although the association between higher socioeconomic status and knowledge of corporate nationality is more pronounced in this particular case, one may still legitimately wonder whether, in a "developed" Western society, quota sampling across economic and educational bounds would indicate such general awareness, among even the most deprived groups, as is illustrated in Table 3.

Affective orientation toward foreign investment

Although if an "attitude" toward foreign investment does indeed exist it does so only as a complex, multidimensional phenomenon, not susceptible to straightforward scaling techniques,[8] disaggregation of investment in Nigeria by origin does generate interesting

Table 3
Percentages giving correct nationality of selected foreign firms

	Enterprises			
Respondents	U.T.C.	Lever Brothers	Total Oil	Mobil Oil
Employment status				
3White collar	24.9	89.0	42.9	61.1
Blue collar[a]	10.6	84.2	24.0	56.4
Students	7.6	82.7	22.2	50.7
Education				
Postsecondary	20.0	88.1	37.5	60.5
No further education	13.0	84.3	27.3	54.3
Annual income				
Over $1960	32.6	93.9	48.0	70.3
$1960 or less	11.1	83.4	26.6	52.9
Preferred criteria for office holders[b]				
Modern	16.4	87.8	33.6	61.0
Traditional	13.6	78.7	23.5	41.2
Preferred method of farming[c]				
Innovative	18.9	87.3	34.3	58.3
Traditional	5.2	80.5	21.2	52.7

[a]Manual workers, plus those currently unemployed.

[b]Respondents were given a list of four criteria for the appointment of officials, two of which were deemed to be modern and two traditional.

[c]Respondents were asked to comment on a story about the introduction of modern techniques to farming. Their answers were classified as either modern or traditional.

discrepancies. The first—and perhaps, most surprising—of these findings, is the unequivocal conclusion that, while there is little animosity directed toward most foreign investors, deep hostility is often displayed toward indigenous enterprise. The second conclusion, less surprising but perhaps more important in its implications, is that where antiforeign sentiment exists, it is primarily directed against those expatriate groups closest economically and socially to the Nigerians themselves, irrespective of their economic influence, rather than against the most economically powerful expatriates.

Table 4 also shows the general unwillingness to take any kind of "strong" position, either for or against foreign investment. Nevertheless, almost 53 percent of the total responses can be construed

Table 4
Percentages responding on items on proforeign sentiment

1. "I don't care who owns a company as long as it provides jobs for Nigerians."

Strongly agree	19.4	
Agree	28.9	
Indifferent	8.6	
Disagree	24.8	
Strongly disagree	18.2	(Missing = 2.9%)

2. "For the good of the economy, it is essential that all foreign companies are eventually owned by Nigerians."

Strongly agree	17.7	
Agree	22.4	
Indifferent	11.6	
Disagree	34.6	
Strongly disagree	13.7	(Missing = 1.0%)

3. "Because Britain has been associated with Nigeria for so long, it is only fair that the U.K. should be given special privileges which other countries do not enjoy."

Strongly agree	5.9	
Agree	16.5	
Indifferent	10.8	
Disagree	34.7	
Strongly disagree	31.9	(Missing = 2.2%)

4. "Do you think that there will ever come a time when all foreigners will have to leave Nigeria?"

Yes	17.7	
No	82.1	(Missing = 2.2%)

5. "Foreign companies offer better employment prospects for Nigerians than do indigenous companies."

Strongly agree	28.7	
Agree	38.9	
Indifferent	9.4	
Disagree	15.4	
Strongly disagree	7.6	(Missing = 7.4%)

6. "Many people seem to feel that the best way to encourage economic growth in Nigeria is by inviting foreign companies to invest here. Do you agree with them?"

Yes	49.8	
No	50.2	(Missing = 4.6%)

7. "Nowadays, foreign companies are no longer interested only in profits—they are beginning to care about their workers and about the development of Nigeria."

Strongly agree	5.4	
Agree	31.1	
Indifferent	13.9	
Disagree	31.3	
Strongly disagree	18.3	(Missing = 4.6%)

as demonstrating support for foreign business and only the item suggesting Britain's right to a privileged economic position evinced a strongly xenophobic response.

Controlling the responses to the questions in Table 4 by the tribal affiliation of the respondents presents interesting patterns in view of the ethnic cleavages in Nigeria. In general, the recently defeated Ibos did seem better disposed toward foreigners than the dominant Yoruba. For example, while 20 percent of the Yoruba felt a time might come when foreigners would have to leave, this sentiment was held by less than one in ten Ibos. Even when age and socioeconomic status were controlled, these differences still remained: for instance, among respondents earning under $1960 per annum, 63.2 percent of the Ibos, compared to only 45 percent of the Yoruba, felt that there was no need for Nigerians to take over all foreign firms. Similarly, among respondents earning less than $1960 per annum, 54.5 percent of the Ibos, compared to 41.8 percent of the Yoruba, were opposed to such total "Nigerianization."

The significance of this disaggregation would seem to be enhanced by the parallel—though not wholly conclusive—finding that, *ceteris paribus,* Yoruba respondents tended to be less well-informed of the origin and extent of foreign investment in the country. There exists, therefore, a suggestive relationship between knowledge of and support for foreign businesses.[9]

One relationship that may help explain the differences in the response patterns between the Yoruba and Ibos suggested itself in the questionnaire. Respondents who scored positively on a scale designed to measure their sense of personal efficacy exhibited more negative feelings toward foreign investors than their less effectual compatriots. It may be that negative feelings toward foreign investors require a secure psyche which can simultaneously harbor memories of a psychologically debilitating colonial past. Thus, the politically and socially dominant Yoruba could apparently feel more secure to harbor less favorable sentiment toward foreign investors compared to the relatively disadvantaged Ibos.

The general impression of favorability toward the bulk of foreign investment is strongly reinforced by the results of a sixteen-point semantic differential test, included in the questionnaire, profiles resulting from which are illustrated in Figure 1. These profiles do, however, also indicate the ambivalence of respondents'

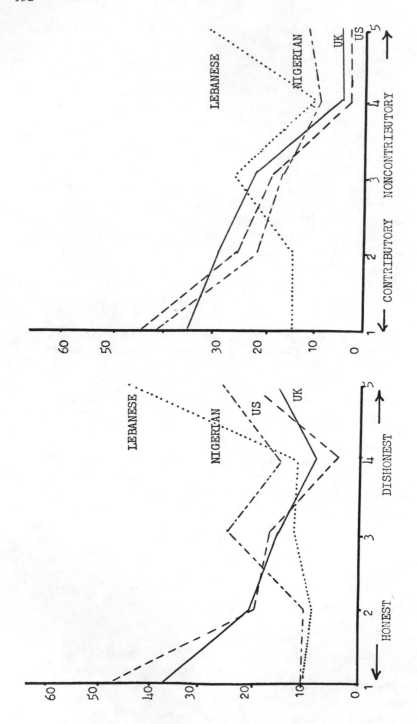

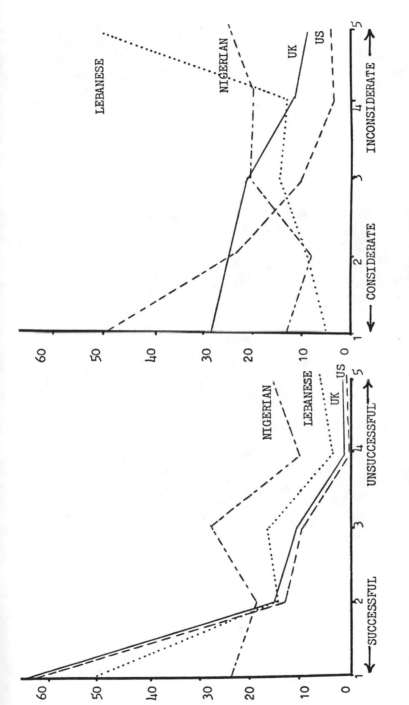

FIGURE 1 : RESPONSE PROFILES OF ALL RESPONDENTS (N=680) TOWARDS FOREIGN
AND INDIGENOUS COMPANIES.

orientations toward local firms and their virtually unmitigated hostility toward the Lebanese.[10] It is also interesting to note how much more willing respondents were to advocate an extreme position when the national group and the criterion under consideration were both specific. In fact, out of all responding, an average of almost 52.5 percent chose an extreme position on each item and only 18.2 percent opted for the neutral mid-point. However, significantly, on those items pertaining to Nigerian companies, the comparable figures were 44.8 and 22.5 percent.

From these profiles, it would seem that little differentiation is made between United Kingdom and U.S. companies, which are both generally considered honest, considerate, contributory, and successful. Where such differences exist, however, U.S. firms tend to be the beneficiaries. Thus, for instance, on the criterion of honesty, 38.7 percent of those responding perceived British firms to be "very honest" as against 48.5 percent for U.S. companies. In contrast to these strongly positive orientations, Lebanese and Nigerian companies seem to be perceived in a negative light. Thus, Lebanese firms were considered to be "very dishonest" by 53.1 percent of the respondents and Nigerian companies by 35.7 percent. Similarly, while 50 percent of those responding classed the Lebanese as "very inconsiderate," almost 37 percent did the same for local firms.

The position of Nigerian firms on these semantic-differential tests is consistent with other prople's findings on the feelings of depressed self-worth prevalent in Nigeria. Only on the dimension of contribution to the economy—where 42.4 percent perceived them to be "very contributory"—did local firms score well. These response patterns suggest that support for foreign firms and negative perceptions of indigenous business are closely related, perhaps reflecting the same postcolonial psychological insecurity. There is abundant evidence that Nigerians have been unable to compete in many commercial areas.[11] Nevertheless, the willingness to accept much of the blame for this, or to transfer it on to the relatively innocuous Levantines, rather than to direct hostility toward the international enterprises which still dominate the Nigerian market, is indicative of the pervasive debilitation associated with colonization and, at the same time, indicates the immediate security of tenure enjoyed by large-scale foreign corporations.

Comparison of Ibo and Yoruba group responses to these semantic-differential items, however, makes such judgments perhaps too facile. While Ibos had appeared more favorably inclined toward foreigners on the items in the main body of the questionnaire, on the specific questions of the semantic-differential test they were (1) marginally less positive toward U.S. and United Kingdom firms, and (2) markedly more negatively disposed toward Nigerian companies on all criteria except that of business success.

Such findings would seem to imply that dissatisfaction with local business might be simply a symptom of a deeper economic or political malaise. However, with the civil war so recent, it is probably also true that, for most Ibos, the terms "Nigerian" and "non-Ibo" are virtually synonymous. Under such circumstances, it is perhaps little wonder that they display such marked hostility. What is more surprising is the similar—though less extreme—pattern of rejection displayed even by the Yoruba.

Ibo ambivalence to foreign investment—as shown by contradictory responses on the profiles and in the main questionnaire—may be a function of their historically nationalistic sentiment, allied to recent political reverses. Although, when asked whether they would vote in a future election, affirmative responses were 15 percent higher among Yoruba, such apoliticism among the Ibo is a new phenomenon. Because they lacked the large-scale permanent social systems associated with the Hausa and Yoruba, they sought to achieve the same kind of cohesion through voluntary associations which became both a rudimentary social security system and the basis for political parties such as the NCNC.[12]

Given this history of nationalism, it might be safest to interpret their support for the more general points concerning foreign investment as a corollary to their war-induced apathy to local, i.e., Yoruba and Hausa, business. Confronted with the specific questions of the semantic-differential test, one might infer that a more deeply-rooted cynicism prevailed.

The scapegoat hypothesis

Nevertheless, whether or not conditions in Nigeria were temporarily biased against local firms, the existence of the Lebanese as a socially sanctioned recipient of nationalist anger might well provide a safety-valve for hostility which might otherwise be directed against the major investors.

The role of the "Cora"[13] in Nigeria is not unlike that of the Indians in East Africa. They constitute an economic and social buffer group between indigenous Nigerians and American and European residents, and one would suggest that the disproportionate
hostility which they clearly evince is a function of this position as
intermediaries. They have historically been primarily engaged in
small-scale retail trade and such technologically unsophisticated
sectors as road haulage. Their primary contacts are directly with
Nigerians and even in terms of residential patterns, they tend to
live—not in the virtually all-white areas of Ikoyi or Victoria Is-
land—but in the marginal, higher density areas of Obalende or
Surulere to which the Nigerian middle class already aspires. At the
same time, however, their small-scale, family-based business operations tend to reinforce the impression of a homogeneous, essentially endogenous and exclusive alien group.[14]

This economic and social proximity—coupled with a form of ethnic exclusivity—is bound to generate resentment. Indeed, in line
with the Berkowitz hypothesis that a "preferred" scapegoat will
be one who has in the past provoked justified hostility,[15] this
antipathy is not without foundation for it is true that the Levantines' easier access to finance has historically helped to exclude
Nigerians from commercial areas eminently within their competence. More important, however, than the validity of anti-Leban-
ese sentiment is the fact that, by attracting hostility from virtually all ethnic and socioeconomic groups, Levantines and Indians
appear to shield other expatriate groups from resentment commensurate with their real economic power. Their presence, therefore, allied with negative perceptions of local enterprise and deep
divisions within Nigerian society, works to counter the potentially
destabilizing impact of the very high awareness levels prevalent
among all groups.

Should the position of the "Cora" within the Nigerian economy
be radically altered—perhaps by their expulsion but, more likely,
as a corollary to the "Nigerianization" of technologically less-
advanced sectors—it is possible that this awareness could translate
itself into a markedly more hostile environment for foreign investors from the major trading nations.[16] For the moment, however, with a scapegoat readily available, it is clear that, even in a
situation where a very high proportion of modern sector employment is dependent—directly or contingently—on a relatively
small number of expatriate concerns, it is not legitimate to infer
that widespread awareness will be associated with a parallel

antipathy. Indeed, currently, the converse holds true. Greater awareness, associated as it is with higher socioeconomic status and education, would seem to be correlated with generally more positive orientations toward foreign business.

NOTES

[1]See S. M. Lipset and S. Rokkan, "Cleavage Structure, Party Systems, and Voter Alignments," in *Party Systems and Voter Alignments: Cross-National Perspectives,* ed. Lipset and Rokkan.

[2]Data was collected while the author was a research associate at the Nigerian Institute of International Affairs, and was gathered through distribution of questionnaires to 680 adult male respondents in the Lagos area. Respondents were chosen on a quota basis, to reflect the ethnic, socioeconomic, and educational heterogeneity of the city. Lagos was selected as the site since, as the national and state capital, and as the country's largest city, it houses over 70 percent of the headquarters of foreign industrial companies and attracts about 33 percent of total foreign investment entering the country. Moreover, population density on Lagos was about 112,000 per square mile in 1960 and is undoubtedly much higher today, reflecting both the difficulties of institution building and the remarkable ethnic mixture represented in the town. Finally, the passage of free primary education acts in the old Western Region, and the existence of a highly developed and relatively sophisticated communications network based on the Lagos-Ibadan axis, make functional literacy rates and political awareness considerably higher than elsewhere in the country.

[3]Peter Kilby, *Industrialization in an Open Society, Nigeria 1945-1966*, p. 62.

[4]*Industrial Survey of Nigeria, 1968,* Federal Office of Statistics, Lagos, 1970. While there is no reason to believe that the sample set used by the government was representative of the manufacturing industry in the country as a whole, the figure of 70 percent for foreign control of the Nigerian economy is widely accepted among the elite and frequently cited in the press.

[5]"Economic and Financial Review," *Central Bank of Nigeria, Lagos,* June 1968, p. 77.

[6]The *1966 Industrial Survey,* Federal Office of Statistics, Lagos, 1969, gave average annual wages of non-Nigerians as $7,000, professional and managerial Nigerians as $843, skilled and semi-skilled workers as $510, and unskilled workers as $308 per annum.

[7]All such response distributions produce chi-squared values significant at or above the 0.05 level.

[8]Such a conclusion is based upon results generated when the 24 items administered as part of the questionnaire, related to respondents' sentiments toward foreign investment, were binarized and subjected to factor analysis.

The orthogonally rotated factor pattern matrix resulting was such that the first four factors explained 15, 9, 9, and 8 percent of the total variance, respectively—an aggregate of just under 42 percent. When the sixteen semantic-differential items were excluded, the first three factors of the orthogonal solution still explained only 47 percent of the total variance.

9This conclusion is reinforced by a fairly clear association between socioeconomic status and favorability to the MNE. Thus, for example, while in general amost 56 percent of respondents earning $1960 per annum or less felt foreign companies to be interested solely in profit-making, theirs was an opinion shared by only 41 percent of those in the higher income bracket.

10Lebanese firms were chosen because, while they probably do not account for more than 5 percent of total foreign investment, they tend to be small-scale, family-based businesses, heavily concentrated in the retail and textile trades.

11In fact, in 1972 the writer found no locally-owned firm operating in Lagos which could trace its identity back to as late as the 1940s.

12R. L. Sklar and C. S. Whitaker, Jr., "The Federal Republic of Nigeria," in *National Unity and Regionalism,* ed. Gwendolyn Carter.

13The term "Cora" is used to denote not only Lebanese but also Syrian and even Indian traders. Its usage is itself indicative of how effective an "out-group" they constitute. Although "European" is used also to connote Americans, no similar derogatory or pejorative epithet has as yet emerged to encapsulate the major foreign investors.

14For instance, the 1972 Annual Conference of the Nigerian Institute of Management, which attracted representatives of over 450 companies, listed no Levantine names among its participants.

15Leonard Berkowitz, "Aggression," in *International Encyclopaedia of the Social Sciences.* A problem of causality clearly exists here. From the immediate evidence it is not clear whether the "Cora" are disliked *sui generis*, or whether hostility is in fact directed mainly at small-scale family-owned businesses—of which many happen to be owned by Levantines. Nevertheless, the combination of close socioeconomic contact and discernible ethnic difference, allied with an acceptance by the Lebanese of their role as an "out-group," makes them a preferred target for "syncretism"—the compounding of several prejudices onto one set of individuals.

16*Nigerian Enterprises Promotion Decree, 1972,* Decree no. 4, Official Gazette, Mar. 1972.

PART III
Counterstrategies

Introduction

The very characteristics of MNEs place them beyond the exclusive reach of any individual government or social group. Under these circumstances, the type and amount of benefits accruing to individual states and social groups depend to a large extent on the bargaining power of both sides. This part deals with the bargaining position of the actors most affected by MNEs—host countries—and the problems they encounter in formulating and implementing effective counterstrategies toward MNEs.

Although counterstrategies can be pursued at various levels, the best solution is one in which the domain of the means of control is as wide as that of the MNEs, that is, global. If an approach at the international level should not be feasible, second-best solutions are alliances of a limited number of countries—either on a regional (e.g., the Andean Common Market) or on a product basis (e.g., OPEC)—and third-best solutions are actions by individual host countries. Each of the chapters in this part addresses itself to counterstrategies at one of these three levels.

Chapter 8 reviews, on the basis of relevant laws in sixteen nations, the instrumentalities available to individual host countries to influence MNE behavior in a desired direction. The available mechanisms are numerous. For instance, a combination of well-defined entry selection criteria (based on the requirements of a long-term economic framework), a sophisticated screening machinery (determining the desirability of each major project), and continuous review of the performance of foreign affiliates (according to well-defined standards) potentially constitutes a powerful set of instruments in the hands of host-country governments resolved to channel MNE activities in appropriate directions. However, in the absence of a global approach, host governments attempting to regulate MNEs, either individually or in coalition with others, have to be careful in striking an acceptable balance between what they have to offer to international business and the severity of their restrictions. In developing countries, too unfavorable a balance may just lead to a decrease in investment inflows. In the case of countries that are also foreign investors, retaliatory measures may result.

Moreover, it has to be realized that the approaches discussed in Chapter 8 suffer from a general and—for a number of countries—serious limitation. Almost all of them require a relatively sophisticated apparatus capable of formulating, implementing, and overseeing an often intricate array of criteria, rules, and provisions—and all this vis-à-vis organizations with access to worldwide resources and talent. It is exactly this capability which most countries—and especially the developing ones—do not possess. A united approach, on the other hand, whether based on territorial contiguity or product identity, promises to be more effective in dealing with a number of problems inherent in most individual attempts to regulate foreign direct investment: it reduces or eliminates costly incentive competition;[1] it pools resources available for dealing with MNEs; and, as a consequence, it increases the bargaining power of each individual party to the common agreement. Chapters 9 and 10 deal with two types of united approaches.

In Chapter 9, Dale B. Furnish examines the Foreign Investment Code of the Andean Common Market which, on a regional basis, attempts to integrate foreign direct investment into a comprehensive, long-term, developmental-emancipatory framework designed to build a strong and independent regional economy. The basic assumptions of the code are that (1) foreign capital and technology have to be acquired selectively; (2) these inputs only become fully effective if they are eventually domestically controlled; and (3) considerable information is required, on the one hand, to make proper choices regarding what, when, and under what conditions foreign direct investment is to be admitted and, on the other, to avoid irregularities by existing foreign affiliates. The provisions of the code most relevant to these objectives, as well as the context in which the objectives have to be seen, are analyzed in detail in Chapter 9.

The Andean Foreign Investment Code is in force to varying degrees in all member countries. Of course, it still has to pass the test of time. But it has already been acknowledged that it has increased the negotiating strength of all the countries involved—an expectation expressly stated in the preamble of the code. Moreover, the comprehensiveness and the detail with which the various problems have been dealt with may well help and inspire other countries, or groups of countries, to move in a similar direction. Over twenty countries have already accredited observers to the Andean group.

As far as raw materials are concerned, an alternative approach to regional arrangements is the organization of supplies. The prototype of such an alliance is, of course, the Organization of Petroleum Exporting Countries (OPEC). Following OPEC's phenomenal success, the discussion has intensified about the extent to which product diplomacy can be used by other countries to improve their economic situation.[2] In Chapter 10, C. Fred Bergsten and Stephen Krasner review the problems involved in creating "One, Two, Many OPECs. . . ." The central issue in this context is the identification of the major determinants of the bargaining power of producers' associations.

Generally speaking, the success of a producers' alliance appears to depend on how effectively important supplies can be withheld. The key variables here are "effective withholding power" and "importance of supplies withheld."

Effective withholding power requires first of all that a relatively small number of countries account for a high percentage of world production and exports. The lower production and export concentration, the more difficult it is to establish and maintain an alliance and to organize, if necessary, production control or buffer stocks. Effective withholding power, moreover, requires the capacity to act jointly. A minimum of centralized organization is therefore usually necessary.[3] Also, with regard to external conditions, an important variable is the retaliatory power of buyers (of both consumer-country governments and MNEs), i.e., their capacity to impose sanctions effectively.

Second, the success of a producers' association depends on the importance of the supplies withheld. Importance is a function of the degree to which a particular product is required by important consuming economies and the extent to which it can be recycled or substituted by readily available alternative products. In other words, the less essential a product or the easier the replacement of an essential product, the more limited are the possibilities of a product-based alliance.

Most of these conditions were fulfilled—almost perfectly—in the case of petroleum. A small number of countries (twelve) accounted in 1973 for about two-thirds of the market economies' oil production and more than four-fifths of their exports. Through OPEC, the oil-producing countries had established and developed their capacity to act jointly. Given the central importance of oil for most developed market economies, their import dependency, and the short-term nonavailability of substitutes, consumer-country governments had little retaliatory power. Although oil companies had to yield varying percentages of equity holdings in their foreign affiliates, they still maintained, as a rule, management control and control over downstream operations; most important, they were able to pass on price increases to consumers. Consequently, they offered little resistance.[4] The oil-producing countries were, therefore, in a position to withhold important supplies effectively.

Bergsten and Krasner discuss the various variables relevant for producers' associations, including associations of petroleum and other raw materials producers. They reach, however, opposing conclusions regarding the prospects for the "opecization" of other natural resources. It is possible that at least part of these differences can be explained by the lack of data on the subject since, so far, hardly any systematic research has been done on the variables (and their interrelationships) relevant to the successful operation of producers' associations. For instance, little information exists on such a basic variable as the price-threshold at which enterprises defect to substitutes—other raw materials as well as lower-grade ores[5]—or at which end-consumers change consumption patterns. This threshold may also determine to what extent producers' associations may have to enter into intergroup alliances or develop parallel strategies, precisely to forestall interproduct substitution. In summary, judgments about the prospects for producers' associations are, at this stage, quite preliminary, but a number of the variables that may enter into such judgments have already been identified.[6]

Independent of the prospects of producers' associations, it should not be overlooked that such an approach would only improve the situation of the relatively few major raw-material suppliers—and even that perhaps at the expense of other developing countries. Regional arrangements, on the other hand, are difficult to establish, particularly where neighboring and conflicting national jealousies or resentments have to be overcome. In addition, it should be kept in mind that an optimal counterstrategy should have the same domain as MNEs, i.e., it should be global. What, then, are the chances and possibilities for a global approach to monitor or possibly even to control MNEs?

This question is discussed, in detail, by N. T. Wang in Chapter 11. Wang proceeds from the premise that any measures taken by international organizations have to observe the primacy of national decision-making. Consequently, such measures have to be basically voluntary in character and should aim mainly at facilitating the conclusion of relevant agreements, the broadening of alternatives, and the provision of better information and expanded technical assistance. Under these premises, Chapter 11 examines how the efforts of the United Nations—to date the most important international initiative dealing with MNEs—can contribute to the establishment of some countervailing power to international business.

Limited as the possibilities at the international level may be, the United Nations has the opportunity of achieving tangible results relatively fast. It has been pointed out throughout this collection that one of the major comparative advantages that MNEs enjoy in a decentralized world of states is their centralized structure and strategy. This situation provides MNEs with a tremendous information advantage vis-à-vis individual states,[7] and it allows them to use, if necessary, their entire intellectual and financial resources in any place they operate, be it for the assessment of investment projects or situations, the evaluation of local laws, or the negotiations of contracts. A well-organized global effort to collect and to analyze MNE-related information and to disseminate it to interested parties, in conjunction with, if so desired, technical assistance in dealing with MNEs, would not only constitute a significant step in the direction of counterbalancing MNEs but would achieve at least that type of control that is vested in equal levels of information and expertise. It would directly improve the general bargaining and control power of host countries and it would place them into a better position to immediately increase (even if only incrementally) their share of the benefits associated with the activities of MNEs.

Many of the problems connected with the transnational character of MNEs, which may constrain the formulation and implementation of governmental policies, are also faced by labor unions. In contradistinction to governments, however, unions do not have legislative power to direct MNE behavior. They are entirely dependent on their bargaining strength. This bargaining strength is increasingly eroding as a growing number of enterprises and industries are outgrowing the organizational reach of any particular labor union and are improving their ability to switch, if necessary, production temporarily from affiliates in one country to those in another.[8]

NOTES

[1]The kind of incentives offered to multinational enterprises are legion. Grant L. Reuber et al., *Private Foreign Investment in Development,* found, for instance, that in 45 percent of the cases of his sample of developing country projects, tariffs were imposed or maintained against competing imports. Tariff concessions on equipment imports, on the other hand, averaged about 40 percent and occurred in about half of the cases surveyed. Similarly, concessions are frequently offered for imports of component parts and raw materials. Other incentives include tax reductions, tax holidays, creation of infrastructure, guarantees against currency inconvertibility, and the like. Reuber et al. conclude that as a result of the competition between developing countries "many of the incentives provided largely cancel each other out" (p. 129).

[2]This interest found its fullest expression in paragraph 4t of resolution 3201 (S-VI), "Declaration on the Establishment of a New International Economic Order," adopted (in May 1974) by the Sixth Special Session of the United Nations General Assembly. The paragraph in question states that the new order should, *inter alia,* facilitate "the role which producers' associations may play within the framework of international co-operation" (contained in United Nations, General Assembly, *Official Records: Sixth Special Session,* Supplement no. 1 (A/9559). The same principle was reaffirmed in Article 5 of the United Nations Charter of Economic Rights and Duties of States (contained in document A/RES/3281 (XXIX), January 15, 1975, mimeographed).

[3]It is probably helpful to have a leader-country with a diversified economy and/or high foreign exchange reserves which, when taking the first step, could sustain at least temporary losses (including those from cheating) if necessary. Territorial contiguity of the prospective group members and the presence of a common external enemy appear, however, to be unimportant. In fact,

territorial noncontiguity might increase the chances that there are no frictions stemming from other sources which could impair cooperation: Guyana and Guinea have no topic of conversation other than bauxite; and both are equally interested in obtaining higher prices and advanced processing facilities.

[4]In fact, according to the board chairman of British Petroleum, the oil companies have become the "tax collecting agency" of the producing countries (quoted in M. A. Adelman, "Is the Oil Shortage Real? Oil Companies as OPEC Tax-Collectors," *Foreign Policy*, p. 70.

[5]The bauxite producing countries, in particular, face this problem since aluminum can also be produced from materials (such as laterites and clay) that are highly abundant in home countries. As the *Economist* (Mar. 1974) candidly observed in reference to the first meeting of the bauxite-exporting countries: "With a fine sense of timing . . . the French aluminium giant, Pechiney-Ugine-Kuhlmann, now claims to have developed a process that will dispense with bauxite." Several other companies, notably Alcoa and Reynolds, are working at similar processes. Alcoa has bought up large areas in Wyoming containing bauxite-bearing clay. Richard S. Reynolds, chairman and president of Reynolds, with the same "fine sense of timing" as Pechiney, attended, during the Conakry meeting, a widely publicized test production run at which laterite ore from Oregon was used to produce alumina. Reynolds, who freely acknowledged that the demonstration was arranged to coincide with the meeting of bauxite-producing countries, found that "it is reassuring to know that we could change overnight if the bauxite cost and supply situation should warrant such action" (quoted in *New York Times*, Mar. 7, 1974).

[6]For a number of minerals, notably manganese, cobalt, nickel, copper, and petroleum, considerations of possible alliances have to take account of a completely new source of supply: the seabed. The technology of ocean mining is complex, sophisticated, and expensive. American technology is most advanced, and offshore oil exploration, until about 1970, was virtually a U.S. monopoly in design, production, and operation. Only a handful of enterprises in the United States, Japan, the Federal Republic of Germany, France, Canada, and Britain is actively developing seabed mining technology, often with government financial support. Large-scale seabed mining appears to be a certainty before the end of the 1970s.

[7]By way of example, the Swiss pharmaceutical company Hoffmann LaRoche sold drugs to the British National Health Service at prices considerably higher than those it charged in Italy for the same product. For years, this practice remained undiscovered, simply because nobody compared prices transnationally.

[8]Illustrative in this context are Malcolm Warner and Louis Turner, "Trade Unions and the Multinational Firm," *Journal of Industrial Relations*, p. 147, who quote the following passage from a report on strikes involving Ford in Britain: "Ford is known to have one of the best early-warning systems in the motor industry and has on occasion pinpointed troubles in supplier firms before production has actually stopped. In some cases, it has beaten strikes by

'pulling' tools and dies in time to start alternative production before employees in the original firm have stopped work." For references on the impact of MNEs on labor unions see the references cited in the bibliography.

Chapter
8
Policies of Governments Toward Foreign Direct Investment
Government of Canada

Introduction: purpose and method

This chapter describes in general terms the kind of approaches governments have taken toward foreign direct investment. The purpose is to provide some idea of the range of policies which prevail and the instruments used to implement them. The countries examined include eleven advanced or relatively advanced industrial countries of Western Europe, the United States, Australia, South Africa, Japan, and Mexico.

There are four considerations which must be taken into account in assessing the findings below. The first is that, in relation to the size of their domestic economies, none of the countries has experienced a degree of foreign control which begins to approach the Canadian situation. The reasons for this vary from case to case. At least two of the countries—Norway and Mexico—appear to have devised restrictive policies at some point in the past because of a particular fear of extensive foreign control by a neighboring country.

Reprinted with permission of Information Canada, from *Foreign Direct Investment in Canada,* by the Government of Canada (Ottawa, 1972), pp. 328-337.

On the other hand, a number of these countries do have a high degree of foreign control in certain high technology and other capital intensive industries. The German petrochemical industry and the British automobile industry, for example, are largely controlled from abroad. But, on the whole, no other country has a situation resembling the Canadian picture.

Secondly, most of the countries surveyed adhere to the OECD Code for the Liberalization of Capital Movements. As they have accepted, in principle, the desirability of freeing capital movements, they normally tend to emphasize the more open aspects of their policies. While Canada is more liberal than most countries, Canada alone among the OECD countries does not adhere to this Code.

Thirdly, these countries include the world's largest exporters of capital, including the United States, United Kingdom, Germany, Switzerland, Sweden, and The Netherlands. As such, they have important vested interests in striving for relative ease of access for the intended overseas investments of their nationals and for ease of repatriation of profits. To varying degrees, this fact serves as a liberalizing pressure in respect of their policies towards capital imports. It seems also to lead them to take a relatively relaxed attitude about the practices of multinational enterprises.

Finally, all countries studied—except the United States, Germany, and Switzerland—have in place a foreign exchange control apparatus. Some use it restrictively, others more liberally. Exchange controls were not implemented in these countries with the primary aim of preserving domestic ownership and control of the economy, but rather for balance of payments reasons. As balance of payments considerations have permitted, most countries have generally tended to rely progressively less on the exchange control mechanism in dealing with current payments. However, as an outgrowth of their earlier balance of payments problems, most countries do have the experience of a foreign exchange control apparatus capable of regulating capital imports.

As each of the countries studied has its own historical experience and special peculiarities, each policy is unique. However, for summary purposes, certain arbitrary lines can be drawn to provide an overview of other countries' policies.

It will be noted that some countries are discussed under more than one of the policy headings below as elements of their practices make it difficult to put the country under any single one. The headings are: (1) open or very open; (2) countries wishing to attract foreign investment, but which bargain about terms and conditions of entry; (3) countries seeking to protect key sectors; (4) restrictive.

Policy approaches

Open or very open

Countries which have very few restrictions on direct foreign investment include the United States, The Netherlands, West Germany, Denmark, and Australia. It should be noted that the first three of these countries are important capital exporters or have major investments abroad. The United States is, of course, the largest capital exporter and bastion of the multinational enterprise and as such had been a proponent in the past of freer movements of capital.

The West German economy is also based upon liberal economic principles. Broader geopolitical reasons may also have strengthened the German willingness to welcome investment from other countries.

The Netherlands is both very anxious to attract foreign capital for economic and regional development purposes and to protect the enormous investments of its multinational giants abroad, such as Shell, Unilever, and Phillips (which are partially controlled in The Netherlands). Denmark and Australia are also anxious to attract foreign capital for economic development purposes.

At the same time, through one device or another, even these countries have from time to time made it difficult for foreigners to invest in particular industries.

Countries wishing to attract foreign investment, but which bargain about terms and conditions of entry

Some countries discussed under this heading are relatively liberal; others are much less so. The main point here is that each uses the apparatus available to it to negotiate to meet the needs of its own economy. The United Kingdom (a major exporter of capital) formally prohibits all investments until the conditions it sets are met and this occasionally involves discussions between the United Kingdom authorities and the investors about a variety of factors in important cases. Similarly the Belgians and the Italians seek to attract foreign investments to one degree or other but bargain at times (but by no means on all foreign investment) to improve the contribution which the investment will make to their particular needs, e.g., bargaining for commitments for export performance and for location in a designated area. Less directly, the Australians seek to convince foreign investors of the desirability of allowing Australian equity participation by regulations affecting access to their capital markets, as outlined more fully below.

France's policy has varied through the last ten years and has normally been rather more nationalistic than the above countries. However, France also bargains about the terms and conditions of foreign entry. Norway's position is in some respects similar to that of the French. The principle, in each case, is that while the foreigner has something of value to the host economy, the host also has an asset the foreigner wants—easy access to its domestic markets.

Countries seeking to protect key sectors

Some of the countries listed below have been or will be referred to under other categories also. The principal countries here are Sweden and Norway, both of which claim to be very liberal, but which in fact exclude or restrict foreign investment across wide and important parts of their economy, especially in resources. In addition, Italy, Austria, France, the United States, and Australia have lesser but still fairly significant parts of their economy which are closed to the foreign investor, or in which the foreigner can obtain only restricted access.

In contrast, the United Kingdom, Denmark, Belgium, West Germany, and Switzerland rely very little on this kind of approach. The selection of key sectors, where this is an important policy element, seems to be based on a few, clearly defined criteria and the considerations apparently vary widely from one country to another. Sectors most frequently designated include banking, insurance, parts of communications and transportation, including public utilities and natural resources.

Restrictive

The prime examples of restrictive policies are those followed by Mexico and Japan, both of which have a very substantially different historical and cultural experience than the other countries considered here. In Mexico, where there was substantial foreign ownership prior to the 1910 revolution, foreign capital is permitted only as a supplement to internal savings.

In Japan, where the foreigner has traditionally been suspect, every effort has been made to hold out foreign participation for as long as possible in order to give domestic industry an opportunity to prepare for competition on an international basis.

In the case of both Mexico and Japan, the degree of foreign investment is very small. It must be further noted that in the case of France, Sweden, and Norway there is a strong desire to ensure that ownership of a fairly wide sector of the economy remains in the hands of the nationals. In all cases, it is apparent that the reasoning is largely due to politico-strategic and/or cultural reasons, and relates rather less to overall economic performance. At the same time, one would be hard pressed to demonstrate conclusively that these economies suffered as a consequence. Indeed, there appears to be little correlation between national economic performance and the degree of a country's liberalism or restrictionism in respect of direct investment inflows.

Policy elements

There are aspects of the experiences of other countries which are being examined as part of the Canadian review of policy and which, therefore, merit further comment here.

A general review provision

Some form of review of foreign direct investment appears to be employed in Norway, France, Japan, Mexico, and the United Kingdom, and to a lesser extent in Italy, Belgium, Sweden, Denmark, Austria, and Australia. In most instances, a foreign exchange control apparatus exists with which to back up statutory requirements about notifications of foreign investment.

In some cases, the review mechanism serves to prevent foreigners from making direct investments in particular industries; that is, permission for such investment is not granted. In Norway and Sweden, for instance, it appears that it is virtually impossible for a foreigner to gain control of wooded lands or paper mills, even though these apparently are not, in any formal sense, key sectors. In Italy, investments may be turned down if the foreigner wishes to invest in an industry in which state ownership is extensive. In other countries, the need to obtain government approval enables the recipient country to bargain about local equity participation, export undertakings, the presence of nationals on the board of directors, location of plant, procurement of services, or whatever other considerations the recipient country judges relevant.

For instance, in Japan the review process begins with the Bank of Japan, which has control of the exchange control apparatus. The bank requires relevant information from would-be foreign investors. It then passes the information to the various ministries concerned, which, in turn meet at a senior interdepartmental level. The file is then passed to the Foreign Investment Council, which includes businessmen, journalists and academics, before a recommendation is made to the Minister of Finance. Changes in the terms and conditions are sometimes negotiated prior to ministerial decision.

A similar approach is followed in France, but with greater emphasis on bargaining and less on rejecting investments. In France, this extends to reviewing licensing agreements (e.g., on technology) to ensure that the terms are reasonable.

In the United Kingdom performance undertakings are sometimes sought in cases of major takeovers. For instance, in the 1967 acquisitions of Rootes by Chrysler and of Pye by Phillips, undertakings were obtained to maintain or to increase exports. On new investment, the United Kingdom does not seem to intervene frequently, if at all.

Domestic borrowing restrictions

Many countries have requirements respecting nonresident direct investment under which all or a part of it must be financed abroad. Such policies are normally justified on balance of payments grounds. In some cases this applies to all investments; in other cases it may apply only to takeovers. The access of nonresident controlled companies to domestic money markets for working capital or for capital for investments in new fixed assets may also be subject to limitation.

In the United Kingdom, takeovers are expected to be entirely financed from abroad and new foreign controlled firms are also expected to be largely self-financing. In France, takeovers by non-resident firms of French companies must be entirely financed from abroad; for new enterprises, at least 50 percent of the financing must be non-French.

In Italy, investments are divided between "productive" and "non-productive." Foreign investments which do not involve creation or expansion of production facilities—for instance, the purchase of existing shares (a share swap or other form of takeover)—are normally deemed to be nonproductive. Nonproductive investments are discouraged by limiting free transferability abroad of interest, dividends, and profits. They are also discouraged by limiting free transfer abroad of the original investment to an amount not exceeding the amount of foreign currency originally imported. It appears also that "productive" investments are freer to raise capital on the Italian capital markets than are "nonproductive" investments.

In Australia, local borrowing by firms is affected by the extent of Australian equity participation in the economy, and in Norway the acceptance of a foreign investment is also affected by the amount of capital imported. There also seem to be similar provisions in South Africa, Mexico, and Japan.

In all cases, the aims seem to include one or more of the following: to strengthen the balance of payments; to use this as an indirect means of discouraging foreign investment or of channelling it into those industries where the host government wishes it; to encourage foreign firms to provide for equity participation by the nationals of the host country, and possibly to prevent displacement of local borrowers.

Other techniques for restricting foreign investment

Several countries have in their companies' legislation provisions which bear on foreign investment. Swedish firms have the right to limit, through their articles of association, the right of non-Swedish nationals to acquire shares in the company. In these cases, non-Swedes are normally restricted to 20 percent interest in aggregate. In practice, 39 of the 40 largest Swedish companies have made use of this provision and thus effectively prevented foreigners from acquiring control.

In Switzerland, corporations can issue their common shares in three forms. "Participation shares" enable a shareholder to participate equally in profits with other common shareholders but not to vote; "registered" common shares are available only to Swiss citizens; "bearer" common shares may be held by citizens of any country. The latter two types have voting rights. Registered shares are always in the majority, thus precluding the acquisition of Swiss firms by foreigners. Japan also requires that companies have different categories of shares, with foreigners being permitted to purchase only a designated category.

Restrictions on the purchase or lease of real property by nonnationals in Norway, Denmark, Sweden, and Switzerland provide the authorities in those countries with the opportunity to bargain over terms or to restrict foreign investment. The extent to which this actually occurs is difficult to document.

Takeovers

In general, national governments tend to distinguish between takeovers by foreigners and the starting up of new enterprises by foreigners. Even some of the more liberal countries, such as West Germany and Australia, have prevented takeovers through ad hoc administrative practices. The Belgian government reviews takeover bids for companies whose shares are publicly traded. In Italy, as already indicated, a takeover is normally deemed to be "nonproductive" unless the enterprise purchased is to be expanded by the acquiring firm. Such nonproductive investment is likely to be discouraged through restrictions on the access of such firms to the domestic money markets for loans and through limitations on repatriation both of profits, interest, other current payments, and of the capital investment itself.

France requires that foreign takeovers be financed entirely through foreign currency. In addition, it has used its review authority to discourage takeovers.

In Switzerland, requirements for nationals on boards of directors, limitations on work permits and land permits, and the technique of using different categories of shares which was referred to above, all make takeovers very difficult.

The constrained share status of almost all leading Swedish companies is an important barrier to the takeover of Swedish firms. Takeovers of Japanese firms are not permitted. In Australia, the government has a policy under which it will intervene to prevent takeovers which are considered contrary to the national interest.

The general philosophy which underpins each of these countries' policies includes one or more of the following: a nationalistic opposition to foreigners; a desire on the part of domestic corporate management to fend off foreign takeovers; a government wish to channel foreign investment into areas where it will be most productive, which means into new investments rather than acquisitions; allowance of takeovers only after negotiations on performance have been successful.

Key sectors

Owing to the widespread restrictions on foreign investment in Mexico and Japan, the key sector analysis cannot be readily applied to those two countries. In Japan, however, even after its recent round of liberalization, distinctions between various categories of industry continue to be made by Japanese authorities.

Sweden and Norway restrict foreign control in real property, waterfalls, minerals, forest resources, and shipping. Denmark restricts foreign participation in financial institutions and farming. The French are most concerned about electronics, information software, and automobiles, and West Germany is concerned about oil refining, automobiles, and electronics. The Italians protect banking, insurance, finance, shipping, and air transportation; the Australians banking and broadcasting. In the United States, foreign participation is prohibited or restricted in shipping, broadcasting, communication satellites, hydroelectric power or activities associated with atomic energy, and banks. In addition, some countries have "catch-all" phrases relating to strategic industries. Moreover, foreigners are excluded from many other industries because of the existence of state monopolies.

The reasons why other governments designate key sectors is seldom made clear. In some cases it obviously reflects historical concern about what were, in the past, industries of great strategic importance, either for military or economic reasons. Thus, most countries ensure that key financial institutions, communications and transportation facilities are under the control of their citizens.

The other general reason seems to reflect a concern about the high technology, high growth industries which may dominate the future. Governments apparently believe that a strong indigenous capacity is important for their national interests. The dilemma here is that it is often the large foreign multinational enterprise which has the most up-to-date technology and is able to make a product available at prices which, in the short run at least, are less than the cost of indigenous development.

Mandatory host country shareholdings

Mandatory local shareholdings is not an issue in Mexico, where the law requires that local shareholders retain a half or more of the shares in virtually all cases, even though the Mexican partners at times may not participate actively in the direction of the enterprise. In the case of Japan, even in those industries which are now liberalized, there is a preference for Japanese shareholdings and in many industries 50 percent or more Japanese equity remains a legal requirement.

In general, nearly all but the most liberal governments tend to look more kindly upon foreign investments in which opportunity is provided for domestic equity ownership—either on a partnership basis or with large single owners.

Thus the French or Italians will be more likely to approve a 51/49 or 50/50 venture than one in which no domestic participation is proposed. Even where investments are permitted, access to local borrowing may not be allowed in the absence of large local shareholdings.

On the other hand, it appears that only Australia attaches importance to local portfolio shareholdings in foreign controlled firms. The degree to which these portfolio holdings are permitted determines whether foreign controlled firms may borrow money in Australia.

Board of directors

Many countries require a majority of nationals on boards of directors. They include the three Scandinavian countries which are examined here. The Australian government emphasizes the importance it attaches to having Australian nationals on boards of directors and in senior management. It does not require this by law, but creates some pressures to obtain such representation. Where foreigners are entitled to up to 50 percent of a Japanese company, management remains entirely Japanese and the percentage of Japanese equity must carry with it an equal number of Japanese directors.

The British also prefer to see a majority of their nationals on boards of directors and while information is not available on some of the other countries, the availability of a bargaining tool has probably led some of them also to impose such requirements.

Conclusions

The foregoing outline illustrates the wide range of approaches to foreign direct investment adopted within the Western economic system and the variety of instruments available for the implementation of government objectives.

Generally, most countries seem to have a sense of national interest in the economic sphere, however inarticulate it may be. What it seems to say is that business enterprise is most easily made to serve the national interest if owned and run by nationals.

Perhaps the single most common instrument which other countries use in dealing with foreign direct investment is some form or other of review or screening mechanism. In some countries, it is used very infrequently as an instrument of intervention. In other cases, the screening mechanism is used more often—either to restrict or to bargain, or both. The review mechanism provides a national government with flexibility to consider foreign direct investment on a case-by-case basis and the vigor with which a review process is applied can be made to vary over time.

In describing the general approach of many other governments toward foreign direct investment in their country, it is by no means intended to suggest that their policies are necessarily optimal ones, or that these countries have defined their national interests in a way which is appropriate to the circumstances of today. The point is, whether one approves or disapproves of the policies, they do represent a national viewpoint.

In recent years, there has been an international trend toward the reduction of barriers to investment flows and increasing nonresident ownership and control of certain industries in a number of countries. This tendency has been due in large part to political pressures exerted by capital exporting countries on the governments of the countries in which they wish to invest. The economies of scale in certain industries, particularly the very high costs of research and product development and innovation in certain high technology industries, have also had an important bearing upon the tendency toward greater foreign ownership and control, a case in point being computer hardware in some Western European countries.

There is thus a tendency toward liberalization, but the pace is slow and uneven. Nor is the liberal trend necessarily a continuous process. Even in the most liberal countries it is likely that if there were a risk of widespread foreign control a halt would be called. This may be reading too much into the policies of other countries, but from isolated measures of the more liberal countries it would appear to be the probable outcome.

Chapter
9
The Andean Common Market's Common Regime for Foreign Investments
Dale B. Furnish

Introduction

The Andean Group (Andean Common Market or ACM) was
organized as a subregion of the Latin American Free Trade
Association (LAFTA) under the agreement of Cartagena   in
1969. ACM represents a new hope in Latin American economic
integration and is certainly the most positive stride forward since
1960. The ACM subregional effort is probably more significant,
however, for the substance of its program than for the fact that it
is composed of a viable group of countries sharing similar dis-
satisfactions with the evolution of LAFTA. In an ambitious
"chronology,"[2] the ACM signatories pledged their new organization to a concentrated program of drafting regulations to control
two of the most sensitive areas of operation that the subregional
effort at development through integration is likely to encounter:
viz., foreign investments[3] and the multinational corporation.[4]
Both are matters of vital concern to the developing countries of
the Third World.[5]

Reprinted in part, by permission, from *Vanderbilt Journal of Transnational
Law,* Vol. 5, no. 2, Spring 1972. Research for this article was assisted by a
faculty grant-in-aid from Arizona State University.

In some ways, the first years of operation may have been the easiest for ACM, despite its commitment to drafting rapidly regulations sufficient to deal with the complex problems of foreign corporate investment. Following the establishment of a functioning bureaucracy, ACM entered a brave initial period of hope. Yet drafting policy standards, while not a simple matter, may be vastly more simple than the task of making them work. Regardless, one notable aspect of the ACM's drafting efforts is that their product may represent the best indicia of current Latin American attitudes and policies. If at all effective, ACM regulations should establish models for years to come.

The case of foreign investment provides a noteworthy illustration. A recent wave of expropriations in South America has foreign investors concerned and edgy,[6] but even the expropriating countries are not happy with the undefined state of affairs that exists. Decision 24 of the ACM, along with its amendments, may represent the most concrete resolution of the foreign investment problem possible in Latin America today, and perhaps even the truest consensus of the entire Third World. This treatment of the ACM's Rules on Foreign Investment will be developed with those considerations in mind; *i.e.,* ACM Decision 24 and amendments are much more than an isolated effort at solving a unique problem. Rather, they will be viewed here as a benchmark and perhaps a landmark piece of legislation in an area of vital importance to the development of the international economy.

The Overall Scheme

The economic theory reflected in the Common Regime is neither new nor unorthodox. It has been developed in recent years by many Latin American economists.[7] In essence, this theory, which has been accepted by the ACM's planners, is that Latin American foreign investment in a majority of cases has evolved in such a way as to create and perpetuate a crippling dependency on the technologically advanced investing nations; *i.e.,* the United States.

The scheme that has been conceived and promulgated by the ACM planners is a common regime that depends for its administration upon the national government of each member state in the subregion; it is not a supranational regime. Individually, no Andean country has had either the clout or the expertise necessary to drive a hard bargain with foreign investors. In large part, they have been forced to rely on the blunt instrument of expropriation to assert themselves. Now the subregion has set out to instigate a comprehensive scheme of controls calculated to bend foreign investment to the needs of each country and the subregion. To accomplish this goal, the drafters of the Common Regime were concerned with coordinating answers to the following inter-related problems:[8]

(1) planned growth of the various industrial sectors to provide balanced development throughout the subregion and in each country;
(2) decisional control of foreign enterprise;
(3) foreign acquisitions of domestic enterprise;
(4) levels of dependency associated with the introduction of foreign technology;
(6) regulation of repatriation of capital and profits; and
(7) policies toward subregional multinational corporations and mixed (foreign and national capital) enterprises.

The Fade-Out

One of the primary tenets of the *dependencia* doctrine is that while foreign enterprise can fill legitimate breaches in the industrial complex of Latin American economies, it often perpetuates the breach by taking over permanent responsibility for providing the "missing" factor when potential domestic competitors succumb to the tendency not to compete with an obviously superior enterprise. Another complaint concerning foreign capital is that it has a history of acquiring the more efficient and progressive domestic enterprises,[9] thus co-opting those national elements that hold the best hope of filling the breaches exploited by foreign investors.

The ACM has responded to these particular problems by including the already well-known fade-out provisions in its Common Regime.[10] It is probably the fade-out provisions, more than any other part of the Common Regime, that have led to its characterization as a scheme of "anti-foreign bias" and the work of "mainly professors and institutional advisors, whose collective attitude toward foreign investment was on the negative side at best."[11] In summary, the fade-out applies to virtually all foreign investments in the manufacturing sector[12] existing or established after July 1, 1971, and means that majority ownership and control must be progressively turned over to national or subregional capital

within fifteen or twenty years, depending on whether the investment is in Chile, Colombia, or Peru or in Bolivia or Ecuador.[13]
In the three larger countries, minimum standards of progressive
fade-out are 15 per cent ownership and control to national investors (including public or private capital from any of the ACM
countries or from the Andean Development Corporation)[14] by
the time production begins, 30 per cent after no more than five
years and 45 per cent after no more than ten years, and 51 per
cent after no more than fifteen years.[15] Bolivia and Ecuador, due
to their relatively less developed status, have a total of 22 years in
which to program foreign divestment. A twenty year period begins
to run two years after production begins, with 5 per cent control
and ownership to be in the hands of national investors three years
after beginning production, 10 per cent at nine years, and 35 per
cent at fifteen years, with a final period of seven years in which to
divest the last 16 per cent up to 51 per cent.[16]

All new investment must come into the ACM on the basis of an
approved fade-out plan, but existing foreign investments have
three years to decide whether to commit themselves to a process
of divestment.[17] To take advantage of the benefits of duty
reduction under the Cartagena Agreement, foreign companies
must agree to fade out.[18] If they choose to divest, they must have
sold at least 15 per cent of control to national capital at the end of
the third year from the effective date of the Common Regime,
June 31, 1974.[19] Otherwise, the time periods and percentages for
fade-out are the same as for new investments, but the grace period
of three years may be important. In the long run, assuming
effective integration, it is unlikely that it will benefit any existing
business to forego participation in the subregional program and
suffer the competition of duty-free products from more efficient
competitors. In the short run, however, an entrepreneur may use
his three years' grace to test the climate for foreign investment in
the ACM. If his evaluation is a pessimistic one, or if he has special
circumstances to consider, he may find it advantageous to maintain 100 per cent control, take his short-term profits while he can
and then assume a loss when forced out at some future date. In
the meantime, such an investor may buy time in the hope that
events or policies will shift in his favor or that the ACM program
will fail to prove effective. Especially if the conditions imposed by
the ACM or the country in which he is situated became
less favorable to foreign investment, he may be no worse off in
fifteen or twenty years than those who choose to apply for participation in the fade-out porgram. Indeed, he will have realized
proportionately greater profits in the meantime.

In time, existing foreign investors who choose not to fade out should be the only foreign controlled enterprises in the manufacturing sectors of the ACM. Possible avenues of circumvention or entry have been carefully foreclosed. Acquisition of existing domestic enterprises is prohibited except where bankruptcy is imminent and no national investor comes forward. Even then, the foreign investor must enter under a fade-out agreement divesting control in fifteen years or less, according to terms negotiated with the competent national authority.[20] Foreign capital may be allowed to participate in existing enterprise to increase its capital. but only so long as it does not take majority control away from national capital.[21]

Foreign enterprise has turned increasingly to internal credit to finance its Latin American operations.[22] This has proved to be a sound business practice because national banks have found established foreign investors to be better credit risks than the usual national borrower. Consequently, loans are relatively easy for the former to obtain. Moreover, inflation may create negative real interest rates—an official policy often utilized to redistribute income, but badly misapplied insofar as the redistribution is to large foreign industry at the expense of national interests. Finally, foreign enterprises may turn to local sources of credit in order to avoid utilizing precious company capital and, where the debt-or has subsidiaries in several countries, it may be able to juggle finances to derive still additional benefits.[23] Under the Common Regime, however, foreign access to local credit is drastically curtailed. Under the original plan, all local credit would have been prohibited except in exceptional circumstances, but a modification before the regulations became effective allows short-term credit for new foreign investment.[24]

The sum of all the Common Regime's provisions on control, acquisitions and finance is to drive foreign investment to the negotiating table with competent local authorities of the country in which the investment would be placed. Since in many cases only one ACM country will be designated as proper for a given investment, no battle of incentives should develop between member countries. By the same mechanism, the bargaining power of the ACM member with the potential investor should steadily increase since a greater market is at stake and the investor cannot seek entry through another country. Thus, the fade-out mechanism should be imposed throughout the dynamic import substitution sectors in order to assure avoidance of crippling *dependencia* by forcing the initiative on national capital.[25]

Several problems with the ACM scheme seem noteworthy. Although the theory seems viable, it ultimately depends upon the existence of sufficient national capital[26] to acquire the progressive percentages of ownership offered by foreign investors as they fade out of ACM enterprises. Wionczek estimates that in 1966-67, foreign investments in the five ACM countries totaled $3,052,000,000. Of this total, $369,000,000 was in manufacturing enterprises.[27] If foreign investors tender shares in accord with their fade-out agreements and available national capital to carry out the purchase is not forthcoming, it is hard to believe that either national or ACM authorities would insist on the sanction of article 32 of the Common Regime, which is designed to take away the benefits of the subregional integration program until the scheduled divestment is complete. More likely, some form of moratorium would be worked out.

Even if sufficient capital is available to make all fade-out purchases on time, the success of the program will still depend upon the vigor with which it is administered in each country by the "competent local authority." There are requirements in the Common Regime that will assist the individual authorities in their vigilance and control: all foreign investments, existing or new, must be registered,[28] and bearer stocks, common in the ACM, must be converted to registered shares.[29] Ultimately, however, registry, vigilance and all other elements of effective control must be generated and sustained by the national authorities. This is an area of the Common Regime that seems particularly amenable to ad hoc modification and shadings of application. Although the general principle that increasing national ownership and control is necessary to combat *dependencia* would probably be accepted by all ACM member countries, there is wide divergence in specific approach to foreign investment.[30] If these differences manifest themselves in varying standards applied by the national authorities responsible for enforcement, the objective of subregional planning and coordination could be defeated.

Technology Transfers, Repatriation and Dependencia

Technology transfers probably constitute the most complex matter taken up by the Common Regime. As in the area of investments generally, ACM planners and economists feel that there is a great lack of knowledge regarding precisely how transfers of technology have been carried out, under what terms, and at what profits to the supplier, with what ultimate effects on internal

policies and interests of recipient states.[31] Nonetheless, it is
generally recognized that the negative effects have been many,
again perhaps because suppliers have been economically rational
in maximizing profits where they found that they could exploit
weak bargaining positions on the part of recipients and lack of
expertise in handling the questions on the part of governments.[32]
Specific complaints against technology transfer include its use as a
hidden means of repatriating capital by the simple expedient of
over charging for an item of technology or by tying unnecessary
technology to a contract for one desired item so that there is
payment for all instead of one. This is of course not the only
method of hidden repatriation that foreign investors have used.[33]
The Common Regime has taken pains to see that most of the
known possibilities for *sub rosa* repatriation are curtailed. Again,
the basic mechanism is one of registration and disclosure.

All agreements on foreign patents, trademark licensing and other
existing[34] or new[35] technical assistance arrangements must be
registered with the designated national authority. All such
contracts are also subject to approval by the recipient national
authority, which must make an appraisal of the "effective contribution" of the technology in question.[36] Apparently, this means
that some measure must be made of the incremental profits that
should result from the use of the technology.[37] To prevent the
inclusion of useless technology in transfer agreements, all such
contracts must include and clearly identify the value of each
element of technology.[38] Transfers of intangible technology may
not be computed as capital contributions to ACM-based
enterprises.[39] In addition, the ACM commission may
intervene to review patent privileges already granted and to set
aside "production processes, products, or groups of products, with
respect to which no patent privileges may be granted in any of the
Member Countries."[40]

The Common Regime specifies a maximum profit of 14 per cent
over capital per year, all of which may be repatriated to the home
company.[41] To guarantee against hidden profits and repatriations
and to control balance of payments, however, the Common
Regime includes several provisions that directly affect
repatriations and external financial arrangements. Foreign
investors must re-export the capital that they have invested as they
divest, and must secure authorization for new investment.[42] Up to
5 per cent of the company's capital may be reinvested each year
without prior authorization, but registration of such investment is
required[43] and anything over that limited percentage must be
applied for as a new investment.[44]

Supervision extends to foreign loans, which may not be contracted for at more than three points over the prevailing rate in the country of contract, with prior authorization and registration in the appropriate agency.[45] In addition, access to internal credit is limited to short-term loans, as defined by ACM regulations.[46] No ACM country can endorse or guarantee any foreign loan for an enterprise that has no state participation.[47]

Repatriation and credit are matters of such central concern because foreign manufacturing investments, perhaps more than any others, have tended to be a drain on host countries' payments credits. Unlike extractive industries and other traditional areas of investment, import substitution generates little or no export income at the same time that it often relies on substantial imports of technology and inputs.[48] Thus, the ACM planners seek to insure that while the fade-out is in progress foreign owners do not exploit past methods of siphoning "non-profit" funds out of the host country, and that in the future they make a reasonable, but not unconscionable, return on investment.

The ACM is concerned with much more than just the use of technology agreements for surreptitious repatriation of capital. Technology is probably the area of the most clearly defined dependence on developed and industrialized nations. Experts in this field initially point out that Latin American purchasers have little knowledge of what they are purchasing, with little conception of alternatives or reasonable pricing. Mauricio Guerrero of the ACM Junta legal staff comments: "Curiously, these [technology] contracts often contain obligations only for the concessionaire and only in exceptional cases impose obligations on the supplier."[49] Typical clauses have included prohibitions against export of products manufactured with the technology in question, the commitment to use only inputs and personnel of the supplier, prohibitions against production of similar products, specified volumes of production, quality control by the supplier, price-fixing, limitations on export, commitments to turn over improvements in technology to the supplier and so forth. All such clauses have been flatly prohibited by the Common Regime.[50] This may be of some help in preventing the sort of situation that Guerrero posits, where a country provides incentives to export a given product while at the same time a supplier of necessary technology for that product demands in his contract with the local producer a clause limiting or prohibiting its export.[51]

A larger and more difficult problem is that of how to develop an indigenous technology to escape the crippling dependency on foreign suppliers from industrialized nations. The Common Regime makes a strong attempt at establishing a system that will achieve that goal, but a foreign supplier cannot be divested of his technology in the same way as can a foreign investment. When one considers the massive commitments of resources and manpower necessary to maintain constantly advancing states of the art in so many varied industries, it is difficult to visualize a time in the near future when the ACM will be able to free itself of reliance on foreign technology in many or most areas.

Nonetheless, the Commission is given broad powers to activate technological development within the ACM. This is to be done primarily through tax and other incentives for technological research and production, "especially that connected with the intensive use of input items of subregional origin or those designed to make efficient use of subregional productive factors," and some unspecified means of channeling domestic savings into national and subregional research and development centers.[52] The Commission has also promulgated a new Industrial Property Law for the ACM, and set up a Subregional Industrial Property Office.[53] Member countries should favor purchases of products that include subregional technology in their manufacture, again under Commission guidelines.[54] Only time will prove whether the effort to develop subregional technology can prosper. In any event, it probably represents the most ambitious of the goals contained in the Common Regime.

NOTES

[1] Acuerdo de Cartagena, signed at Bogotá, Colombia, 26 May 1969 [hereafter Acuerdo]. An English translation may be found in 8 *Int'l L. Materials* 910 (1969). The subregional agreement was approved by the Permanent Executive Committee of LAFTA in its "Resolución" 179 of 9 July 1969, as compatible with the Treaty of Montevideo. The printed record of the discussions and resolution in *Derecho de la Integración*, No. 6 at 118-36 (1970), indicates that the issue of subregional integration was settled beforehand by "Resoluciones" 202, 203 and 222 of the contracting parties to LAFTA.

[2] For a concise presentation of ACM's deadlines, see *Business Latin America* "The Andean Common Market" 37 (published by Bus. Int'l 1970).

[3]See Decision 24 of the ACM Commission, promulgated 31 December 1970. Decisions 37 of 24 June 1970 and 37-A of 17 July 1970 amended the original regulations. Properly titled Common Regime of Treatment of Foreign Capital and of Trademarks, Patents, Licenses, and Royalties [hereafter Common Regime] , the English translation of the final version is available in *11 Int'l L. Materials* 126 (1972). The official decrees of each country in approving the Common Regime are collected in *Grupo Andino, No.* 9 (1971).

[4]See Decision 46 of the ACM Commission, approved 31 December 1971, to enter into effect by 30 June 1972. See generally Peruvian Times, Dec. 31, 1971, at 3.

[5]See, *e.g.,* C. Fulda & W. Schwartz, *Regulation of International Trade and Investment: Cases and Materials* 479-536 (1970).

[6]See, *e.g.,* Wesley, "Expropriation Challenge in Latin America: Prospects for Accord on Standards and Procedures." 46 *Tul. L. Rev.* 232 (1971); "Symposium—Foreign Investment in Latin America." 11 *Va. J. Int'l L.* 175 (1971); Eder, "Expropriation: Hickenlooper and Hereafter," 4 *Int'l Lawyer* 611 (1970): "Foreign Investment in Latin America: Past Policies and Future Trends" (Proceedings of a Regional Meeting of the American Society of International Law, published in 1970 by *Va. J. Int'l L.).*

[7]For those whose interest is more general, the author found two recent articles especially helpful, in addition to Hirschman, "How to Divest in Latin America and Why," in *Essays in International Finance,* No. 76 (1969). Sunkel "Big Business and *Dependencia," 50 Foreign Affairs* 517 (1972); Garcia, "Industrialización y Dependencia en América Latina," *38 Trimestre Económico* 731 (1971).

There is an abundance of material on the subject. Among the more prominent sources are: Cardoso & Faletto, *Dependencia y Desarrollo en América Latina* (1969); Dos Santos, *El Nuevo Caracter de la Dependencia* (1969); Furtado, *Los Estados Unidos y el Subdesarrollo de América Latina* (1970); Sunkel & Paz, *El Subdesarrollo Latinoamericano y la Teoría del Subdesarrollo* (1970). In addition, the Latin American journals contain many articles by these and other authors on the subjects of foreign investment and *dependencia.*

[8]This is a hybrid list gleaned primarily from Wionczek and Guerrero, "El Régimen Común de la Inversión Extranjera en el Grupo Andino," *Derecho de la Integración,* No. 8 at 11 (1971).

[9]See Wionczek, "Problems Involved in the Establishment of a Common Agreement for Foreign Investment in the Andean Common Market" (1970), at 7-26 (country-by-country analysis indicating that about half to a third of foreign investments in the manufacturing sectors have been acquisitions of existing enterprises in ACM countries).

10*Common Regime,* arts. 27-37.

11 18*Bus. Int'l,* "Supplement toThe Andean Common Market" 2 (1971).

12An exception is made for those foreign enterprises (any business having less than 51% national investment, as defined in article 1 of the Common Regime) that do not wish to participate in the advantages of the subregional duty-free commercial traffic. *Common Regime*, arts. 27, 34.

13Common Regime, art. 30.

14Common Regime, art. 35. This is a modification of the original provision, which would have required a first refusal to the host state on each divestment. The change is probably due to Colombia's strong opposition to the original provision. See *Peruvian Times,* July 2, 1971, at 3.

15Common Regime, art. 30. The standards set out here are the most lenient permitted. Any country may impose stricter time periods or greater percentages of divestment. *Id.* art. 33.

16Common Regime, art. 30.

17Common Regime, art. 28.

18Common Regime, art. 27. The basis for control is through certificates of origin, which will be issued only to companies that have achieved mixed or national status (as defined in article 1) or are in the process of transforming themselves to achieve it. *Id.,* art. 24.

19Common Regime, art. 28.

20Common Regime, art. 3.

21Common Regime, art. 4. In some cases, national capital must constitute not less than 80% of control.

22See M. Wionczek, *La Banca Extranjera en América Latina* (1970).

23See *Guerrero,* supra note 8, at 22.

24Common Regime, art. 17. Like other provisions in the ACM regulations, this article probably reflects Peruvian legislation, in this case Decree-Law 18858 of 19 May 1971. If the ACM follows the general outline of Peru's approach, short-term credit may be permitted to the total of the company's capital and reserves, but only for loans of a year or less. When the term is over a year, short-term credit in Peru is limited to three times the value of the locally-owned portion of the enterprise. See *Peruvian Times,* July 2, 1971, at 3. The ACM will promulgate its own regulations by Commission decision. Common Regime, art. 17.

[25] Article 31 of the *Common Regime* contains the required elements of the agreement to be negotiated between national authorities and foreign investors.

[26] For the purposes of figuring fade-out percentages, "national investors" include the Andean Development Corporation or investors from any ACM country. *Common Regime,* art. 30.

[27] M. Wionczek, *El Grupo Andino y la Inversión Extranjera* 6-7 (1970).

[28] Common Regime, art. 5, Temporary Provision B.

[29] Common Regime, art. 45.

[30] See *Peruvian Times,* January 8, 1971, at 3-4.

[31] The best overviews and analyses of the subject, which bring together most of the existing data and thought, are easily Vaitsos, *Strategic Choices in the Commercialization of Technology: The Point of View of Developing Countries* (1970); Vaitsos, *Transfer of Resources and Preservation of Monopoly Rents* (1970); and Sábato, *Producción y Comercialización de Tecnología* (1970).

[32] See Aracama-Zorraquín, "El Derecho de las Patentes en América Latina," *Derecho de la Integración,* No. 9 at 75 (1971).

[33] The most commonly cited sources of returns on investment in Latin America are the U.S. Department of Commerce and the Council for the Americas. See *Peruvian Times,* April 23, 1971, at 6; May, "The Effects of United States and Other Foreign Investments in Latin America" (published by the Council of the Americas 1970). Wionczek, "Problems Involved in the Establishment of a Common Agreement for Foreign Investment in the Andean Common Market," supra note 9.

[34] Common Regime, Temporary Provision E.

[35] Common Regime, art. 6(f).

[36] Common Regime, art. 18. Without such prior approval no remittance of royalties in foreign exchange will be permitted. *Id.,* art. 21.

[37] See Schliesser, "Restrictions on Foreign Investments in the Andean Common Market," 5 *Int'l Lawyer* 586, 596 (1971).

[38] Common Regime, art. 19. Clauses providing for royalty payments on unused patents or trademarks are prohibited. *Id.,* arts. 20 (g) and 25(d).

[39] Common Regime, art. 21.

[40]Common Regime, art. 26.

[41]Common Regime, art. 37. The figure of 14% return should not be a disincentive to invest in Latin America. If figures or profits from other areas are reliable, 14.1% is the highest profit being made by U.S. investors in any part of the world except for recently reported returns of 28.7% in the Middle and Far East. There may be some question whether the 14% profit is a binding figure for ACM countries and for all foreign investments. In applying the Common Regime in Ecuador, that country specifically excepted the basic products (petroleum and other minerals and forest exploitation) from the 14% limitation, citing article 40, which would appear to support Ecuador's right to unilaterally make such a decision. See Supreme Decree No. 1029 of 13 July 1971, art. 2, in *Grupo Andino*, No. 8 (1971). Article 37, on the other hand, would appear to require ACM Commission authorization for any deviation from 14% regardless of the circumstances. One possibility is that since articles 37 and 40 are in different chapters of the Common Regime, they are not mutually exclusive, and apply only to the subject matter of their respective chapters.

[42]Common Regime, arts. 7-10.

[43]Common Regime, art. 13.

[44]Common Regime, art. 12.

[45]Common Regime, arts. 14-16.

[46]Common Regime, art. 17.

[47]Common Regime, art. 15.

[48]See Guerrero, supra note 8, at 16-17.

[49]Guerrero, supra note 8, at 20.

[50]Common Regime, arts. 20,25.

[51]Guerrero, supra note 8, at 21.

[52]Common Regime, art. 23.

[53]Common Regime, Temporary Provisions F and G.

[54]Common Regime, art. 24.

One, Two, Many OPECs . . .?

C. Fred Bergsten and
Stephen D. Krasner

The Threat from the Third World
C. Fred Bergsten

The United States is rapidly joining the rest of the industrialized
countries in depending on the Third World for a critical share of
its energy supplies and other natural resources. For oil alone, annual U.S. imports are expected to rise by $20 billion by the end of
the decade. But it is not only much-publicized oil; accelerating imports of other raw materials will raise these figures significantly.

Four countries control more than 80 percent of the exportable
supply of world copper, have already organized, and have already
begun to use their oligopoly power. Two countries account for
more than 70 percent of world tin exports, and four countries
raise the total close to 95 percent. Four countries combine for
more than 50 percent of the world supply of natural rubber. Four
countries possess over one-half the world supply of bauxite, and
the inclusion of Australia (which might well join the "Third
World" for such purposes) brings the total above 90 percent. In
coffee, the four major suppliers have begun to collude (even within the framework of the International Coffee Agreement, which
includes the main consuming countries) to boost prices. A few
countries are coming to dominate each of the regional markets
for timber, the closest present approximation to a truly vanishing

Reprinted in part, with permission, from *Foreign Policy*, no. 11 (Summer
1973), pp. 107-111.

resource. The percentages are less, but still quite impressive, for several other key raw materials and agricultural products. And the United States already meets an overwhelming share of its needs for most of these commodities from imports, or will soon be doing so.

A wide range of Third World countries thus have sizable potential for strategic market power. They could use that power against all buyers, or in a discriminatory way through differential pricing or supply conditions—for example, to avoid higher costs to other LDCs [less-developed countries] or against the United States alone to favor Europe or Japan.

Supplying countries could exercise maximum leverage through withholding supplies altogether, at least from a single customer such as the United States. Withholding is a feasible policy when there are no substitute products available on short notice, and when the foreign exchange reserves of the suppliers become sizable enough that they have no need for current earnings.

The suppliers would be even more likely to use their monopoly power to charge higher prices for their raw materials, directly or through such techniques as insisting that they process the materials themselves. Either withholding or price-gouging could hurt U.S. security. The threat of either could pressure the United States to compromise its positions on international political and economic issues. Either would hurt the U.S. efforts to combat domestic inflation and restore equilibrium in our international balance of payments.

The price and balance-of-payments effects on the United States of withholding or price-gouging by suppliers of raw materials could not be attacked through conventional policy instruments. Domestic demand for raw materials could be dampened only at the cost of additional unemployment. Foreign suppliers are outside the jurisdiction of U.S. price controls. Substitution of domestic resources would also raise costs significantly. Stockpile sales help only for a short time. Devaluations make resource imports more costly without much dampening their volume. Such actions could thus cause major new problems for the U.S. economy and international position.

Such Third World leverage could have a double bite on the United States if used discriminatorily against it, thereby benefiting the competitive positions of Europe and Japan. Such discriminatory action, triggered either by the suppliers or by our industrialized competitors, is by no means impossible. It was attempted in oil by some Arab countries in 1967 and has been actively sought at least by Italy and France in the recent past. The spectre of "cannibalistic competition" among the rich for natural resources is unfortunately a real possibility which suggests that the owners of those resources have tremendous clout.

The Third World suppliers could also cause major problems by the way in which they use their huge export earnings. Oil earnings alone could rise to at least $50 billion per year by the end of the decade. It is hard to see how more than $20 billion of the total can be spent on imports. These countries could thus add $30 billion *per year* to their portfolios seeking profitable (or mischievous) outlets. They could use the money to disrupt international money markets overtly, and we have already seen that they generate great monetary instability, perhaps without consciously trying, by pushing the world toward a multiple reserve currency system. Aimed specifically at particular currencies, they could seek to force the United States (or anyone else) to adopt policies which clashed with its national objectives of the moment—as a few Arab countries, from a much weaker financial base, attacked the United Kingdom by converting sterling balances in June 1967 and again in 1971.[1] At a minimum, the uncertain destination of these huge resources will add to the already formidable problems faced by the international monetary system, which can affect the United States quite adversely.

The oil situation is, of course, the prototype. The concerted action of the OPEC countries in raising oil prices has raised energy costs throughout the world and dramatically increased their revenues. Such extortion by the oil producers—including such "normal" LDCs as Nigeria, Indonesia, Iran, and Venezuela—is likely to continue. This economic pressure is unlikely to be reduced as a result of the takeover of the production facilities by the OPEC countries from the international companies,[2] because the countries themselves—including "opposition" politicians in each—have well learned from the companies that *each* benefits from getting the highest possible price for *all*, and that price-cutting by one would be counterproductive because it would quickly be emulated by the others to preserve existing market shares. Equally important is the fact that OPEC has shown other countries how to do it. Oil may be merely the start.

To be sure, each of the specific commodity situations presents dif- ferent and complex problems. There are serious obstacles to con- certed supplier action: the economic option of using substitutes for some of the commodities, the political problem of achieving adequate cooperation among the suppliers, and the risk of overt retaliation by the industrialized world (or just the United States).

But the two obstacles specific to commodity action can be largely overcome within the Third World itself. Subtle pricing and other marketing strategies could boost consumer costs and producer gains significantly without pushing consumer countries to the de- velopment of substitutes, which requires heavy initial investments and start-up costs. Concerted action by copper, tin, and bauxite producers would sharply reduce the risk to each that cheaper alu- minum or tin would substitute for higher priced copper, or vice versa. An alliance among the producers of coffee, cocoa, and tea could preempt substitution by drinkers around the world. Objec- tive calculations of the benefits to all producers could provide a basis for "equitable" division of the spoils.

All that is needed to permit political cooperation is increased knowledge of the market and the potential gains from concerted action, self-confidence, and leadership. Whether such action actu- ally eventuates would seem to depend quite importantly on the policy milieu of the future. The countries involved will certainly be more likely to act if the industrialized world frustrates their ef- forts to achieve their goals more constructively, and if they are barred from participating effectively in global decisions which vi- tally affect their own destinies. They are more likely to act against the United States alone if the United States is the most obstinate or neglectful of all. Even a perception of such obstinacy or ne- glect, sufficiently plausible to be widely believed in both the Third World and the industrialized countries themselves, could trigger action. It would seem far better for the United States, and for all the industrialized countries, to try to preempt such risks by taking initiatives to help these countries fulfill their aspirations by more stable means.

Oil is the Exception
Stephen D. Krasner

Petroleum is the exception, not the rule. In other commodity markets Third World states acting alone will not be able to artificially limit supplies. Natural scarcities, corporate oligopolies, or commodity agreements between exporting and importing areas may bring higher prices, but no other group of less-developed countries (LDCs) possesses the attributes that permit the oil-rich Arab sheikdoms to *independently* regulate the world market for a major raw material.

In any market where some producers see the possibility of restraining trade, there is tension between competitive and cooperative behavior. Each producer wants to maximize *his own returns.* This can be done in two ways. By cooperating, producers can increase the joint revenues of the entire industry. With a larger pie, all suppliers can procure greater benefits. Alternatively, a producer can raise his profits by increasing his share of the market even if the size of the pie remains the same or decreases.

Competition is more likely. Durable collusion requires sharing the burden of market control. Equally important, once agreement is reached, cartel members must be confident that commitments will be kept. If cheating takes place, loyal oligopolists, confronting a residual market, may be worse off than if they had followed competitive policies. To avoid such risks, would-be cartelists are likely to abandon cooperation if they distrust their partners. The suspicion of cheating becomes a self-fulfilling prophecy. It must be minimized for markets to be controlled successfully.

Since World War II, a group of oil-exporters have been the only Third World states to effectively limit the supply of a major raw material. The attributes that distinguish these countries from other materials producers are their enormous foreign exchange holdings,

Reprinted in part, with permission, from *Foreign Policy*, no. 14 (Spring 1974), pp. 68-81.

a common external enemy, and tacit assistance from multinational companies. No other group of exporting states is likely to find itself in an analogous situation.

Past failures

Oil's uniqueness does not signify an absence of other efforts. In 1962, cocoa-exporting states formed the Cocoa Producers Alliance (COPAL). In October 1964, Ghana, the Ivory Coast, the Cameroons, Nigeria, Brazil, and Togo agreed to limit their cocoa sales to levels that would keep prices above twenty cents per pound. They failed, and for Ghana, the largest producer, the failure was disastrous. The Ivory Coast and the Cameroons did not, from the outset, abide by the agreement. By January, the other producing countries held large stocks of cocoa and confronted a weak market. Because of pressing economic demands, Ghana, in particular, could not continue to restrict sales. Controls were formally abandoned in January 1965, and the resulting glut, coupled with predictions of a large harvest, sent prices tumbling to a low of eleven cents per pound by June. The consequent drop in foreign earnings contributed to the overthrow of the Nkrumah regime.

Prior to the 1962 signing of the International Coffee Agreement, the producing states made numerous efforts to regulate the market on their own. Colombia and Brazil, the two largest exporters, signed a "gentlemen's agreement" in 1955. It lasted for only a few months. This was followed by a series of arrangements that included ever larger numbers of exporting countries. They were ineffectual. Before 1962, only Brazil and Colombia actually withheld coffee from the market. Other producers were either unwilling or unable to share the burden of control.

Copper-exporting states have made several abortive efforts to raise prices. In 1967, Zambia, Zaire, Chile, and Peru formed the Intergovernmental Council of Copper Exporting States (CIPEC). Since then, they have at one time or another attempted to reach agreement on a buffer stock, open market purchases, target prices, production limitations, and export controls. CIPEC's only success came in 1969, when an announcement that a master plan had been agreed upon temporarily halted declining prices. Buyers quickly learned to treat such press releases lightly, and industry publications openly disparaged later threats from the exporting states.

Agreement has eluded the copper exporters because they have not decided how to share the burden of intervention, cannot trust each other to adhere to controls, have had no mechanism for enforcing agreements, and, at least while Allende was in power, had profound ideological differences.

Producers of natural fibers—sisal, henequen, jute, kenaf, and abaca—and of tea have formed voluntary export control organizations under the auspices of the Food and Agricultural Organization. With the exception of some success in stabilizing the sisal and henequen markets from 1968 to 1970, these arrangements have had little impact on price levels. Differing interests, the absence of enforcement mechanisms, and, in the case of fibers, competition from synthetics, have prevented effective price manipulation.

Even the petroleum producers had little success in regulating supplies, as opposed to raising taxes, before 1973. In the late 1960s, efforts were made through OPEC to establish export quotas. They failed. Saudi Arabia, Iran, and other Middle East countries resisted proposals that would have reduced the market advantage they derived from their low production costs. Before the Middle East war only Kuwait and Libya had restricted output.

Recent developments in the petroleum market offer the only example of effective collusion, independently implemented by Third World countries. Even its limits must be recognized. Present shortages are the result not of an OPEC cartel, nor even an Arab cartel, but of actions taken by four countries—Libya, Kuwait, Abu Dhabi, and, most importantly, Saudi Arabia. Whether the producing countries will be able to sustain market control remains to be seen.

Attempts to form cartels are being made by other groups. With the collapse of the International Coffee Agreement, Brazil, Colombia, the Ivory Coast, and Portugal (Angola) formed an international marketing company. Other countries have pledged various levels of stock retention. Major bauxite-exporting states have announced plans to establish their own organization. The copper producers have initiated contacts with OPEC, and continue to discuss possibilities for intervention. Is oil a harbinger of things to come?

Conditions favoring collusion

There is no satisfactory theory of oligopoly behavior. Theoretically, it is not possible to state definitively when collusion will take place. Conditions that make durable cartel behavior more likely can, however, be specified. They are: price inelastic demand, high barriers to entry, high market concentration, shared experience among producers, lack of consumer resistance, ability to work with an extended time horizon, and shared values. Precisely what probabilities of success are associated with what levels of each of these indicators is something we do not know. Even if all the conditions favoring collusion are present, we cannot say that it will definitely take place. Market control is an art, not a science. There are a series of random and extraneous factors, such as leadership, strikes, and natural disasters, that cannot be systematically predicted.

By comparing oil with other commodities we can, however, begin to answer the question of whether the threat from the Third World is real. If the attributes of other groups of exporters are similar to those of the Arab states that have controlled oil supplies, then there are grounds for maintaining that a new era is upon us. Past failures in copper, cocoa, tea, fibers, and coffee must be interpreted as preliminary experiences that will lead to durable collusion. Relations between less- and more-developed areas will be transformed.

If, on the other hand, it turns out that oil exporters have unique characteristics, then current fears are probably unwarranted. The Third World will not be able to strike at the economic jugular of the industrialized states.

Two basic market conditions must be present if supply restrictions are to result in increased foreign exchange earnings: demand and supply must be unresponsive to price.

1. *Demand unresponsive to price:* If consumers stop buying when prices are raised, then production curtailments are self-defeating. Any increase in per unit price is more than offset by a decline in total sales.[3] (In economic jargon, the price elasticity of demand is greater than unity.) The less responsive demand is to price, the greater the benefits of collusion.

It is difficult to establish precise numerical relationships between demand and price for raw materials because of changes in taste and quality over time. Studies indicate, however, that only the producers of natural rubber, citrus fruits, bananas, natural fibers, and possibly tin, confront market conditions that would make export controls self-defeating. The demand for other raw materials is not very responsive to price.[4] Like oil exporters, most other producers face a demand structure that would make it possible for them to increase their foreign exchange earnings if they could effectively cooperate.

2. *Supply unresponsive to price:* Collusion is more likely in an industry where there are effective economic or technical barriers to the entry of new producers. If higher prices prompt large increases in production, then collusion is, at best, attractive only in the short term. Additional supplies will rapidly erode the market share of members of the cartel, and they may eventually be left with a lower level of receipts than they enjoyed under free market conditions.

Estimates of the responsiveness of supplies to price for raw materials are even more difficult to come by than those for demand. The development of additional sources of raw materials often involves new technologies whose costs cannot be precisely defined. In the medium term, however, there are significant impediments to greatly expanding production in most major raw materials. Large investments and lead times of several years are needed to bring new supplies of most minerals to the market. Crops can be grown efficiently only in certain climatic and soil conditions, and some, such as coffee, require four to five years before new plantings bear fruit. The benefits of collusion in other raw materials, as well as in petroleum, would not immediately be dispelled by new output.

Hence the basic market prerequisites for oligopoly behavior are present for many other raw materials as well as for petroleum. Their existence alone does not determine when collusion will take place, for then it would be impossible to explain why efforts at market control have failed. Other conditions favoring cooperation must be investigated.

3. *Limited number of producers:* The smaller the number of producers, the greater the probability of collusion. Where the level of market concentration is high, each supplier is more likely to realize that his actions affect others. With fewer producers, the

organizational costs of establishing a cartel are less. It is also easier to identify and detect cheating.

Table 1 shows the percentage of world exports and world production accounted for by the four largest LDC exporters of nine major commodities. Oil is several points below the general average for both measures, and ranks seventh in terms of export market concentration. If the number of major producers were the critical determinant of the ability of less-developed states to successfully collude, one would have expected tin or cocoa, rather than oil, to be in the forefront.

4. *Shared experience among producers:* The greater the level of shared experience among producers, the more aware they will be of their mutual interdependence. Shared experience also makes it more likely that producers will agree on principles that enable them to allocate the burden of market control.

Although the joint negotiations carried out throughout OPEC provided an important fund of shared experience for oil exporters, other groups of commodity producers have had similar or more intense exchanges. Through OPEC, the producing states secured marginally greater revenues by getting the companies to change the tax treatment of royalties, and halt a decline in posted prices. OPEC's membership as a whole has never, however, grappled successfully with the question of quota allocation. Market restrictions are now being carried out not by an OPEC cartel, but by a wealthy Arab cartel. Producing states that have participated in international commodity agreements in tin, coffee, sugar, and now cocoa have been forced to agree among themselves on prices, aggregate supplies, and specific production allocations— a shared experience much more relevant to establishing a successful cartel than bargaining with unresisting corporations. The level of shared experience among petroleum producers does not distinguish them from several other groups of exporting states.

5. *Lack of consumer resistance:* Collusion is more likely if buyers do not cooperate with each other, play one producer off against another, or retaliate by, for instance, raising the price of their exports. One of the striking aspects of the history of raw-materials markets is the absence of concerted resistance to restrictive arrangements by the governments of consuming areas. Aside from Herbert Hoover's efforts to combat rubber, potash, and other foreign cartels while secretary of commerce in the 1920s, no one

Table 1

Market shares of the four largest LDC producers
(percentages)

	Tin	Coffee	Cocoa	Sugar	Rubber	Tea	Petroleum	Iron ore	Copper	Mean
World production	70	49	58	14	30	36	32	11	25	36
World exports	82	55	73	45	60	66	52	30	61	58

Sources and explanations: Figures for sugar, cocoa, tea, coffee, and rubber from Food and Agriculture Organization of the United Nations' *Trade Yearbook, 1971* and *FAO Commodity Review and Outlook, 1971-72*; for petroleum from British Petroleum Corporation's *BP Statistical Review of the World Oil Industry, 1971* (London); for copper, tin, and iron ore from *Metal Bulletin Handbook, 1972* (London: Metal Bulletin Books Ltd., 1972). All figures are for 1970. Values for rubber include synthetic rubber.

Table 2

Ratio of reserves to annual imports by groups of commodity-producing states

	Tin	Coffee	Cocoa	Sugar	Rubber	Tea	Petroleum	Iron ore	Copper
Number of countries	5	12	6	5	4	2	10	6	4
Ratio of reserves to annual imports	.48	.32	.29	.20	.44	.38	1.33	.16	.39

Sources and explanations: All values are averages of the scores for major exporters of the designated commodity weighted by their level of production. Levels of production were taken from the United Nations' *Statistical Yearbook, 1971*. Whenever available, 1970 figures were used. The ratio of reserves to imports for groups of commodity-producing countries was derived from figures in the International Monetary Fund's *International Financial Statistics, 1972 Supplement*.

in American government has seriously tried to dismantle any market control arrangement. Governments of consumer nations have often abetted collusion by supporting the oligopolistic practices of multinational corporations, or by protecting high cost domestic producers. They have joined commodity agreements designed to regulate international markets. Like other raw-material exporters, petroleum-producing countries have not met resistance from the governments of industrial states.

Corporate behavior has not been so consistent. In some cases processors have actively resisted attempts to exercise market control. Cocoa companies played a significant role in thwarting COPAL in 1964. Companies in other industries have been neutral. The coffee roasters, for instance, never seriously opposed higher prices even when they came through an international agreement that required the participation of the American government.

In the petroleum market, corporate behavior has facilitated collusion among exporting countries. The oil companies have willingly participated in a tax structure that discourages competitive behavior, have regulated output themselves, have created an artificial pricing system, and have capitulated to demands for price increases. In dealing with the oil companies, OPEC's members hit mush and, following Lenin's dictum, pushed on. The benefits petroleum-exporting states have derived from their association with multinational corporations surpass those bestowed on any other group of Third World exporters. Tacit assistance from multinational corporations is the first characteristic that distinguishes the oil market from that of other raw materials.

6. *Ability to take a long-term perspective:* Collusion maximizes returns only over the long term. Any member of a coalition can increase short-run earnings by cheating. There will always be some time lag between an initial breach and the decision by other partners to abandon established production levels. A producer that does not have the resources, either financial or political, to take an extended outlook will always be an unreliable coalition member. The future is meaningless since he cannot survive without maximizing present returns.

If we examine the ability of raw materials exporters to work with an extended time horizon, a second and more critical distinction between oil and other commodities is evident. Table 2 gives the ratio of reserves to annual imports by groups of commodity-producing states.

As a group, the petroleum exporters have by far the largest amount of wealth in excess of current needs. The figures for Saudi Arabia, which had more than two years' worth of reserves at the end of 1972, and Libya, with more than three years' worth, are particularly striking. For these states there was little risk in curtailing production. Even if prices had not responded as favorably as they have, they would still have had enough cushion to weather any temporary reversals.

The inability to take an extended time horizon has been a critical impediment to effective oligopoly behavior outside the oil market. Joining cartels is a tenuous and risky business. For the political leaders of Third World states, foreign exchange earnings are a potent political resource. Not only are these states poorer than industrialized areas, but their governments procure a smaller percentage of the country's wealth. For the poorest states, taxes on foreign trade are the major source of government revenue. Less-developed states are tempted to cheat because their resources often cannot meet current political demands. If one country does cheat, others may be left holding large stocks in a declining market—a situation that can lead to political as well as economic collapse. The relationship between a high reserve to import ratio and successful collusion is not fortuitous.

7. *Shared values:* If a group of producers share salient noneconomic values, the probability for successful cooperation is increased. Such values can strengthen trust, and provide sanctions against cheating.

Here too, the group of oil-exporting states that has limited output stands apart from countries exporting other raw materials. The Middle East dispute has been the most bitter and durable conflict in the postwar international system. King Faisal, in particular, had a strong ideological commitment to changing the present status of Jerusalem. The 1973 war was a catalytic event that triggered substantial export curtailments.

Hence there are three characteristics that distinguish the oil-exporting states that have curtailed production: tacit assistance from multinational corporations, surfeit revenues, and a highly salient shared value. No other group of Third World producers now possesses, or is likely to possess in the forseeable future, similar advantages.

This does not definitely rule out the formation of other cartels.

While demand and supply unresponsiveness, market shares, time horizons, shared values, and consumer resistance are likely to remain at existing levels, the success of OPEC has dramatically increased one value associated with successful collusion—the level of shared experience. Oil stands as an example for the rest of the Third World. It is heady stuff. The oil minister of Saudi Arabia dictates his terms to the United States; the Japanese bow to Abu Dhabi. Outstanding leadership might overcome distrust. Random events such as strikes in industrial areas could demonstrate the potential for higher prices if supplies were restricted. Countries that are major suppliers on the world market of commodities that are of secondary importance to their own economies—such as Brazil (coffee) and Nigeria (cocoa)—might bear the burden of market restriction, even if it were unprofitable, to secure broader political or economic aims.

The Threat Is Real
C. Fred Bergsten

Stephen Krasner seeks to minimize "The Threat From The Third World" which I described in *Foreign Policy* 11. He concludes that "the Third World is not in a position to squeeze [the primary product needs of the industrialized countries] very hard," because "petroleum is the exception, not the rule." Unfortunately for the consuming countries, Krasner is wrong. As Zuhayr Mikdashi points out,[5] collusion *could* work—and could add dramatically to both the raging inflation and rising unemployment which are spreading rapidly across most of the globe.

First, it should be noted that neither Krasner nor anyone else has yet contradicted my view that there are a number of economic issues other than natural resources (investments, markets, supplies of manufactured goods, agreements on monetary reform and trade liberalization, environmental protection, etc.) on which the Third World *can* hold us up. For example, the developing countries, even

Reprinted with permission from *Foreign Policy*, no. 14 (Spring, 1974), pp. 84-90.

those whose "objective economic interests" suggest a contrary course, have adopted a common position on the seabeds in opposition to that of the United States. Likewise, they have adopted a set of views on monetary reform, contrary to those of the United States, on which they seem unlikely to relent. And Krasner does not deal with several of the commodities for which, as I indicated, cartelization is most likely, such as bauxite and timber. So these points stand unchallenged in print, at least so far.

Second, there is growing evidence that my analysis is all too correct with regard to natural resources. OPEC has succeeded beyond my wildest fears. The bauxite producers have explicitly decided to form their own "OPEC." The coffee exporters have successfully held production off the market to boost prices, and are so confident that they let the International Coffee Agreement with the consuming countries expire. The rubber producers have agreed to regular consultation. Krasner says that the market scoffs at threats from the copper exporters, but they are in contact with OPEC and something has driven the price of that commodity to unheard-of levels. Mikdashi's doubts that copper can be cartelized because "the copper exported by CIPEC countries represented less than a quarter of total world copper supply" is not very comforting, because Krasner's Table 1 reveals that the comparable number for OPEC oil is, at 32 percent, only slightly higher. The Shah of Iran has publicly suggested that other Third World countries emulate OPEC, and offered them assistance to do so.

Indeed, all of Krasner's examples of unsuccessful cartelization efforts come from an era which now seems light-years away. Shortages of supply have replaced shortages of demand as the dominant force in world economics for the first time in almost 50 years, and the power position of suppliers and consumers has thus changed dramatically. Détente has removed much of the security blanket which smothered international economic conflict in the past. The successes of many developing countries on a variety of fronts, and especially of OPEC itself, have provided them with the skills and the courage to effectively promote their own interests. There is indeed a very real and growing threat from the Third World unless the industrialized countries, particularly the United States, both stand up to the producer cartels and begin to adopt far more cooperative policies toward it.

On the issue of additional producer cartels, Krasner himself disposes of most of the potential differences between oil and other commodities. He concludes, however, that there are two distinguishing features which set oil apart: the flush foreign exchange positions of the oil producers, which enable them to afford the risks of cartelization, and their "shared value" concerning Israel. Neither point in fact distinguishes OPEC from potential emulators.

The foreign exchange argument

The foreign exchange argument fails for four reasons: some of the key oil producers are *not* flush, some of the leaders of other potential cartels *are* flush, reserve holdings do not tell the whole story of a country's ability to risk failure in a cartelization effort anyway, and, most important, none of these considerations is very important if the likelihood of successful cartelization is high.

Iran is crucial to OPEC, as the second largest oil producer, but its reserves equal less than three months' imports and it spends virtually all of its earnings for development. So do Iraq, Algeria, Venezuela, Nigeria, and Indonesia, which along with Iran account for 60 percent of OPEC output. Yet OPEC has obviously succeeded; reserve levels thus need not be high for even the most important cartel members.

The reason is that oil was a setup for cartelization, with very little risk involved. The same situation holds for several other commodities as well. But a country can undertake even a risky cartelization effort for a particular commodity if its *over-all economic position* is strong enough to stand failure.

If its economy is solely or heavily dependent on the commodity in question, as is Saudi Arabia's on oil, the risk *is* high unless its reserve cushion is also very high. But the risks are much lower if the potential cartelizer has a highly diversified economy, and if its reserve position does not then determine whether it can undertake the effort. This is precisely why Brazil, which has developed both an impressive manufacturing base and a highly diversified range of primary exports, as well as the world's eighth-largest reserves, can hold an umbrella over the coffee market now whereas it could not do so a decade ago. Colombia can even help, because coffee now provides less than one-half its export earnings and its reserves equal six months' imports. Krasner's Table 2 is thus misleading: it needs to be weighted by the dependence of the producing countries

on the commodities in question to portray an accurate picture of
how likely they are to initiate cartels.

In addition to "safe" export earnings, a diversified economic base
sharply increases the likelihood that the country can borrow sizable sums from the international capital markets to supplement its
reserves. The Third World obtained over $8 billion in Eurocredits
in 1972, and perhaps $10-$12 billion in 1973. So there is every
likelihood that cartelization efforts can be underwritten by foreign
loans as well as by national reserves and ongoing earnings from
other exports of goods and services.

One source of financing for emulators of OPEC might be OPEC.
The huge increase in oil prices obviously hobbles the development
efforts of many countries in the Third World. But the Shah seems
to reject the obvious alternatives of dual pricing for oil and com-
pensatory grants to the beleaguered, because those options could
undermine his own cartel and deplete his own reserves, respectively. Hence he has called on other developing countries to restore
their terms of trade by raising their own export prices, and offered
to help them do so. Underwriting such an effort would, in one fell
swoop, establish OPEC as leader of the entire Third World and provide a handsome return on invested capital if the cartels worked.

These considerations of economic invulnerability are far more important for potential cartel leaders than rank and file members.
There will always be cheating by smaller countries, as Krasner suggests, but the output decisions of one or two leaders determine
whether the price umbrella can be held. How then do the potential
leaders, and to a lesser extent members of other potential cartels,
meet these criteria?

For tin, Malaysia accounts for one-half of world exports, has reserves which exceed seven months' imports, and relies on that commodity for only 20 percent of its export earnings. That same country accounts for 38 percent of world rubber exports, but rubber
provides only one-third of its export earnings. Australia, which has
announced that it will attend the organizational meeting of the
bauxite "OPEC" and has spoken publicly of developing a "resources diplomacy," is a leading exporter of bauxite, iron ore, and
lead, and has a widely diversified economic base and the world's
ninth largest reserves. (The other bauxite producers are less afflu-
ent, but this appears to be the commodity least susceptible to substitutes and hence the least risky to cartelize, especially if the tin

and copper producers move along similar lines.) Thailand is an important factor in the tin and rubber markets. Each of these commodities represents less than 15 percent of total Thai exports, and its reserves exceed eight months' imports. Each of the four main copper exporters relies heavily on that commodity, but Zambia, the largest exporter, has substantial reserves as do Peru and Zaire. There are many other similar examples. "Surfeit reserves" are *not* a distinguishing characteristic of great significance for the petroleum oligopoly.

"Shared values"

The issue of "shared values"—hatred for Israel—is even more easily disposed of. OPEC is comprised of countries with sharp political *differences.* Iran has always been *close* to Israel. There remains deep hostility between Iran and Iraq, Iran and Kuwait, and Iraq and Kuwait. Iran and Saudi Arabia are leading rivals for dominance of the Persian Gulf. Libya under Qaddafi and Saudi Arabia have bitterly competed for leadership of the entire Arab world. Venezuela and Nigeria have none of the so-called "shared values."

Yet OPEC has clearly succeeded, and was in fact a highly successful cartel well over two years *before* the latest war submerged at least some of these differences. It nicely survives the failure of Iran, Iraq, Libya, and all non-Arabs to join the production cutbacks to pressure the West over Israel. There is only one explanation: the common economic gain for all participants from raising their prices and avoiding the production increases which would undermine such action—a motive which could readily trigger similar action wherever the economics permit.

Indeed, the only political prerequisite for producer cartels is the absence of overt hostility, and none seems to exist among the members of any of the potential emulators of OPEC. Few of those countries (e.g., Bolivia and Malaysia for tin, Guinea and Guyana for bauxite) have any reason even to talk to each other *except* for their common interest in maximizing their economic returns from a commodity which they happen to have in common. So "shared values" hardly set OPEC apart.

In fact, producer cartels look more feasible in other commodities than in oil. Fewer countries need to collude. Capital, technological, and marketing complexities may be more easily mastered. As already indicated, other potential cartelizers are frequently more diversified economically and less antagonistic politically. I continue to fear that oil is only the beginning, particularly in view of the dramatic demonstration effect of OPEC's success and the utter failure of the consuming countries to respond with common action of their own.

NOTES

[1]Feeling no responsibility for the system, they hold their assets in whichever national currency appears most likely to appreciate in value and/or has the highest yield at the moment—switching rapidly among currencies (and even buying gold in the free market) as the situation changes. Some of these oil countries which are members of the IMF have even opted out of the SDR scheme, which was a first step toward reducing such problems. For the problems involved, see C. Fred Bergsten, "Reforming the Dollar: An International Monetary Policy for the United States," especially pp. 9-13.

[2]As argued by Theodore H. Moran, "Coups and Costs," *Foreign Policy*, 8 (Fall 1972), pp. 129-137.

[3]It is assumed throughout this paper that exporting states seek to maximize foreign exchange earnings rather than profits. Cost considerations have been ignored.

[4]A study by Houthaker and Magee, *Review of Economics and Statistics*, 51 (May 1969), p. 121, estimated the elasticities of demand for U.S. crude materials imports and crude food imports to be -.18 and -.21 respectively. The elasticity of demand for cocoa has been estimated at -.41, of tea from -.05 to -.25, of coffee from -.25 to -.44 and of copper from -.10 to -.30.

For cocoa, see F. Helmut Weymar, *The Dynamics of the World Cocoa Market*, p. 100; for tea, Goutam K. Sarkar, *The World Tea Economy*, pp. 72-73; for coffee, U.S. Federal Trade Commission, *Economic Report of the Investigation of Coffee Prices*, p. 510, and Rex F. Daly, "Coffee Consumption and Prices in the United States," *Agricultural Economic Research*, p. 62; for copper, IBRD estimates.

[5]Zuhayr Mikdashi, "Collusion could Work," *Foreign Policy*, 14(Spring 1974), pp. 57-68.

11

The International Community and Transnational Corporations

N. T. Wang

In recent years, transnational corporations have become one of the most widely discussed topics. This sudden surge of interest reflects a widespread disquiet about the state of the world and a searching reappraisal of existing values and institutions. With the critical re-examination of the foundations of modern industrial, as well as the less developed, societies, and the searching questioning of the abilities of these societies to fulfill basic human needs, the growth and spread of transnational corporations are no longer equated with progress and development. Every crisis, whether it is external or internal disequilibrium, shortage of food or energy, has been linked with the operations, if not the misconduct, of some transnational corporations. In the developing host countries especially,

---

This chapter summarizes the main points made at several lectures delivered at the Brookings Institution, Columbia University, the University of Pennsylvania, and the University of Virginia. The views expressed here do not necessarily reflect those of the United Nations Secretariat, with which the author is presently associated.

The term "transnational corporations," unless otherwise specified, is used here in the broad sense of "enterprises which own or control production or service facilities outside the country in which they are based," and is therefore interchangeable with the term "multinational corporations." For alternative definitions, see United Nations, *Multinational Corporations in World Development.*

transnational corporations are often looked upon as a manifestation of foreign intrusion reminiscent of colonialism, contributing to indigenous underdevelopment by draining off natural resources, distorting the development path, or even interfering in domestic politics.

At the same time, as the world ponders the destiny of mankind and goes about the task of development, the capabilities of transnational corporations are recognized. As the developing nations gain self-confidence in the management of their own affairs, transnational corporations are increasingly viewed as a resource which, under certain conditions, can aid development. The flood of co-operative arrangements between some of the socialist countries and transnational corporations, moreover, suggests transideological possibilities and flexible responses on the part of the corporations.

While opinions continue to be sharply divided on the positive and negative effects of transnational corporations on world development, and their true causal relationships, a surprisingly large area of consensus is emerging with respect to what the international community could and should usefully do.

The emerging consensus

The primacy of national decision-making

It might appear paradoxical that the first point of general consensus on transnational corporations in the international context is the primacy of national decision-making. This is, however, inescapable since the sovereignty of nation-states is a basic tenet in international life. Noninterference in the domestic affairs of other states is generally accepted even though one state may totally disagree with another on how such affairs should be managed. Supranational organizations are a rare exception to intergovernmental organizations where the main decisions remain in the hands of the sovereign states. International bodies such as the United Nations seek voluntary compliance for their decisions through persuasion and the pressure of public opinion; enforcement by sanctions in these bodies is the exception rather than the rule.

The fiercely nationalistic bias in the present international system reflects, of course, the pluralistic character of the world's political and social creeds and has been reinforced by the breakdown of the colonial regimes. While a political theorist may rightly question the suitability of the whole concept of national sovereignty to the maintenance of international order in a world which is both capable of self-destruction and daily growing smaller, a practical international program must be based on this fundamental fact of life, at least for the immediate future, rather than on some form of ideal system.

Given the different styles and models of development of the various nation-states, the roles to be played by transnational corporations in their development are correspondingly different. Some nation-states have little to do with transnational corporations in their development; others want them to make a significant contribution. And the types of transnational corporations that are of interest to particular nations are equally diverse. The very large transnational corporations are evidently pervasive, but the relatively small ones figure importantly in many developing nations whose economic size is no larger than that of a moderately sized city in the United States. The firms engaged in natural resources and manufacturing industries are clearly most prevalent in host countries, but the growth of conglomerates and service industries (e.g., transportation, communications, tourism, and multinational banking) has reached significant proportions in certain cases. "Transnational enterprises" which are owned and operated from their home bases by home-state nationals across national borders are the predominant forms encountered by most host countries, but "multinational" firms owned and controlled by many nationals can no longer be ignored.[1]

The diversity of sovereign states, both in their attitudes toward transnational corporations and in the actual role that they permit these corporations to play, severely limits the possible choices for action which will be acceptable to the international community as a whole. Consequently, this very diversity is also a source of unity of approach in international action—if there is to be any action at all.

Limitations of corporate social responsibility

A corollary to the primacy of national decision-making are the inherent limitations of corporate social responsibility. This is not to deny the limitations of a purely legalistic approach. Nor is this to deny the value of good corporate behavior, including sensitivity to the human and environmental implications of corporate activity. Such behavior is neither prescribed in all the detail by society nor necessarily in conflict with good business even from the viewpoint of the firm. At the same time, if a country is beset with mass un-employment and the maldistribution of income, it is hardly the re-sponsibility of transnational corporations to provide full employ-ment or establish distributive justice. Nor is it the responsibility of transnational corporations to set environmental safeguards or stan-dards for consumer or worker protection. Evidently, it is not up to an enterprise to determine whether its emission of pollutants is within safe margin or to stop producing cigarettes because of health hazards. Such goals and standards, including the social ac-countability of transnational corporations, must be the concern of the society as a whole. The socially responsible behavior of trans-national corporations must be defined in the first instance by the requirements of accountability to society. Such behavior can be in-duced or required by society, although, obviously, care must be taken that the constraints imposed are not so onerous as to impair unintentionally the efficient functioning of transnational corpora-tions and their very raison d'être.

Transnational corporations for development

The question arises as to how the activities of transnational cor-porations are to be geared to the goals of development. Decisions have to be made as to whether transnational corporations are to be encouraged to play any role, and if so, for what goals and in what sectors. Thus, emphasis may be placed on access to world financial sources or markets, the continuous supply of new technology, or management know-how. It may be placed on depressed areas or export industries. At the same time, the conditions for local fi-nancing, outward remittance, the training of local labor, the health and safety of workers, etc., may be specified. Particular sectors, such as national defense, communications, inland transport, or banking may be reserved for nationals. Participation and fade-out arrangements may be negotiated.

Insofar as a clear national policy concerning the activities of trans-national corporations does not exist, the basis for evaluating their performance is correspondingly lacking. Indeed, if a nation pur-sues an inappropriate policy, such as an over-valuation of curren-cy, transnational corporations can hardly be expected to promote exports. If purchasing power is concentrated in the hands of a few, transnational corporations are unlikely to cater to the low-income groups.

The channeling of the activities of transnational corporations for development depends on a set of overall policies as well as deliberate policies toward these corporations. The conditions of success rest on an understanding of the functioning of the economy as a whole as well as the nature of transnational corporations and their responses to particular circumstances.

A most important constraint on the effectiveness of policies toward transnational corporations in most developing countries is their relatively weak bargaining position. It is true that the sovereign power of a state cannot be compared with the economic power of a transnational corporation. Even a small country can regulate its resident transnational corporations or nationalize them. The recent examples of the strong bargaining position of petroleum-producing countries illustrates the possibility that some small developing countries can have great bargaining power. Nevertheless, many host countries lack knowledge of precisely what they are bargaining about or for. They are frequently uncertain about their own resources and about the capabilities of the party at the opposite side of the bargaining table. Thus, a free-for-all encouragement of foreign investment may attract little net capital inflow. Even when a deliberate choice is being made among sources of investment, the alternatives open to them are often unknown. Over 80 percent of direct foreign investment of many developing countries originates from a single home country. Many new cooperative arrangements, such as joint ownership and control, management contracts, and coproduction arrangements, have hardly been explored.

The relatively new sources and novel forms are not, of course, always superior. Like new drugs the side effects may be less apparent or well known. The proliferation of foreign investors in manufacturing may, for example, also mean the introduction of a profusion of models and hamper standardization and economies of scale. The separation or "depackaging" of direct investment into simply the purchase of technology, the contracting for management services, and financing from other sources may inhibit the continuous supply of new technology and access to worldwide markets and finance. Fade-out arrangements may discourage long-term projects. Even general control and regulation require a degree of administrative competence and fairness so that they do not turn into instruments of bureaucratic obstruction and even corruption. Moreover, less stringent and more attractive conditions often exist in other host countries, especially in the developed countries.

The lacuna in international institutions

If the developing nations are often ill-equipped to make effective use of transnational corporations for development, international institutions have hardly begun to play a constructive role for this purpose. In theory, transnational corporations, being international in scope and effect, are a natural subject for international scrutiny. In fact, the existing institutions have not been designed for such a purpose. Only recently have questions been raised as to whether the international trade and money regimes have adequately taken into account the operations of transnational corporations, despite the evident importance of intracorporate transfers and capital movements to these regimes. Indeed, in contrast to trade and money, where the international community at least had the foresight to establish institutions and rules of the game and to consider how they might evolve in the light of changing requirements, no comparable arrangements have been made with respect to transnational corporations or international investment.

Proposals for the international control and regulation of transnational corporations through such an organization as the International Trade Organization (ITO), envisaged by the Havana Charter in 1948,[2] have not attracted the needed support mainly because a commensurable degree of coherence among nations and confidence in international institutions do not as yet exist. A more modest approach is thus indicated.

Agenda for international action

The international action currently under consideration is indeed modest and moderate.[3] The sharp tone and colorful rhetoric which frequently attract much attention in international debate are thus deceptive; they reflect more the mood of particular nations or the virtuosity of orators rather than actual prospects for action on a world scale.

Even at the regional level, where the interests of both home and host countries are represented[4] and the degree of homogeneity among countries is relatively high, no precipitous action appears to be in prospect. At the European Community level, where countries may be both home and host, the proposals for action on transnational corporations mainly concern the elimination of tax conflicts and evasion, the protection of workers in mass layoffs, the maintenance of competition, the disclosure of information on the activities of these corporations, and the adoption of a European Company Law.[5] It is recognized that such action will be fully effective only to the extent that rules at the international level exist for a homogeneous framework for operation of transnational corporations, whatever their origin and their field of activity.

At the Organisation for Economic Co-operation and Development (OECD), apart from considerations of the operations of transnational corporations by the various functional committees,[6] the consideration of a code of conduct is one of the first tasks of the Committee for International Investment and Multinational Enterprises created early in 1975.

It is significant that parallel initiatives are being pursued at the truly international level of the United Nations. The new impetus started with an Economic and Social Council resolution, adopted in 1972, calling for the appointment of a Group of Eminent Persons to study the role of multinational corporations and their impact on development and international relations. The purpose of the resolution is action-oriented.[7] In June 1974 the group issued its report which contains a series of recommendations which constituted a basis for international consideration and action.[8] On August 2, 1975, the Economic and Social Council adopted resolution 1908 (LVII) on the impact of transnational corporations on the development process and on international relations, this was followed by another resolution, 1913 (LVII), adopted on December 11, 1974.

The new international machinery

The key decision in these ECOSOC resolutions is the establishment of a Commission on Transnational Corporations and a United Nations Centre on Transnational Corporations. The Commission has three distinguishing characteristics. First, it is within the framework of the Economic and Social Council to the end that the functions of the council (envisaged by the United

Nations Charter) can be fulfilled better, both as a permanent machinery and a coordinating body. Second, the members consist of
high-level experts, although they are appointed by states rather
than by the Secretary-General as originally proposed by the Group
of Eminent Persons. Third, benefiting from the experience of the
Group of Eminent Persons, there would be consultation and hear-
ing procedures which would encourage interested parties, including transnational corporations, labor unions, consumer groups, and
scholars to be involved in the work and to present their views. At
the first session of the Commission in March 1975, a work program
was adopted which is annexed to this chapter for ready reference
(pp. 229-245).

Toward a general agreement on transnational corporations

A chief objective of the Commission is to formulate a Code of
Conduct[9] which could in the longer run evolve into a General
Agreement on transnational corporations. This clearly provides
for institutional evolution since the agreement would in itself call
for new international machinery. Insofar as such an agreement is
yet to be negotiated, the precise substance and form are open. The
agreement would undoubtedly include a set of rules concerning
transnational corporations and possibly also governments and
would make provisions for administering the rules. These rules
are admittedly more complicated than those concerning trade or
money partly because the issues involved are even more political.
For instance, the rights and duties of states and those of transnational corporations cannot be considered in a similar vein. Even
the economic issues are extremely complicated as they intertwine
with virtually all other issues, including trade and money matters.

There is, therefore, a dilemma: the rules might be so general as to
be meaningless or so specific and fragmented as to be ineffectual
in the large. The solution of the dilemma lies in an evolutionary
approach. As a first step, the rules of conduct or guidelines could
be stated in general terms. Even these would go beyond those now
in existence. For example, they would go further than the rules of
conduct drafted by private business (such as the International
Chamber of Commerce (ICC) Guidelines[10] and the Pacific Basin
Charter on International Investments),[11] or by a group of host
countries (such as the investment codes of the Andean Group),[12]
or those under discussion by a group of developed countries as the
Organisation for Economic Co-operation and Development[13] in
terms of country coverage or substance. Evidently, the rules

drafted and negotiated with a broader international participation would better reflect the interests of all parties concerned. While the developing host countries are well represented within the United Nations framework, the consensus of the home countries is essential if the rules are to have operational significance, and the cooperation of transnational corporations will facilitate smooth functioning and implementation of the rules.

Even as a first step, efforts need not be limited to the preparation of a set of general rules. A number of specific areas can be tackled and progress in these areas would constitute the building blocks for a general agreement in more concrete terms.

Indeed, in the field of taxation, rudiments of guidelines have already been drafted by a United Nations Expert Group on Tax Treaties between Developed and Developing Countries. These guidelines better reflect the interests of developing countries than does the pioneer work of the OECD.[14] Further work could refine and elaborate the guidelines and cover hitherto neglected areas. Tax evasion or avoidance and transfer pricing are already receiving increasing attention. More bold global approaches for alleviating or eliminating overlapping or underlapping of taxes may also be explored.[15]

In the area of restrictive business practices, work has already been initiated at the United Nations Conference on Trade and Development (UNCTAD) to prepare a draft of international guidelines and a model law aiming at the control of a number of these practices.[16] With respect to the transfer of technology, work has also been initiated by UNCTAD to prepare a draft code of conduct.[17]

In the field of labor, the International Labour Organization (ILO) has pioneered the negotiation of minimum international standards. A recent report by an ad hoc group of experts on multinational enterprises has stimulated further work in this area.[18]

With respect to legal issues, the United Nations Commission on International Trade Law has sought information from governments and international agencies and suggestions for future action.[19]

All this work and possible action are mutually complementary and can be drawn upon and coordinated in a concerted effort.

Design for better information

Whether in the field of taxation, restrictive business practices, transfer pricing, the transfer of technology, the general improvement of the contribution of transnational corporations to development, or the introduction of measures for accountability of these corporations, the availability of information is crucial to the understanding of the issues and the formulation of concrete action concerning them. Thus, measures to combat tax avoidance or evasion must be based on information on tax systems and on the payment and nonpayment of taxes by whom and in what categories. Artificial transfer pricing is revealed if accounting conventions are disclosed and book entries of the subsidiaries and headquarters can be compared with world prices. Rational choices of technologies can be made if alternatives and their implications are known. Regulation of transnational corporations must be based on an understanding of the operations and behavior of these corporations. Yet, much of the pertinent information is available neither to the international community nor to the countries concerned.

One of the first tasks of international action must, therefore, be the development of an information base. A United Nations Centre on Transnational corporations has therefore been established within the United Nations Secretariat so that the Commission on Transnational Corporations will receive the continuous support to fulfill its functions. Apart from the collection of existing information, some of the pertinent information will have to be carefully developed. For instance, corporate reports are mainly designed for the shareholders; they are not necessarily informative, from the point of view of the host or home countries, on questions such as employment creation, training of local labor at different levels of skill, or the precise technology transferred. The establishment of a system of International Standard Accounting (and the issuance of corporate reports with an additional column in accordance with the standard) and the disclosure of agreements concluded between governments and transnational corporations constitutes an important part of the work program.

At the same time, it is realized that certain kinds of information can be developed only through research or some investigatory process. For example, the possibility of artificial transfer pricing may not be revealed by standard reporting; it may only be discovered by a detailed evaluation of the record of the corporation.

Evidently it is neither possible nor desirable to compile all conceivable information. Where confidentiality is a consideration, the conditions of access and disclosure are also a subject of negotiation and must be carefully defined. At any rate the selection and analysis of information is a major international undertaking which must be carried out on a continuing basis. The capacity thus developed at the international level would constitute a key to intelligent deliberations by the international community, to technical cooperation with developing countries, and redressing the imbalance in the bargaining positions.

Measures for enforcement

The evolutionary character of the content of the rules of conduct also applies to their administration or enforcement. Thus, in the first stages, the international machinery may mainly serve the purpose of a forum in which opinions may be expressed and problems discussed. The existence of a set of rules, even in general terms, would provide a framework for the discussions and give substance to the concept of accountability.[20] It would also form the basis for review and reporting. When the rules are formalized into a General Agreement, more definitive procedures for consultation, investigation and accountability can be specified. Even here a fairly broad spectrum between a relatively loose machinery for enforcement, as in the General Agreement on Trade and Tariffs (GATT) and a more strictly defined one, as in the proposed ITO, can be visualized. For instance, complaints and conflicts could be dealt with by third-party study groups or by procedures for adjudication. Noncompliance can be dealt with by public disclosure, withdrawal of certain rights, or specific sanctions. These are not necessarily mutually exclusive, especially if progress in different areas is uneven. And many intermediate positions and mixes are possible.

Nor is the evolutionary process necessarily always in one direction. It is conceivable that preventive measures at the international, as well as the national and regional, levels may be so effective that the need for detailed control and regulation of the activities of transnational corporations may decrease after a point.

At the same time, some sequences appear to follow naturally. For instance, the registration of transnational corporations with the United Nations prior to the establishment of a general agreement or an international company law would imply an unwarranted stamp of international approval without adequate means of supervision or regulation. The establishment of international arbitration machinery before the acceptance by many host countries of the principle of arbitration involving disputes between a state and a private party is likely to be of limited application. The provision for petitions by governments and transnational corporations in disputes before a United Nations body presumes judicial functions for the international organization or at least a set of mutually accepted rules in a general agreement.

Concluding remarks

The inherent contradictions between the global requirements for efficiency and the nationalistic divisions, between the profit motive of a firm and the welfare objectives of the state, are apparent. Yet, in a pluralistic world, the choice is hardly ever one versus the other. Global welfare is certainly increasingly relevant on this small planet, but national interests remain paramount as independent nationhood is as yet a new experience for most of the world. Transnational corporations have no intrinsic claim for their existence other than for the service of society, but society will be deprived of an instrument of development if the functioning of transnational corporations is impaired without the creation of alternative instruments. Transnational corporations possess enormous capabilities which can be channeled for development, but few would make investments in countries where the need is most urgent, as in the least developed.

Within the international context it is not surprising that the weight of current opinion is both moderate and constructive, although it appears biased in favor of the adversaries to both extremes. While recognizing the primacy of national decision-making, the need for international action is also appreciated, precisely because there are possibilities of conflicts in goals and practices. In attempting to resolve the potential conflicts, the emphasis is placed on institutional arrangements within which the issues can be dealt with and procedures worked out. While some of the more controversial problems remain to be solved, these arrangements, if implemented, would constitute a pathbreaking step in international economic life. From the point of view of the international community as a whole, it would be the first time that the subject of transnational corporations would be considered as seriously as trade and money.

Viewed from the standpoint of host countries, an important countervailing power would have been established through the international community and their bargaining power would have been strengthened, especially by the broadening of alternatives, better information, and expanded technical cooperation. As for the home countries and transnational corporations, the development of meaningful dialogues with all parties concerned could reduce potential conflicts and lessen the chances of unilateral action. These potential benefits can be realized, however, only by serious preparation in all the technical aspects and by painstaking negotiations.

NOTES

[1] The definitions in this sentence are in accordance with Latin American usage; some other writers, however, use the terms "transnational" and "multinational" in the opposite sense. The discussion in this chapter illustrates why the concept of transnational corporation used in the international context is broader than that used for some particular purposes of research in a national or regional framework. As a general rule, the concept adopted should fit the facts and not define away important phenomena or problems. For example, a "transnational enterprise" as defined above would exclude many petroleum companies formed by international consortia and would raise questions about firms with different nationals on the board of directors, owned by many nationals and traded in various capital markets. An industrial corporation may exclude companies, such as ITT or Control Data, which derive a significant portion of earnings from insurance, finance, or other services, especially after mergers.

[2] United Nations Conference on Trade and Employment, *Final Act and Related Documents.*

[3] See also the views expressed at the Düsseldorf Conference on Multinational Corporations, Don Wallace, Jr., ed., *International Control of Investment: The Düsseldorf Conference on Multinational Corporations.*

[4] For regional programs of host countries, such as the Andean pact, see elsewhere in this Collection.

[5] Commission of the European Communities, "Multinational Undertakings and Community Regulations."

[6] Including fiscal, industry, and restrictive business committees. See for example, OECD, "Interim Report of the Industry Committee on International Enterprises," which summarizes the work of the Working Party on International Enterprises to the end of 1972 and was derestricted in February 1974.

[7] Resolution 1721 (LIII).

[8]United Nations, *Impact of Multinational Corporations on Development and on International Relations.* The group was assisted in its work by a report of the United Nations on *Multinational Corporations in World Development,* which contains a discussion of the dimensions of the problem as well as possible international programs of action.

[9]For further discussions, see my paper on "The Design of an International Code of Conduct for Transnational Corporations."

[10]International Chamber of Commerce, *Guidelines for International Investment.*

[11]Special International Committee on the Pacific Basin Charter, "The Pacific Basin Charter on International Investments," *Fortune,* Sept. 1972, 52-53.

[12]Andean Group, *Historia Documental del Acuerdo de Cartagena* (Lima; Junta del Acuerdo de Cartagena, n.d.).

[13]In 1973, the OECD began consideration of "guidelines" for government policies concerning transnational corporations and "standards of behavior" for these corporations. The issues have been discussed by the Executive Committee in Special Session. Both the Business and Industry Advisory Committee (BIAC) to the OECD, representing the business community, and the Trade Union Advisory Committee (TUAC) to the OECD, representing organized labor, have assisted in the work.

[14]United Nations, *Tax Treaties between Developed and Developing Countries,* (E.74.XVI.5); and Organisation for Economic Co-operation and Development, *Draft Double Taxation Convention.*

[15]See United Nations, *Tax Treaties between Developed and Developing Countries, Fifth Report.*

[16]See *Report of the Ad Hoc Group of Experts on Restrictive Business Practices,* United Nations document (TD/B/C.2/119). For a private effort, see also, Richard J. Fine, "The Control of Restrictive Business Practices in International Trade," pp. 635-676.

[17]The recognition of the importance of transfer of technology in the work of UNCTAD is indicated by the decision of the fourteenth session of the Trade and Development Board to transform the Intergovernmental Group entrusted with the matter into a permanent main Committee of the Board.

[18]See International Labour Office, *Multinational Enterprises and Social Policy.* The International Labour Office has also formulated a research project on the Impact of Multinational Firms on Employment and Incomes in the Developing Countries.

[19]See "Multinational Enterprises: Current Status of Work," mimeographed, United Nations document (A/CN.9/90), April 22, 1974.

[20]The concept of accountability is, therefore, also to be understood in the evolutionary sense, as the rules of conduct.

Excerpts from the Report on the First Session of the Commission on Transnational Corporations

Conclusions and recommendations of the Commission

Introduction

1. Taking fully into account General Assembly resolutions 3201 (S-VI) and 3202 (S-VI) of 1 May 1974 on the Declaration and the Program of Action for the establishment of a New International Economic Order, in particular the relevant provisions on transnational corporations, and resolution 3281 (XXIX) of 12 December 1974 on the Charter of Economic Rights and Duties of States, and giving due regard to the guidelines contained in those resolutions, the Commission on Transnational Corporations, in conformity with paragraph 7 of Economic and Social Council resolution 1913 (LVII) of 5 December 1974, is requested to submit a detailed program of work concerning the whole range of issues related to transnational corporations to the Council at its sixtieth session. Since that session will take place in the spring of 1976 and the Commission must meet again before that date, according to paragraph 2 of the same resolution, the Commission decided to establish a preliminary program of work at its current session so that the Information and Research Centre on Transnational Corporations could start operating as early as possible and to wait until the next session of the Commission, in early 1976, to formulate, in the light of accumulated experience, the detailed program of work that must be submitted to the Council at its sixtieth session.

2. The Commission will be the forum within the United Nations system for the comprehensive and in-depth consideration of issues relating to transnational corporations, without prejudice to the work undertaken within the United Nations in related fields.

Excerpted from the *Official Records: Fifty-ninth Session,* Supplement no. 12, of the United Nations Economic and Social Council, document E/5655 (New York, 1975).

3. The Commission desired that the Secretary-General should take early steps to set up the Information and Research Centre.

A. Identification of the areas of concern regarding the activities of transnational corporations

4. If the Commission and the Information and Research Centre are to serve all the interests of the countries concerned with the full range of issues relating to transnational corporations, and in particular the subject of the regulation and supervision of their activities, it is of the greatest importance that the areas of concern regarding the activities of transnational corporations be clearly spelled out.

5. The Commission decided during its first session to make a preliminary identification of areas of concern, fully recognizing that they might require subsequent additions and revisions. These areas of concern of host and home Governments will be found in annexes I and II of the present report. Issues requiring the attention of the Commission are identified also in annex III. The members of the Commission from the developing countries, the socialist countries and others intend that the areas of concern listed in annex I should serve as preliminary guidelines for the work of the Commission and the Information and Research Centre, while a number of countries intend that annex II should also serve a similar purpose. Annex III should also be considered for this objective. The Commission expects that the preliminary identification may lead, through future consultations and revisions, to the identification of areas of concern agreeable to all its members.

B. Draft program of work

6. The program of work of the Commission should be focused on the following five areas:

(a) Preliminary work with the purpose of formulating a code of conduct;

(b) Establishment of a comprehensive information system;

(c) Research on the political, economic, and social effects of the operations and practices of transnational corporations;

(d) Organization and coordination, at the request of Governments, of technical cooperation programs concerning transnational corporations;

(e) Work leading to a definition of transnational corporations.
7. In pursuance of the guidelines conveyed by the Economic and Social Council in paragraph 7 of its resolution 1913 (LVII), in accordance with which the detailed draft program of work should include a statement of its proposed priorities, the Commission has selected specific activities for priority attention, bearing in mind the limitations imposed by the budget on the tasks which the Information and Research Centre can undertake.

[8. An order of priority is assigned below in the work of the Commission.] *

C. Preliminary work with the objective of formulating a code of conduct

9. The Commission decided that among the various tasks it would undertake in the next few years the priority would be assigned to the formulation of the code of conduct [to be observed by] [dealing with] transnational corporations.

10. At a preliminary stage the Commission would concentrate on defining a set of fundamental rules of conduct, taking into account the principles contained in the document (E/C.10/L.2) submitted by a number of countries at the current session, as well as of any additional proposals outlining principles relevant to the issue that might be submitted in future by other countries.

11. In order to advance as much as possible the work toward that objective, the Information and Research Centre must undertake the following work in the immediate future and submit related reports at the second session of the Commission:
    (a) A comparative study of existing international codes of conduct or guidelines drafted with the purpose of influencing and/ or regulating the operations and practices of transnational corporations, including the study of relevant materials underlying such codes;
    (b) A comparative study of existing national and regional legislation and regulations enacted with the purpose of regulating

---

*As indicated in the introduction, this report, containing certain conclusions and recommendations, reflects the progress of work by the Commission on the elaboration of a detailed program of work and on its modalities of work. The texts between brackets have not yet been agreed upon.

the operations and activities of transnational corporations;

 (c) Suggestions as to possible methods of intersessional work by the Commission which would further the task of drafting a code of conduct;

 [(d) Collection and analysis of material relevant to the formulation of a code of conduct.]

D. Establishment of a comprehensive information system

12. The establishment of a comprehensive information system must have the following objectives:

 (a) To further understanding of the nature and the political, economic and social effects of the activities of transnational corporations in home countries and host countries and in international relations, particularly between developed and developing nations;

 (b) To strengthen the capacity of host countries, in particular of developing countries, in their dealings with transnational corporations;

 (c) To collect and analyse material relating to the [evolution and development] [formulation] of a code of conduct.

13. Considering that there was a vast amount of information available in Governments, academic centers, business councils, and international organizations regarding transnational corporations and their activities, a high-priority task to be undertaken by the Information and Research Centre would be a survey, by means of a questionnaire and other methods, to determine what information on transnational corporations was available, and where, throughout the world. The survey would permit identification of sources of information at the national and international level, be they governmental, private or academic organizations; the periodicity on which this information was collected and published; the level of aggregation of statistical data available; information disclosure requirements; experience of other international organizations in the collection of information concerning the nature and activities of transnational corporations.

14. Work for the survey should be started as soon as the Information and Research Centre obtained the necessary technical staff, so that at the second session of the Commission a preliminary report on the subject could be examined by its members. On the basis of the results of the survey, the Information and Research Centre

should be able to point out gaps and problems regarding the a-
vailability, disclosure, analysis and dissemination of information,
so that at the next session, member countries of the Commission
could decide on priority areas for the collection of information in
accordance with specific areas of concern.

15. The Information and Research Centre should not necessarily
wait until the survey was ready to start collecting information.
Therefore, in its first years of operation, the Information and Research Centre should start making efforts in two directions:

(a) Development of a classification system of information relevant to concerns of member countries, in particular, but not limited to, those of the developing countries;

(b) Collection of information of a general or specific nature
at the aggregate and enterprise levels on the following priority areas, where information gaps were most pressing:

1. Transfer pricing and taxation;

2. Short-term capital movements by transnational corporations;

3. Restrictive business practices (other than those already
covered by the United Nations Conference on Trade and Development (UNCTAD));

4. Corporate ownership and alternative forms of business participation;

5. Market concentration (giving special consideration to acquisition of participation and merger);

6. Relative use by transnational corporations of home, international and host country's financial markets in their operations
and investments;

7. Alternative forms of management and control;

8. Political activities of transnational corporations;

9. Social impact of transnational corporations;

10. Impact of transnational corporations on freedom of labor
organizations, trade union rights, labor standards and working
conditions;

[11. The effect on operations of transnational corporations
of the presence or absence of a stable investment climate.]

16. The information should be obtained in the first instance from
relevant bodies of the United Nations system. Wherever the United Nations system as such was not itself collecting any of the information, the Information and Research Centre should collect it
directly from the appropriate sources.

[17. In order to ensure that the information system should be as comprehensive as possible, the Economic and Social Council should invite all States Members of the United Nations to cooperate with the Information and Research Centre in its task of collecting information and to examine the adequacy of their domestic legislative and regulatory powers to obtain from transnational corporations information about their operations and activities.]

E. Studies on the political, economic and social effects of the operations and practices of transnational corporations

18. The Commission should undertake studies concerning specific subjects that require analysis, in the light of the report which the Information and Research Centre would submit in 1976 to the Commission on available information and in the light of the state of research on transnational corporations by public, private and academic research institutions throughout the world.

19. With a view to facilitating the aggregation and comparison of financial data relating to the operations of transnational corporations, the Information and Research Centre should establish an Expert Group of professional accountants, auditors and financial managers to explore the possibility of working out standard forms for the presentation of the financial relations between transnational corporations and the associated enterprises.

20. In order to determine the current state of research on those areas of concern regarding the activities of transnational corporations, a simultaneous survey to that in the field of information, as mentioned in paragraph 13 above, should be undertaken and completed in the near future. Such a survey should attempt to establish what significant research on transnational corporations had been undertaken in recent years related with the areas of concern, what research was currently under way, and whether the information was complete and comprehensive. A preliminary report should be submitted at the second session of the Commission in 1976.

21. Meanwhile the Information and Research Centre should concentrate on research on the following areas:
(a) Studies on the role and effects of transnational corporations in sectors of economic activity that so far had been insufficiently covered by research projects, such as in the case of

agricultural, extractive, land development, shipping, trade, banking, insurance and tourism activities;

(b) Obstacles to strengthening the bargaining capacity of Governments in their relations with transnational corporations;

(c) Lessons to be obtained from national and regional legislation, mechanisms and arrangements that had permitted the strengthening of the bargaining capacity of Governments in their relations with transnational corporations;

(d) A study of the measures adopted by host countries to strengthen the competitive position of national enterprises vis-à-vis transnational corporations;

(e) Studies described in paragraph 11 above to support the work directed toward the formulation of a code of conduct [to be observed by] [dealing with] transnational corporations;

(f) Studies of the political, economic, and social impact of the operations and activities of the transnational corporations.

F. Technical cooperation

22. The Commission decided to endorse the general approach to the program of technical cooperation as described in paragraphs 30-49 of the report of the Secretary-General (E/C.10/2). However, a more detailed program would have to be formulated in the light of the aforementioned areas of concern and of the specific requirements of developing countries.

23. Each country concerned with the operations and practices of transnational corporations should inform the Information and Research Centre before the end of 1975 what its basic requirements of technical assistance were both in the fields of manpower training and consultancy services, so that the Centre could prepare a proposal for the next session of the Commission, taking into consideration the overall requirements of technical assistance and the availability of funds and specialized [staff resources] [persons] from the United Nations system. The ultimate responsibility for the technical cooperation program should lie with the Centre.

G. Definition of transnational corporations

24. The Information and Research Centre would endeavor to collect available definitions on transnational corporations and background work that had been done by the Organisation for Economic

Co-operation and Development (OECD), other international organizations and some well-known academic centers throughout the world.

25. While such work was being collected, the Information and Research Centre should concentrate on identifying the common characteristics of the transnational corporations which played a significant role in the internationalization of the world economy, without prejudice to such definition as might eventually be proposed. Such a study should cover at least the five leading transnational corporations in each industrial sector.

H. Modalities

26. The Commission discussed the identification by the Secretary-General and all States Members of the United Nations of persons who might later, as required by its program of work, be considered for selection by the Commission to assist it and participate in its discussions in a manner to be decided by it at its second session. It suggested that the Secretary-General and States Members might, in the meantime, begin to give preliminary consideration to identifying persons they might wish to suggest to the Commission at the appropriate time.

27. The Commission recommended that summary records be provided for its future sessions. At its 11th meeting, the Commission heard a statement of the financial implications (E/C.10/5) of the recommendation.

Annex 1
List of areas of concern regarding the operations and activities of transnational corporations
Note submitted by the Group of 77

1. Preferential treatment demanded by transnational corporations (TNCs) in relation to national enterprises.

2. Lack of adjustments by TNCs to the legislation of the host countries in the matters *inter alia* of foreign investment and policies concerning credits exchange, fiscal matters, prices and polimercial matters, industrial property, and labor policies.

3. The negative attitudes by TNCs toward the renegotiations of original concessions if such exist and if this should be considered necessary by the Government of the host country.

4. The refusal of TNCs to accept exclusive jurisdiction of domestic law in cases of litigation.

5. Direct or indirect interference in the internal affairs of host countries by TNCs.

6. Requests by TNCs to Governments of the country of origin to intercede with the host Government, with actions of a political or economic nature in support of their private interests.

7. The refusal of TNCs to accept the exclusive jurisdiction of domestic law in the question of compensation on nationalization.

8. Extension by TNCs of laws and regulations of the country of origin to the host country.

9. The activities of TNCs as instruments of foreign policy, including for intelligence purposes, contrary to the interests of the host country.

10. The contribution of TNCs in the maintenance of racist and colonial regime and support of policies of *apartheid* and foreign occupation.

11. The role of TNCs in the illegal traffic of arms.

12. Obstruction by TNCs of the efforts of the host country to assume its rightful responsibility and exercise effective control over the development and management of its resources in contravention of the accepted principle of permanent sovereignty of countries over their natural resources.

13. Tendency of TNCs not to conform to the national policies, objectives and priorities for development set forth by the Governments of host countries.

14. Withholding of information of their activities by TNCs making host countries unable to carry out effective supervision and regulation of those activities.

15. Excessive outflow of financial resources from host countries due to practices of TNCs and failure to generate expected foreign exchange earnings in the host country.

16. Acquisition and control by TNCs of national, locally capitalized enterprises through controlled provision of technology among other means.

17. Superimposition of imported technology without any adaptation to local conditions, creating various types of distortions.

18. Failure by TNCs to promote research and development in host countries.

19. Obstruction or limitation by TNCs to access by host countries

to world technology.

20. Imposition of restrictive commercial practices, *inter alia,* on affiliates in developing countries as a price for technical know-how.

21. Lack of respect of the sociocultural identity of host countries.

Annex 2

Areas of concern which relate to relations between transnational corporations and governments

Note submitted by the delegations of France, the Federal Republic of Germany, Italy, the United Kingdom of Great Britain and Northern Ireland, and the United States of America

Preamble

1. The following is a selection of areas of concern which, in the opinion of the delegations having prepared this document, deserve particular consideration, although not all of these delegations necessarily share all the concerns mentioned herein. These cover broadly effects on economic and social development of the activities and operations of transnational corporations (TNCs) within the framework set by Governments, including positive and negative impacts.

List of areas of concern

2. Areas of concern of particular importance are set out below. The list is nonexhaustive and may be added to or modified in the light of experience.

(1) The extent to which host country legislation and regulations may discriminate (either in favor of TNCs or against TNCs as compared to domestic enterprises) in the treatment of enterprises on the basis of whether or not such enterprises are under foreign control; the extent to which any such discriminatory treatment affects the activities of TNCs as well as the contributions of TNCs to the development objectives of host countries.

(2) The extent to which expropriation of properties undertaken for public purposes related to internal requirements of the countries concerned are nondiscriminatory in application and are accompanied by prompt, adequate and effective compensation.

(3) The extent to which recourse to international arbitration (including that provided by the International Centre for Settlement of Investment Disputes) or other dispute settlement organizations or procedures play a role in the settlement of disputes arising out of the activities of TNCs.

(4) The effect of the presence or absence of a stable investment climate as a factor affecting the ability of TNCs to contribute effectively to development.

(5) The observance and nonobservance of contracts and agreements between TNCs and Governments, the consequential issues which arise in the case of nonobservance by either party, and the role which contracts may play in the creation of a stable investment climate.

(6) The role which freedom or restriction of establishment by TNCs in countries can have in assisting or hampering economic and industrial development.

(7) The extent to which domestic laws, regulations and practices on social policies help or hinder development of labor relations activities in TNCs.

(8) The extent to which the social policies practised by TNCs help or hinder development of labor relations activities in countries in which they operate.

(9) The effects of TNC operations and activities on employment possibilities and whether these give rise to benefits (e.g., job creation) or nonbenefits (e.g., strain on indigenous resources of host countries).

(10) The extent to which the presence or absence of declared points of contact within both TNCs and host Governments have assisted or hindered development of an effective and continuing dialogue between the parties concerned.

(11) The effect of TNC operations and activities on the social and cultural identities of host countries, the positive or negative impacts which these can have on such countries and the extent to which host countries make their expectations known in these respects.

(12) The extent to which existing codes of conduct and guidelines concerned with any aspect of the range of issues relating to the activities of TNCs may already exist, including the study of materials underlying such codes and guidelines, commentaries thereon and the implementation and/or effects of such codes and guidelines upon TNCs and Governments.

(13) Issues relating to cooperation between host Governments and TNCs to ensure the fullest possible attainment of their respective objectives when TNCs invest in host countries, including

the extent to which TNCs and host countries state their needs and objectives in a sufficiently clear manner and how such cooperation may be improved for their mutual benefit.

(14) The need to define more clearly the areas of acceptable and unacceptable political activities on the part of TNCs.

(15) The role played by TNCs and Governments in the transfer of technology to host countries, including the types of technology involved, conditions imposed by TNCs and Governments in connexion with such transfers, and the positive and negative effects of technology transfers and the framework within which they are made on host country development objectives and the viability of the investment concerned.

(16) The role played by TNCs in fostering development and growth of related industries in host countries and the positive and negative effects of the activities of TNCs on the existing patterns of indigenous supply and production.

(17) The extent to which TNCs endeavor to participate in or ignore local business and regional organizations of host countries, host country regulation of such participation where these exist, and the consequences of TNC and host country actions in this area.

(18) The extent to which TNCs seek to promote indigenization of their operations and activities in host countries, including appointment of staff at all levels, and the extent to which policies adopted by host Governments help or hinder this process.

(19) The extent to which TNCs may help to improve or make worse the working conditions of employees, including workers' health and safety, and the extent to which host Governments make clear their requirements and/or expectations in these respects.

(20) Identification of those countries having declared policies on conservation and protection of the environment, and the extent to which these may or may not be observed by TNCs operating therein.

(21) The appropriateness or otherwise of the forms in which TNCs allow for participation in the equity of their operations in host countries, and relevant host country policies and the extent to which these are made known.

(22) The extent to which TNCs take host countries' interests into account in the repatriation of capital, remittance of profits, payments of dividends, royalties, and management fees, the extent to which the levels at which these are made are constrained by Governments and the effect this may have on the development process.

(23) The extent to which domestic commercial policies (e.g., in relation to restrictive business practices) have been developed by host Governments, whether appropriate machinery has been set up by them within which TNCs and Governments may discuss problems of mutual interest and, if so, the extent to which TNCs and/or Governments use these facilities when it would be appropriate for them to do so.

Annex 3
Issues requiring the attention of the Commission and the Information and Research Centre on transnational corporations
Note submitted by the People's Republic of Bulgaria, the German Democratic Republic, the Ukrainian Soviet Socialist Republic, and the Union of Soviet Socialist Republics

Supporting the list of areas of concern regarding the activities of transnational corporations (TNCs) contained in Annex 1 the aforementioned socialist countries propose the following issues requiring the attention of the Commission and the Information Research Centre:

1. The negative attitude of TNCs toward the freedom of organization of workers, labor conditions and the full exercise of trade union rights.

2. The negative impact of TNCs on economic relations between States, particularly by short-term massive capital movements and price policy, aggravating inflation, the monetary and the raw material situation.

Appendix:
Statistical Tables

Reprinted with permission from United Nations, *Multinational Corporations in World Development* (New York, 1973), document number ST/ECA/190 and Corr. 1. Since not all tables from the United Nations' document have been reprinted, the numbering of the tables has been adapted.

Table 1. The 650 largest industrial corporations[a] of the market economies, by country and by size (sales in millions of dollars), 1971

Country[b]	Number of corporations with sales[c] of					
	Over 10,000	5,000 - 10,000	1,000 - 4,999	500 - 999	300 - 499	Total
United States........	3	9	115	115	116	358
Japan...............	-	-	16	31	27	74
United Kingdom.......	-	1	14	22	24	61
Federal Republic of Germany............	-	-	18	10	17	45
France..............	-	-	13	9	10	32
Canada..............	-	-	2	7	8	17
Sweden..............	-	-	2	6	5	13
Switzerland.........	-	-	4	2	2	8
Italy...............	-	-	4	2	-	6
Netherlands.........	-	1	1	2	2	6
Belgium.............	-	-	1	2	2	5
Australia...........	-	-	1	1	2	4
South Africa........	-	-	-	1	2	3
Spain...............	-	-	-	-	3	3
Argentina...........	-	-	-	1	1	2
Austria.............	-	-	-	-	2	2
India...............	-	-	-	1	1	2
Brazil..............	-	-	1	-	-	1
Luxembourg..........	-	-	1	-	-	1
Mexico..............	-	-	1	-	-	1
Netherlands Antilles.	-	-	-	1	-	1
Zaire...............	-	-	-	-	1	1
Zambia..............	-	-	-	-	1	1
Netherlands-United Kingdom.....	1	1	-	-	-	2
United Kingdom-Italy.	-	-	1	-	-	1
TOTAL, number of corporations......	4	12	195	213	226	650
TOTAL, sales (millions of dollars)........	76,131	83,807	379,297	147,703	86,069	773,007

Source: Centre for Development Planning, Projections and Policies of the Department of Economic and Social Affairs of the United Nations Secretariat, based on the listing in Fortune, July and August 1972, of the 500 largest industrial corporations in the United States and the 300 largest industrial corporations outside the United States.

a/ Almost all the corporations included are multinational, according to the definition adopted in the text.

b/ Countries are arranged in descending order of total number of corporations listed.

c/ Sales are based on figures adjusted by Fortune and are not necessarily identical with those reported by corporations.

Table 2. Selected multinational manufacturing corporations[a] of
market economies: a profile of foreign content [b] of the
corporation's total operations and assets

(Number)

Foreign content	Sales	Assets	Production	Earnings	Employment	Total
More than 75 per cent						
United Kingdom.....	2	1	-	3	2	8
Switzerland........	3	-	-	-	3	6
United States......	-	-	2	3	-	5
Sweden.............	3	-	-	-	-	3
Belgium............	2	-	-	-	-	2
Netherlands-						
United Kingdom...	1	-	-	-	1	2
50 - 74 per cent						
United States......	2	2	1	7	7	19
United Kingdom.....	-	-	-	1	-	1
Federal Republic of						
Germany..........	4	-	-	-	-	4
Sweden.............	3	-	-	-	-	3
Japan..............	2	-	-	-	2	4
France.............	2	-	-	-	-	2
Italy..............	1	-	-	-	-	1
Netherlands........	-	-	-	-	2	2
Belgium............	1	-	-	-	-	1
Brazil.............	1	-	-	-	-	1
25 - 49 per cent						
United States......	14	5	3	7	11	40
Japan..............	15	-	-	-	1	16
Federal Republic of						
Germany..........	13	-	-	-	1	14
France.............	8	-	-	-	-	8
United Kingdom.....	-	-	-	2	-	2
Italy..............	2	1	-	-	-	3
Sweden.............	3	-	-	-	-	3
Belgium............	1	-	-	-	-	1
10 - 24 per cent						
United States......	6	4	-	2	1	13
Federal Republic of						
Germany..........	7	-	-	-	-	7
France.............	6	-	-	-	-	6
Japan..............	2	-	-	-	-	2
United Kingdom.....	-	-	-	-	-	-
Less than 10 per cent						
United States......	1	5	2	-	2	10
Federal Republic of						
Germany..........	3	-	-	-	-	3
Sweden.............	1	-	-	-	-	1
TOTAL						193

Source: Centre for Development Planning, Projections and Policies of the Department of Economic and Social Affairs of the United Nations Secretariat, based on table 1; Belgium's 500 largest companies (Brussels, 1969); Entreprise, No. 878, 6-12 July, 1972; Rolf Jungnickel, "Wie multinational sind die deutschen Unternehmen?" in Wirtschafts dienst, No. 4, 1972; Wilhelm Grotkopp and Ernst Schmacke, Die Grossen 500 (Düsseldorf, 1971); Commerzbank, Auslandsfertigung (Frankfurt, 1971); Bank of Tokyo, The President Directory 1973 (Tokyo, 1972); Financial Times, 30 March 1973; Vision, 15 December 1971; Sveriges 500 Största Företag (Stockholm, 1970); Max Iklé, Die Schweiz als internationaler Bank- und Finanzplatz (Zürich, 1970); Schweizer Bankgesellschaft, Die grössten Unternehmen der Schweiz (1971); Financial Times, 15 May 1973; J.M. Stopford, "The foreign investments of United Kingdom firms", London Graduate School of Business Studies, 1973, (mimeo); Multinational Corporations, Hearings before the Subcommittee on International Trade of the Committee on Finance, United States Senate, 93rd Congress, First Session, February/March 1973; Nicholas K. Bruck and Francis A. Lees, "Foreign content of United States corporate activities", Financial Analyst Journal, September-October 1966; Forbes, 15 May 1973; Chemical and Engineering News, 20 December 1971; Moody's Industrial Manual, 1973; Sidney E. Rolfe, The International Corporation (Paris, 1969); Charles Levinson, Capital, Inflation and the Multinationals (London, 1971); Yearbook of International Organizations, 12th ed., 1968-1969, and 13th ed., 1970-1971; Institut für Marxistische Studien und Forschung, Internationale Konzerne und Arbeiterklasse (Frankfurt, 1971); Heinz Aszkenazy, Les grandes sociétés européennes (Brussels, 1971); Mirovaja ekonomika i mezdunarodnyje otnosenija, No. 9, 1970.

a/ Selected from the 650 largest industrial corporations of table 1, for which information on at least one measure of foreign content could be obtained. When information could be obtained on more than one measure, the highest figure was used to classify the corporation according to its percentage of foreign content.

b/ "Foreign content" refers to the ratio of the value of foreign sales, assets, production, earnings, or number of foreign employees with respect to the totals.

Table 3. Foreign content of operations and assets of manufacturing
corporations of market economies with sales of over $1 billion, 1971

Rank[a]	Company	Nationality	Total sales (millions of dollars)	Foreign content as percentage of					Number of subsidiary countries[c]
				Sales[b]	Production	Assets	Earnings	Employment	
1	General Motors	USA	28,264	19[i]	..[e]	15[g]	19[h]	27[e]	21
2	Standard Oil (N.J.)	USA	18,701	50[i]	81[e]	52[h]	52[i]	...	25
3	Ford Motors	USA	16,433	26[i]	36[h]	40[i]	24[i]	48[i]	30
4	Royal Dutch/Shell Group	Neth.-UK	12,734	79[i]	...	..[n]	..[i]	70[i]	43
5	General Electric	USA	9,429	16[i]	...	15[i]	20[i]	...	32
6	International Business Machines	USA	8,274	39[i]	...	27[h]	50[i]	36[e]	80
7	Mobil Oil	USA	8,243	45[i]	..[e]	46[h]	51[i]	51[h]	62
8	Chrysler	USA	7,999	24[i]	22[e]	31[i]	..[e]	24[e]	26
9	Texaco	USA	7,529	40[i]	65[e]	..[n]	25[e]	..[i]	30
10	Unilever	Neth.-UK	7,483	80[i]	...	60[n]	...	94[i]	31
11	International Telephone and Telegraph Corp	USA	7,346	42[i]	60[h]	61[h]	35[i]	72[h]	40
12	Western Electric	USA	6,045	..[i]	..[e]	..[n]	..[i]	...	...
13	Gulf Oil	USA	5,940	45[i]	75[e]	38[n]	21[i]	..[i]	61
14	British Petroleum	UK	5,191	88[i]	...	...	...	83[i]	52
15	Philips' Gloeilampenfabrieken	Neth.	5,189	...	67[h]	53[h]	...	73[i]	29
16	Standard Oil of Calif.	USA	5,143	45[i]	46[i]	9[h]	43[h]	29[h]	26
17	Volkswagenwerk	FRG	4,967	69[i]	25[i]	...	...	18[i]	12
18	United States Steel	USA	4,928	...	...	...	...	...	...
19	Westinghouse Electric	USA	4,630	...	...	...	...	...	...
20	Nippon Steel	Japan	4,088	31[e]	...	...	...	2[e]	5
21	Standard Oil (Ind.)	USA	4,054	...	...	16[e]	...	...	24
22	Shell Oil (subsidiary of Royal Dutch/Shell)	USA	3,892	...	...	...	...	...	...
23	E.I. du Pont de Nemours	USA	3,848	18[i]	12[n]	12[e]	...	..[i]	20
24	Siemens	FRG	3,815	39[i]	17[i]	...	...	23[i]	52
25	ICI (Imperial Chemical Industries)	UK	3,717	35[i]	42[h]	25[h]	...	27[i]	46
26	RCA	USA	3,711	...	...	...	...	...	18
27	Hitachi	Japan	3,633	...	...	...	...	...	...
28	Goodyear Tire and Rubber	USA	3,602	30[e]	...	22[e]	30[e]	..[h]	22
29	Nestle	Switz.	3,541	98[i]	...	90[h]	...	96[h]	15
30	Farbwerke Hoechst	FRG	3,487	42[i]	17[i]	..[j]	...	...	43
31	Daimler-Benz	FRG	3,460	44[i]	12[i]	28[i]	...	...	12
32	Ling-Temco-Vought	USA	3,359	..[e]	...	..[e]	...	..[e]	...
33	Toyota Motors	Japan	3,308	31[e]	...	1[i]	...	11[e]	6
34	Montedison	Italy	3,270	37[h]	...	...	...	...	14
35	British Steel	UK	3,216	...	...	...	...	...	18
36	BASF	FRG	3,210	47[i]	17[i]	..[n]	..[i]	18[i]	14
37	Procter and Gamble	USA	3,178	25[i]	...	16[n]	25[i]	...	24
38	Atlantic Richfield	USA	3,135	...	...	...	...	...	12
39	Mitsubishi Heavy Industries	Japan	3,129	...	...	...	...	...	...
40	Nissan Motor	Japan	3,129	28[e]	...	1[e]	...	6[e]	10
41	Continental Oil	USA	3,051	...	...	20[d]	...	...	27
42	Boeing	USA	3,040	..[i]	..[n]	..[n]	..[e]	..[n]	...
43	Union Carbide	USA	3,038	29[i]	25[n]	26[n]	22[e]	43[h]	34
44	International Harvester	USA	3,016	25[i]	19[h]	26[h]	10[e]	32[e]	20
45	Swift	USA	2,996	16[i]	...	...	...	...	...
46	Eastman Kodak	USA	2,976	33[k]	20[h]	27[k]	19[i]	40[k]	25

Rank[a]	Company	Nationality	Total sales (millions of dollars)	Foreign content as percentage of: Sales[b]	Production	Assets	Earnings	Employment	Number of subsidiary countries[c]
47	Bethlehem Steel.......	USA	2,964	2[e]	...	...	...	...	...
48	Kraftco..............	USA	2,960	...	...	...	...	...	16
49	Fiat..................	Italy	2,943	36[j]	...	43[j]	...	...	25
50	August Thyssen-Hütte..	FRG	2,904	21[j]	...	...	...	...	17
51	Lockheed Aircraft.....	USA	2,852	3[d]	...	...	...	...	10
52	Tenneco..............	USA	2,841	...	...	...	...	...	14
53	British Leyland Motors	UK	2,836	14[j]	...	...	...	12[j]	33
54	Renault..............	France	2,747	41[k]	...	...	...	...	23
55	AEG-Telefunken........	FRG	2,690	29[j]	8[j]	...	...	10[j]	31
56	Matsushita Electric Industrial..........	Japan	2,687	23[k]	...	...	...	1[k]	27
57	Bayer.................	FRG	2,649	54[j]	19[j]	...	...	16[j]	3
58	Greyhound.............	USA	2,616	...	...	...	...	...	...
59	Tokyo Shibaura Electric............	Japan	2,553	13[k]	...	1[k]	...	15[k]	22
60	Firestone Tire and Rubber..............	USA	2,484	...	...	...	26[e]	24[d]	33
61	Litton Industries.....	USA	2,466	17[j]	...	...	...	...	13
62	Pechiney Ugine Kuhlmann............	France	2,462	12[k]	...	...	...	...	29
63	Occidental Petroleum..	USA	2,400	46[j]	...	...	...	...	21
64	Cie Francaise des Petroles............	France	2,395	49[k]	...	...	...	...	28
65	Dunlop Pirelli Union..	Italy-UK	2,365	52[k]	...	...	87[k]	...	28
66	Phillips Petroleum....	USA	2,363	...	42[e]	...	...	...	37
67	Akzo..................	Neth.	2,307	84[i]	...	...	...	66[i]	19
68	General Foods.........	USA	2,282	21[j]	...	18[h]	3[e]	...	20
69	British-American Tobacco............	UK	2,262	93[j]	100[i]	82[j]	92[h]	84[j]	54
70	General Electric......	UK	2,218	24[j]	10[h]	...	...	13[j]	36
71	North American Rockwell............	USA	2,211	...	...	...	...	...	...
72	Rhone Poulenc.........	France	2,181	47[i]	24[h]	...	...	...	27
73	Caterpillar Tractor...	USA	2,175	53[j]	14[h]	25[g]	...	17[d]	14
74	ENI...................	Italy	2,172	...	...	...	...	18[i]	39
75	National Coal Board...	UK	2,159	-	-	-	-	-	-
76	Nippon Kokan..........	Japan	2,122	29[k]	...	...	...	1[k]	4
77	BHP (Broken Hill Proprietary)........	Australia	2,100	-	-	-	-	-	-
78	Singer................	USA	2,099	37[j]	...	54[h]	75[j]	66[h]	30
79	Monsanto..............	USA	2,087	24[j]	...	25[d]	31[j]	...	23
80	Continental Can.......	USA	2,082	...	...	...	...	...	11
81	Borden................	USA	2,070	7[d]	...	12[d]	13[d]	...	...
82	McDonnell Douglas.....	USA	2,069	...	...	...	...	...	...
83	Dow Chemical..........	USA	2,053	40[j]	25[h]	...	45[j]	22[d]	24
84	W.R. Grace............	USA	2,049	35[j]	34[h]	...	39[j]	60[e]	18
85	Ruhrkohle.............	FRG	2,043	22[j]	...	...	...	...	...
86	United Aircraft.......	USA	2,029	11[d]	...	...	...	...	...
87	Rapid American........	USA	1,991	...	...	...	...	...	...
88	Union Oil of Calif....	USA	1,981	...	...	...	...	8[d]	...
89	International Paper...	USA	1,970	10[i]	...	...	...	...	11
90	Gutehoffnungshütte....	FRG	1,962	38[i]	...	...	...	...	19
91	Xerox.................	USA	1,961	30[j]	...	...	38[j]	38[j]	23
92	Honeywell.............	USA	1,946	35[k]	...	20[d]	...	24[d]	24
93	Sun Oil...............	USA	1,939	...	...	...	...	...	21
94	Saint-Gobain-Pont-à Mousson............	France	1,914	19[k]	...	...	...	...	13
95	American Can..........	USA	1,897	...	...	...	...	...	24
96	General Dynamics......	USA	1,869	...	...	...	...	...	16

Rank[a]	Company	Nationality	Total sales (millions of dollars)	Foreign content as percentage of: Sales[b]	Production	Assets	Earnings	Employment	Number of subsidiary countries[c]
97	Ciba-Geigy............	Switz.	1,843	98[i]	...	...	...	71[h]	37
98	Krupp-Konzern.........	FRG	1,843	23[j]	3[j]	...	...	3[j]	15
99	Minnesota Mining and Manufacturing...	USA	1,829	36[j]	30[h]	29[h]	29[h]	40[h]	29
100	Beatrice Foods........	USA	1,827	4[d]	...	...	5[d]	...	13
101	ELF Group.............	France	1,825	...	...	...	...	...	...
102	Mannesmann............	FRG	1,823	41[j]	11[j]	...	...	12[j]	15
103	R.J. Reynolds Industries..........	USA	1,816	...	...	...	...	...	...
104	Cities Service........	USA	1,810	...	...	...	...	...	25
105	Citroën...............	France	1,792	33[k]	...	...	...	...	13
106	Bolse Cascade.........	USA	1,786	...	...	...	...	...	...
107	Ralston Purina........	USA	1,746	...	...	...	...	...	26
108	Sperry Rand...........	USA	1,739	34[j]	...	28[h]	...	42[h]	27
109	Coca-Cola.............	USA	1,729	31[j]	...	30[d]	11[d]	...	11
110	Burlington Industries.	USA	1,727	4[h]	...	8[h]	...	...	...
111	Cie Générale d' Electricité.........	France	1,699	20[k]	...	...	...	...	14
112	Courtaulds............	UK	1,696	22[j]	...	...	...	16[j]	31
113	Armco Steel...........	USA	1,696	...	...	3[d]	...	11[d]	...
114	Consolidated Foods....	USA	1,689	...	...	...	...	...	10
115	Peugeot...............	France	1,685	36[k]	...	...	...	...	...
116	Uniroyal..............	USA	1,678	27[j]	...	30[h]	75[j]	...	20
117	American Brands.......	USA	1,627	...	...	...	...	...	...
118	Ashland Oil...........	USA	1,614	1[d]	...	4[d]	2[d]	2[d]	17
119	Bendix................	USA	1,613	49[e]	14[h]	10[h]	...	...	20
120	Robert Bosch..........	FRG	1,607	39[j]	8[j]	...	...	20[j]	23
121	ARBED.................	Luxembourg	1,604	...	...	...	...	...	...
122	Textron...............	USA	1,604	26[d]	...	...	...	...	13
123	U.S. Plywood-Champion Papers....	USA	1,600	...	...	...	...	...	...
124	Brown Boveri..........	Switz.	1,599	76[j]	...	...	...	82[h]	11
125	Sumitomo Metal Industries.........	Japan	1,598	37[k]	...	...	...	...	3
126	Gulf and Western Industries.........	USA	1,566	...	...	...	...	...	14
127	TRW...................	USA	1,544	...	...	...	...	...	16
128	Associated British Foods..............	UK	1,525	32[j]	...	...	34[j]	24[j]	...
129	National Steel.......	USA	1,522	...	...	...	...	...	...
130	Owens-Illinois.......	USA	1,508	...	...	10[d]	9[d]	27[d]	15
131	CPC International....	USA	1,500	50[j]	46[h]	27[h]	51[j]	...	22
132	Michelin.............	France	1,500	50[i]	...	...	...	...	13
133	Rheinstahl...........	FRG	1,483	23[i]	...	...	...	...	...
134	Kobe Steel...........	Japan	1,466	...	...	...	...	...	...
135	National Cash Register...........	USA	1,466	45[j]	41[h]	35[h]	60[h]	...	42
136	United Brands........	USA	1,449	...	...	...	...	...	...
137	Georgia-Pacific......	USA	1,447	...	...	...	...	...	...
138	Aluminium Co. of America............	USA	1,441	...	...	7[d]	...	...	28
139	Hoesch...............	FRG	1,431	26[i]	...	...	...	...	14
140	Alcan Aluminium......	Canada	1,431	...	...	42[h]	...	...	33[g]
141	American Home Products............	USA	1,429	19[d]	...	14[d]	14[d]	...	27
142	American Standard....	USA	1,410	36[j]	28[h]	30[h]	33[j]	...	21
143	U.S. Industries......	USA	1,407	45[e]	...	...	5[e]	...	...
144	Hoffmann-LaRoche.....	Switz.	1,402	80[j]	...	...	...	83[h]	...
145	Standard Oil (Ohio)..	USA	1,394	...	...	...	...	...	...

Rank[a]	Company	Nationality	Total sales (millions of dollars)	Sales[b]	Production	Assets	Earnings	Employment	Number of subsidiary countries[c]
146	Republic Steel........	USA	1,385	...	...	...	...	...	...
147	GKN (Guest, Keen and Nettlefolds)........	UK	1,377	16[j]	...	31[j]	38[j]	21[j]	27
148	KF (Kooperativa Förbundet).............	Sweden	1,376	9[i]	...	...	...	...	13
149	FMC...................	USA	1,354	9[d]	...	...	...	...	19
150	Petrofina.............	Belgium	1,350	90[i]	...	...	...	...	21
151	Amerada Hess..........	USA	1,349	..[i]	...	...	...	...	...
152	Warner-Lambert........	USA	1,346	36[j]	33[h]	32[h]	33[g]	...	47
153	Getty Oil.............	USA	1,343	...	...	...	...	...	19
154	Reed International....	UK	1,330	...	...	...	...	..[j]	13
155	Allied Chemical.......	USA	1,326	...	...	...	...	6[d]	14
156	Colgate-Palmolive.....	USA	1,310	52[j]	...	50[h]	88[d]	70[d]	55
157	Raytheon..............	USA	1,308	6[d]	...	...	13[h]	13[h]	18
158	Genesco...............	USA	1,307	...	...	...	...	...	13
159	B.F. Goodrich.........	USA	1,300	...	...	..[d]	...	...	24
160	Weyerhaeuser..........	USA	1,300	...	...	2[d]	...	...	12
161	Mitsubishi Electric...	Japan	1,294	..[k]	...	...	...	..[k]	...
162	Taiyo Fishery.........	Japan	1,292	13[k]	...	..[d]	...	21[d]	25
163	American Cyanamid.....	USA	1,283	18[j]	...	18[d]	20[h]	17[d]	27
164	Signal Companies......	USA	1,281	...	...	...	...	...	16
165	Ishikawajima-Harima Heavy Industries....	Japan	1,280	32[k]	...	-	...	13[k]	8
166	Whirlpool.............	USA	1,274	...	...	4[d]	...	...	...
167	Inland Steel..........	USA	1,254	...	...	...	...	...	...
168	Columbia Broadcasting System..............	USA	1,248	..[j]	..[j]	...	...	...	19
169	Metallgesellschaft....	FRG	1,248	22[j]	6[j]	...	...	...	17
170	Thomson Brandt........	France	1,246	23[k]	...	...	...	...	...
171	PPG Industries........	USA	1,238	..[j]	...	22[h]	18[e]	...	10
172	Celanese..............	USA	1,236	19[j]	...	9[d]	...	...	21
173	American Motors.......	USA	1,232	..[j]	...	...	...	...	10
174	Pepsi Co.	USA	1,225	34[d]	...	...	...	52[d]	25
175	Pemes (Petróleos Mexicanos)...........	Mexico	1,214	...	...	...	...	...	...
176	Philip Morris.........	USA	1,210	..[g]	...	...	...	...	11
177	Volvo.................	Sweden	1,196	69[g]	26[h]	...	...	...	13
178	Deere.................	USA	1,188	...	...	...	...	..[d]	14
179	Marathon Oil..........	USA	1,182	...	...	...	...	4[d]	...
180	Imperial Tobacco Group................	UK	1,173	5[j]	...	...	...	11[j]	13
181	Kawasaki Steel........	Japan	1,162	27[k]	...	...	...	14[k]	18
182	Hawker Siddeley Group.	UK	1,151	36[j]	...	40[j]	...	18[j]	20
183	Borg-Warner...........	USA	1,148	...	...	...	...	...	21
184	Carnation.............	USA	1,148	...	...	...	...	...	...
185	Olin..................	USA	1,145	...	...	...	...	...	18
186	Idemitsu Kosan........	Japan	1,145	..[e]	...	...	...	...	...
187	Johnson and Johnson...	USA	1,140	25[e]	...	27[e]	25[d]	40[d]	18
188	General Mills.........	USA	1,120	...	...	...	...	...	...
189	Teledyne..............	USA	1,102	...	...	...	...	...	...
190	Mitsubishi Chemical Industries...........	Japan	1,095	...	...	...	...	...	...
191	Reynolds Metal........	USA	1,093	54[i]	28[h]	32[d]	4[d]	...	...
192	Usinor................	France	1,092	18[j]	...	...	...	...	...
193	Rio Tinto-Zinc........	UK	1,087	74[j]	...	82[j]	71[j]	71[j]	20
194	Italsider.............	Italy	1,080	...	7[j]	...	...	...	...
195	British Insulated Callender's Cables..	UK	1,080	35[j]	...	...	55[j]	36[j]	17

Rank[a]	Company	Nationality	Total sales (millions of dollars)	Sales[b]	Production	Assets	Earnings	Employment	Number of subsidiary countries[c]
				Foreign content as percentage of					
196	Nabisco	USA	1,070	...	...	...	...	...	16
197	Wendel-Sidelor	France	1,067	37[k]	...	...	...	...	...
198	Bristol-Myers	USA	1,066	...	...	...	...	...	15
199	Combustion Engineering	USA	1,066	...	...	...	...	...	12
200	Salzgitter	FRG	1,061	...	...	...	...	...	12
201	Standard Brands	USA	1,057	5[d]	...	9[d]	10[d]	...	26
202	Mead	USA	1,056	...	...	...	...	...	13
203	Kennecott Copper	USA	1,053	...	...	...	...	...	13
204	Norton Simon	USA	1,052	...	...	...	...	...	...
205	Petróleo Brasileiro (Petrobras)	Brazil	1,044	74[l]	...	...	...	...	...
206	Ogden	USA	1,043	...	...	...	...	...	...
207	Eaton	USA	1,036	23[h]	...	25[h]	22[h]	35[e]	...
208	Henkel	FRG	1,033	...	...	...	8[a]	29[i]	8
209	Campbell Soup	USA	1,032	...	...	...	...	...	7
210	Massey-Ferguson	Canada	1,029	90[g]	62[g]	84[g]	...	...	22
211	Iowa Beef Processors	USA	1,015	...	...	...	...	...	...

Source: See table 2.

a/ Corporations are ranked in descending order of sales.

b/ Total sales to third parties (non-affiliate firms) outside the home country.

c/ Countries in which the parent corporation has at least one affiliate, except in the case of Japan, where the number of foreign affiliates is reported.

d/ 1964. g/ 1967. j/ 1970.

e/ 1965. h/ 1968. k/ 1971.

f/ 1966. i/ 1969. l/ 1972.

Table 4. Multinational corporations of selected developed market economies: parent corporations and affiliate networks by home country, 1968-1969

Home country[a]	Total parent		Parent corporations with affiliates in				Affiliates	
	Number	Percentage	1 country	2-9 countries	10-19 countries	Over 20 countries	Minimum number[b]	Percentage
United States	2,468	33.9	1,228	949	216	75	9,691	35.5
United Kingdom	1,692	23.3	725	809	108	50	7,116	26.1
Federal Republic of Germany	954	13.1	448	452	43	11	2,916	10.7
France	538	7.4	211	275	42	10	2,023	7.4
Switzerland	447	6.1	213	202	26	6	1,456	5.3
Netherlands	268	3.7	92	149	20	7	1,118	4.1
Sweden	255	3.5	93	129	24	9	1,159	4.2
Belgium	235	3.2	137	88	8	2	594	2.2
Denmark	128	1.8	54	69	4	1	354	1.3
Italy	120	1.7	57	54	3	6	459	1.7
Norway	94	1.3	54	36	4	-	220	0.8
Austria	39	0.5	21	16	2	-	105	0.4
Luxembourg	18	0.2	10	7	1	-	55	0.2
Spain	15	0.2	11	4	-	-	26	0.1
Portugal	5	0.1	3	2	-	-	8	-
TOTAL	7,276	100.0	3,357	3,241	501	177	27,300	100.0

Source: Centre for Development Planning, Projections and Policies of the Department of Economic and Social Affairs of the United Nations Secretariat, based on Yearbook of International Organisations, 13th ed., 1970-1971.

a/ Countries are arranged in descending order of number of parent corporations.

b/ "Minimum number of affiliates" refers to the number of "links" between parent corporations and host countries. Two or more affiliates of a particular corporation in a given foreign country are counted as one "link".

Table 5. Market economies: stock of foreign direct investment (book value), 1967, 1971
(Millions of dollars and percentage)

Country a/	1967		1971 b/	
	Millions of dollars	Percent-age share	Millions of dollars	Percent-age share
United States...............	59,486	55.0	86,001	52.0
United Kingdom..............	17,521	16.2	24,019	14.5
France......................	6,000	5.5	9,540	5.8
Federal Republic of Germany.	3,015	2.8	7,276	4.4
Switzerland.................	4,250 c/	3.9	6,760	4.1
Canada......................	3,728	3.4	5,930	3.6
Japan.......................	1,458	1.3	4,480 d/	2.7
Netherlands.................	2,250	2.1	3,580	2.2
Sweden e/	1,514	1.4	3,450	2.1
Italy.......................	2,110 f/	1.9	3,350	2.0
Belgium.....................	2,040 f/	1.9	3,250	2.0
Australia...................	380 f/	0.4	610	0.4
Portugal....................	200 f/	0.2	320	0.2
Denmark.....................	190 f/	0.2	310	0.2
Norway......................	60 f/	0.0	90	0.0
Austria.....................	30 f/	0.0	40	0.0
Other g/	4,000 g/	3.7	6,000	3.6
TOTAL	108,200	100.0	165,000	100.0

Source: Centre for Development Planning, Projections and Policies of the Department of Economic and Social Affairs of the United Nations Secretariat, based on table 9 ; Organisation for Economic Co-operation and Development, Stock of Private Direct Investments by DAC Countries in Developing Countries, End 1967 (Paris, 1972); United States Department of Commerce, Survey of Current Business, various issues; Bundesministerium für Wirtschaft, Runderlass Aussenwirtschaft, various issues; Handelskammer Hamburg, Deutsche Direktinvestitionen in Ausland (1969); Bank of England, Quarterly Bulletin, various issues; Hans-Eckart Scharrer, ed., Förderung privater Direktinvestitionen (Hamburg, 1972); Toyo Keizai, Statistics Monthly, vol. 32, June 1972; Canadian Department of Industry, Trade and Commerce, "Direct investment abroad by Canada, 1964-1967" (mimeo) (Ottawa, 1971); Skandinaviska Enskilda Banken, Quarterly Review, No. 2, 1972.

Note: According to the Organisation for Economic Co-operation and Development, op. cit., "...by the stock of foreign investment...is understood the net book value to the direct investor of affiliates (subsidiaries, branches and associates) in LDC's...Governments of DAC member countries decline all responsibility for the accuracy of the estimates of the Secretariat which in some cases are known to differ from confidential information available to the national authorities... Any analysis of detailed data in the paper should therefore be done with the utmost caution...", p. 4.

a/ Countries are arranged in descending order of book value of direct investment in 1971.

b/ Estimated (except for United States, United Kingdom, Federal Republic of Germany, Japan and Sweden) by applying the average growth rate of the United States, United Kingdom and Federal Republic of Germany between 1966 and 1971.

c/ Data from another source for 1965 ($4,052 million) and 1969 ($6,043 million) seem to indicate that the 1967 and 1971 figures are probably relatively accurate. See, Max Iklé, Die Schweiz als internationaler Bank und Finanzplatz (Zurich 1970).

d/ Financial Times, 4 June 1973.

e/ The figures for Sweden are for 1965 and 1970 instead of 1967 and 1971 and they are in current prices for total assets of majority-owned manufacturing subsidiaries.

f/ Data on book value of foreign direct investment are only available for developing countries. Since the distribution of the minimum number of affiliates between developing countries and developed market economies correlates highly with the distribution of book value, the total book value has been estimated on the basis of the distribution of their minimum number of affiliates. For Australia, the average distribution of the total minimum number of affiliates has been applied.

g/ Estimated, including developing countries.

Table 6. United States multinational corporations: average size[a]
of foreign affiliates by sector and area, 1966

(Thousands of dollars)

Sector	World total	Developing countries b/	Developed market economies
Mining and smelting......	8,330	7,668	8,906
Petroleum................	8,746	8,981	8,486
Manufacturing............	2,361	1,399	2,761
Public utilities.........	2,165	2,646	1,397
Trade....................	1,114	1,219	1,070
Other....................	818	477	1,044
TOTAL, all sectors	2,350	2,186	2,440

Source: Centre for Development Planning, Projections and Policies of the Department of Economic and Social Affairs of the United Nations Secretariat, based on United States Department of Commerce, Survey of Current Business, October 1968; and United States Direct Investments Abroad, 1966, Part I: Balance of Payments Data, (Washington, D.C., 1970).

a/ Book value divided by number of affiliates.

b/ Includes international shipping.

Table 7. Average size^{a/} of United States and United Kingdom foreign
affiliates by area, in selected years

(Thousands of dollars)

Area	United States			United Kingdom	
	1950	1957	1966	1965	1968
Developed market economies......	1,221	2,299	2,413	1,822	2,105
Canada........................	1,825	3,171	3,172	2,903	3,282
Western Europe................	769	1,564	1,885	920	1,063
European Economic Community.	631	1,371	1,867	925	1,172
United Kingdom..............	1,219	2,342	2,449	-	-
Japan...;.....................	.333	1,350	1,424	551	771
Southern hemisphere...........	1,019	1,846	1,657	2,429	2,879
United States................	-	-	-	3,001	3,867
Unallocated.....................				5,372	3,954
Developing countries^{b/}..........	2,083	2,548	2,096	1,600	1,575
Africa........................	840	1,344	2,158	1,479	1,412
Asia..........................	1,956	2,615	2,037	1,506	1,424
Western hemisphere...........	2,220	2,639	2,106	2,027	2,299
Unallocated....................	...	8,748	4,710	467	5,298
TOTAL	1,589	2,472	2,350	1,742	1,919

Source: Centre for Development Planning, Projections and Policies of the
Department of Economic and Social Affairs of the United Nations Secretariat,
based on United States Department of Commerce, United States Direct Investments
Abroad, 1966, Part I: Balance of Payments Data, (Washington, D.C., 1970) and
Survey of Current Business, various issues; United Kingdom Department of Trade
and Industry, Trade and Industry, various issues.

a/ Book value of foreign direct investment divided by number of affiliates.

b/ The developing countries comprise the countries and territories of
Africa (other than South Africa), Asia and the Pacific (other than Australia,
China, the Democratic People's Republic of Korea, the Democratic Republic of
Viet-Nam, Japan, Mongolia, New Zealand and Turkey) and Central and South America
and the Caribbean (other than Puerto Rico and the United States Virgin Islands).

Table 8. Selected developed market economies: direct investment flows,
inward and outward, 1960, 1965-1971

(Millions of dollars)

Country and region		Direct investment flow							
		1960	1965	1966	1967	1968	1969	1970	1971
North America									
Canada..............	Outward	-52	-116	-5	-116	-209	-344	-283	-303
	Inward	691	495	731	639	547	669	800	877
United States........	Outward	-1,674	-3,468	-3,661	-3,137	-3,209	-3,254	-4,440	-4,765
	Inward	140	57	86	258	319	832	1,030	-67
Western Europe									
European Economic Community									
Belgium-Luxembourg.	Outward	...	-40	-8	-52	-52	-14	-156	...
	Inward	...	142	140	230	250	276	318	...
France a/..........	Outward	-100 b/	-233	-170	-354	-343	-193	-373	-346
	Inward	176 b/	334	293	342	196	295	622	524
Federal Republic of Germany.............	Outward	-116	-263	-307	-260	-397	-545	-686	...
	Inward	169	823	860	703	370	347	299	...
Italy..............	Outward	-10 b/	-178	-97	-234	-261	-283	-109	...
	Inward	197	286	315	262	332	418	606	...
Netherlands........	Outward	-134	-148	-256	-298	-342	-498	-512	...
	Inward	42	153	158	254	324	354	536	...
United Kingdom........	Outward	-700	-862	-773	-770	-984	-1,313	-1,166	...
	Inward	745	551	546	461	657	765	761	...

Other

		1	2	3	4	5	6	7	8
Denmark	Outward	-9	-15	-6	—	-9	-15	-29	⋯
	Inward	27	90	43	110	-24	124	104	⋯
Finland	Outward	⋯	-3	-4	-8	-24	-18	-52	⋯
	Inward	⋯	5	6	12	9	20	18	⋯
Norway	Outward	-3	-2	-7	18	-10	-16	-32	⋯
	Inward	22	23	28	70	33	27	26	⋯
Portugal	Outward	⋯	—	—	—	—	-1	-7	⋯
	Inward	⋯	24	28	13	27	24	21	⋯
Spain	Outward	—	-7	-6	-6	-9	-13	-43	-25
	Inward	36	123	134	186	152	200	222	201
Sweden	Outward	-29	-102	-118	-110	-45	-237	-195	-172
	Inward	20	87	139	101	105	155	108	81
Japan	Outward	-79	-77	-107	-123	-220	-206	-355	-360
	Inward	6	47	30	45	76	72	94	210
Southern hemisphere									
Australia	Outward	⋯	-20	-32	-55	-59	-124	-114	⋯
	Inward	⋯	127	464	485	659	660	926	⋯
New Zealand	Outward	⋯	-1	1	—	-1	-4	-1	1
	Inward	⋯	-3	-1	8	-5	—	23	54
South Africa	Outward	⋯	-4	-32	-10	-31	-28	-20	-41
	Inward	⋯	109	149	92	287	262	410	336
TOTAL [c]	Outward	-2,906	-5,510	-5,588	-5,515	-6,205	-7,106	-8,518	⋯
	Inward	2,271	3,483	4,149	4,271	4,314	5,500	6,862	⋯

Source: Centre for Development Planning, Projections and Policies of the Department of Economic and Social Affairs of the United Nations Secretariat, based on Organisation for Economic Co-operation and Development, Policy Perspectives for International Trade and Economic Relations (Paris, OECD, 1972); International Monetary Fund, Balance of Payments Yearbook, various issues.

a/ 1961-1966 covers transactions of metropolitan France with the non-franc area only, 1967-1971 covers transactions of metropolitan France with the rest of the world.

b/ 1961 figures.

c/ 1960, only 12 countries with available data are included.

Table 9. Selected developed market economies: stock of foreign
direct investment, 1960-1971

(Millions of dollars and percentage)

Year	Japan	Federal Republic of Germany	United Kingdom	United States
A. Book value (millions of dollars)				
1960.................	289.0	758.1	11,988.2	32,765
1961.................	453.8	968.7[a]	12,912.1	34,664
1962.................	535.2	1,239.6	13,649.1	37,149
1963.................	679.2	1,527.3	14,646.2	40,686
1964.................	799.5	1,811.7	16,415.6	44,386
1965.................	956.2	2,076.1	16,796.5	49,328
1966.................	1,183.2	2,513.2	17,531.4	54,711
1967.................	1,458.1	3,015.0	17,521.1[a]	59,486
1968.................	2,015.3	3,587.0	18,478.8	64,983
1969.................	2,682.9	4,774.5[a]	20,043.2	71,016
1970.................	3,596.3	5,774.5	21,390.5	78,090
1971.................	4,480.0[a]	7,276.9[a]	24,019.0[a]	86,001
B. Average annual rate of growth (percentage)				
1960-1965............	27.0	22.3	7.0	8.5
1965-1971............	29.4	23.2	6.1	9.7
1960-1971............	28.3	22.8	6.5	9.2

Source: Centre for Development Planning, Projections and Policies of the Department of Economic and Social Affairs of the United Nations Secretariat, based on Hans-Eckart Scharrer, ed., Förderung privater Direktinvestitionen (Hamburg, 1972); Toyo Keizai, Statistics Monthly, vol. 32, June 1972; Bundesministerium für Wirtschaft, Runderlass Aussenwirtschaft, various issues; Bank of England, Quarterly Bulletin, various issues; United States Department of Commerce, Survey of Current Business, various issues; Financial Times, 6 April 1973.

a/ Exchange rate change.

Table 10. Multinational corporations of selected developed market
economies: number of affiliates and distribution by area,
1968 or 1969

Home countries[a]	Minimum number of affiliates[b]	Distribution of affiliates by area				
		World (percentages)		Developing countries		
		Developed market economies	Developing countries	Africa	Western hemi- sphere	Asia[c]
United States.....	9,691	74.7	25.3	8.3	72.8	18.8
United Kingdom....	7,116	68.2	31.8	40.0	28.5	31.5
Federal Republic of Germany.......	2,916	82.2	17.8	21.8	49.9	28.3
France...........	2,023	59.7	40.3	66.6	24.1	9.2
Switzerland.......	1,456	85.7	14.4	15.8	60.3	23.9
Sweden...........	1,159	83.4	16.6	10.4	66.7	22.9
Netherlands.......	1,118	72.6	27.4	27.8	47.4	24.8
Belgium...........	594	69.7	30.3	69.4	21.7	8.9
Italy.............	459	67.3	32.7	30.0	56.0	14.0
Denmark...........	354	84.8	15.2	27.8	35.2	37.0
Norway...........	220	84.6	15.5	47.1	26.5	26.5
Austria...........	105	81.0	19.0	5.0	50.0	45.0
Luxembourg........	55	85.5	14.5	37.5	62.5	-
Spain.............	26	73.1	26.9	14.3	85.7	-
Portugal..........	8	50.0	50.0	75.0	25.0	-
TOTAL	27,300	73.6	26.4	29.3	47.9	22.8

Source: See table 4.

a/ Countries are arranged in descending order of minimum number of affiliates.

b/ This column reports only the number of "links" from parent corporations to
host countries. Two or more affiliates of a particular corporation in a given
foreign country are counted as one "link".

c/ Including Oceania (other than Australia and New Zealand), Turkey, Cyprus.

Table 11. Development Assistance Committee countries: estimated stock of
foreign direct investment, by country of origin and region of investment,
end 1967

(Millions of dollars and percentage)

Country of origin a/	World (total book value,b/ millions of dollars)	Total book value (millions of dollars)	Developing countries c/					
			Africa	Central America	South America	Middle East	Asia	Total developing
			(percentage share)						
United States..	59,486	16,703	2.3	7.4	12.4	3.0	3.0	28.1
United Kingdom.	17,521	6,582	11.3	4.7	5.0	4.8	11.8	37.6
France.........	6,000	2,689	28.8	1.0	6.8	2.7	5.5	44.8
Netherlands....	2,250	1,694	14.4	8.2	33.6	7.7	11.4	75.3
Canada.........	3,728	1,453	1.5	13.3	22.7	0.2	1.3	39.0
Federal Republic of Germany....	3,015	1,018	4.6	3.4	22.8	0.8	2.2	33.8
Japan..........	1,458	700	0.9	6.9	20.9	5.8	13.5	48.0
Italy..........	2,110	696	11.7	1.0	17.6	1.2	1.4	33.0
Belgium........	2,040	613	23.6	-	5.5	0.1	0.8	30.0
Switzerland....	4,250	565	1.4	3.4	6.7	0.1	1.7	13.3
Sweden.........	1,514	180	5.3	0.8	4.6	-	1.2	11.9
Australia......	380	100	-	-	-	-	26.3	26.3
Portugal.......	200	99	...	...	3.0	...	...	49.5
Denmark........	190	29	8.7	1.5	1.2	1.0	2.7	15.3
Norway.........	60	9	5.0	-	10.0	-	-	15.0
Austria........	30	5	-	-	16.7	-	-	16.7
TOTAL, DAC countries	104,232	33,135	6.3	6.1	11.6	3.0	4.8	31.8

Source: Centre for Development Planning, Projections and Policies of the
Department of Economic and Social Affairs of the United Nations Secretariat,
based on table 5 and Organisation for Economic Co-operation and Development,
Stock of Private Direct Investments by DAC Countries in Developing Countries,
end 1967 (Paris, 1972).
  a/ Countries are arranged in descending order of value of total investment
stock in developing countries.
  b/ Not including centrally planned economies; see also table 5.
  c/ Countries included in developing regions, throughout tables, based on
OECD figures, are listed in table 23.

Table 12. Development Assistance Committee countries: estimated stock of foreign investment by sector, end 1966

(Value and percentage)

Sector	Total world a/ Value (millions of dollars)	Per-cent-age	Area of investment Developed market economies Value (millions of dollars)	Per-cent-age	Developing countries Value (millions of dollars)	Per-cent-age	Developing countries (percentage of total world)
Petroleum............	25,942	28.9	14,050	23.6	11,892	39.7	45.8
Mining and smelting.	5,923	6.6	3,122	5.2	2,801	9.3	47.3
Manufacturing.......	36,246	40.5	28,199	47.3	8,047	26.9	22.2
Other...............	21,472	24.0	14,242	23.9	7,230	24.1	33.7
TOTAL	89,583	100.0	59,613	100.0	29,970	100.0	33.5

Source: Centre for Development Planning, Projections and Policies of the Department of Economic and Social Affairs of the United Nations Secretariat, based on Organisation for Economic Co-operation and Development, as tabulated in Sidney E. Rolfe, The International Corporation (Paris, 1969).

a/ Not including centrally planned economies.

Table 13. Development Assistance Committee countries: estimated stock of
foreign direct investment in developing countries, by sector and developing
region, end 1967

(Value and percentage)

Sector[a]	Total (millions of dollars)	Share in total stock of DAC countries (percentage)	Distribution among developing regions (percentage)			
			Africa	Western hemi-sphere	Middle East	Asia
Petroleum............	10,962	33.1	23.7	40.9	25.3	10.1
Manufacturing........	9,627	29.1	12.8	69.1	2.0	16.1
Mining and smelting..	3,554	10.7	36.0	56.7	0.2	7.1
Trade................	2,601	7.8	15.3	64.1	1.2	19.4
Agriculture..........	2,046	6.2	24.3	29.7	0.1	45.9
Public utilities.....	1,570	4.7	4.2	87.3	0.7	7.8
Transport............	676	2.0	32.8	54.4	2.7	10.1
Banking..............	588	1.8	23.9	48.7	4.7	22.7
Tourism..............	448	1.4	9.8	57.9	4.0	28.3
Others..............	1,063	3.2	10.4	69.2	2.2	18.2
TOTAL	33,135	100.0	19.9	55.6	9.4	15.1

Source: Centre for Development Planning, Projections and Policies of the
Department of Economic and Social Affairs of the United Nations Secretariat,
based on Organisation for Economic Co-operation and Development, Stock of
Private Direct Investments by DAC Countries in Developing Countries, end 1967
(Paris, 1972).

a/ Sectors are arranged in descending order of value of stock of direct
private investment in developing regions.

Table 14. Selected developed market economies: stock of foreign direct
investment by sector and industry, 1965 and 1970

(Value and percentage)

Sector and industry	Federal Republic of Germany (end 1970)		Japan (end 1970)		United Kingdom (end 1965)		United States (end 1970)	
	Millions of dollars	Per-cent-age	Millions of dollars	Per-cent-age	Millions of dollars	Per-cent-age	Millions of dollars	Per-cent-age
Distribution by sector								
All sectors, TOTAL	5,775	100.0	3,596	100.0	16,797	100.0	78,090	100.0
Mining..........	260	4.5)	1,127	31.3	(760	4.5	6,137	7.9
Petroleum.......	164	2.8)			(3,853	22.9	21,790	27.9
Others..........	908	15.7	1,506	41.9	6,290	37.4	17,932	23.0
Manufacturing...	4,443	76.9	963	26.8	5,894	35.1	32,231	41.3
Distribution by industry								
Manufacturing, TOTAL	4,443	100.0	963	100.0	5,894	100.0	32,231	100.0
Food products...	234	5.3	61	6.3	583	9.9	2,680	8.3
Textiles........	110	2.5	190	19.7	98	1.7	-	-
Lumber, pulp....	63	1.4	212	22.0	129	2.2	-	-
Chemicals.......	1,589	35.8	60	6.2	594	10.1	6,272	19.5
Steel, non-ferrous metals.	436	9.8	138	14.3	377	6.4	3,576	11.1
Machinery.......	428	9.6	67	7.0	943	16.0	4,012	12.4
Electrical products.......	677	15.2	71	7.4	519	8.8	2,606	8.1
Transport products.......	563	12.7	103	10.7	850	14.4	5,871	18.2
Others..........	343	7.7	61	6.3	1,801	30.5	7,214	22.4

Source: Centre for Development Planning, Projections and Policies of the
Department of Economic and Social Affairs of the United Nations Secretariat,
based on Bundesministerium für Wirtschaft, Runderlass Aussenwirtschaft,
1 April 1971; Hans-Eckart Scharrer, ed., Förderung privater Direktinvestitionen
(Hamburg, 1972); Japanese Ministry of International Trade and Industry, White Paper
on Foreign Trade, 1972; United Kingdom Board of Trade, Board of Trade Journal,
26 January 1968; United States Department of Commerce, Survey of Current Business,
various issues.

Table 15. Multinational corporations of selected developed market economies:
ownership patterns of foreign affiliates

(Number and percentage)

Form of ownership	Home country					
	United States[a]		United Kingdom[b]		Japan[c]	
	Affiliates in developed market economies	Affiliates in developing countries	Affiliates in developed market economies	Affiliates in developing countries	Affiliates in developed market economies	Affiliates in developing countries
Wholly owned (more than 95 per cent)						
Number......	3,570	1,573	1,875	1,274	570	325
Percentage..	67.0	60.6	60.0	62.7	64.4	23.2
Majority owned (50 - 95 per cent)						
Number......	936	521	493	260	164	519
Percentage..	17.6	20.1	15.8	12.8	18.5	37.1
Minority owned (less than 50 per cent)						
Number......	373	287	761	499	128	492
Percentage..	7.0	11.0	24.3	24.5	14.5	35.2

Source: Centre for Development Planning, Projections and Policies of the Department of Economic and Social Affairs of the United Nations Secretariat, based on Toyo Keizai, Statistics Monthly, vol. 32, June 1972; United Kingdom Board of Trade, Board of Trade Journal, 26 January 1968; James W. Vaupel and Joan P. Curhan, The Making of Multinational Enterprise, (Boston, 1969).

a/ 1967. Percentages do not add up to 100 because in a number of cases the form of ownership is unknown.

b/ End of 1965. "Wholly owned" is defined as 100 per cent owned. Branches are included. In terms of book value, 90.3 per cent of United Kingdom foreign direct investment in developing countries and 91.6 per cent of such investment in developed market economies is placed with affiliates which are at least 50 per cent owned by the parent corporation.

c/ 1970. Percentages do not add up to 100 because in a number of cases the form of ownership is unknown.

Table 16. Ownership patterns of foreign affiliates in selected developed
market economies

(Number, value in millions of dollars and percentage)

	Wholly owned (more than 95 per cent)	Majority owned (50 - 95 per cent)	Minority owned (less than 50 per cent)
Affiliates in			
Australia[a]			
Manufacturing			
Number..................	1,641	516	148
Percentage..............	71.2	22.4	6.4
Value...................	1,402	455	171
Percentage..............	69.1	22.5	8.4
Mining			
Number..................	44	15	13
Percentage..............	61.1	20.8	18.1
Value...................	178	82	20
Percentage..............	63.7	29.2	7.0
Austria[b]			
Number..................	720	345	225
Percentage..............	55.8	26.7	17.4
Value...................	162	44	38
Percentage..............	66.3	18.1	15.6
Belgium[c]			
Value...................	1,422	216	283
Percentage..............	74.0	11.2	14.7
France[d]			
United States-owned			
Number..................	181	94	43
Percentage..............	56.9	29.6	13.5
Others			
Number..................	66	93	40
Percentage..............	33.2	46.7	20.1
Federal Republic of Germany[e]			
Number..................	5,020	1,108	1,633
Percentage..............	64.7	14.3	21.0
Value...................	4,720	535	674
Percentage..............	79.6	9.0	11.4
Japan[f]			
United States-owned			
Number..................	16	28	23
Percentage.............	23.9	41.8	34.3
Others			
Number.................	10	15	8
Percentage.............	30.3	45.5	24.2
New Zealand[f]			
Number.................	421	120	33
Percentage.............	73.4	20.9	5.7

United Kingdom[g]/
  United States-owned

Number..................	384	52	105
Percentage..............	71.0	9.6	19.4
Value...................	2,726	517	370
Percentage..............	75.4	14.3	10.2

Others

Number..................	277	51	62
Percentage..............	71.0	13.1	15.9
Value...................	1,278	480	63
Percentage..............	70.2	26.3	3.5

Source: Centre for Development Planning, Projections and Policies of the Department of Economic and Social Affairs of the United Nations Secretariat, based on Australian Bureau of Census and Statistics, "Overseas participation in Australian mining industry, 1967" and "Overseas participation in Australian manufacturing industry, 1962-1963 and 1966-1967" (mimeos), (Canberra); Oskar Grünwald and Ferdinand Lacina, Auslandskapital in der österreichischen Wirtschaft (Vienna, 1970); Banque Nationale de Belgique, Bulletin d'Information et de Documentation, vol. 2, October 1970; Société d'Editions Economiques et Financières, Les Maisons Financières Françaises (Paris, 1966); Deutsche Bundesbank, Monthly Report, January 1972; Bank of Tokyo, The President Directory, 1973 (Tokyo, 1972); Roderick S. Deane, Foreign Investment in New Zealand Manufacturing (Wellington, 1970); United Kingdom Board of Trade, Board of Trade Journal, 26 January 1968.

a/ 1966-1967 for manufacturing; 1967 for mining. "Wholly owned" is defined as 75 per cent or more owned. "Value" is in terms of value of production.

b/ 1969. Limited liability companies only. "Wholly owned" is defined as 100 per cent owned. "Value" is in terms of nominal capital.

c/ 1960-1967. "Wholly owned" is defined as 100 per cent owned. "Value" is in terms of book value.

d/ 1965.

e/ End of 1970. "Wholly owned" is defined as 90 per cent or more owned. "Value" is in terms of nominal capital.

f/ 1964. "Wholly owned" is defined as 100 per cent owned.

g/ End of 1965. "Wholly owned" is defined as 100 per cent owned. Branches are included. "Value" in terms of book value.

Table 17. Market economies: international production and exports, 1971
(Millions of dollars)

Country[a]	Stock of foreign direct invest-ment (book value)	Estimated international production [b]	Exports	International production as percentage of exports
United States..........	86,000	172,000	43,492	395.5
United Kingdom.........	24,020	48,000	22,367	214.6
France.................	9,540	19,100	20,420	93.5
Federal Republic of Germany..............	7,270	14,600	39,040	37.4
Switzerland............	6,760	13,500	5,728	235.7
Canada.................	5,930	11,900	17,582	67.7
Japan..................	4,480	9,000	24,019	37.5
Netherlands............	3,580	7,200	13,927	51.7
Sweden.................	3,450	6,900	7,465	92.4
Italy..................	3,350	6,700	15,111	44.3
Belgium................	3,250	6,500	12,392[c]	52.4
Australia..............	610	1,200	5,070	23.7
Portugal...............	320	600	1,052	57.0
Denmark................	310	600	3,685	16.3
Norway.................	90	200	2,563	7.8
Austria................	40	100	3,169	3.2
TOTAL, above	159,000	318,000	237,082	133.7
Other	6,000	12,000	74,818	16.0
TOTAL, market economies	165,000	330,000	311,900	105.8

Source: Centre for Development Planning, Projections and Policies of the Department of Economic and Social Affairs of the United Nations Secretariat, based on table 5 and Monthly Bulletin of Statistics (United Nations publication), vol. XXVII, April 1973.

a/ Countries are listed in descending order of book value of foreign direct investment.

b/ Estimated international production equals the book value of foreign direct investment multiplied by the factor 2.0. The estimate of this factor was derived as follows: the ratio of foreign sales to book value of foreign direct investment has been estimated from 1970 United States data on gross sales of majority-owned foreign affiliates and book value of United States foreign direct investment. "Gross sales of majority-owned foreign affiliates" (approximately $157 billion) includes transactions between foreign affiliates and parent corporations (approximately $20.3 billion) and inter-foreign affiliate sales (approximately $28.1 billion), which together account for about 30 per cent of gross foreign affiliate sales. The book value of United States foreign direct investment in 1970 amounted to $78.1 billion. The resulting ratio of gross sales to book value is 2:1. This ratio has been used to estimate the international production of non-United States foreign affiliates.

c/ Includes Luxembourg.

Table 18. Selected developed market economies: direct investment flow and
flow of investment income, annual average, 1968-1970

(Millions of dollars)

Country [a]	Direct investment flow			Income on direct investment		
	Inward	Outward	Net	Inward	Outward	Net
United States.....	727.0	-3,621.0	-2,894.0	8,107.0	-866.3	7,240.7
United Kingdom....	727.7	-1,154.3	-426.6	1,535.0	-781.7	753.3
Federal Republic of Germany.......	338.7	-542.7	-204.0	49.3	-547.7	-498.4
Netherlands.......	404.7	-450.7	-46.0	496.0	-192.7	303.3
France............	371.0	-303.0	68.0	268.0	-33.2	234.8
Canada............	651.3	-273.7	377.6	171.0	-579.3	-408.3
Japan.............	80.7	-260.3	-179.6	56.0 [b]	-89.3 [b]	-33.3
Italy.............	452.0	-217.7	234.3	344.7 [b]	-325.0 [b]	19.7
Sweden............	122.7	-159.0	-36.3	52.7	-25.0	27.7
Australia.........	748.3	-99.0	649.3	53.0	-566.7	-513.7
Belgium-Luxembourg	281.3	-74.0	207.3	301.7 [b]	-282.0 [b]	19.7
Finland...........	15.7	-31.3	-15.6	-	-7.7	-7.7
South Africa......	319.7	-26.3	293.4	109.3	-365.0	-255.7
Spain.............	191.3	-21.7	169.6	2.3	-16.7	-14.4
Norway............	28.7	-19.3	9.4	23.0	-17.7	5.3
Denmark...........	68.0	-17.7	50.3	18.0	-24.3	-6.3
Austria c/	48.0	-7.3	40.7	4.7	-29.3	-24.6
Portugal..........	24.0	-2.7	21.3	...	...	...
New Zealand.......	6.0	-2.0	4.0	-	-28.7	-28.7
Greece............	146.0	-	146.0	9.3	-47.0	-37.7

Source: Centre for Development Planning, Projections and Policies of the
Department of Economic and Social Affairs of the United Nations Secretariat,
based on Organisation for Economic Co-operation and Development, Policy
Perspectives for International Trade and Economic Relations (Paris, 1972);
International Monetary Fund, Balance of Payments Yearbook (Washington, D.C.),
various issues.

a/ Countries are arranged in descending order of outward direct investment
flow.

b/ Estimated.

c/ 1969-1970.

Table 19. Stock of foreign direct investment in the United States, and stock of United States direct investment abroad, by country and sector, 1962, 1971

(Millions of dollars and percentage)

Country and sector	Foreign direct investment in the United States		Average annual rate of growth between 1962-1971 (percentage)	United States direct investment abroad		Average annual rate of growth between 1962-1971 (percentage)	Book value of foreign direct investment in the United States as a percentage of book value of United States direct investment abroad	
	1962	1971a/		1962	1971a/		1962	1971a/
TOTAL (millions of dollars)...........	7,612	13,704	6.8	37,145	86,000	9.8	20.5	15.9
Percentage distribution by country and area								
Canada..............	27.1	24.4	5.5	32.7	27.9	7.9	17.0	13.9
Europe..............	68.9	73.5	7.5	23.8	32.1	13.5	59.3	36.5
United Kingdom....	32.5	32.4	6.7	10.2	10.4	10.0	65.0	49.6
European Economic Community.........	22.0	27.4	9.4	9.9	15.8	15.6	45.6	27.7
Belgium-Luxembourg...........	2.1	2.5	8.9	0.8	2.1	22.9	55.8	18.8
France............	2.4	2.3	6.2	2.7	3.5	13.0	18.2	10.5
Federal Republic of Germany......	2.0	5.6	19.7	4.0	6.1	15.1	10.3	14.7
Italy.............	1.3	0.8	1.0	1.4	2.2	14.7	18.5	5.9
Netherlands......	14.2	16.2	8.3	1.0	1.9	18.2	292.4	133.1
Other western Europe	14.4	13.8	6.2	3.7	5.9	15.8	80.3	36.9
Sweden............	2.4	1.7	2.8	0.5	0.8	16.4	101.7	33.2
Switzerland.......	11.0	11.2	7.0	1.5	2.2	14.5	190.6	81.6
Other.............	1.1	0.9	4.2	1.7	3.0	16.6	13.1	4.7
Developing western hemisphere.........	2.0	2.3	8.4	25.6	18.3	5.8	1.6	2.0
Other, unallocated..	2.0	-	-	17.9	21.6	12.1	2.2	-
TOTAL	100.0	100.0	-	100.0	100.0	-		
By sector								
Petroleum...........	18.6	22.7	9.1	34.1	28.2	7.5	11.2	13.8
Manufacturing.......	37.9	49.3	9.9	35.6	41.3	11.6	21.8	19.0
Other...............	43.5	28.0	1.7	30.3	30.5	9.9	29.3	14.6
TOTAL	100.0	100.0	-	100.0	100.0	-		

Source: Centre for Development Planning, Projections and Policies of the Department of Economic and Social Affairs of the United Nations Secretariat, based on United States Department of Commerce, Survey of Current Business, various issues.

a/ Preliminary.

Table 20. Stock of foreign direct investment in selected developed market
economies, by country of origin and sector

(Millions of dollars and percentage)

Item	Canada (1967)	Federal Republic of Germany (1970)	United Kingdom[a] (1965)
TOTAL, value	19,166	5,861	5,549
Distribution by country of origin, percentage			
Canada......................	–	1.4	12.0
Federal Republic of Germany...	...	–	0.6
France......................	...	5.7	2.0
Netherlands.................	...	13.1	4.8
Switzerland.................	...	13.5	8.4
United Kingdom..............	10.4	10.2	
United States..............	82.1	42.7	66.0
Other......................	7.5	13.4	6.4
TOTAL	100.0	100.0	100.0
Distribution by sector, percentage			
Manufacturing..............	41.5	57.9	82.3
Petroleum..................	25.4	18.0[b]	...
Mining and smelting........	12.3	4.3	...
Trade......................	6.1	8.9[c]	12.3
Financial..................	10.5	4.9	...
Other......................	4.2	6.0	5.4
TOTAL	100.0	100.0	100.0

Source: Centre for Development Planning, Projections and Policies of the
Department of Economic and Social Affairs of the United Nations Secretariat,
based on Canadian Foreign Investment Division, "Foreign direct investment in
Canada since the Second World War" (Amendment List Number 2), mimeo (Ottawa,
1970); Deutsche Bundesbank, Monthly Report, January 1972; United Kingdom Board
of Trade, Board of Trade Journal, 26 January 1968.

a/ Excluding oil, insurance and banking.

b/ Petroleum extraction, processing and distribution.

c/ Distributive trade (excluding petroleum distribution) and transport
and telecommunications.

Table 21. Selected developed market economies: foreign content[a]/ of selected industrial sectors [b]/

Country and area	Foreign content			
	Very high (75 to 100 per cent)	High (50 to 75 per cent)	Medium (25 to 50 per cent)	Low (Less than 25 per cent)
North America				
Canada	Tobacco and cigarettes.....(1968-A) Coal and petroleum........(1968-A) Chemicals.....(1968-A) Rubber products.(1968-A) Transport equipment.....(1968-A) Oil refining....(1969-A)	Non-metallic minerals......(1968-A) Iron and steel..(1968-A) Machinery......(1968-A) Electrical machinery.....(1968-A) Others.....(1968-A) Mining..........(1969-A)	Wood products..(1968-A) Pulp and paper products.....(1968-A) Metal products..(1968-A) Textiles.......(1968-A) Food...........(1968-A)	Leather products...(1968-A) Printing.........(1968-A) Furniture.......(1968-A) Non-financial services........(1969-A) Retailing........(1969-A) Construction.....(1969-A)
Western Europe				
Belgium........	Timber processing....(1967-A) Cars.....(US 1965-B)	Plastics.......(1969-B)	Refining....(US 1969-B) Iron and steel.....(1968-B)	Food.............(1968-B) Pulp and paper products.....(1968-B) Non-metallic minerals.....(1968-B) Textiles.......(1968-B)
France.........	Electric power office equipment....(1968-B) Elevators......(1968-B) Photographic films ....(1968-B) Detergents.....(1968-B)	Mineral oil.(US 1966-B)	Building machinery....(1968-B) Gasoline......(1968-B) Electrical components production....(1968-B) Organic chemicals....(1968-B) Pharmaceuticals(1968-B) Transport equipment....(1968-B) Food processing(1968-B) Precision equipment....(1968-B)	Refining........(US 1969-B) Cars............(US 1966-B)

Country and area	Foreign content			
	Very high (75 to 100 per cent)	High (50 to 75 per cent)	Medium (25 to 50 per cent)	Low (Less than 25 per cent)
Western Europe (continued)				
Federal Republic of Germany......	Petroleum and gas........(1970-A) Computers and electronics (US 1967-B)	Food..........(1970-A) Beverages and tobacco......(1970-A) Rubber products(1970-A) Electrical machinery....(1970-A) Plastics......(1970-A) Insurance and finance......(1970-A)	Refining....(US 1969-B) Chemicals......(1970-A) Stones and ceramics......(1970-A) Leather products......(1970-A) Pulp and paper products......(1970-A) Glass......(US 1967-B) Metal products.(1970-A) Textiles......(1970-A) Machinery......(1966-A) Cars......(1967-B) Public utilities......(1970-A)	Cosmetics..........(1967-B) Tyres............(US 1967-B) Packing industry......(US 1967-B) Iron and non-ferrous metal....(1968-A) Footwear......(1966-A) Commerce......(1970-A) Agriculture......(1970-A) Mining......(1968-A) Real estate......(1970-A) Services......(1970-A)
Italy........		Cosmetics...(US 1965-A) Rubber products......(1966-A)	Petroleum and gas......(US 1970-B) Refining....(US 1969-B) Wood products..(1966-A) Pharmaceut-icals......(US 1970-B) Textiles......(1966-A) Telecommuni-cation equip-ment......(1970-B)	Food..........(1966-A) Coffee and paste(US 1965-B) Soft drinks......(1965-A) Tobacco and cigarettes......(1965-A) Synthetic rubber(US 1965-A) Chemicals......(US 1970-B) Pulp and paper products......(1966-A) Non-metallic minerals......(1966-A) Iron and steel....(1966-A) Canning......(US 1965-B)

United Kingdom

Razor blades....(1966-B)
Typewriters..(US 1966-B)
Computers and
electronics (US 1966-B)
Boot and shoe
machinery.....(1966-B)
Sewing machines.(1966-B)
Electric razors.(1966-B)
Spark plugs.....(1966-B)
Products for
photography.(US 1966-B)
Breakfast
cereals........(1966-B)

Frozen foods...(1966-B)
Tractors..(US 1970/1-B)
Refrigerators..(1966-B)

Tobacco and
cigar-
ettes....(US 1970/1-B)
Synthetic
fibres.......(1966-B)
Soap and deter-
gents....(US 1970/1-B)
Pharmaceuti-
cals.....(US 1970/1-B)
Agricultural
equip-
ment.....(US 1970/1-B)
Transport
equipment....(1966-B)
Cars.....(US 1970/1-B)
Lifts and
elevators....(1966-B)
Photographic
equipment....(1966-B)
Dental equip-
ment........(1966-B)
Plastics.(US 1970/1-B)
Mining.......(1966-B)
Petroleum.US 1970/1-B)
Tyres.......(1966-B)

Foods........(US 1970/1-B)
Soft drinks...(US 1970/1-B)
Chemicals.....(US 1970/1-B)
Stones and
ceramics.....(US 1970/1-B)
Leather
products......(US 1965-A)
Rubber
products.....(US 1970/1-B)
Printing......(US 1970/1-B)
Pulp and paper
products....(US 1970/1-B)
Metal products(US 1970/1-B)
Textiles.....(US 1970/1-B)
Machinery.....(US 1970/1-B)
Pump valves and
compressors..(US 1970/1-B)
Machine tools.(US 1970.1-B)
Electrical
machinery....(US 1970/1-B)
Telecommuni-
cation
equipment....(US 1970/1-B)

Others.........(1966-A)
Finance and
insurance.......(1966-A)
Commerce.......(US 1970-B)
Public utilities...(1966-A)
Agriculture......(1966-A)
Mining.........(1966-A)

| | Foreign content | | | |
Country and area	Very high (75 to 100 per cent)	High (50 to 75 per cent)	Medium (25 to 50 per cent)	Low (Less than 25 per cent)
Austria.......		Electrical machinery.....(1969-C)	Pulp and paper products......(1969-C)	Food..........(1969-C) Mineral fuels..(1969-C) Chemicals......(1969-C) Stones and ceramics.......(1969-C) Wood products..(1969-C) Textiles.......(1969-C) Agricultural equipment......(1969-C) Transport equipment......(1969-C) Clothing.......(1969-C) Mining.........(1969-C) Leather products..(1969-C) Glass..........(1969-C) Metal products....(1969-C)
Norway........				Machinery.........(1970-A) Transport equipment(1970-A)
Other				
Australia....	Oils, minerals..(1967-B) Soap and detergent.............(1965-A) Pharmaceuticals.(1967-B) Telecommunication equipment......(1965-A) Transport equipment......(1967-B) Motor vehicles (con-	Printing.......(1965-A) Iron and non-ferrous metal (1967-B) Musical instruments........(1967-B) White lead, paints, varnishes, other chemicals....(1967-B)	Food..........(1965-A) Meat freezing..(1967-B) Beverages and tobacco......(1965-A) Tobacco and cigarettes....(1965-A) Refining.......(1965-A) Rubber products(1967-B) Packing	Timber processing..(1965-A) Pulp and paper products...........(1965-A) Textiles.........(1967-B) Machines and transport equipment....(1967-B) Plastics..........(1965-A)

struction and
assembly).....(1967-B)
Industrial and
heavy chemicals,
acids..........(1967-B)

Australia....

industry......(1967-B)
Glass.........(1965-A)
Iron and steel.(1965-A)
Agricultural
equipment.....(1967-B)
Electrical
machinery.....(1967-B)
Electrical
appliances....(1967-B)

Clothing......(1965-A)
Footwear......(1965-A)
Wireless and
amplifying
apparatus.....(1967-B)

Japan ....

Coal and
petroleum.....(1968-B)
Gas and
petroleum.....(1971-B)

Food..........(1968-B)
Chemicals.....(1971-B)
Stones and
ceramics......(1970-A)
Leather products...(1970-A)
Pharmaceuticals....(1968-B)
Iron and steel.....(1970-A)
Iron and non-
ferrous metals...(1971-B)
Textiles......(1970-A)
Machinery.........(1970-A)
Electrical
machinery.......(1968-B)
Transport equipment(1970-A)
Cars.............(1968-B)
Commerce.........(1970-A)
Services.........(1970-A)
Rubber products...(1971-B)

Source: Centre for Development Planning, Projections and Policies of the Department of Economic and Social Affairs of the United Nations Secretariat, based on ANZ Banking Group Limited, "Foreign investment and multinational corporations in Australia" (Canberra, 1971) mimeo; Australian Commonwealth Treasury, Overseas Investment in Australia (Canberra, 1972); Banco di Roma, Review of Economic Conditions in Italy, September 1972; Bank of Japan, Manual of

Foreign Investment in Japan (Tokyo, 1970); Bank of Tokyo, The President Directory, 1973 (Tokyo, 1972); Banque Nationale de Belgique, Bulletin d'information et de documentation, October 1970; Jack N. Behrman, Some Patterns in the Rise of the Multinational Enterprise (Chapel Hill, 1969); K. Blauhorn, Jetzt kauft uns Amerika (Munich, 1968); Deutsche Bundesbank, Monthly Report, various issues; John H. Dunning, United States Industry in Britain (London, 1972); Government of Canada, Foreign Direct Investment in Canada, (Ottawa, 1972); O. Grünwald and F. Lacina, Auslandskapital in der österreichischen Wirtschaft (Vienna, 1970); Rainer Hellmann, The Challenge to U.S. Dominance of the International Corporation (New York, 1970); Industrial Bank of Japan, Survey of Japanese Finance and Industry, vol. XXIII, 1971; I. Litvak and C. Maule, ed. Foreign Investment: The Experience of Host Countries (New York, 1970); Organisation for Economic Co-operation and Development, Gaps in Technology - Analytical Report (Paris, 1970); S. Rolfe and W. Damm, ed., The Multinational Corporation in the World Economy, (New York, 1970); A. Stonehill, Foreign Ownership in Norwegian Enterprises (Oslo, 1965); D. van den Bulcke, Les enterprises étrangères dans l'industrie Belge (Ghent, 1971); E.L. Wheelwright, "Development and dependence: the Australian problem", The Australian Quarterly, vol. 43, September 1971; Business International, Investing, Licensing and Trading Conditions Abroad, various issues.

a/ Ratio of foreign to total assets, equity capital, employment, production or sales. Within the brackets, A refers to assets or equity capital, such capital in the case of Italy referring to nominal capital and in the case of Norway to the face value of shares held, B to production and C to employment. US indicates that data are for United States share only; they are provided to give an indication of minimum foreign content.

b/ The absence of a particular sector or industry does not necessarily mean that it has no foreign content. The table is illustrative rather than exhaustive.

Table 22. Manufacturing industries in selected host countries: share of United States plant and equipment expenditures in gross fixed capital formation of industry, 1966 and 1970

(Percentage)

Industry	Belgium-Luxembourg 1966	Belgium-Luxembourg 1970	Canada 1966	Canada 1970a/	France 1966	France 1970	Federal Republic of Germany 1966	Federal Republic of Germany 1970b/	United Kingdom 1966	United Kingdom 1970
All manufacturing .... of which:	17.0	14.1	42.7	32.2	4.3c/	5.8c/	9.2	12.3	16.3	20.9
Food...................	...	...	22.5	23.5	1.9	0.9	1.4	2.0	4.6	4.4
Chemicals..............	23.3	24.9	36.6	68.1	1.9d/	2.1d/	5.1	10.4	15.8	17.9
Primary and fabricated metals................					1.7	1.0e/	1.8	8.4	11.3	21.1e/
Non-electrical machinery..............	19.3	12.0	54.0	57.8	15.4	23.3	19.4	27.8	21.5	29.0
Electrical machinery.... Transportation equipment	...	...	47.2	39.7	8.8	9.8	37.8	27.8	47.6	45.5
Paper and allied products...............	...	...			...	...	...	...	...	...
All other manufacturing...	10.6	10.8	7.9	13.6	1.0	2.8	1.1	2.7	11.6	18.2

Source: Centre for Development Planning, Projections and Policies of the Department of Economic and Social Affairs of the United Nations Secretariat, based on United States Senate, Committee on Finance, Implications of Multinational Firms for World Trade and Investment and for United States Trade and Labor (Washington, D.C., 1973).

a/ Based on "intentions" data from Canadian Survey.
b/ Gross fixed capital formation is estimated.
c/ Including mining operations in metal industries.
d/ Including rubber.
e/ Partly estimated.

Table 23. Developing countries: distribution among Development Assistance Committee
countries of stock of foreign direct investment, end 1967

(Millions of dollars and percentage)

Country and region a/	DAC total (millions of dollars)	Percentage share in total investment in region	Share in total investment by DAC countries (percentage)			
			Country accounting for 50 per cent or more	Other main investing countries		
All developing countries	33,134.6		US..... 50.4	UK......19.9	France....8.1	Neth.....5.1
Africa	6,591.1	100.0	-	UK......30.0	France...26.3	US.......20.8 Belgium.. 7.3
Nigeria........	1,108.8	16.8	UK..... 53.8	US......16.4	Neth. ...14.5	
Algeria........	702.5	10.7	France. 71.7	US......16.4		
Libyan Arab Republic......	578.2	8.8	US..... 77.7	UK......10.9		
Zaire (Congo-Kinshasa).....	480.7	7.3	Belgium 87.8	Neth.... 4.4		
Zambia.........	421.1	6.4	UK..... 79.6	US......19.2		
Liberia........	299.5	4.5	US..... 57.8	Sweden..21.7		
Gabon..........	265.2	4.0	France. 73.4	US......10.9		
Ghana..........	260.4	4.0	UK..... 59.1	US......24.6		
Rhodesia.......	237.3	3.6	UK..... 88.3	US..... 4.2		
Ivory Coast....	201.6	3.1	France. 80.0	US...... 3.7		
Angola.........	193.3	2.9	-	UK......48.6	Portugal.28.5	US.......17.6
Morocco........	179.3	2.7	-	France..45.2	US.......19.5	Italy....15.6
Kenya..........	172.1	2.6	UK..... 78.8	US...... 8.7		
Senegal........	153.8	2.3	France. 87.4	US...... 4.4		
Cameroon.......	149.5	2.3	France. 75.1	UK......11.9		
Tunisia........	135.1	2.0	-	France..39.2	Italy....28.5	Sweden...10.4 US....... 9.6
Mozambique.....	102.2	1.6	UK..... 50.1	Port. ..37.2		
Mauritania.....	101.1	1.5	France. 68.8	UK......16.2		
Guinea.........	92.9	1.4	-	US......38.5	France...23.1	Switz....20.5
Congo (Congo-Brazzaville)..	90.1	1.4	France. 83.4	Belgium 6.1		
Malagasy Rep...	72.4	1.1	France. 76.5	US...... 8.3		
Sierra Leone...	68.1	1.0	UK..... 84.4	US......13.2		
United Republic of Tanzania...	60.4	0.9	-	UK......46.7	Italy....18.2	Denmark..12.9 FRG...... 5.6
United Arab Republic......	58.0	0.9	US..... 70.7	Italy...26.7		
Ethiopia.......	50.3	0.8	-	France..43.7	US.......23.9	UK.......15.9
Uganda.........	48.0	0.7	-	UK......48.1	Canada...31.3	US....... 4.2
Togo...........	42.4	0.6	France. 56.6	US......30.7		
Sudan..........	36.7	0.6	UK..... 74.9	Neth. ..13.6		
Central African Republic.......	36.6	0.6	France. 91.8	US..... 4.1		
Malawi.........	30.0	0.5	UK..... 92.7	US..... 6.7		
Swaziland......	29.0	0.4	UK..... 96.6	US..... 3.4		
Niger..........	23.3	0.4	France. 95.7	US..... 2.1		
Dahomey........	17.9	0.3	France. 57.0	Italy.. 25.7		
Chad...........	17.8	0.3	France. 80.4	Neth... 8.4		
Upper Volta.....	16.2	0.2	France. 75.3	UK..... 12.3		
Rwanda.........	15.2	0.2	Belgium 86.8	Italy.. 6.6		
Burundi........	14.2	0.2	Belgium 84.5	Canada. 7.1		
Somalia........	12.6	0.2	Italy.. 83.3	US..... 7.9		
Mali...........	6.5	0.1	France. 76.9	US..... 7.7		
Territory of the Afars and the Issars (French Somalia).......	5.5	0.1	France. 90.9	Neth... 5.5		
Botswana.......	2.5	0.0	UK..... 88.0	Neth... 12.0		
Gambia.........	2.3	0.0	UK..... 87.0	US..... 4.3		
Lesotho........	0.5	0.0	UK..... 60.0	US..... 20.0		

Country and region a/	DAC total (millions of dollars)	Percent- age share in total invest- ment in region	Share in total investment by DAC countries (percentage)			
			Country accounting for 50 per cent or more	Other main investing countries		
Asia	4,991.5	100.0		UK..... 41.5	US.......35.6	France... 6.6
India...........	1,308.7	26.2	UK..... 64.6	US..... 20.6		
Philippines.....	722.7	14.5	US..... 88.4	Neth... 3.8		
Malaysia........	679.4	13.6	UK..... 74.3	US..... 11.9		
Pakistan........	346.0	6.9	UK..... 59.5	US..... 22.3		
Hong Kong.......	285.1	5.7	-	UK..... 41.4	US...... 38.6	
Indonesia.......	254.0	5.1	US..... 73.2	France. 9.4		
Thailand........	213.7	4.3	-	US..... 40.2	UK...... 20.1	Japan... 19.7
Singapore.......	183.3	3.7	-	UK..... 33.8	US..... 33.3	Neth... 23.5
Papua-New Guinea	161.5	3.2	-	Austra- lia... 48.3	UK...... 34.1	
Viet-Nam, Rep.of	152.1	3.0	France. 65.7	US..... 27.0		
Sri Lanka.......	144.1	2.9	UK..... 95.1	US..... 1.4		
Brunei..........	85.5	1.7	Neth... 56.1	UK..... 43.9		
Khmer Republic.	83.9	1.7	France. 88.2	Belgium 5.9		
New Caledonia...	81.0	1.6	France. 91.4	US..... 7.4		
Korea, Rep. of..	78.0	1.6	US..... 92.3	Japan.. 4.2		
Ryukyu..........	18.0	0.4	US..... 66.7	Japan.. 33.3		
Afghanistan.....	12.0	0.2	US..... 54.2	FRG.... 33.3		
French Polynesia	11.0	0.2	France. 72.7	US..... 27.3		
Burma...........	9.7	0.2	UK..... 92.8	Denmark 7.2		
Laos............	8.3	0.2	-	France 36.6	US...... 36.6	Japan....12.2
Nepal...........	4.0	0.1	US..... 50.0	UK..... 35.0		
Bhutan..........	-	-	-	-		
Other...........	149.5	3.0	US..... 70.9	Japan.. 18.7		
Middle East......	3,102.7	100.0	US..... 57.3	UK..... 27.1		
Saudi Arabia....	866.0	27.9	US..... 90.4	Japan.. 9.2		
Iran............	713.5	23.0	-	US..... 45.1	UK...... 35.1	
Kuwait..........	620.7	20.0	US..... 54.4	UK..... 45.4		
Iraq............	186.7	6.0	-	UK..... 37.5	France.. 23.6	US...... 23.6
Bahrain.........	122.0	3.9	US..... 91.8	UK..... 8.2		
Israel..........	108.7	3.5	US..... 59.8	UK..... 14.7	Neth.... 8.3	
Abu Dhabi.......	102.5	3.3	UK..... 51.2	France. 26.3	US...... 13.7	
Lebanon.........	89.9	2.9	US..... 54.5	France. 21.7	UK...... 14.3	
Qatar...........	89.0	2.9	-	UK..... 40.5	Neth.... 33.7	US...... 12.9
Muscat and Oman.	70.0	2.3	Neth... 52.1	UK..... 37.9		
Southern Yemen and Aden.......	68.0	2.2	UK.... 100.0			
Syrian Arab Republic.......	35.2	1.1	US..... 56.8	UK..... 19.9	France.. 14.2	
Jordan..........	24.0	0.8	US..... 75.0	UK..... 20.0		
Dubai...........	6.5	0.2	-	US..... 46.2	UK...... 38.4	
Western hemi- sphere..........	18,449.3	100.0	US..... 63.8	UK..... 9.2	Canada.. 7.3	
Brazil..........	3,727.9	20.2	-	US..... 35.6 FRG..... 13.9	Canada.. 16.8 Japan.... 5.7	France... 7.1 UK....... 4.8
Venezuela.......	3,495.0	18.9	US..... 73.1	UK..... 10.1		
Argentina.......	1,821.4	9.9	US..... 55.8	Italy.. 11.3	UK...... 9.5	France... 5.7
Mexico..........	1,786.5	9.7	US..... 76.4	UK..... 6.5		
West Indies b/ .	1,109.7	6.0	-	US..... 42.2	UK...... 34.2	Canada...20.4
Chile...........	963.1	5.2	US..... 91.3	Japan... 3.6		
Panama..........	830.3	4.5	US..... 90.8	FRG..... 1.5		
Peru............	782.4	4.2	US..... 84.4	Japan... 3.8		
Colombia........	727.7	3.9	US..... 86.2	Neth.... 3.5		
Trinidad and Tobago.........	686.8	3.7	US..... 75.8	UK......17.8		
Jamaica.........	670.9	3.6	US..... 70.7	Canada..18.3		
Netherlands- Antilles.......	381.5	2.1	-	US..... 36.2	Neth.... 26.9	UK.......16.8

Country and region a/	DAC total (millions of dollars)	Percentage share in total investment in region	Share in total investment by DAC countries (percentage)		
			Country accounting for 50 per cent or more	Other main investing countries	
Guyana..........	189.0	1.0	-	Canada. 41.0	UK...... 34.1 US.......24.6
Honduras........	168.8	0.9	US..... 97.7	UK..... 1.4	
Dominican Republic.......	157.9	0.9	US..... 81.1	Canada. 17.1	
Guatemala.......	146.5	0.8	US..... 84.4	Canada. 6.1	
Bolivia.........	143.5	0.8	US..... 82.9	UK..... 8.4	
Costa Rica......	135.5	0.7	US..... 89.3	UK..... 5.9	
Surinam.........	99.6	0.5	US..... 56.7	Neth... 42.8	
Ecuador.........	82.0	0.4	US..... 58.5	UK..... 26.8	
El Salvador.....	77.5	0.4	US..... 58.1	Canada. 16.8	Japan.... 9.0
Nicaragua.......	72.8	0.4	US..... 63.9	Canada. 27.5	
Uruguay.........	60.1	0.3	US..... 71.5	FRG.... 9.7	
Haiti...........	36.2	0.2	US..... 56.6	France. 19.3	Canada...17.1
Paraguay........	34.7	0.2	US..... 57.6	UK..... 29.1	
British Honduras	28.5	0.2	UK..... 70.2	US..... 17.5	
French Antilles.	26.5	0.1	France. 71 7	US..... 18.9	
French Guyana...	7.0	0.0	France 100.0		

Source: Centre for Development Planning, Projections and Policies of the Department of Economic and Social Affairs of the United Nations Secretariat, based on Organisation for Economic Co-operation and Development, Stock of Private Direct Investments by DAC Countries in Developing Countries, end 1967 (Paris, 1972).

a/ Countries are arranged within regions in descending order of share in total investment in region by DAC countries.

b/ Includes Leeward Islands, Windward Islands, Bahamas, Barbados and Bermuda.

Table 24. 187 United States multinational corporations: method of entry into host country

(Number of affiliates and percentage)

	Total affiliates			Acquisitions a/			Acquisitions as percentage of total		
	Pre-1946	1946-1957	1958-1967	Pre-1945	1946-1957	1958-1967	Pre-1946	1946-1957	1958-1967
Developed market economies									
Canada...............	537	414	639	158	187	370	29.4	45.2	57.9
Western Europe.........	1,105	693	2,754	255	194	1,193	23.2	28.0	43.3
Southern hemisphere b/ ...	152	185	511	30	57	240	19.7	30.8	47.0
Japan................	17	43	198	5	17	53	29.4	39.5	26.8
Developing countries									
Western hemisphere......	508	735	1,309	110	157	477	21.7	21.4	36.4
Asia and Africa c/	103	176	491	17	23	109	16.5	13.1	22.2
TOTAL	2,422	2,246	5,898	576	635	2,442	23.8	28.3	41.4

Source: Centre for Development Planning, Projections and Policies of the Department of Economic and Social Affairs of the United Nations Secretariat, based on James W. Vaupel and Joan P. Curhan, The Making of Multinational Enterprise (Boston, 1969).

a/ Acquisition refers to purchases by United States corporations of domestic companies previously under local control.

b/ Including Australia, New Zealand, Republic of South Africa, Rhodesia.

c/ Excluding Rhodesia.

Table 25. United States and United Kingdom: average returns[a] on book
value of foreign direct investment by area and investing country

(Percentage)

Area of investment	United States Average (1965-1968)		United Kingdom Average (1965-1968)
	All sectors	Exclud-ing petroleum	Exclud-ing petroleum
Developed market economies	7.9	9.6	9.3
United States.....................	-	-	8.6
Canada............................	8.0	8.6	11.3
Europe[b]	7.1	10.0	7.9
Japan.............................	14.2	20.2	...
Southern hemisphere..............	9.7	12.0	9.5
Developing countries	17.5	11.0	9.8
Western hemisphere..............	12.1	11.1	8.7
Asia...........................	34.7	11.7)	
Africa.........................	22.3	7.7)	10.4
European developing countries[c]..	...	...)	
Unallocated......................	8.5	11.6	...
TOTAL	10.7	10.0	9.5

Source: Centre for Development Planning, Projections and Policies of the
Department of Economic and Social Affairs of the United Nations Secretariat,
based on United States Department of Commerce, Survey of Current Business,
various issues; United Kingdom Government Statistical Service, Business Monitor,
M4, Overseas Transactions, 1969 (London, 1971).

a/ Adjusted earnings (branch earnings + dividends + interest + reinvested
earnings) over book value at year end.

b/ United States data include all European countries, other than Eastern
Europe. United Kingdom data include European developed countries as defined by
the Organisation for Economic Co-operation and Development.

c/ As defined by the Organisation for Economic Co-operation and Development.

Table 26. United States and United Kingdom: royalty and fee receipts and payments, 1966, 1968, 1970, 1971

(Millions of dollars)

Country	Affiliate firms (direct investment)				Non-affiliate firms				Total			
	1966	1968	1970	1971	1966	1968	1970	1971	1966	1968	1970	1971
United States												
Receipts.....	1,030	1,245	1,620	1,874	353	461	600	695	1,383	1,707	2,220	2,569
Payments.....	64	80	111	91	76	107	119	125	140	187	230	216
Balance.....	966	1,166	1,509	1,783	277	354	481	570	1,243	1,520	1,990	2,353
United Kingdom												
Receipts.....	54 (12)a/	63 (12)	86 (20)	...	101 (27)	110 (36)	133 (40)	...	155 (38)	172 (48)	218 (60)	...
Payments.....	73 (56)a/	99 (78)	136 (111)	...	51 (31)	59 (30)	68 (38)	...	124 (87)	156 (108)	205 (145)	...
Balance.....	-19	-36	-50	...	50	51	65	...	31	16	13	...

Source: Centre for Development Planning, Projections and Policies of the Department of Economic and Social Affairs of the United Nations Secretariat, based on United States Department of Commerce, Survey of Current Business, various issues; United Kingdom Department of Trade and Industry, Trade and Industry (formerly Board of Trade Journal), various issues.

a/ In parentheses, receipts from and payments to the United States.

Table 27. United States manufacturing and mining affiliates in Central
and South America: local sales and exports, 1965, 1968

(Millions of dollars and percentage)

	Manufacturing affiliates		Mining affiliates	
	1965	1968	1965	1968
Total sales (millions of dollars)...	5,526	7,966	1,345	1,814
Total exports (millions of dollars).	415	753	1,105	1,497
Ratio of exports to sales (percentage).....................	7.5	9.4	82.2	82.5
Ratio of exports to United States to total exports of affiliates (percentage).....................	24.3	28.1	48.4	46.4

Source: Centre for Development Planning, Projections and Policies of the
Department of Economic and Social Affairs of the United Nations Secretariat,
based on United States, Department of Commerce, Survey of Current Business,
October 1970.

Table 28. Selected developing countries: current inflow of foreign direct
investment and outflow of income on accumulated past direct investment, a/
by region, 1965-1970

(Millions of dollars)

Region	1965	1966	1967	1968	1969	1970
Africa, total						
A. Inflow.............	182.2b/	163.7	241.5	201.6	235.5	270.7
B. Outflow............	380.8b/	718.8	708.6	963.7	924.3	996.2
C. Balance............	-198.6	-555.1	-467.1	-762.1	-688.8	-725.5
Non-oil producing countries c/						
A. Inflow...........	133.5	74.7	61.5	53.6	46.5	42.7
B. Outflow..........	49.3	53.8	56.6	57.7	56.3	60.2
C. Balance..........	84.2	20.9	4.9	-4.1	-9.8	-17.5
Oil-producing countries d/						
A. Inflow...........	48.7b/	89.0	180.0	148.0	189.0	228.0
B. Outflow..........	331.5b/	665.0	652.0	906.0	868.0	936.0
C. Balance..........	-282.8	-576.0	-472.0	-758.0	-679.0	-708.0
Western hemisphere, total						
A. Inflow.............	723.3	780.5	647.5	1,011.4	1,088.6	1,141.9
B. Outflow............	1,437.9	1,752.7	1,793.4	2,021.4	2,093.0	1,943.7
C. Balance............	-714.6	-972.2	-1,145.9	-1,010.0	-1,004.4	-801.8
Non-oil producing countries e/						
A. Inflow...........	642.3	671.5	567.5	827.4	964.6	1,067.9
B. Outflow..........	722.9	1,043.7	1,119.4	1,291.4	1,418.0	1,382.7
C. Balance..........	-80.6	-372.2	-551.9	-464.0	-453.4	-314.8

Region	1965	1966	1967	1968	1969	1970
Oil-producing countries						
A. Inflow...........	81.0	109.0	80.0	184.0	124.0	74.0
B. Outflow..........	715.0	709.0	674.0	730.0	675.0	561.0
C. Balance..........	-634.0	-600.0	-594.0	-546.0	-551.0	-487.0
Asia and West Asia, total						
A. Inflow.............	436.9	271.2	185.0	159.0	189.5	200.1
B. Outflow............	1,367.4	1,592.4	1,744.2	1,997.5	2,138.5	2,401.9
C. Balance............	-930.5	-1,321.2	-1,559.2	-1,838.5	-1,949.0	-2,201.8
Non-oil producing countries g/						
A. Inflow...........	131.0	95.2	60.0	94.0	116.5	180.1
B. Outflow..........	168.7	150.4	204.2	239.5	246.5	235.9
C. Balance..........	-37.7	-55.2	-144.2	-145.5	-130.0	-55.8
Oil-producing countries h/						
A. Inflow...........	305.9	176.0	125.0	65.0	73.0	20.0
B. Outflow..........	1,198.7	1,442.0	1,540.0	1,758.0	1,892.0	2,166.0
C. Balance..........	-892.8	-1,266.0	-1,415.0	-1,693.0	-1,819.0	-2,146.0
Selected developing countrics, total						
A. Inflow.............	1,342.4 b/	1,215.4	1,074.0	1,372.0	1,513.6	1,612.7
B. Outflow............	3,186.1 b/	4,063.9	4,246.2	4,982.6	5,155.8	5,341.8
C. Balance............	-1,843.7	-2,848.5	-3,172.2	-3,610.6	-3,642.2	-3,729.1
Non-oil producing countries, total						
A. Inflow...........	906.8	841.4	689.0	975.0	1,127.6	1,290.7
B. Outflow..........	940.9	1,247.9	1,380.2	1,588.6	1,720.8	1,678.8
C. Balance..........	-34.1	-406.5	-691.2	-613.6	-593.2	-388.1
Oil-producing countries, total						
A. Inflow...........	435.6 b/	374.0	385.0	397.0	386.0	322.0
B. Outflow..........	2,245.2 b/	2,816.0	2,866.0	3,394.0	3,435.0	3,663.0
C. Balance..........	-1,809.6	-2,442.0	-2,481.0	-2,997.0	-3,049.0	-3,341.0

Source: Centre for Development Planning, Projections and Policies of the Department of Economic and Social Affairs of the United Nations Secretariat, based on International Monetary Fund, Balance of Payments Yearbook (Washington, D.C.).

a/ All statistics - inflows and outflows - are expressed in gross figures.
b/ Excluding Algeria.
c/ Ethiopia, Ivory Coast, Malawi, Mauritius, Sierra Leone, Sudan, Tunisia.
d/ Algeria, Libyan Arab Republic, Nigeria.
e/ Argentina, Barbados, Bolivia, Brazil, Chile, Colombia, Costa Rica, Ecuador, El Salvador, Guatemala, Guyana, Haiti, Honduras, Jamaica, Mexico, Nicaragua, Panama, Paraguay, Peru, Surinam, Trinidad and Tobago.
f/ Venezuela.
g/ Indonesia, Israel, Lebanon, Philippines, Sri Lanka, Thailand, Republic of Viet-Nam.
h/ Iran, Iraq, Saudi Arabia.

Bibliography

"Acuerdo de Cartagena," 26 May 1969. Translated in *International Legal Materials*, 8 (1969), 910.

Adám, György. "New Trends in International Business: Worldwide Sourcing and Dedomiciling." *Acta Oeconomica,* 7 (1971), 319-367.

—————————— "The Big International Firm and the Socialist Countries and Interpretation." Paper presented at the Colloque Internationale, C.N.R.S., Rennes, 1972. Mimeographed.

——————————. "Some Implications and Concomitants of Worldwide Sourcing." *Acta Oeconomica,* 8 (1972), 309-323.

Adebahr, Hubertus. "Auslandskapital in der Bundesrepublik Deutschland." *Schmollers Jahrbuch,* 86 (1966), 469-484.

Adelman, M. A. "Is the Oil Shortage Real? Oil Companies as OPEC Tax-Collectors." *Foreign Policy,* 9 (1972), 69-107.

Ady, Peter, ed. *Private Foreign Investment and the Developing World.* New York: Praeger, 1971.

Aharoni, Yair. *The Foreign Investment Decision Process.* Boston: Harvard Business School, 1966.

——————————. "On the Definition of a Multinational Corporation." *Quarterly Review of Economics and Business,* 11 (1971), 27-37.

Ahooja, Krishna. "Investment Legislation in Africa." *Journal of World Trade Law,* 2 (1968), 495-520.

Akkache, Ahmed. *Capitaux Etrangers et Libération Economique: L'Experience Algerienne.* Paris: Maspero, 1971.

Alnasrawi, Abbas. "Collective Bargaining Power in OPEC." *Journal of World Trade Law,* 7 (1973), 188-207.

Amin, Samir. "Le Commerce International et les Flux Internationaux de Capitaux." *L'Homme et la Société,* 15 (1970), 77-103.

——————————. *L'Accumulation à l'Echelle Mondiale. Critique de la Théorie du Sous-développement.* Ifan-Dakar and Paris: Anthropos, 1971.

Amuzegar, Jahangir. "The Oil Story: Facts, Fiction, and Fair Play." *Foreign Affairs,* 51 (1973), 676-689.

ANZ Banking Group Limited. "Foreign Investment and Multinational Corporations in Australia." Mimeographed. Canberra, 1971.

Araujo, Orlando. *Venezuela: Die Gewalt als Voraussetzung der Freiheit.* Frankfurt: Suhrkamp, 1971.

Arditi, Nelson. *Les Investissements Etrangers en Turquie.* Geneva: Librairie Droz, 1970.

Aronson, Jonathan David. "The Multinational Corporation, the Nation-State, and the International Systems. A Bibliography." Mimeographed. Stanford: Stanford University, Department of Political Science, 1974.

Arosalo, Uolevi, and Väyrynen, Raimo. "Financial and Industrial Oligarchy: Present Structure and Some Trends." *Journal of Peace Research,* 10 (1973), 1-35.

Arpan, Jeffrey S. *International Intracorporate Pricing.* New York: Praeger, 1971.

Arrighi, Giovanni. "International Corporations, Labour Aristocracies and Economic Development in Tropical Africa." In *Imperialism and Underdevelopment; A Reader,* edited by Robert I. Rhodes. New York and London: Monthly Review Press, 1971.

Ashworth, William. *A Short History of the International Economy Since 1850.* London: Longman, 1962.

Aszkenazy, Heinz. *Les Grandes Sociétés Europeenes.* Brussels: CRISP' 1971.

Atkey, Ronald J. "Foreign Investment Disputes: Access of Private Individuals to International Tribunals." *Canadian Yearbook of International Law,* 5 (1967), 229-240.

Australia, Commonwealth of. *Report of the Committee of Economic Enquiry.* 2 vols. Canberra: Commonwealth of Australia, 1965.

——————————. Treasury. *Overseas Investment in Australia.* Canberra: Australian Government Publishing Service, 1972.

Bacon, Jeremy. *Corporate Directorship Practices: Membership and Committees of the Board.* New York: The Conference Board, 1973.

Babson, Steve. "The Multinational Corporation and Labor." *Review of Radical Political Economics,* 5 (1973), 19-36.

Baker, James C., and Bradford, M. Gerald. *American Banks Abroad: Edge Act Companies and Multinational Banking.* New York: Praeger, 1974.

Balasubramanyam, V. N. *International Transfer of Technology to India.* New York: Praeger, 1973.

Ball, George W. "Cosmocorp: The Importance of Being Stateless." *Columbia Journal of World Business,* 2 (1967), 25-30.

——————————. "Making World Corporations into World Citizens." (*War/Peace Report,* 8 (1968), 8-10.

——————————. "Toward a World Economy." *Dun's Review,* 91 (1968), 19-20.

Bank of Japan. *Manual of Foreign Investment in Japan.* Tokyo: Bank of Japan, 1970.

Bank of Tokyo. *The President Directory 1973.* Tokyo: Bank of Tokyo, 1972.

Banque Nationale de Belgique. "Les Investissements Etrangers dans les Enterprises Industrielles en Belgique." *Bulletin d'Information et de Documentation,* 2 (1970), 461-498.

Baran, Paul A. *The Political Economy of Growth.* New York: Monthly Review Press, 1957.

——————————, and Sweezy, Paul M. *Monopoly Capital: An Essay on the American Social and Economic Order.* New York: Monthly Review Press, 1966.

Baranson, Jack. *International Transfer of Automotive Technology to Developing Countries.* New York: UNITAR, 1971.

_____. "Technology Transfer Through the International Firm." *American Economic Review,* 60 (1970), 435-440.

_____. "Transfer of Technical Knowledge by International Corporations to Developing Economies." *American Economic Review, Papers and Proceedings,* 56 (1966), 259-267.

Barber, Richard J. *The American Corporation: Its Power, Its Money, Its Politics.* New York: Dutton, 1970.

Barkin, Solomon, et al., eds. *International Labor.* New York: Harper & Row, 1967.

Baum, Daniel J. "Global Corporation: An American Challenge to the Nation-State." *Iowa Law Review,* 55 (1969-1970), 410-437.

_____. *The Banks of Canada in the Commonwealth Caribbean: Economic Nationalism and Multinational Enterprises of a Medium Power.* New York: Praeger, 1974.

Behrendt, Hans. "Private Auslandsinvestitionen der Monopole in den Entwicklungsländern: Instrument des Neokolonialismus." *Deutsche Aussenpolitik,* 13 (1968), 980-989.

Behrman, Jack N. *Decision Criteria for Foreign Direct Investment in Latin America.* New York: Council of the Americas, 1974.

_____. *Direct Manufacturing Investment, Exports and the Balance of Payments.* New York: NFTC, 1968.

_____. "International Divestment: Panacea or Pitfall?" *Looking Ahead,* 18 (1970), 1-12.

_____. *National Interests and the Multinational Enterprise: Tensions Among the North Atlantic Countries.* Englewood Cliffs, N.J.: Prentice-Hall, 1970.

_____. "New Orientation in International Trade and Investment." In *Trade and Investment Policies for the Seventies: New Challenges for the Atlantic Area and Japan,* edited by Pierre Uri. New York: Praeger, 1971.

_____. *The Role of International Companies in Latin American Integration: Autos and Petrochemicals.* Lexington, Mass.: Lexington Books, 1972.

_____. "Sharing International Production Through the Multinational Enterprise and Sectoral Integration." *Law and Policy in International Business,* 4 (1972), 1-36.

_____. *Some Patterns in the Rise of the Multinational Enterprise.* Chapel Hill: University of North Carolina Press, 1969.

_____. "U.S. Government Encouragement of Private Direct Investment Abroad." In *United States Private and Government Investment Abroad,* edited by Raymond F. Mikesell. Eugene: University of Oregon Press, 1962.

_____. *U.S. International Business and Governments.* New York: McGraw-Hill, 1971.

Beigie, Carl E. "Foreign Investment in Canada: The Shade is Gray." *Columbia Journal of World Business,* 7 (1972), 23-32.

Belgium's 500 Largest Companies. Brussels: A. S. OKonomisk Literatur, 1969.

Benning, Bernhard. "Auslandskapital in der Bundesrepublik Deutschland. Umfang der ausländischen Direktinvestitionen und Einflüsse auf Volkswirtschaft und Kreditwirtschaft." *Schmollers Jahrbuch,* 86 (1966), 435-445.

Bergmann, Leopold. "Multinational Corporations and Labour in the EEC: A Survey of Research and Developments." Prepared for the ILO Research Meeting on Multinational Corporations and Labour, Geneva, December 1973. Mimeographed.

Bergsten, C. Fred. "Reforming the Dollar: An International Monetary Policy for the United States." Council on Foreign Relations Paper on International Affairs, no. 2. New York: Council on Foreign Relations, 1972.

Berkowitz, Leonard. "Aggression." *International Encyclopedia of the Social Sciences.* New York: Macmillan-Free Press, 1968.

Berman, Harold J., and Garson, John R. "United States Export Controls: Past, Present and Future." *Columbia Law Review,* 67 (1967), 791-890.

Bertin, Gilles Y. *L'Investissement des Firmes Etrangers en France (1945-1962).* Paris: Presses Universitaires de France, 1963.

——————————. "Foreign Investment in France." In *Foreign Investment: The Experience of Host Countries,* edited by I. A. Litvak and C. J. Maule. New York: Praeger, 1970.

——————————. "Les Causes de la Croissance des Enterprises à l'Etranger." *Revue Economique,* 23 (1972), 616-647.

——————————. "Les Entreprises Multinationales et les Etats Nationaux: Zones de Tension et Recherche de Solutions." *Analyse & Prévision,* 10 (1970), 669-674.

——————————. et al. *L'Expansion Internationale des Grandes Enterprises.* Rennes: G.R.E.F.I., 1972.

Bertrand Russell Peace Foundation. *Subversion in Chile: A Case Study in U.S. Corporate Intrigue in the Third World.* Nottingham: The Russell Press, 1972.

Bettelheim, Charles. "Economic Inequalities Between Nations and International Solidarity." *Monthly Review,* 22 (1970), 19-24.

Blake, David H. "Corporate Structure and International Unionism." *Columbia Journal of World Business,* 7 (1972), 19-26.

——————————. "Labor's Multinational Opportunities." *Foreign Policy,* 12 (1973), 132-143.

——————————. "The Multinationalization of Industrial Relations." *Journal of International Business Studies,* 3 (1972), 17-32.

——————————. ed. "The Multinational Corporation." *Annals of the American Academy of Political and Social Sciences,* 403 (1972), whole issue.

Blanchard, Daniel. "The Threat to U.S. Private Investment in Latin America." *Journal of International Law and Economics,* 5 (1971), 221-237.

Blauhorn, K. *Jetzt kauft uns Amerika!* Munich: Heyne Verlag, 1968.

Blough, Roy. *International Business: Environment and Adaptation.* New York: McGraw-Hill, 1966.

Böckstiegel, Karl Heinz. "Arbitration of Disputes Between States and Private Enterprises in the International Chamber of Commerce." *American Journal of International Law,* 59 (1965), 579-586.

Boddewyn, Jean. *International Business-Government Affairs: U.S. Corporate Experience Abroad.* New York: American Management Association, 1973.

——————. *Western European Policies Toward U.S. Investors.* Institute of Finance *Bulletin,* New York University, 1974.

Bohrisch, Alexander. *Probleme privater Auslandsinvestitionen in Mexico.* Hamburg: Übersee-Verlag, 1969.

Bonham, John M. "Private Long-Range Foreign Investment and U.S. Balance of Payments, 1950-1956." *Rocky Mountain Social Science Journal,* 6 (1969), 47-56.

Bonin, Bernard. *L'Investissement Etranger à Long Term au Canada.* Montreal: Les Presses de l'Ecole des Hautes Etudes Commerciales, 1967.

Bornschier, Volker. "Multinationale Wirtschaftskorporationen: Eine Form organizationeller Überschichtung im Weltmasstab." Mimeographed. Zürich: Soziologisches Institut der Universität, 1973.

Braindorge, Jacques. "L'Avenir des Relations Entre Firmes Multinationales et Etats Nationaux." *Analyse & Prévision,* 10 (1970), 723-736.

Branco, Raul. "Rational Development of Sea-bed Resources: Issues and Conflicts." *Ocean Management,* 1 (1973), 41-54.

——————. "The Tax Revenue Potential of Manganese Nodules." *Ocean Development and International Law Journal,* 1 (1973), 201-208.

Brash, Donald T. *American Investment in Australian Industry.* Canberra: Australian National University Press, 1966.

Brewster, Havelock. "The Growth of Employment and Export-biased Underdevelopment: Trinidad." *Social and Economic Studies,* 21 (1972), 153-170.

Brewster, Kingman. *Antitrust and American Business Abroad.* New York: McGraw-Hill, 1958.

Brimmer, Andrew F. "Eurodollar Flows and the Efficiency of U.S. Monetary Policy." Paper presented at Conference on Wall Street and the Economy, 1969, New York, The New School for Social Research.

Brooke, Michael Z., and Remmers, H. Lee. *The Strategy of Multinational Enterprise: Organization and Finance.* New York: American Elsevier, 1970.

——————. eds. *The Multinational Company in Europe: Some Key Problems.* London: Longman, 1972.

Brown, Courtney C., ed. *World Business: Promise and Problems.* New York, Macmillan, 1970.

Brown, Martin S., and Butler, John. *The Production, Marketing, and Consumption of Copper and Aluminum.* New York: Praeger, 1968.

Brubaker, Sterling. *Trends in the World Aluminum Industry.* Baltimore: The Johns Hopkins Press, 1967.

Bruck, Nicholas K., and Lees, Francis A. "Foreign Content of United States Corporate Activities." *Financial Analyst Journal,* Sept.-Oct. 1966, 127-132.

——————. *Foreign Investment, Capital Controls, and the Balance of Payments.* Institute of Finance *Bulletin,* New York University, 1968.

Brudenius, Claes. "The Anatomy of Imperialism: The Case of the Multinational Mining Corporations in Peru." *Journal of Peace Research,* 9 (1972), 189-208.

Bundesanstalt für Bodenforschung (BfB)',and Deutsches Institut für Wirtschaftsforschung (DIfW). *Untersuchungen über Angebot und Nachfrage mineralischer Rohstoffe: Aluminium.* Berlin and Hannover:(BfB)and DIfW, 1973.

Burger, Erwin. "Steuerpolitische Massnahmen der Industrieländer zur Förderung von privaten Direktinvestitionen in Entwicklungsländern." Ph.D. dissertation, University of Cologne, 1968.

Burtis, David; Lavipour, Farid G.; Ricciardi, Steven; and Sauvant, Karl P., eds. *Multinational Corporation—Nation-State Interaction: An Annotated Bibliography.* Philadelphia: Foreign Policy Research Institute, 1971.

Business International. *The Effects of U.S. Corporate Foreign Investment 1960-1970.* New York: Business International, 1972.

──────────. *The Effects of U.S. Corporate Foreign Investment 1960-1972.* New York: Business International, 1974.

──────────. *Organizing the Worldwide Corporation.* New York: Business International, 1970.

──────────. *Setting Intercorporate Pricing Policies.* New York: Business International, 1973.

Canada, Government of. *Foreign Direct Investment in Canada (Gray Report).* Ottawa: Information Canada, 1972.

──────────. *Foreign Ownership and the Structure of Canadian Industry.* Ottawa: Information Canada, 1968.

Canada, Canadian Department of Industry, Trade and Commerce. "Canada's International Investment Position, 1926 to 1967." Mimeographed. Ottawa, 1971.

──────────. "Direct Investment Abroad by Canada, 1964-1967." Mimeographed. Ottawa, February 1971.

Canada, Canadian Foreign Investment Division. "Foreign Direct Investment in Canada Since the Second World War." Mimeographed. Ottawa, 1970.

Cardoso, Fernando H., and Faletto Enzo. *Dependencia y desarrollo en América Latina.* Mexico City: Siglo Veintiuno Editores, 1969.

Carlsen, John. "Danish Private Business and the Developing Countries." Mimeographed. Copenhagen: Institute for Development Research, 1973.

──────────. "Danish Private Investment in Kenya." Mimeographed. Copenhagen: Institute for Development Research, 1973.

Carter, Cnendolen, ed. *National Unity and Regionalism.* New York: Cornell University Press, 1966.

Casas, Juan Carlos. *Las Multinacionales y el Comercio Latinoamericano.* Mexico: CEMLA, 1973.

Casserini, Karl. "L'internationalisation de la Production et les Syndicats." *Revue Economique et Sociale (Lausanne),* 25 (1967), 189-201.

Catherwood, H. F. R. "American Companies in Britain: The Advantages and the Problems." *Atlantic Community Quarterly,* 7 (1969), 405-413.

Chandler, Alfred D. *Strategy and Structure.* Cambridge: MIT Press, 1962.

Chang, Y. S. *The Transfer of Technology: Economics of Offshore Assembly. The Case of Semiconductor Industry.* New York: UNITAR, 1971.

Christen, R. M. *Die amerikanischen Auslandsinvestitionen in der Nachkriegs-zeit, ihre Motive und Wirkungen.* Winterthur: Keller, 1966.
Chudnovsky, D. "International Corporations and the Theory of Imperialism." *Bulletin of the Conference of Socialist Economists,* (1973), 12-22.
Chudson, Walter A. *The International Transfer of Commercial Technology to Developing Countries.* New York: UNITAR, 1971.
——————. and Wells, Louis T. *The Acquisition of Proprietary Technology by Developing Countries from Multinational Enterprises.* New York: United Nations, 1974.
Cockcroft, James D.; Frank, A. G.; and Johnson, Dale L. *Dependence and Underdevelopment: Latin America's Political Economy.* Garden City, N. Y.: Doubleday, 1972.
Comité Européen pour le Progrès Economique et Social (CEPES). *Grenzüberschreitende Unternehmungskooperation in der EWG.* Stuttgart: Forkel-Verlag, 1968.
Commerzbank. *Auslandsfertigung.* Frankfurt: Commerzbank, 1971.
Commission of the European Communities (CEC). *First Report on the Development of the Competition Policy.* Brussels: CEC, 1972.
——————. Fourth General Report on the Activities of the Communities, 1970. Brussels: CEC, 1971.
——————. *Industrial Policy in the Community. Memorandum from the Commission to the Council.* Brussels: CEC, 1970.
——————. *L'industrie Electronique des Pays de la Communauté et les Investissements Americains.* Brussels: CEC, 1969.
——————. "Multinational Undertakings and Community Regulations." Commission Communication to the Council, COM (73) 1930 (1973). Mimeographed.
——————. *Second Report on the Development of the Competition Policy.* Brussels: CEC, 1973.
——————. *Third General Report on the Activities of the Communities, 1969.* Brussels: CEC, 1970.
Confédération Générale du Travail (CGT). *The CGT and the Multinational Companies.* Paris: CGT, 1973.
CONICYT-Corfo. *Estudio de los Contratos de Compra de Tecnologia.* Santiago: CONICYT-Corfo, 1971.
Corcoran, James. "The Trading with the Enemy Act and the Controlled Canadian Corporation." *McGill Law Journal,* 14 (1968), 174-208.
Council of the Americas (CoA). *The Effects of United States and other Foreign Investment in Latin America.* New York: CoA, 1971.
——————. *The Andean Pact: Definition, Design, and Analysis.* New York: CoA, 1974.
Craig, William. "Applications of the Trading with the Enemy Act to Foreign Corporations Owned by Americans: Reflections on Fruehauf V. Massardy." *Harvard Law Review,* 83 (1969-1970), 597-601.
Critiques de l'Economie Politique. La Formation du Sousdéveloppement, April-June 1971, whole issue.
Dahl, Frederick. "International Operations of U.S. Banks: Growth and Public Policy Implications." *Law and Contemporary Problems,* 32 (1967), 100-130.

d'Alauro, Orlando. "Les Effects Actuels et Potentials des Investissements Directs de Provenance Etrangère sur les Balances des Paiements des Pays de la C. E. E." In *La Politique Industrielle de l'Europe Integrée et l'Apport des Capitaux Extérieurs,* edited by Maurice Byé. Paris: Presses Universitaires de France, 1968.

Daly, Rex F. "Coffee Consumption and Prices in the United States." *Agricultural Economic Research,* 10 (July 1958), 61-71.

Daniels, John D. *Recent Foreign Direct Manufacturing Investment in the United States.* New York: Praeger, 1971.

Davis, Steven. "U.S. Banks Abroad: One-stop Shopping?" *Harvard Business Review,* 49 (1971), 75-84.

Dean, Arthur. "The Impact of Antitrust Regulation upon the Multinational Corporation." *SAIS Review,* 13 (1969), 4-17.

de Cecco, Marcello. "Der Einfluss der multinationalen Gesellschaften auf die Wirtschaftspolitik der unterentwickelten Länder." In *Kapitalismus in den siebziger Jahren, Referate vom Kongress in Tilburg im Sept. 1970,* pp. 172-197. Frankfurt: Europäische Verlagsanstalt, 1971.

de Jong, Fritz. "L'influence de l'Investissement Direct Etranger sur la Balance des Paiements des Pays-Bas." In *La Politique Industrielle de l'Europe Integrée et l'Apport des Capitaux Extérieurs,* edited by Maurice Byé. Paris: Presses Universitaires de France, 1968.

deKadt, Emanuel, ed. *Patterns of Foreign Influence in the Caribbean.* London: Oxford University Press, 1972.

Delilez, Jean-Pierre. "Internationalisation." *Economie et Politique,* 212 (1972), 53-71.

Demas, William G. *The Economics of Development in Small Countries with Special Reference to the Caribbean.* Montreal: McGill University Press, 1965.

Demerara Bauxite Co., Ltd. "Where Did the Money Go? The Demba Record in Guyana, 1919-1969," September 1970.

Departamento Nacionál de Planeación. *Transferencia de Tecnología.* Bogota: Departamento Nacionál de Planeación, 1970.

Desai, Ashok. *Foreign Technology and Investment.* New Delhi: National Council of Applied Economic Research, 1971.

de Seynes, Philippe. "Multinational Corporations: A View from the United Nations." Address given at the Annual Meeting of the Academy of International Business, New York, 1973. Mimeographed.

——————. "The Role of International Organizations and Multinational Corporations." Address given at the Wharton School Multinational Lecture Series, Philadelphia, 1973. Mimeographed.

de Sousa, Eduardo F. "Internationales Kapital in Nambia." *Blätter für deutsche und internationale Politik,* 12 (1972), 1315-1324.

Deutsch-schwedische Handelskammer. *Ausländische Unternehmensniederlassungen in Schweden und schwedische Unternehmensniederlassungen in Ausland.* Stockholm: Tysksvenska handelskammaren, 1968.

Devadhar, Y. C. "The Role of Foreign Private Capital in India's Economic Development: An Assessment of Policy and Performance." *International Studies,* 8 (1966-1967), 242-276.

Dickie, Robert B. *Foreign Investment in France: A Case Study.* Dobbs Ferry, N.Y.: Oceana Publications, 1970.

Diebold Group. *Business and Developing Countries.* New York: Praeger, 1974.

DIVO Institut. *Amerikanische Tochtergesellschaften in der Bundesrepublik: Analyse und kritische Würdigung.* Frankfurt: DIVO Institut, 1968.

Doggart, Tony, and Voûte, Carroline. *Tax Havens and Offshore Funds.* London: Economist Intelligence Unit, 1971.

Doman, Nicholas. "New Developments in the Field of Nationalization." *New York University Journal of International Law and Politics,* 3 (1970), 306-322.

Donaghue, Hugh P. "Control Data's Joint Venture in Romania." *Columbia Journal of World Business,* 8 (1973), 83-89.

Donner, Frederic G. *The World-Wide Industrial Enterprise: Its Challenge and Promise.* New York: McGraw-Hill, 1967.

Donovan, Peter. "Antitrust Consideration in the Organization and Operations of American Business Abroad." *Boston College Industrial and Commercial Law Review,* 9 (1968), 239-353.

Drysdale, Peter. *Direct Foreign Investment in Asia and the Pacific.* Toronto: University of Toronto Press, 1972.

Dubashi, J. *Research and Industry: Seven Case Histories.* New Delhi: Economic and Scientific Research Council, 1966.

Duerr, Michael G. *R & D in the Multinational Company.* New York: National Industrial Conference Board, 1970.

Dunning, John H. *American Investment in British Manufacturing Industry.* London: George Allen & Unwin, 1958.

——————. "The Determinants of International Production." *Oxford Economic Papers (New Series),* 25 (1973), 280-336.

——————. *The Role of American Investment in the British Economy.* London: PEP, 1969.

——————. *Studies in International Investment.* London: George Allen & Unwin, 1970.

——————. *United States Industry in Britain.* London: Economists' Advisory Group Research Study, 1972.

——————. *U.S. Industry in Britain.* EAG/FT Profile no. 1, London, 1973.

——————. "U.S. Manufacturing Affiliates in the U.K.: A Statistical Profile." *EAG, Financial Times Occasional Paper,* 1972.

——————. ed. *Economic Analysis and the Multinational Enterprise.* London: George Allen & Unwin, 1974.

——————. ed. *International Investment: Selected Readings.* Harmondsworth, Eng.: Penguin, 1972.

——————. ed. *The Multinational Enterprise.* London: George Allen & Unwin, 1971.

Durand-Reville, Luc. *Les Investissements Privés au Service du Tiers-Monde.* Paris: Editions France-Empire, 1970.

Ebert, R. R. "Multinational Coordination of Labor Objectives in the Automobile Unions." *Ohio State University Bulletin of Business Research,* 44 (1969), 1-3; 7-9.

Economic Commission for Europe (ECE). "Analytical Report on Industrial Co-operation Among ECE Countries." Mimeographed. United Nations document (E/ECE/844), Geneva, March 14, 1973.
──────────. Analytical Report on the State of Intra-European Trade. New York: United Nations, 1971.
Economic Commission for Latin America (ECLA). Economic Survey of Latin America. New York: United Nations, 1972.
──────────. The Process of Industrial Development in Latin America. New York: United Nations, 1965.
Economist Intelligence Unit. The Growth and Spread of Multinational Companies. QER special, October 1969, April 1971.
Eder, George. "Expropriation: Hickenlooper and Hereafter." International Lawyer, 4 (1970), 611-645.
Edwards, Corwin D. "The World of Antitrust." Columbia Journal of World Business, 4 (1969), 11-25.
Edwards, John. "The International Tin Agreement." Journal of World Trade Law, 3 (1969), 237-250.
Eells, Richard. Global Corporation: The Emerging System of World Economic Power. New York: Interbook, 1972.
Ehrlich, Robert. "Amerikanische Direktinvestitionen in Österreich." Monatsberichte, supplement no. 89, edited by Oesterreichisches Institut für Wirtschaftsforschung, December 1970.
Eiteman, David K., and Stonehill, Arthur I. Multinational Business Finance. Reading, Mass.: Addison-Wesley, 1973.
Eliasson, Gunnar. "Swedish Enterprise in Europe." Mimeographed. Stockholm: Sveriges Industriforbund, 1971.
Elsenhans, Hartmut, and Junne, Gerd. "Einige Aspekte des gegenwärtigen Wandels der internationalen Arbeitsteilung." Mimeographed. Berlin: Freie Universität, Fachbereich Politische Wissenschaft, 1973.
Emergency Committee for American Trade (ECAT). The Role of the Multinational Corporation (MNC) in the United States and World Economies. 2 vols. Washington, D. C.: ECAT, 1972.
Emmanuel, Arghiri. "The Delusions of Internationalism." Monthly Review, 22 (1970), 13-18.
──────────. L'échange Inégal: Essai sur les Antagonismes dans les Rapports Economiques Internationaux. Paris: Maspero, 1972.
Endres, Ulla. "Auswahlbibliographie Multinationale Konzerne." In Multinationale Konzerne, edited by Otto Kreye. Munich: Hanser, 1974.
Evan, Harry Z. "The Multinational Oil Company and the Nation State." Journal of World Trade Law, 4 (1970), 666-685.
Evan, William M. "The Organization-Set: Toward a Theory of Interorganizational Relations." In Approaches to Organizational Design, edited by James D. Thompson. Pittsburgh: University of Pittsburgh, 1966.
──────────. "An Organization-Set Model of Interorganizational Relations." In Interorganizational Decision Making, edited by M. F. Tuite, Roger Chisholm, and Michael Radnor. Chicago: Aldine, 1972.
──────────. Organization Theory: Systems, Structures, and Environments. New York: John Wiley, 1976.

Evan, William M.; Hilton, Andrew C.; Irwin, Patrick H.; Saghafi-nejad, Taghi; and Sauvant, Karl P. "The Effects of Multinational Enterprises on the Modernization Process of Developing Countries: A Comparative Study." Mimeographed. Philadelphia: University of Pennsylvania, 1973.

Faith, Nicholas. *The Infiltrators: The European Business Invasion of America.* London: Hamish Hamilton, 1971.

Fajnzylber, Fernando. *Sistema industrial y exportación de manufacturas: análisis de la experiencia brasilera.* Santiago: ECLA, 1970.

Falsami, Robert C. "The Multinational Cocoa Agreement." *Law and Policy in International Business,* 5 (1973), 999-1017.

Fann, K. T., and Hodges, Donald C., eds. *Readings in U.S. Imperialism.* Boston: Porter Sargent, 1971.

Fatouros, A. A. "The Computer and the Mud Hut: Notes on Multinational Enterprise in Developing Countries." *Columbia Journal of Transnational Law,* 10 (1971), 325-363.

Fayerweather, John. "Elite Attitudes Toward Multinational Firms." *International Studies Quarterly,* 16 (1972), 472-490.

————————. *Foreign Investment in Canada.* New York: International Arts and Sciences Press, 1973.

————————. *International Business Management: A Conceptual Framework.* New York: McGraw-Hill, 1968.

Feis, Herbert. *Europe: The World's Banker, 1870 1914.* New Haven: Yale University Press, 1931.

Feld, Werner J. *Nongovernmental Forces and World Politics.* New York: Praeger, 1973.

————————. "Political Aspects of Transnational Business Collaboration in the Common Market." *International Organization,* 24 (1970), 109-138.

————————. *Transnational Business Collaboration Among Common Market Countries.* New York: Praeger, 1970.

Ferrer, Aldo. "Foreign Enterprises and National Development." *Comments on Argentine Trade,* 50 (1971), 12-16.

Ferris, Paul. *The Money Men of Europe.* New York: Macmillan, 1969.

Fine, Richard J. "The Control of Restrictive Business Practices in International Trade—A Viable Proposal for an International Trade Organization." *International Lawyer,* 7 (1973), 635-676.

First, Ruth; Steele, Jonathan; and Gurney, Christabel. *The South African Connection: Western Investment in Apartheid.* London: Temple Smith, 1972.

Foch, René. *Europe and Technology: A Political View.* Paris: Atlantic Institute, 1970.

Foot, D. K. "Overseas Investment: The Economic Effects." *Economic Activity in Western Australia,* 40 (1966), 22-32.

"Foreign Investment in Latin America: Past Policies and Future Trends," in "Proceedings of a Regional Meeting of the American Society of International Law." *Virginia Journal of International Law,* 1970.

Forsyth, David. "Foreign-Owned Firms and Labour Relations: A Regional Perspective." *British Journal of Industrial Relations,* 10 (1973), 20-28.

Forsyth, David. *U.S. Investment in Scotland.* New York: Praeger, 1972.

Fowler, Henry H. "National Interest and Multinational Business." *California Management Review,* 8 (1965), 3-12.

Frank, A. G. *Capitalism and Underdevelopment in Latin America.* New York: Monthly Review Press, 1969.

——————. *Lumpenbourgeoisie: Lumpen Development.* New York: Monthly Review Press, 1972.

Franko, Lawrence G. "Who Manages Multinational Enterprises?" *Columbia Journal of World Buisness,* 8 (Summer 1973), 30-42.

Frerichs, Karl; Idel, Klaus; Jüttner, Heinrich; and Wolf, Alfred. *Analyse der internationalen industriellen Zusammenarbeit.* Opladen: Westdeutscher Verlag, 1973.

Friedman, Wolfgang M. "The Contractual Joint Venture." *Columbia Journal of World Business,* 7 (1972), 57-63.

Fulda, Carl H., and Schwartz, Warren F. *Regulation of International Trade and Investment.* New York: The Foundation Press, 1970.

Furtado, Celso. *Development and Underdevelopment.* Berkeley: University of California Press, 1971.

——————. *Los Estados Unidos y el subdesarrollo de América Latina.* Lima: Campodónico Ediciones, 1971.

Furuhashi, Yusaku. "Foreign Capital in Japan." *Columbia Journal of World Business,* 7 (1972), 50-56.

Gabriel, Peter. "Adaptation: The Name of the MNCs' Game." *Columbia Journal of World Business,* 7 (1972), 7-14.

——————. *The International Transfer of Corporate Skills.* Boston: Harvard Business School, 1967.

Galtung, Johan. "A Structural Theory of Imperialism." *Journal of Peace Research,* 8 (1971), 81-118.

Ganoe, Charles. "Banking Consortia: Are They Here to Stay?" *Columbia Journal of World Business,* 7 (1972), 51-58.

Gantzel, Klaus Jürgen, ed. *Zur Multinationalisierung des Kapitals.* Hamburg: Deutsche Vereinigung für Politische Wissenschaft, 1976.

Gennard, John. *Multinational Corporations and British Labour: A Review of Attitudes and Responses.* London: British-North American Committee, 1972.

Gensous, P. "Die Gewerkschaften und die multinationalen Gesellschaften." *Weltgewerkschaftsbewegung,* 6-7 (1971).

Gervais, Jacques. *La France Face au Investissements Etrangers. Analyse par Secteurs.* Paris: Editions de l'Enterprise Moderne, 1963.

Gilles, Paquet, ed. *The Multinational Firm and the Nation-State.* Don Mills: Collier-Macmillan, 1972.

Girvan, Norman. "Bauxite: The Need to Nationalize, Part II." *Review of Black Political Economy,* 2 (Winter 1972), 81-101.

——————. *The Caribbean Bauxite Industry.* Jamaica: University of the West Indies, 1967.

——————. *Foreign Capital and Economic Underdevelopment in Jamaica.* Jamaica: University of the West Indies, 1971.

——————. "Multinational Corporations and Dependent Underdevelopment in Mineral Export Economies." Mimeographed. New Haven: Yale University, 1970.

Girvan, Norman. "Why We Need to Nationalize Bauxite and How." In *Readings in Political Economy of the Caribbean,* edited by Norman Girvan and Owen Jefferson. Kingston: Ebony Business Printers, 1971.

──────────. and Jefferson, Owen, eds. *Readings in Political Economy of the Caribbean.* Kingston: Ebony Business Printers, 1971.

Glickman, Richard B., and Sukijasovic, Miodag. "Yugoslav Worker Management and its Effect on Foreign Investment." *Harvard International Law Journal,* 12 (1971), 260-311.

Goldberg, Paul M., and Kindleberger, Charles P. "Toward a GATT for Investment: A Proposal for Supervision of the International Corporation." *Law and Policy in International Business,* 2 (1970), 295-325.

Gordon, Walter L. *A Choice for Canada: Independence or Colonial Status.* Toronto: McClelland and Stewart, 1966.

Gray, H. Peter. *The Economics of Business Investment Abroad.* New York: Crane, 1972.

──────────. and Makinen, Gail E. "The Balance-of-Payments Contributions of Multinational Corporations." *Journal of Business,* 40 (1967), 339-343.

Grant, Cedric H. *Company Towns in the Caribbean: A Preliminary Analysis of Christianburg-Wismar-Mackenzie.* Georgetown: Government Printery, 1970.

──────────. "Political Sequel to Alcan Nationalisation in Guyana: The International Aspects." *Social and Economic Studies,* 22 (1973), 249-271.

Greene, James, and Duerr, Michael G. *Intercompany Transactions in the Multinational Firm.* New York: National Industrial Conference Board, 1970

Grosche, Günter, and Lehmann-Richter, Rolf. *Die Gewinne aus deutschen Direktinvestitionen in Entwicklungsländern.* Düsseldorf: Bertelsmann Universitätsverlag, 1970.

Grotkopp, Wilhelm, and Schmacke, Ernst. *Die grossen 500.* Düsseldorf: Droste Verlag, 1971.

Groves, Roderick. "Expropriation in Latin America: Some Observations." *Inter-American Economic Affairs,* 23 (1969), 47-66.

Gruber, William; Mehta, Dileep; and Vernon, Raymond. "The R & D Factor in International Trade and International Investment of United States Industries." *The Journal of Political Economy,* 75 (1967), 20-37.

Grünwald, Oskar, and Lacina, Ferdinand. *Auslandskapital in der österreichischen Wirtschaft.* Vienna: Europa Verlag, 1970.

Günter, Hans, ed. *Transnational Industrial Relations: The Impact of Multinational Corporations and Economic Regionalism on Industrial Relations.* London: Macmillan, 1972.

Halliday, Jon, and McCormack, Gavan. Japanese Imperialism Today: Co-prosperity in Greater East Asia. Harmondsworth, Eng.: Penguin Books, 1973.

Hartmann, Heinz. *Amerikanische Firmen in Deutschland.* Cologne and Opladen: Westdeutscher Verlag, 1963.

Hastedt, Pedro G. *Deutsche Direktinvestitionen in Lateinamerika.* Göttingen: Verlag Otto Schwartz, 1970.

Haubold, Dietmar. *Direktinvestitionen und Zahlungsbilanz.* Hamburg: Verlag Weltarchiv, 1972.

Hawkins, Robert G. *Job Displacement and the Multinational Firm: A Methodological Review.* Washington, D.C.: Center for Multinational Studies, 1972.

────────── . *U.S. Multinational Investment in Manufacturing and Domestic Economic Performance.* Washington, D.C.: Center for Multinational Studies, 1972.

Hederer, G.; Hoffman, C. D., and Kumar, B. "The Internationalization of German Business." *Columbia Journal of World Business,* 7 (1972), 38-44.

Heldring, F. "Multinational Banking Strives for Identity." *Columbia Journal of World Business,* 3 (1968), 49-53.

Helfgott, Roy B. "Multinational Corporations and Manpower Utilization in Developing Nations." *Journal of Developing Areas,* 7 (1973), 235-246.

Hellman, Rainer. *Amerika auf dem Europamarkt.* Baden-Baden: Nomos Verlagsgesellschaft, 1966.

────────── . *The Challenge to U.S. Dominance of the International Corporation.* New York: Dunellen, 1970.

Herzog, Philippe. "Nouveau Développements de l'Internationalisation du Capital." *Economie et Politique,* 198 (1971), 125-158.

Hinfrey, Colin. "Foreign Influences in Guyana: The Struggle for Independence." In *Patterns of Foreign Influence in the Caribbean,* edited by Emanuel de Kadt. London: Oxford University Press, 1972.

Hirschman, Albert O. *How to Divest in Latin America and Why.* Princeton: Princeton University, 1969.

────────── . "The Political Economy of Import-Substituting Industrialization in Latin America." *Quarterly Journal of Economics,* 2 (1968), 1-32.

Hobbing, Enno. "The World Corporation: A Catalytic Agent?" *Columbia Journal of World Business,* 6 (1971), 45-51.

Holbik, Karel. "Canada's Economic Sovereignty and United States Investment." *Quarterly Review of Economics and Business,* 10 (1970), 5-16.

Hornbostel, Peter A. "Investment Guarantees: Bureaucracy Clogs the Flow." *Columbia Journal of World Business,* 4 (1969), 37-47.

Holt, John B. "Joint Ventures in Yugoslavia: West German and American Experiences." *MSU Business Topics,* 21 (1973), 51-63.

────────── . "New Roles for Western Multinationals in Eastern Europe." *Columbia Journal of World Business,* 8 (1973), 131-139.

Houthaker, H. S., and Magee, F. P. "Income and Price Elasticities in World Trade." *Review of Economics and Statistics,* 51 (May 1969), 111-125.

Hu, Y. S. *The Impact of U.S. Investment in Europe: A Case Study of the Automotive and Computer Industries.* New York: Praeger, 1973.

Hufbauer, G. C., and Adler, F. M. *Overseas Manufacturing Investment and the Balance of Payments.* Washington, D.C.: Government Printing Office, 1968.

Huggins, H. D. *Aluminium in Changing Communities.* London: André Deutsch, 1965.

Hughes, Helen, ed. *Prospects for Partnership.* Baltimore: Johns Hopkins University Press, 1973.

Hughes, Helen, and You, Poh Seng, eds. *Foreign Investment and Industrialisation in Singapore.* Canberra: Australian National University Press, 1969.

Hugill, J. A. C. "The Industry Cooperative Programme." Testimony before the United Nations Group of Eminent Persons to Study the Impact of Multinational Corporations, Geneva, November 1973. Mimeographed.

Huntington, Samuel P. "Transnational Organizations in World Politics." *World Politics,* 25 (1973), 333-368.

Hveem, Helge.*The Global Dominance System.* Oslo: International Peace Research Institute, forthcoming.

──────────. "The Global Dominance System: Notes on a Theory of Global Political Economy." *Journal of Peace Research,* 10 (1973), 319-340.

──────────. "International Anti-Domination Struggle and the 'Opecization' of Raw Materials." Mimeographed. Oslo: International Peace Research Institute, 1974.

Hymer, Stephen. "La Grande Corporation Multinationale." *Revue Economique (Paris),* 19 (1968), 949-972.

──────────. "The Internationalization of Capital." *Journal of Economic Issues,* 6 (1972), 91-111.

──────────. "The International Operations of National Firms: A Study of Direct Investment." Ph.D. dissertation, Massachusetts Institute of Technology, 1960.

Ihara, T. "Die japanischen Investitionsbewegungen vom und ins Ausland." *Aussenwirtschaft,* (1971), 100-121.

Iklé, Max. *Die Schweiz als internationaler Bank- und Finanzplatz.* Zürich: Orell Füssli Verlag, 1970.

"Indonesia: Profile of a Neocolony." *Tricontinental,* 5 (1970), 3-15.

Industrial Reorganisation Corporation (IRC). *The 1969/70 Report & Accounts.* London: IRC, 1970.

Ingram, George M. *Nationalization of U.S. Property in South America.* New York: Praeger, 1974.

Institut für Marxistische Studien und Forschungen (IMSF). *Internationale Konzerne und Arbeiterklasse: Dokumente; Statistiken; Analysen.* Frankfurt: IMSF, 1971.

International Centre for Settlement of Investment Disputes (ICSID). *Investment Laws of the World.* Dobbs Ferry, N.Y.: Oceana, 1973.

International Chamber of Commerce (ICC). *Guidelines for International Investment.* Paris: ICC, 1972.

──────────. *The International Corporation and the Transfer of Technology.* Paris: ICC, 1972.

──────────. *Realities: Multinational Enterprises Respond on Basic Issues.* Paris: ICC, 1974.

International Confederation of Free Trade Unions (ICFTU). *The Multinational Challenge.* Brussels: ICFTU, 1971.

International Labour Office (ILO). *Multinational Enterprises and Social Policy.* Geneva: ILO, 1973.

International Research Associates and International Advertising Association. *1970 World Advertising Expenditures.* New York: International Research Associates, 1972.

Iskander, Marwan. *The Arab Oil Question.* Beirut: Middle East Economic Consultants, 1974.

Jagauribe, Hélio. *La dependencia político-econômica de America Latina.* Mexico City: Siglo Veintiuno Editores, 1969.

Jager, Elizabeth. "Multinationalism and Labor: For Whose Benefit?" *Columbia Journal of World Business,* 5 (1970), 56-64.

Jalée, Pierre. *Le Tiers Monde dans l'Economie Mondiale.* Paris: Maspero, 1968.

——————. *L'Imperialisme en 1970.* Paris: Maspero, 1969.

Japan External Trade Organization (JETRO). *Japan into the Multinationalization Era.* Tokyo: JETRO, 1973.

Japan Tariff Association. *The Customs Tariff of Japan, 1962.* Tokyo: Japan Tariff Association, 1962.

Japanese Trade and Industry Ministry (MITI). *Special Report on Foreign Owned Firms in Japan.* Tokyo: MITI, 1968.

Johnstone, Allan W. *United States Direct Investment in France: An Investigation of the French Charges.* Cambridge: MIT Press, 1965.

Judet, P., and Palloix, Christian. *Grandes Firmes Multinationales et Transfer des Technologies.* Grenoble: IREP, 1972.

Julien, Claude. *L'Empire Americain.* Paris: B. Grasset, 1968.

Jung, Volker, and Piehl, Ernst. "Die Entwicklung der internationalen Strukturen der westeuropäischen Gewerkschaften." *WSI-Mitteilungen,* 6 (1972), 191-198.

Jungnickel, Rolf, and Koopmann, Georg. "Deutsche Unternehmen in Entwicklungsländern." *Wirtschaftsdienst,* 53 (1973), 461-464.

——————. and Koopmann, Georg. "Wie multinational sind die deutschen Unternehmen?" *Wirtschaftsdienst,* no. 4(1972), 191-195.

——————. Koopmann, Georg; Matthies, Klaus; and Sutter, R. *Die deutschen multinationalen Unternehmen: Der Internationalisierungsprozess der deutschen Industrie.* Frankfurt: Athenäum, 1974.

——————. and Matthies, Klaus. *Multinationale Unternehmen und Gewerkschaften.* Hamburg: Weltarchiv, 1973.

Junne, Gerd, and Nour, Salua. "Zur Analyse internationaler Abhängigkeiten." Mimeographed. Berlin: Freie Universität, 1972.

Kamin, Alfred, ed. *Western European Labor and the American Corporation.* Washington, D.C.: Bureau of National Affairs, 1970.

Kanenas. "Wide Limits and 'Equitable' Distribution of Seabed Resources." *Ocean Development and International Law Journal,* 1 (1973), 137-157.

Kaplan, Marcos, ed. *Corporaciones publicas multinacionales.* Mexico: Fondo de Cultura Economica, 1972.

Kapoor, Ashok. *International Business Negotiations: A Study in India.* New York: New York University Press, 1970.

——————. and Grub, Phillip, eds. *The Multinational Enterprise in Transition. Selected Readings and Essays.* Princeton, N.H.: Darwin, 1972.

Kates, Peat, Marwick and Co. "Foreign Ownership and the Advertising Industry." Mimeographed. Province of Ontario, Canada, June 1973.

Katz, Jorge. "Importación de Tecnología. Aprendizaje Local e Industrialización Dependiente." *Documento de Trabajo.* Buenos Aires: Instituto Torcuato di Tella, 1972.

——————. "Le Industria Farmsceutica Argentina. Estructura y Comportamiento." *Documento de Trabajo.* Buenos Aires: Instituto Torcuato di Tella, 1973.

Katz, Jorge. "Patentes, Corporaciones Multinacionales y Tecnología: Un Examen Crítico de la Legislación Internacionál." *Desarrollo Economico,* 12 (1972), 105-150.

Kauder, Louis M. *International Allocations of Income, Problems of Administration and Compliance.* United Nations document (ST/SG/AC.8/L.5), September 27, 1973.

Keller, Ernst. "Multinational Corporations in World Development." Hearings before the United Nations Group of Eminent Persons to Study the Impact of Multinational Corporations, New York, September 1973. Mimeographed.

Kendall, Donald. "Corporate Ownership: The International Dimension." *Columbia Journal of World Business,* 4 (1969), 59-65.

Keohane, Robert O., and Nye, Joseph S., Jr., eds. *Transnational Relations and World Politics.* Cambridge: Harvard University Press, 1972.

Kidron, Michael. *Foreign Investments in India.* London: Oxford University Press, 1965.

Kilby, Peter. *Industrialization in an Open Society: Nigeria 1945-1966.* London: Cambridge University Press, 1969.

Kindleberger, Charles P. *American Business Abroad: Six Lectures on Direct Investment.* New Haven: Yale University Press, 1969.

_____. "European Integration and the International Corporation." *Columbia Journal of World Business,* 1 (1966), 65-73.

_____. ed. *The International Corporation: A Symposium.* Cambridge: MIT Press, 1970.

_____. "The International Firm and the International Capital Market." *Southern Economic Journal,* 39 (1971), 223-230.

Kirschen, E.; Bloch, H. S.; and Bassett, W. B. *Financial Integration in Western Europe.* New York: Columbia University Press, 1969.

Klijnstra. G. D. A., and Woodroofe, Sir Ernest G. "Statement to the United Nations Economic and Social Council Group of Eminent Persons." Hearings before the United Nations Group of Eminent Persons to Study the Impact of Multinational Corporations, Geneva, November 1973. Mimeographed.

Klopstock, Fred H. "The Euro-dollar Market: Some Unresolved Issues." *Essays in International Finance* (Princeton University), 65 (1968), 1-21.

_____. "Euro-dollars in the Liquidity and Reserve Management of United States Banks." *Federal Reserve Bank of New York Monthly Review,* 50 (1968), 130-138.

Knickerbocker, Frederick T. *Oligopolistic Reaction and Multinational Enterprises.* Boston: Harvard Business School, 1973.

Kolde, Endel J. *International Business Enterprise.* Englewood Cliffs, N.J.: Prentice-Hall, 1973.

Köpke, Günter. "Multinationale Unternehmen und Gewerkschaften." *Gewerkschaftliche Monatshefte,* 7 (1971), 391-399.

Koopmann, George. *Die internationalen Unternehmen in der Theorie.* Hamburg: HWWA-Institut, 1973.

Koszul, Julien-Pierre. "American Banks in Europe." In *The International Corporation: A Symposium,* edited by Charles P. Kindleberger. Cambridge: MIT Press, 1970.

Krasner, Stephen D. "Manipulating International Commodity Markets: Brazilian Coffee Policy, 1906-1962." *Public Policy,* 21 (1973), 493-524.

——————. "Trade in Raw Materials: The Benefits of Capitalism." Paper presented at the International Studies Association Convention, New York, March 16, 1973. Mimeographed.

Kretschmar, Robert S., Jr., and Foor, Robin. *The Potential for Joint Ventures in Eastern Europe.* New York: Praeger, 1972.

Kreye, Otto, ed. *Multinationale Konzerne.* Munich: Hanser, 1974.

Kroeber, Alfred L., amd Parsons, Talcott. "The Concepts of Culture and of Social Systems." *American Sociological Review,* 23 (October 1958), 582-583.

Kujawa, Duane. *International Labor Relations Management in the Automotive Industry: A Comparative Study of Chrysler, Ford, and General Motors.* New York: Praeger, 1971.

——————. ed. *American Labor and the Multinational Corporation.* New York: Praeger, 1973.

Kurian, Matthew. *Impact of Foreign Capital on the Indian Economy.* New Delhi: People's Publishing House, 1966.

Lagos, Gustavo. *International Stratification and Underdeveloped Countries.* Chapel Hill: University of North Carolina Press, 1963.

Landau, Henry. "Protection of Private Foreign Investment in Less Developed Countries: Its Reality and Effectiveness." *William and Mary Law Review,* 9 (1968), 804-823.

Langley, Kathleen. "The International Petroleum Industry and the Developing World: A Review Essay." *Journal of Developing Countries,* 5 (1971), 109-122.

Lattes, Robert. *Mille Milliards de Dollars.* Paris: Editions et Publications Premiers, 1969.

Layton, Christopher. *Cross-Frontier Mergers in Europe.* Bath: Bath University Press, 1971.

——————. *Trans-Atlantic Investments.* Paris: Atlantic Institute, 1966.

Lau, Stephen F. *The Chilean Response to Foreign Investment.* New York, Praeger, 1972.

Lea, Sperry, and Webley, Simon. *Multinational Corporations in Developed Countries: A Review of Recent Research and Policy Thinking.* Washington, D.C.: British-North American Committee, 1973.

Levinson, Charles. *Capital, Inflation, and the Multinationals.* London: George Allen & Unwin, 1971.

Levitt, Karl. *Silent Surrender: The Multinational Corporation in Canada.* Toronto: Macmillan of Canada, 1970.

Levy, Walter J. "Oil Power." *Foreign Affairs,* 49 (1971), 652-669.

L'Impérialisme, Colloque d'Alger. University d'Alger, N'S.E.D., 1970.

Lindfors, Grace V., ed. *Bibliography: Cases and Other Materials for the Teaching of Multinational Business.* Boston: Harvard Business School. 1966.

Lipset, Seymour M., and Rokkan, S. "Cleavage Structure, Party Systems, and Voter Alignments." In *Party Systems and Voter Alignments: Cross-National Perspectives,* edited by Seymour M. Lipset and S. Rokkan. New York: Free Press, 1967.

Lipset, Seymour M., and Rokkan, S., eds. *Party Systems and Voter Alignments: Cross-National Perspectives.* New York: Free Press, 1967.

Little, Jane Sneddon. "The Euro-dollar Market: Its Nature and Impact." *New England Business Review* (Federal Reserve Bank of Boston), 50 (1969), 9.

Litvak, I. A., and Maule, C. J. "Guidelines for the Multinational Corporation. *Columbia Journal of World Business*, 3 (1968), 35-42.

_____. "The Multinational Firm and Conflicting National Interests." *Journal of World Trade Law*, 3 (1969), 309-318.

_____. eds. *Foreign Investment: The Experience of Host Countries.* New York: Praeger, 1970.

Lodgaard, Sverre. "Industrial Cooperation, Consumption Patterns, and Division of Labor in the East-West Setting." *Journal of Peace Research*, 10 (1973), 387-399.

McAllister, Breck P. "Current Developments in United States Antitrust Law and Restrictive Business Practice Law in Western Europe." In *Symposium*, sponsored by the International Comparative Law Center of the Southwestern Legal Foundation. New York: Matthew Bender and Co., 1968.

McCreary, Edward. *The Americanization of Europe.* Garden City, N.Y.: Doubleday, 1964.

McDonough, Peter. "Foreign Investment and Political Control in Brazil." Paper presented at the Yale University Conference on the Multinational Corporation as an Instrument of Development—Political Considerations, New Haven, May 1974. Mimeographed.

_____. "Political Implications of Economic Concentration in Brazil." Paper presented at the Ninth World Congress of the International Political Science Association, Montreal, August 19-25, 1973.

MacDougall, Iver C. "Antitrust Abroad—Room for Compromise." *Conference Board Record*, 5 (1968), 2-4.

McLaughlin, Russell U. *Foreign Investment and Development in Liberia.* New York: Praeger, 1966.

McMillan, James, and Harris, Bernard. *The American Take-over of Britain.* London: L. Frewin, 1968.

McNulty, Nancy G. *Training Managers: The International Guide.* New York: Haper and Row, 1969.

Magdoff, Harry. *The Age of Imperialism.* New York: Monthly Review Press, 1969.

Maisonrouge, Jacques G. "Statement to the United Nations Economic and Social Council Group of Eminent Persons." Hearings before the United Nations Group of Eminent Persons to Study the Impact of Multinational Corporations, New York, September 1973. Mimeographed.

Makinen, Gail E. "The 'Payoff' Period of Direct Foreign Investment." *The Journal of Business*, 43 (1970), 395-409.

Malles, Paul. "The Multinational Corporation and Industrial Relations: The European Approach." *Industrial Relations*, 26 (1971), 64-81.

Mandel, Ernest. *Die EWG und die Konkurrenz Europe-Amerika.* Frankfurt: Europäische Verlagsanstalt, 1968.

_____. *Der Spätkapitalismus.* Frankfurt: Suhrkamp, 1972.

Manser, W. A. P. *The Financial Role of Multinational Enterprise.* Paris: ICC, 1973.

Manuali, Louis. *La France Face à l'Implantation Etrangère.* Paris: Editions S.E.F., 1967.

Martyn, Howe. "Social Benefits of Multinational Manufacturing." *Michigan Business Review,* 21 (1969), 26-32.

Mason, R. Hal. *The Transfer of Technology and the Factor Proportion Problem: The Philippines and Mexico.* New York: UNITAR, 1971.

Mastrapasqua, Frank. "U.S. Bank Expansion Via Foreign Branching: Monetary Policy Implications." New York University *Bulletin* 87 (1973).

Matthöfer, Hans. "Internationale Kapitalkonzentration und Gewerkschaftsbewegung." *Gewerkschaftliche Monatshefte,* (1971), 469-476.

Maximowa, M. "Die Veränderung der Produktivkräfte des Kapitalismus und die Internationalisierung des Wirtschaftslebens." *Sowjetwissenschaft. Gesellschaftswiss. Beiträge,* 1971, 151-66.

Meeker, Guy. "Fade-out Joint Venture: Can It Work for Latin America?" *Inter-American Economic Affairs,* 24 (1971), 25-42.

Meerhaeghe, M. A. G. van. *International Economic Institutions.* London: Longman, 1971.

——————. *International Economics.* London: Longman, 1972.

Mennis, Bernard, and Sauvant, Karl P. "Describing and Explaining Support for Regional Governmental Integration: An Investigation of German Business Elite Attitudes Toward the European Community." *International Organisation,* 29(Autumn 1975), 973-996.

——————. *Emerging Forms of Transnational Community: Transnational Business Enterprises and Regional Integration.* Lexington, Mass.: D. C. Heath, 1976.

——————. "Multinational Corporations, Managers and the Development of Regional Identifications in Western Europe." *Annals of the American Academy of Political and Social Sciences,* 403 (1972), 22-33.

——————. "Regional Integration in Western Europe and the Multinational Corporation: A Preliminary Analysis." Paper presented at the American Political Science Association Annual Meeting, Washington, D.C., 1972. Mimeographed.

Merten, H. L., and Voigt, K. *Auslandskapital in Handel und Vertrieb.* Cologne: Rationalisierungs-Gemeinschaft des Handels, 1973.

Merton, Robert K. *Social Theory and Social Structure.* New York: Free Press, 1957.

Metallgesellschaft. *Metal Statistics 1961-1971.* Frankfurt: Metallgesellschaft, 1972.

Meyer, Herbert E. "What It's Like to Do Business With the Russians." *Fortune,* 84 (1972), 167-169, 234-238.

Michaelis, Hans. "Memorandum über eine europäische Rohstoffversogungspolitik." Mimeographed. Brussels: CEC, 1972.

Michalet, Charles-Albert. *L'Entreprise Plurinationale.* Paris: Dunod Economie, 1969.

——————. "La Multinationalisation des Entreprises Françaises." *Revue Economique,* 23 (1972), 648-668.

Michalet, Charles-Albert, and Delapierre, Michel. *La Multinationalisation des Entreprises Francaises.* Paris: Gauthier-Villars, 1973.

Michel, Roland. *Les Investissements Americains en Belgique.* Brussels: CRISP, 1970.

Mielke, Siegfried. "Multinationale Konzerne—internationale Kapitalstrategie ohne Grenzen?" *Aus Politik und Zeitgeschichte, Beilage zur Wochenzeitung das Parlament* B 11/74, March 16, 1974, 3-29.

Mikdashi, Zuhayr. *The Community of Oil Exporting Countries: A Study in Governmental Co-operation.* London: George Allen & Unwin, 1972.

——————. "Co-operation Among Oil Exporting Countries with Special Reference to Arab Countries: A Political Economy Analysis." *International Organization,* 28 (1974), 1-30.

Mikesell, Raymond F., ed. *Foreign Investment in the Petroleum and Mineral Industries: Case Studies of Investor-Host Country Relations.* Baltimore: Johns Hopkins University Press, 1971.

Minkner, Mechthild, and Bohrisch, Alexander. *Investitionsklima und Auslandskapital in Argentinien.* Hamburg: Institut für Iberoamerika-Kunde, 1970.

Mitchell, Alison K. "Foreign Investment Legislation in Africa." *Finance and Development,* 7 (1970), 7-11.

Modelski, George, ed. "Multinational Corporations and World Order." *International Studies Quarterly,* 16 (1972), whole issue.

Moore, G. S. "International Growth: Challenge to U.S. Banks." *National Banking Review,* 1 (1963), 1-14.

Moran, Theodore H. "Foreign Expansion as an Institutional Necessity for U.S. Corporate Capitalism: The Search for a Radical Model." *World Politics,* 25 (1973), 369-386.

——————. "A Model of National Interest, Balance of Power, and International Exploitation in Large Natural Resource Investments." Mimeographed. Washington, D.C.: The Brookings Institution, 1973.

——————. "New Deal or Raw Deal in Raw Materials." *Foreign Policy,* 5 (1971-72), 119-134.

——————. "The Politics of Oil: Coups and Costs." *Foreign Policy,* 8 (1972), 129-137.

——————."Transnational Strategies of Protection and Defence by Multinational Corporations: Spreading the Risk and Raising the Cost for Nationalization in Natural Resources. "*International Organization,* 27 (1973), 273-287.

Moyer, Reed. "Impact of U.S. Investments on Britain." *California Management Review,* 13 (1971), 69-76.

Mueller-Ohlsen, Lotte. "Die ausländischen Investitionen in Frankreich-Vorteil oder Gefahr für die französische Wirtschaft?" *Weltwirtschaftliches Archiv,* 102 (1969), 121-149.

Muldau, Bernd. *U.S.-Investitionen in der EWG.* Hamburg: Verlag Weltarchiv, 1966.

Müller, Ronald. "Poverty Is the Product." *Foreign Policy,* 13 (1973-74), 71-103.

Murray, J. Alex, and Gerace, Mary C. "Canadian Attitudes Toward the U.S. Presence." *Public Opinion Quarterly,* 36 (1972), 388-397.

Murray, J. Alex, and Kubota, Akira. "What Canadians Think of U.S. Investment." *International Review,* 12 (1973), 35-41.

Murray, Robin. "The Internationalization of Capital and the Nation-State." *New Left Review,* 67 (1971), 84-109.

————————. "Underdevelopment, International Firms and the International Division of Labour." In *Towards a New World Economy,* edited by Jan Tinbergen. Rotterdam: University Press, 1972.

Nadler, Paul S. "The Territorial Hunger of Our Major Banks." *Harvard Business Review,* 52 (1974), 87-98.

National Academy of Sciences (NAS). *U.S. International Firms and R, D and E in Developing Countries.* Washington, D.C.: NAS, 1973.

National Association of Manufacturers (NAM). *U.S. Stake in World Trade and Investment.* New York: NAM, 1972.

National Foreign Trade Council (NFTC). *The Impact of U.S. Direct Investment on U.S. Employment and Trade.* New York: NFTC, 1971.

National Industrial Conference Board (NICB). *Obstacles and Incentives to Private Foreign Investment, 1967-1968.* Vol. 2. *Incentives, Assurances, and Guarantees.* New York: NICB, 1969.

National Science Foundation. *Research and Development in Industry, 1969.* NSF publication NSF 71-18. Washington, D.C.: NSF, 1971.

Nearing, Scott, and Freeman, Joseph. *Dollar Diplomacy: A Study in American Imperialism.* New York: Viking Press, 1926.

Nehls, Katja. *Internationale Konzerne: Monopolmacht Klassenkampf.* Berlin: IPW-Forschungshefte Jg. 8, 1973.

————————. *Kapitalexport und Kapitalverflechtung.* Frankfurt: Marxistische Blätter, 1970.

————————. *Voraussetzungen, Formen und Bedeutung der westdeutschen Kapitalexporte 1952 bis 1958.* East Berlin: Akademie-Verlag, 1963.

Nehrt, Lee Charles. *International Finance for Multinational Business.* Scranton, Pa.: International Textbook Co., 1967.

————————. Truitt, J. Frederick; and Wright, Richard. *International Business Research: Past, Present and Future.* Bloomington: Indiana University Graduate School of Business, 1970.

Neusüss, Christel. *Imperialismus und Weltmarktbewegung des Kapitals. Kritik der Leninschen Imperialsmustheorie und Grundzüge einer Theorie des Verhältnisses zwischen den kapitalistischen Metropolen.* Erlangen: Politladen, 1972.

Newlyn, W. T., and Rowan, D. C. *Money and Banking in British Colonial Africa.* Oxford: Clarendon Press, 1954.

North American Congress on Latin America (NACLA). *Yanqui Dollar: The Contribution of U.S. Private Investment to Underdevelopment in Latin America.* New York: NACLA, 1971.

O'Connor, James. "International Corporations and Economic Underdevelopment." *Science & Society,* 34 (1970), 42-60.

Oliver, Covey. "The Andean Foreign Investment Code: A New Phase in the Quest for Normative Order as to Direct Foreign Investment." *American Journal of International Law,* 66 (1972), 763-784.

Oppenheim, Peter. *International Banking.* New York: American Institute of Banking, 1969.

Organisation for Economic Co-operation and Development (OECD). *Development Co-operation, 1972 Review.* Paris: OECD, 1972.

_____. *Development Co-operation, 1973 Review.* Paris: OECD, 1973.

_____. *Draft Double Taxation Convention.* Paris: OECD, 1963.

_____. *Fiscal Incentives for Private Investment in Developing Countries.* Paris: OECD, 1965.

_____. *Foreign Investment and Its Impact in Developing Countries.* Paris: OECD, 1968.

_____. *Gaps in Technology: Analytical Report.* Paris: OECD, 1970.

_____. "Interim Report of the Industry Committee on International Enterprises." Mimeographed. Paris: OECD, 1974.

_____. *Investing in Developing Countries.* Paris: OECD, 1970.

_____. *Investing in Developing Countries.* Paris: OECD, 1972.

_____. *Market Power and the Law: Report of the OECD Committee of Experts on Restrictive Business Practices.* Paris: OECD, 1970.

_____. *Policy Perspectives for International Trade and Economic Relations.* Report by the High Level Group on Trade and Related Problems to the Secretary-General of OECD. Paris: OECD, 1972.

_____. *Private Foreign Investments and Their Impact on Developing Countries.* Paris: OECD, 1973.

_____. *Problems and Prospects of the Primary Aluminium Industry.* Paris: OECD, 1973.

_____. "The Relation of Expropriatory Action by Developing Countries to Foreign Private Investment Flows." Mimeographed. (CD/R/72:5), 1972.

_____. *Restrictive Business Practices Relating to Patents and Licenses.* Paris: OECD, 1972.

_____. *Stock of Private Direct Investments by DAC Countries, end 1967.* Paris: OECD, 1972.

Osterberg, David, and Ajami, Fouad. "The Multinational Corporation: Expanding the Frontiers of World Politics." *Journal of Conflict Resolution,* 15 (1971), 457-470.

Ozawa, Terutomo. *Transfer of Technology from Japan to Developing Countries.* New York: UNITAR, 1971.

Pachter, Henry. "The Problems of Imperialism." *Dissent,* 17 (1970), 461-488.

Pacific Basin Economic Council. "The Pacific Basin Charter on International Investments." *Fortune,* (July 1972), 52-53.

Palloix, Christian. *L'Economie Mondiale Capitaliste.* Paris: Maspero, 1971.

_____. *Firmes Multinationales et Analyse du Capitalisme Contemporain.* Grenoble: Institut de Recherche Economique et de Planification (IREP), 1971.

_____. *Les Firmes Multinationales et le Procès d'Internationalisation.* Paris: Maspero, 1973.

_____. "Imperialisme et Mode de Production Capitaliste." *L'Homme et la Société,* 12 (1969), 175-194.

Palloix, Christian. *Internationalisation du Capital et Stratégie des Firmes Multinationales.* Grenoble: IREP, 1972.

_____. *Note de Recherche sur le Procès d'Internationalisation.* Grenoble: IREP, 1972.

Parada, Carlos Bazdresch. "La politica actuel hacia la inversión extranjera directa." *Comercio Exterior,* 22 (November 1972), 1012-1017.

Parsons, Talcott. "Order and Community in the International Social System." In *International Politics and Foreign Policies,* edited by James N. Rosenau. New York: Free Press, 1961.

Pavitt, Kenneth. "Multinational Enterprise and Transfer of Technology." In *The Multinational Enterprise,* edited by John H. Dunning. London: George Allen & Unwin, 1971.

Penner, Rudolph G. "Benefits of Foreign Investment in Canada, 1950 to 1956." *Canadian Journal of Economic and Political Science,* 32 (1966), 172-183.

Penrose, Edith T. *The Large International Firm in Developing Countries: The International Petroleum Industry.* London: George Allen & Unwin, 1968.

Penzin, D. "New Moves by Oil Imperialism." *International Affairs* (Moscow), 5 (1973), 47-53.

_____. "Oil and Independence." *International Affairs* (Moscow), 10 (1972), 34-40.

Perlmutter, Howard V. "A Content Analysis of Existing Investment Codes." Mimeographed. Philadelphia: University of Pennsylvania, 1974.

_____. "Emerging East-West Ventures: The Transideological Enterprise." *Columbia Journal of World Business,* 4 (1969), 39-50.

_____. "Entreprise Internationale—Trois Conceptions." *Revue Economique et Sociale,* 23 (1965), 151-165.

_____. "Nations, Syndicats et Firmes Multinationales." *Analyse et Prévision,* 9 (1970), 221-236.

_____. "Super-Giant Firms in the Future." *Wharton Quarterly,* 3 (1968), 8-14.

_____; Root, Franklin R.; and Plante, Leo V. "Responses of U.S.-based MNCs to Alternative Public Policy Futures." *Columbia Journal of World Business,* 8 (1973), 78-86.

Petersman, Ernst V. "Das internationale Kakaoabkommen 1972." *Zeitschrift für ausländisches öffentliches Recht und Völkerrecht,* 33 (1973), 489-502.

Petras, James F., and LaPorte, Robert, Jr. "Can We Do Business With Radical Nationalists? Chile: No." *Foreign Policy,* 7 (1972), 132-158.

Perroux, Francois. *Independence de l'Economie Nationale et Interdependence des Nations.* Paris: Aubier-Montaigne, 1972.

Peyrelevade, Jean. "Les Entreprises Multinationales et les Marchés Monetaires Internationaux." *Revue d'Economie Politique,* 82 (1972), 1198-1215.

Phatak, Arvind V. *Managing Multinational Corporations.* New York: Praeger, 1974.

Piehl, Ernst. "Multinationale Konzerne und internationale Gewerkschaftsbewegung." In *Politik und Zeitgeschichte, Beilage zur Wochenzeitung Das Parlament,* B 11/74, March 16, 1974, 25-45.

_____. *Multinationale Konzerne und internationale Gewerkschaftsbewegung.* Frankfurt: Europäische Verlagsanstalt, 1974.

Pincus, Joseph, and Edwards, Donald E. "The Outlook for United States Foreign Direct Investment in the Andean Pact Countries in the Seventies." *Journal of International Business Studies,* 3 (1972), 69-94.

Pinelo, Adalberto J. *The Multinational Corporation as a Force in Latin American Politics. A Case Study of the International Petroleum Company in Peru.* New York: Praeger, 1973.

Pinto, C. W. "Settlement of Investment Disputes: The World Bank's Convention." *Harvard Law Journal,* 13 (1967), 337-348.

Pisar, Samuel. *Coexistence and Commerce.* New York: McGraw-Hill, 1970.
───────. "Trade and Investment Policy Toward Communist Countries." In *U.S. International Economic Policy in an Interdependent World.* Vol. 2. Paper submitted to the Commission on International Trade and Investment Policy. Washington, D.C.: Government Printing Office, 1971.

Polk, Judd. "The Internationalization of Production." Mimeographed. Washington, D.C.: United States Council of the International Chamber of Commerce, 1969.
───────; Meister, Irene; and Veit, Lawrence. *U.S. Production Abroad and the Balance of Payments: A Survey of Corporate Investment Experience.* New York: Educational Industrial Conference Board, 1966.

Potter, David R. "The London Dollar CD—Liquid Tool for International Cash Management." *Columbia Journal of World Business,* 8 (1973), 2-10.

Preiswerk, A. Roy. "Neokolonialismus oder Selbstkolonisierung? Die Kulturbegegnung in den europäisch-afrikanischen Beziehungen." *Europa Archiv,* 28 (1973), 845-853.

Pringle, Robin. "Why American Banks Go Abroad." *Bankers' Magazine,* 150 (1967), 48-58.
───────. "Why American Banks Go Overseas." *The Banker,* 116 (1966), 770-785.

Quandt, William B. "Can We Do Business With Radical Nationalists? Algeria: Yes." *Foreign Policy,* 7 (1972), 108-131.

Quijano, Anibal. *Nationalism and Capitalism in Peru: A Study in Neo-Imperialism.* New York: Monthly Review Press, 1971.

Quinn, James B. "Technology Transfer by Multinational Companies." *Harvard Business Review,* 47 (1969), 147-161.

Reddaway, W. B. et al. *Effects of U.K. Direct Investment Overseas.* Interim and Final Reports. Cambridge: Cambridge University Press, 1967, 1968.

Reuber, Grant L., et al. *Private Foreign Investment in Development.* Oxford: Clarendon Press, 1973.

Rheinisch-Westfälisches Institut für Praktische Wirtschaftsforschung. *Die Kapitalverflechtung der Montanindustrie in Nordrhein-Westfalen mit dem Ausland.* Cologne and Opladen: Westdeutscher Verlag, 1967.

Rhodes, John B. "U.S. Investment Abroad: Who Is Going Where, How and Why." *Columbia Journal of World Business,* 7 (1972), 33-40.
───────. "Upturn in Foreign Activity By U.S. Business." *Columbia Journal of World Business,* 8 (Summer 1973), 19-24.

Robbins, Sidney M., and Stobaugh, Robert B. "How the Multinationals Play the Money Game." *Fortune,* 38 (1973), 59-62, 138.
───────. *Money in the Multinational Enterprise.* New York: Basic Books, 1973.

Roberts, B. C. "Multinational Collective Bargaining: A European Prospect?" *British Journal of Industrial Relations,* 11 (1973), 1-19.

Robinson, Richard D. *International Business Management.* New York: Holt, Rinehart and Winston, 1973.

Robinson, Stuart. *Multinational Banking.* Leyden: Sijthoff, 1972.

Robock, Stefan H., and Simmonds, Kenneth. "International Business: How Big Is It?" *Columbia Journal of World Business,* 5 (1970), 6-19.

——————————. *International Business and Multinational Enterprises.* Homewood, Ill.: Richard D. Irwin, 1973.

Rogers, Christopher D. "International Commodity Agreements." *Lloyds Bank Review,* 108 (1973), 33-47.

Rolfe, Sidney E. *The International Corporation.* Paris: ICC, 1969.

——————————. *The Multinational Corporation.* New York: Foreign Policy Association, 1970.

——————————, and Damm, Walter, eds. *The Multinational Corporation in the World Economy: Direct Investment in Perspective.* New York: Praeger, 1970.

Romania, Chamber of Commerce of the Socialist Republic of, ed. *Romania— Trade and Economic Cooperation.* Bucharest: Chamber of Commerce of the Socialist Republic of Romania, n.d.

Root, Franklin R. "The Expropriation Experience of American Companies." *Business Horizons,* 11 (1968), 69-74.

——————————. *International Trade and Investment.* Cincinnati, Ohio: South-Western Publishing Co., 1973.

——————————. "Public Policy and the Multinational Corporation." *Business Horizons,* 17 (1974), 67-78.

——————————. "Public Policy Expectations of Multinational Managers." *MSU Business Topics,* 2 (1973), 5-12.

——————————. "The Role of International Business in the Diffusion of Technological Innovation." *The Economic and Business Bulletin,* 17 (1968), 17-25.

Rosane, R. E. "Bauxite in Guyana: The Role of Demerara Bauxite Company, Limited in Guyana Over Fifty-Three Years." Mimeographed. Georgetown, 1969.

Rosenau, James N., ed. *International Politics and Foreign Policies.* New York: Free Press, 1961.

Rosenstein-Rodan, P. N. "Multinational Investment in the Framework of Latin American Integration." In *Multinational Investment in the Economic Development and the Integration of Latin America,* edited by Inter-American Development Bank (IDB). Washington, D.C.: IDB, 1968.

Rostow, W. W. *The Stages of Economic Growth.* Cambridge: Cambridge University Press, 1960.

Rouhani, Fuad. *A History of O.P.E.C.* New York: Praeger, 1971.

Rowthorn, Robert. "Imperialism in the Seventies: Unity or Rivalry?" *New Left Review,* 69 (1971), 31-54.

Rubin, Seymour J. "The International Firm and the Rational Jurisdiction." In *The International Corporation: A Symposium,* edited by Charles P. Kindleberger. Cambridge: MIT Press, 1970.

Ruttenberg, Stanley H. *Needed: A Constructive Foreign Trade Policy.* Washington, D.C.: Industrial Union Department, AFL-CIO, 1971.

Safarian, A. E. *Foreign Ownership of Canadian Industry.* Toronto: McGraw-Hill, 1966.

Salera, Virgil. "The Definition of a Multinational Corporation." *Quarterly Review of Economics and Business,* 11 (1971).

──────────. "Liquidate U.S. Direct Investments?" *Inter American Economic Affairs,* 24 (1970), 31-39.

──────────. *Multinational Business.* Boston: Houghton Mifflin, 1969.

──────────. "On Host Countries' Direct Investment Guidelines." *Inter-American Economic Affairs,* 23 (1969), 67-81.

Samuelsson, Hans-Fredrik. *Foreign Direct Investment in Sweden 1965-1970.* Stockholm: Industriens Utredningsinstitut, 1973.

Sarkar, Goutam K. *The World Tea Economy.* Delhi: Oxford University Press, 1972.

Sarosi, Eva. "Zur industriellen Kooperation zwischen Österreich und Ungarn." *Forschungsberichte* no. 2. Österreichisches Institut für Wirtschaftsforschung, Abteilung Internationale Wirtschaftsvergleiche, July 1972.

Sauvant, Karl P. "Multinational Enterprises and the Transmission of Culture: The International Supply of Advertising Services and Business Education." *Journal of Peace Research,* 13 (1976), no. 1.

──────────. "Multinationale Unternehmen und die Transformation des gegenwärtigen Staatensystems." *Politische Vierteljahresschrift,* 13 (1972), 196-242.

──────────, and Mennis, Bernard. "Corporate Internationalization and German Enterprises: A Social Profile of German Managers and Their Attitudes Regarding the European Community and Future Company Strategies." Paper presented at Institut für Führungslehre, Technische Akademie, Wuppertal, 1973. Mimeographed.

──────────. "Zum Managerbewusstsein in multinationalen Unternehmen vor dem Hintergrund europäischer Integration." In *Zur Multinationalisierung des Kapitals,* edited by Klaus Jürgen Gantzel. Hamburg: Deutsche Vereinigung für Politische Wissenschaft, 1976.

Sayers, Richard S. *Banking in Western Europe.* Oxford: Clarendon, 1962.

Scafuri, Allison. "United States Antitrust Laws in Relation to American Business Operating in the Common Market." *Boston College Industrial and Commercial Law Review,* 6 (1965), 561-567.

Scharrer, Hans E., ed. *Förderung privater Direktinvestitionen.* Hamburg: Verlag Weltarchiv, 1972.

Schatz, Sayre P. "Crude Private Neo-Imperialism: A New Pattern in Africa." *Journal of Modern African Studies,* 7 (1969), 677-688.

Schiller, Herbert I. "Madison Avenue Imperialism." *Trans-Action,* 8 (March 1971), 52-58.

Schliesser, Peter. "Restrictions on Foreign Investment in the Andean Common Market." *International Lawyer,* 5 (July 1971), 586-598.

Schlupp, Friedrich; Nour, Salua; and Junne, Gerd. "Zur Theorie und Ideologie internationaler Interdependenz." *Politische Vierteljahresschrift,* 14 (1973), 245-308.

Schmill, Erick. *Les Investissements Etrangers en France.* Paris: Editions Cujas, 1966.

Schoeller, Wolfgang. "Werttransfer und Unterentwicklung. Bemerkungen zu Aspekten der neueren Diskussion um Weltmarkt, Unterentwicklung und Akkumulation des Kapitals in unterentwickelten Ländern (anhand von E. Mandel: Der Spätkapitalismus)." *Probleme des Klassenkampfs,* 6 (1973), 99-120.

Schreiber, Jordan C. *U.S. Corporate Investment in Taiwan.* New York: Dunellen, 1970.

Schwarzenberger, George. *Foreign Investments and International Law.* London: Stevens, 1969.

Schweizer Bankgesellschaft. *Die grössten Unternehmen der Schweiz.* Zürich: Schweizer Bankgesellschaft, 1971.

Schwendiman, J. S. *Strategic and Long-Range Planning for the Multinational Corporation.* New York: Praeger, 1974.

Seifert, Hubertus. *Die deutschen Direktinvestitionen im Ausland.* Cologne and Opladen: Westdeutscher Verlag, 1967.

Senghaas, Dieter, ed. *Imperialismus und strukturelle Gewalt Analysen über abhängige Reproduktion.* Frankfurt: Suhrkamp, 1972.

——————————, ed. *Peripherer Kapitalismus: Analysen über Abhängigkeit und Unterentwicklung.* Frankfurt: Suhrkamp, 1974.

Servan-Schreiber, Jean-Jacques. *The American Challenge.* New York: Atheneum, 1968.

Shaker, Frank. "The Multinational Corporation: The New Imperialism?" *Columbia Journal of World Business,* 5 (1970), 80-84.

Shawinigan Engineering Company Limited. "Power Development Survey in Guyana for United Nations. Tiboku Hydro-electric Development Feasibility Study." Mimeographed. Aug. 1968.

Shihata, Ibrahim F. "International Responses to Investment Problems." *L'Egypte Contemporaine,* 64 (1973), 53-66.

Sieber, Eugen H. "Die internationale Unternehmung." Gegenwartsfragen der Unternehmensführung. In *Festschrift zum 65. Geburtstag von Wilhelm Hasenack,* edited by H. J. Engeleite. Herne-Berlin: Verlag neue Wirtschafts-Briefe, 1966.

Singer, Hans W. "U.S. Foreign Investment in Underdeveloped Areas: The Distribution of Gains Between Investing and Borrowing Countries." *American Economic Review,* 40 (1950), 473-485.

Simmonds, Kenneth. "Multinational? Well, Not Quite." *Columbia Journal of World Business,* 1 (1966), 115-122.

Sklar, R. L., and Whitaker, C. S., Jr. "The Federal Republic of Nigeria." In *National Unity and Regionalism,* edited by Cnendolen Carter. New York: Cornell University Press, 1966.

Skorov, G. "The Transfer of Technology and Neocolonialist Maneuvers." *International Affairs* (Moscow), 5 (1972), 55-62.

Special International Committee on the Pacific Basin Charter. "The Pacific Basin Charter on International Investments." *Fortune,* Sept. 1972, 52-53.

Spencer, Daniel L., and Woroniak, Alexander, eds. *The Transfer of Technology to Developing Countries.* New York: Praeger, 1967.

Spieker, Wolfgang. "Möglichkeiten des Arbeitnehmereinflusses in multinationalen Unternehmen." *Gewerkschaftliche Monatshefte,* 24 (1973), 105-113.

Standke, Klaus-Heinrich. *Amerikanische Investitionspolitik in der EWG.* Berlin: Beuth-Vertrieb, 1965.

Stamper, John W. "Aluminum." In *Mineral Facts and Problems, 1970.* Washington, D.C.: Government Printing Office, 1971.

Statistics Canada. *Corporations and Labour Unions Returns Act, 1970.* Ottawa: Statistics Canada, 1973.

Steiner, George A., and Cannon, Warren M. *Multinational Corporate Planning.* New York: Macmillan, 1966.

Stephenson, Hugh. *The Coming Clash: The Impact of the International Corporation on the Nation State.* London: Weidenfeld and Nicolson, 1972.

Steuer, M. D., et al. *The Impact of Foreign Direct Investment on the United Kingdom.* London: Her Majesty's Stationery Office, 1973.

Stevens, Guy V. G. "The Determinants of Investment." In *Economic Analysis and the Multinational Enterprise,* edited by John H. Dunning. London: George Allen & Unwin, 1974.

Steward, C. F., and Simmons, G. B. *A Bibliography of International Business.* New York: Columbia University Press, 1964.

Stobaugh, Robert B. *The International Transfer of Technology in the Establishment of the Petrochemical Industry in Developing Countries.* New York: UNITAR, 1971.

Stonehill, Arthur. *Foreign Ownership in Norwegian Enterprises.* Oslo: Central Bureau of Statistics of Norway, 1965.

Stopford, J. M. "The Foreign Investments of United Kingdom Firms." Mimeographed. London: London Graduate School of Business Studies, 1973.

Stopford, John M., and Wells, Louis T., Jr. *Managing the Multinational Enterprise.* New York: Basic Books, 1972.

Streeten, P. P., and Lall, S. "Main Findings of a Study of Private Foreign Investment in Selected Developing Countries." Mimeographed. UNCTAD document (TD/B/C.3/111), 1973.

──────────. "Some Reflections on Government Policies Concerning Private Foreign Investment." Mimeographed. United Nations document (TD/B/C.3 (VI) Misc. 7), May 28, 1973.

Stubenitsky, Frank. *American Direct Investment in the Netherlands Industry: A Survey of the Year 1966.* Rotterdam: Rotterdam University Press, 1970.

Sukijasovic, Miodrag. *Yugoslav Foreign Investment Legislation at Work: Experiences So Far.* Belgrade: Institute for International Politics and Economics, 1970.

Sunkel, Osvaldo. "Big Business and 'Dependencia.'" *Foreign Affairs,* 50 (1972), 517-531.

──────────. "Intégration Capitaliste Transnationale et Désintégration Nationale en Amérique Latine." *Politique Etrangère,* 35 (1970), 641-700.

──────────. "Latin American Underdevelopment in the Year 2000." In *Economics and World Order from the 1970's to the 1990's,* edited by Jagdish N. Bhagwati. New York: Macmillan, 1972.

Sunkel, Osvaldo. "National Development Policy and External Dependence in Latin America." *Journal of Development Studies,* 6 (1969), 23-48.

—————————. "Notes on the United Nations Report 'Multinational Corporations in World Development.'" Hearings before the United Nations Group of Eminent Persons to Study the Impact of Multinational Corporations, New York, Sept. 1973. Mimeographed.

—————————. *Obstacles to Change in Latin America.* London: Oxford University Press, 1965.

—————————. "The Structural Background of Development Problems in Latin America." *Weltwirtschaftliches Archiv,* 97 (1966), 22-63.

Sveriges 500 Stösta Företag. Stockholm: A. S. Ekonomisk Literatur, 1970.

Swedenborg, Birgitta. *Den svenska industrins investeringer i utlandet.* Uppsala: Almqvist & Wiksell, 1973.

Swoboda, Alexander K. "The Euro-dollar Market: An Interpretation." *Essays in International Finance,* (Princeton University), (1968), 1-47.

Tacke, Gerd. "Statement to the Group of Eminent Persons Established by the Economic and Social Council of the United Nations to Study the Impact of Multinational Corporations on Development and on International Relations." Presented in Geneva, Nov. 1973. Mimeographed.

Tahmassebi, Ahmad. "Zur Situation der erdöl exportierenden Länder des Nahen Ostens." *Probleme des Klassenkampfs,* 4 (1974), 253-272.

Tanzer, Michael. *The Political Economy of International Oil and the Underdeveloped Countries.* Boston: Beacon Press, 1969.

Task Force on the Structure of Canadian Industry. *Foreign Ownership and the Structure of Canadian Industry* (The Watkins Report). Ottawa: Privy Council Office, 1970.

Testa, Victór. *Empresas multinacionales e imperialismo.* Buenos Aires: Siglo, 1973.

Thackeray, John. "Not So Multinational After All." *Interplay,* 1968, 23-25.

Thompson, James D., ed. *Approaches to Organizational Design.* Pittsburgh: University of Pittsburgh, 1966.

Topping, Francis K. *Comparative Tariffs and Trade: The United States and the European Common Market.* Washington, D.C.: Committee for Economic Development, 1963.

Traité Marxiste d'Economie Politique. Paris: Editions Sociales, 1971.

Truitt, Frederick. *Expropriation of Private Foreign Investment.* Bloomington, Ind.: Graduate School of Business, 1974.

—————————. "Expropriation of Foreign Investments: Summary of the Post World War II Experience of American and British Investors in the Less Developed Countries." *Journal of International Business Studies,* 1 (1970), 21-34.

Tsurumi, Yoshi. "Japanese Direct Investment in Indonesia: Toward New Indonesian Policies of Foreign Direct Investment." Mimeographed. Cambridge: Developing Advisory Service, Harvard University, 1973.

—————————. "Japanese Multinational Firms." *Journal of World Trade Law,* 7 (1973), 74-90.

—————————. "The Strategic Framework for Japanese Investments in the United States." *Columbia Journal of World Business,* 8 (1973), 19-25.

Tudyka, Kurt. *Multinational Corporations and Labour Unions.* Nijmegen: SUN, 1973.

Tugendhat, Cristopher. *The Multinationals.* London: Eyre and Spottiswoode, 1971.

Tuite, M. F.; Chisholm, Roger; and Radnor, Michael, eds. *Interorganizational Decision Making.* Chicago: Aldine Publishing Co., 1972.

Turner, Louis. *Invisible Empires.* New York: Harcourt Brace Jovanovich, 1971.

——————. *Multinational Companies and the Third World.* New York: Hill and Wang, 1973.

——————. *Politics and the Multinational Company.* London: Fabian Society, 1969.

Tyler, Gus. "Labor's Multinational Pains." *Foreign Policy,* 12 (1972), 113-131.

Tyagunenko, V. "Neocolonialism and the International Capitalist Division of Labour." *International Affairs* (Moscow), 1971, 9-14.

United Nations. "Additional Notes on the Possible Economic Implications of Mineral Production from the International Sea-Bed Area." Mimeographed. (A/AC.138/73), May 12, 1972.

——————. "Charter of Economic Rights and Duties of States." Mimeographed. (A/RES/3281 [XXXIX]), Jan. 15, 1975.

——————. "Economic Significance in Terms of Sea-Bed Mineral Resources Proposed for National Jurisdiction." Mimeographed. (A/AC.138/87), June 4, 1973.

——————. "Establishing Transfer Prices in Allocation of Taxable Income Among Countries." (ST/SG/AC.8/I.3), Sept 14, 1973.

——————. "The Expansion of International Enterprises and Their Influence on Development in Latin America." In *Economic Survey of Latin America, 1970.* Part 4. New York: UN, 1972.

——————. *Foreign Investment in Developing Countries.* New York: UN, 1968.

——————. *Guidelines for Tax Treaties Between Developed and Developing Countries.* New York: UN, 1974.

——————. *The Impact of Multinational Corporations on Development and on International Relations.* New York: UN, 1974.

——————. *Implementation of the International Development Strategy: Papers for the First Over-All Review and Appraisal of Progress during the Second United Nations Development Decade.* Vol. 2. New York: UN, 1973.

——————. *Investment Laws and Regulations in Africa.* New York: UN, 1965.

——————. "Multinational Corporations. A Selected Bibliography." (ST/LIB/30), Aug. 27, 1973.

——————. *Multinational Corporations in World Development.* New York: UN, 1973.

——————. "Multinational Enterprises: Current Status of Work." Mimeographed. (A/CN./90), Apr. 22, 1974.

——————. "Permanent Sovereignty over Natural Resources." Mimeographed. (E/5170), June 7, 1972.

United Nations. "Permanent Sovereignty over Natural Resources." Mimeographed. (E/5425), Oct. 3, 1973.

───────────. *Provisional Verbatim Record of the Two Thousand and Ninety-Sixth Meeting, Twenty-Seventh Session, New York.* (A/PV.2096). Dec. 4, 1972.

───────────. *Report of the Group of Eminent Persons to Study the Impact of Multinational Corporations on Development and on International Relations.* New York: UN, 1974.

───────────. "Sea-Bed Resources: Recent Developments." Mimeographed. (A/AC.138/90), July 3, 1973.

───────────. "Study of the Problems of Raw Materials and Development. The Hypothetical Impact of Commodity Price Movements in World Trade." Mimeographed. (A/9544/Add.2), Apr. 12, 1974.

───────────. *Summary of Statements Made at Public Hearings Conducted by the Group of Eminent Persons Studying the Impact of Multinational Corporations on Development and International Relations.* New York: UN, 1974.

───────────. *Tax Treaties between Developed and Developing Countries. Fifth Report.* New York: UN, 1975.

United Nations Conference on Trade and Development (UNCTAD). "Exploitation of the Mineral Resources of the Sea-bed Beyond National Jurisdiction. Issues of International Commodity Policy: Case Studies of Cobalt." Mimeographed. (TD/B/449 and Add. 1), June 1973.

───────────. *The Kennedy Round Estimated Effects on Tariff Barriers.* New York: UN, 1968.

───────────. *Private Foreign Investment in its Relationship to Development.* (TD/134), 1972.

───────────. *Restrictive Business Practices in Relation to the Trade and Development of Developing Countries: Report of Ad Hoc Group of Experts on Restrictive Business Practices.* Geneva: UNCTAD, 1973.

United Nations Conference on Trade and Employment. *Final Act and Related Documents.* Havana: UN, 1948.

United Nations, General Assembly. "Declaration on the Establishment of a New International Economic Order." *Official Records: Sixth Special Session.* Supplement no. 1, (A/9559).

U.S. Chamber of Commerce. *United States Multinational Enterprise.* Washington, D.C.: U.S. Chamber of Commerce, 1972.

U.S. Commission on International Trade and Investment Policy (Williams Commission). *United States International Economic Policy in an Interdependent World.* 3 vols. Washington, D.C.: Government Printing Office, 1971.

U.S. Congress, House. *The Overseas Private Investment Corporation: A Critical Analysis.* Prepared for the Committee on Foreign Affairs by the Foreign Affairs Division, Congressional Research Service, Library of Congress. Washington, D.C.: Government Printing Office, 1973.

───────────, Committee on Foreign Affairs. *Expropriation of American-Owned Property by Foreign Governments in the Twentieth Century.* Washington, D.C.: Government Printing Office, 1963.

U.S. Congress, House, Committee on Foreign Affairs. *Overseas Private Invest-ment Corporation: Hearings* before a subcommittee of the Committee on Foreign Affairs, May 22, 29, 31, June 5, 7, 12, 13, 19, and 20, 1973. Washington, D.C.: Government Printing Office, 1973.

——————, Committee on Foreign Affairs, Subcommittee on Foreign Economic Policy. *The Overseas Private Investment Corporation.* Washing-ton, D.C.: Government Printing Office, 1973.

U.S. Congress, Senate, Committee on Finance. *Implications of Multinational Firms for World Trade and Investment and for U.S. Trade and Labor.* Washington, D.C.: Government Printing Office, 1973.

——————, Committee on Finance. *The Multinational Corporation and the World Economy.* Washington, D.C.: Government Printing Office, 1973.

——————, Committee on Finance. *Multinational Corporations.* Wash-ington, D.C.: Government Printing Office, 1973.

——————, Committee on Finance. *Multinational Corporations.* Hear-ings before the Subcommittee on International Trade of the Committee on Finance, Feb. 26, 27, 28, Mar. 1 and 6, 1973. Washington, D.C.: Gov-ernment Printing Office, 1973.

——————, Committee on Foreign Relations. "The International Tel-ephone and Telegraph Company and Chile, 1970-1971," in *Multinational Corporations and United States Foreign Policy: Hearings* before the Sub-committee on Multinational Corporations of the Committee on Foreign Relations, March 20, 21, 22, 27, 28, 29, and April 2, 1973. 2 vols. Wash-ington, D.C.: Government Printing Office, 1973.

——————, Committee on Foreign Relations. *Multinational Corpora-tions and United States Foreign Policy: Hearings* before the Subcommit-tee on Multinational Corporations of the Committee on Foreign Rela-tions, July 18, 19, 20, 30, 31, and August 1, 1973. Washington, D.C.: Government Printing Office, 1973.

——————, Committee on Foreign Relations. *The Overseas Private In-vestment Corporation Amendments Act: Report on S. 295.* Washington, D.C.: Government Printing Office, 1974.

——————, Committee on Foreign Relations, Subcommittee on Inter-national Corporations. *The Overseas Private Investment Corporation Re-port to the Committee on Foreign Relations by the Subcommittee on Multinational Corporations.* Washington, D.C.: Government Printing Of-fice, 1973.

U.S. Department of Commerce. *The Multinational Corporation. Studies on U.S. Foreign Investment.* Vol. 1. Washington, D.C.: Government Printing Office, 1972.

——————. *The Multinational Corporation. Studies on U.S. Foreign Investment.* Vol. 2. Washington, D.C.: Government Printing Office, 1973.

——————. *U.S. Business Investment in Foreign Countries, 1960.* Washington D.C.: Government Printing Office, 1960.

——————, Bureau of Economic Analysis. *Special Survey of U.S. Mul-tinational Companies, 1970.* Springfield, Va.: National Technical Infor-mation Service, 1972.

U.S. Department of Commerce, Office of Business Economics. *United States Direct Investments Abroad, 1966.* Part I: *Balance of Payments Data.* Washington, D.C.: Government Printing Office, 1971.

——————, Office of Business Economics. *United States Direct Investment Abroad, 1966.* Part II: *Investment Position, Financial and Operating Data.* Group 1. *Preliminary Report on Foreign Affiliates of the U.S. Petroleum Industry.* Springfield, Va.: National Technical Information Service (NTIS), 1971.

——————, Office of Business Economics. *United States Direct Investments Abroad, 1966.* Part II: *Investment Position, Financial and Operating Data.* Group 2: *Preliminary Report on Foreign Affiliates of U.S. Manufacturing Industries.* Springfield, Va.: NTIS, 1972.

——————, Office of Business Economics. *United States Direct Investments Abroad, 1966.* Part II: *Investment Position, Financial and Operating Data.* Group 3: *Preliminary Report on Foreign Affiliates of U.S. Reporters in U.S. Industries Other than Manufacturing and Petroleum.* Springfield, Va.: NTIS, 1972.

U.S. Department of the Interior, Bureau of Mines. *Minerals Yearbook 1971.* Washington, D.C.: Government Printing Office, 1973.

U.S. Department of State. "Nationalization, Expropriation, and Other Takings of United States and Certain Foreign Property Since 1960." Mimeographed. Washington, D.C.: 1971.

——————. "Disputes Involving U.S. Foreign Direct Investment: July 1, 1971 through July 31, 1973." Mimeographed. Washington, D.C.: 1974.

U.S. Federal Trade Commission. *Economic Report of the Investigation of Coffee Prices.* Washington, D.C.: Government Printing Office, 1954.

U.S. Tariff Commission. *Economic Factors Affecting the Use of Items 807.00 and 806.30 of the Tariff Schedules of the United States.* Tariff Commission Publication 339. Washington, D.C.: 1970..

Uri, Pierre, ed. *Trade and Investment Policies for the Seventies: New Challenges for the Atlantic Area and Japan.* New York: Praeger, 1971.

Vagts, Detlev F. "The Multinational Enterprise: A New Challenge for Transnational Law." *Harvard Law Review,* 83 (1970), 739-792.

Vaitsos, Constantine V. "Bargaining and the Distribution of Returns in the Purchase of Technology by Developing Countries." Institute of Development Studies *Bulletin,* 3 (1970), 16-23.

——————. *Considerations on Technological Requirements in Developing Countries with Observations on Technology Licensing Arrangements.* New York: UNIDO, 1972.

——————. "Foreign Investment Policies and Economic Development in Latin America." *Journal of World Trade Law,* 7 (November-December 1973), 619-665.

——————. "The Process of Commercialization of Technology in the Andean Pact: A Synthesis." Mimeographed. Lima: October 1971.

——————. "Stretégie des Choix dans le Commerce de la Technologie: Le Point de Vue des Pays en Voie de Développement." *Economies et Sociétés,* 6 (1972), 2133-2166.

Vaitsos, Constantine V. *Transfer of Resources and Preservation of Monopoly Rents.* Cambridge: Harvard University Press, 1970.

Van den Bulcke, Daniel. *Les Entreprises Étrangères dans L'industrie Belge.* Ghent: University of Ghent, 1971.

—————————. *The Foreign Companies in Belgian Industry.* Ghent: Belgian Productivity Centre, 1973.

Varon, Bension, and Takeuchi, Kenji. "Developing Countries and Non-Fuel Minerals." *Foreign Affairs,* 52 (1974), 497-510.

Vaupel, James W., and Curhan, Joan P. *The Making of Multinational Enterprise.* Boston: Harvard Business School, 1969.

—————————. *The World's Multinational Enterprises.* Boston: Harvard Business School, 1973.

Vernon, Raymond. "Antitrust and International Business." *Harvard Business Review,* 46 (1968), 78-87.

—————————. "Conflict and Resolution Between Foreign Direct Investors and Less Developed Countries." *Public Policy,* 17 (1968), 333-351.

—————————, ed. *The Economic and Political Consequences of Multinational Enterprises: An Anthology.* Boston: Harvard Business School, 1972.

—————————. "Economic Sovereignty at Bay." *Foreign Affairs,* 47 (1968), 110-122.

—————————. "Foreign-Owned Enterprise in the Developing Countries." *Public Policy,* 15 (1966), 361-380.

—————————, ed. *How Latin America Views the U.S. Investor.* New York: Praeger, 1966.

—————————. "International Investment and International Trade in the Product Cycle." *Quarterly Journal of Economics,* 80 (1966), 190-207.

—————————. *Manager in the International Economy.* Englewood Cliffs, N.J.: Prentice-Hall, 1966.

—————————. *Multinational Enterprise and National Security.* London: Institute for Strategic Studies, 1971.

—————————. "Multinational Enterprise and National Sovereignty." *Harvard Business Review,* 45 (1967), 156-172.

—————————. "Progress Report, Calendar Year 1970. Harvard Business School Multinational Enterprise Project." *Journal of Common Market Studies,* 9 (1971), 322-332.

—————————. *Restrictive Business Practices. The Operation of Multinational United States Enterprises in Developing Countries: Their Role in Trade and Development.* New York: UN, 1972.

—————————. *Sovereignty at Bay: The Multinational Spread of U.S. Enterprises.* New York: Basic Books, 1971.

Vetrov, A. "Economic Ties Between Socialist and Capitalist States." *International Affairs* (Moscow), 16 (1970), 7-11.

—————————. "Strengthening of All-European Business Contacts." *International Affairs* (Moscow), 19 (1973), 67-74.

Walker, Charls. "Expropriation of Foreign Private Investments." Statement by the Under-Secretary of the Treasury before the Subcommittee on International Finance of the House Banking and Currency Committee, July 6, 1971.

Wallace, Don, Jr., ed. *International Control of Foreign Investment. The Düsseldorf Conference on Multinational Corporations.* New York: Praeger, 1974.

Wang, N. T. "The Design of an International Code of Conduct for Transnational Corporations." Paper presented to the Seventh World Law Conference, October 12-17, 1975, Washington, D.C., forthcoming in *Journal of International Law and Economics.*

Warner, Malcolm, and Turner, Louis. "Trade Unions and the Multinational Firm." *Journal of Industrial Relations,* 14 (1972), 143-170.

Warren, William. "The Internationalization of Capital and the Nation State: A Comment." *New Left Review,* 67 (1971), 83-88.

Watkins, Melville H. "The Canadian Experience with Foreign Direct Investment." *Law and Contemporary Problems,* 34 (1969), 126-134.

——————. "Impact of Foreign Investment: The Canadian-U.S. Case." *Columbia Journal of World Business,* 4 (1969), 23-28.

Weber, André-Paul. "Entreprise Multinationale et Pratiques Restrictives." *Revue Economique,* 23 (1972), 669-694.

Wessely, Kurt. "Westliche Investitionen in sozialistischen Staaten." *Aussenwirtschaft,* 3-4 (1973), 179-208.

Weymar, F. Helmut. *The Dynamics of the World Cocoa Market.* Cambridge: MIT Press, 1968.

Wheelwright, E. L. "Development and Dependence: The Australian Problem." *The Australian Quarterly,* 43 (Sept. 1971), 22-39.

Wilkins, Mira. *The Emergence of Multinational Enterprise: American Business Abroad from the Colonial Era to 1914.* Cambridge: Harvard University Press, 1970.

Williams, B. R. *Technology, Investment and Growth.* London: Chapman and Hall, 1967.

Wilszynski, Joseph. *The Economics of East-West Trade.* New York: Praeger, 1969.

Wionczek, Miguel S. *La banca extranjera en América Latina.* Lima: Instituto de Estudios Peruanos, 1970.

——————. *Lateinamerika und das ausländische Kapital.* Hamburg: Übersee Verlag, 1969.

Wolf, Thomas A. *East-West Economic Relations and the Multinational Corporation,* Occasional Paper no. 5. Mimeographed. Washington, D.C.: Center for Multinational Studies, 1973.

——————. *U.S. East-West Trade Policy: Economic Warfare Versus Economic Welfare.* Boston: D. C. Heath, 1972.

——————, and Hawkins, Robert G. "The Evolving Policy of East-West Trade." In *The United States and International Markets,* edited by Robert G. Hawkins and Ingo Walter. Boston: D. C. Heath, 1972.

Wolff, Richard D. "The Foreign Expansion of U.S. Banks." *Monthly Review,* 23 (1971), 17-30.

——————. "Modern Imperialism: The View from the Metropolis." *American Economic Review,* 60 (1970), 225-230.

Wortzel, Lawrence H. *Technology Transfer in the Pharmaceutical Industry.* New York: UNITAR, 1971.

Yaniv, S. M. "Arrangements for the Transfer of Operative Technology to Developing Countries: Progress Report of the Secretary-General," Annex II, "Case Study of Israel." United Nations (E/4452/Add. 2), March 1, 1968.

Yearbook of International Organizations. 13th ed. Union of International Associations, 1970-1971.

Yoshino, M. Y. "Japanese Foreign Direct Investment." Mimeographed. Cambridge: Harvard Business School, November 1972.

Yugoslav Chamber of Economy, Institute of Comparative Law. *The Legal System of Foreign Capital Investments in Yugoslav Enterprises.* Belgrade: Yugoslav Chamber of Commerce, 1972.

Yugoslavia, Government of. "Law on Foreign Investment in Domestic Organization of Associated Labor." Presidential Decree. *Official Gazette,* 314 (April 19, 1973).

Zenoff, David B., and Zwick, Jack. *International Financial Management.* Englewood Cliffs, N.J.: Prentice-Hall, 1969.

Zwick, Jack. *Foreign Banking in the United States.* Washington, D.C.: Government Printing Office, 1966.

Subject Index

Access to markets, 96

Accountability, xiii, 218, 224, 225
See also Control of MNEs

Acquisitions, 174, 175, 176-177, Appendix Table 24

Adaptation of MNEs, Ch. 5

Advertising, 43-44, 57-67, 70-71
concentration of, 62-63, 67; expenditures in, 58-59; and foreign presence in host countries, 59, 62, 64-67; functions of, 57-58; internationalization of, 58; U.S. dominance in, 59-67

Alcan, 98, Ch. 6
diversification policy of, 123-125; and division of labor, 123; situation of, 123-126
See also Guyana; Guyana-Alcan conflict; Demba; Aluminum industry

Alternative strategies open to MNEs, 95-97, Chs. 5, 6
and MNE autonomy, 96, 104-107; and MNE protective strategies, 96-97
See also Location of production facilities; Geographical diversification of supply; Public policy vis-à-vis MNEs; Responsiveness of MNEs to home country public policies

Alumina, *see* Aluminum industry

Aluminum industry, 98, Ch. 6
capital intensiveness in, 113; concentration of enterprises in, 112-119; and concentration of producing countries, 112-119; and dis-
tribution of benefits, 119-120; and forward and backward linkages, 119-120; locational preferences in, 113; structure and main characteristics of, 98,112,120; vertical integration in, 112
See also Alcan; Producers' associations, individual resources; Bauxite

Anaconda, 97

Andean Common Market, 161, 162-163, Ch. 9, 222
See also Andean Common Market, investment code

Andean Common Market, investment code, 162-163, Ch. 9
and Andean Development Corporation, 184; and capital repatriation, 187; overall scheme of, 182-183; and sources of credit, 185, 188; and supervision of foreign loans, 188
See also Fade-out; Acquisitions; Dependencia; Transfer of technology; Restrictive business clauses

Banking, 5-6, 14-15, 19

Bargaining strength, xi, 111, 123, 161, 162, 166, 186, 219, 225
See also Control of MNEs; Dominance structures; constraints on counterstrategies

Barriers to entry, 97, 119, 203

Bauxite, *see* Aluminum industry

Business culture, 4-5, Ch. 3
basis of transfer potential for, 41-42, 43, 68-69; content of, 41, 63, 66-68; linkages in transfer pro-

Names Index